Television Histories

Television Histories

Shaping
Collective Memory
in the Media Age

Edited by
Gary R. Edgerton *and* Peter C. Rollins

THE UNIVERSITY PRESS OF KENTUCKY

Publication of this volume was made possible in part
by a grant from the National Endowment for the Humanities.

Scholarly publisher for the Commonwealth,
serving Bellarmine University, Berea College, Centre
College of Kentucky, Eastern Kentucky University,
The Filson Club Historical Society, Georgetown College,
Kentucky Historical Society, Kentucky State University,
Morehead State University, Murray State University,
Northern Kentucky University, Transylvania University,
University of Kentucky, University of Louisville,
and Western Kentucky University.
All rights reserved.

Editorial and Sales Offices: The University Press of Kentucky
663 South Limestone Street, Lexington, Kentucky 40508-4008

05 04 03 02 01   5 4 3 2 1

Library of Congress Cataloging-in-Publication Data

Television histories : shaping collective memory in the media age /
Gary R. Edgerton and Peter C. Rollins, editors.
      p.   cm.
Includes bibliographical references and index.
ISBN 0-8131-2190-6
1. Television and history. 2. Historical television programs—
History and criticism. 3. Television broadcasting of news. I.
Edgerton, Gary R. (Gary Richard), 1952– . II. Rollins, Peter C.
PN1992.56 .T45   2001   00–012272
791.45'658—dc21

This book is printed on acid-free recycled paper meeting
the requirements of the American National Standard
for Permanence in Paper for Printed Library Materials.

Manufactured in the United States of America.

Contents

Television as Historian

A Different Kind of
History Altogether

Gary R. Edgerton

History on television is a vast enterprise, spanning commercial and public networks, corporate and independent producers. As we rapidly enter the twenty-first century, a significant increase in historical programming exists on television screens throughout the United States, mostly in the form of biographies and quasi-biographical documentaries, which coincides with a marked rise of interest in history among the general population. This introduction will explore some of the parameters and implications of "television as historian," propose seven general assumptions about the nature of this widespread phenomenon, and end with some concluding observations concerning the enduring relationship between *professional history* and *popular history* as well as the challenges and opportunities this linkage poses for "television and history" scholarship in the future.

My first and most basic assumption is that television is the principal means by which most people learn about history today. Television must be understood (and seldom is) as the primary way that children and adults form their understanding of the past. Just as television has profoundly affected and altered every aspect of contemporary life—from the family to education, government, business, and religion—the medium's nonfictional and fictional portrayals have similarly transformed the way tens of millions of viewers think about historical figures and events. Most people, for example, recall the Gulf War and the major individuals associated with that conflict through the lens of television, just as their frame of reference regarding slavery has been deeply influenced by TV miniseries such as *Roots* (1977) and *Africans in America*

(1998), along with theatrical films such as *Amistad* (1997), which characteristically has been seen by more people on TV than in theaters.[1]

Second, history on television is now big business. There are over one hundred
broadcast and cable networks in America alone, and roughly 90 percent of
these services resulted from the dramatic rise of cable and satellite TV over
the last twenty-five years. Scores of cable networks have become closely identified with documentaries in general and historical documentaries in particular for two main reasons: (1) Nonfiction is relatively cost-effective to
produce when compared to fictional programming (i.e., according to the
latest estimates, per-hour budgets for a dramatic TV episode approximate
$1 million, while documentaries average $500,000 and reality-based programs $300,000); and, (2) even more importantly, many of these shows that
have some historical dimension are just as popular with audiences as sitcoms,
hour-long dramas, and movie reruns in syndication.[2]

Fifteen biographical programs are currently thriving on U.S. television,
for example, with a half-dozen more already in preparation.[3] Most of these
existing series are also among the most watched shows on their respective
networks. The forerunner and acknowledged prototype is A&E's (The Arts
and Entertainment Network) *Biography,* which averages a nightly viewership
of nearly three million, spawning videotapes, CDs, a magazine called *Biography* with two million readers, and a newly launched all-biography channel.
The index of historical (and contemporary) individuals and couples featured
on *Biography*—from Thomas Jefferson to Jackie Robinson to Pocahontas
and John Smith to Abraham and Mary Todd Lincoln—is sweeping and
diverse. At the same time, this series typically relies on highly derivative
stylistics, which are a pastiche of techniques borrowed from TV news, prime-
time dramatic storytelling, and PBS nonfiction à la Ken Burns. All told,
A&E's *Biography* is a representative example of how history is often framed
in highly conventional and melodramatic ways on TV, mainly to be marketed and sold directly to American consumers as a commodity.

*Third, the technical and stylistic features of television as a medium strongly
influence the kinds of historical representations that are produced.* History on TV
tends to stress the twin dictates of *narrative* and *biography,* which ideally
expresses television's inveterate tendency towards personalizing all social,
cultural, and (for our purposes) historical matters within the highly controlled and viewer-involving confines of a well-constructed plot structure.
The scholarly literature on television has established *intimacy* and *immediacy*
(among other aesthetics) as inherent properties of the medium.[4] In the case
of intimacy, for instance, the limitations of the relatively smaller TV screen
that is typically watched within the privacy of the home environment have

long ago resulted in an evident preference for intimate shot types (i.e., primarily close-ups and medium shots), fashioning most fictional and nonfictional historical portrayals in the style of personal dramas or melodramas played out between a manageable number of protagonists and antagonists. When successful, audiences closely identify with the historical "actors" and stories being presented, and, likewise, respond in intimate ways in the privacy of their own homes.

Television's immediacy usually works in tandem with this tendency toward intimacy. Both TV and film are incapable of rendering temporal dimensions with much precision. They have no grammatical analogues for the past and future tenses of written language and, thus, amplify the present sense of immediacy out of proportion. The illusion created in television watching is often suggested by the cliché "being there," which is exactly what David Grubin, celebrated producer of such historical documentaries as *LBJ* (1992), *FDR* (1994), *TR, The Story of Theodore Roosevelt* (1996), and *Truman* (1997) is talking about when he says, "You are not learning about history when you are watching . . . you feel like you're experiencing it."[5] "Television as historian," in this regard, is best understood as personifying Marshall McLuhan's eminently useful—though often misunderstood—metaphor, "the medium is the message."

Fourth, the improbable rise and immense popularity of history on TV is also the result of its affinity and ability to embody current concerns and priorities within the stories it telecasts about the past. Television's unwavering allegiance to the present tense is not only one of the medium's grammatical imperatives, it is also an implicit challenge to one of the traditional touchstones of academic history. Professional historians have customarily employed the rigors of their craft to avoid *presentism* as much as possible, which is the assumption that the past is being judged largely by the standards of the present. The revisionist work of postmodernist historians like Hayden White have lately challenged this principle in academic circles.[6] White and others have argued that historiography is much more about telling stories inspired by contemporary perspectives than recapturing and conveying any kind of objective truth about the past.[7] This alternative scholarly outlook has gained increased momentum in some quarters over the last generation, even calling into question whether or not there is an authentic, knowable history at all beyond the subjectivity of the present. Most popular historians for their part, such as television producers and filmmakers, take this postmodernist viewpoint one step further. They tacitly embrace presentism through the back door by concentrating only on those people, events, and issues that are most relevant to themselves and their target audiences.

The recent revising of the "prime-time Indian," ranging from fictions (e.g., CBS's *Dr. Quinn, Medicine Woman*, 1993–1998) to docudramas (e.g., TNT's *Crazy Horse*, 1996) to documentaries (e.g., Kevin Costner's *500 Nations*, 1995; Ric Burns's *The Way West*, 1995; Ken Burns and Stephen Ives's *The West*, 1996), along with literally dozens of other programming examples, is a telling case in point. Televised (and filmic) representations from the 1990s largely employ Native American characters as emblems for a wide assortment of mainstream multicultural, environmental, and New Age spiritual concerns, rather than reconstructing the old small-screen stereotypes primarily on the basis of the existing historical record.[8] "Television as historian," in general, is less committed to rendering a factually accurate depiction as its highest priority than to animating the past for millions by accentuating those matters that are most relevant and engaging to audiences in the present. On the most elementary level, this preference is commercially motivated and often results in an increasing number of viewers, but in a deeper vein the more fundamental goal of most popular historians is to utilize aspects of the historical account as their way of making better sense out of the current social and cultural conditions.

Horace Newcomb recognized this tendency twenty-five years ago in his seminal article "Toward a Television Aesthetic," when he identified *a special sense of history* as one of the representative characteristics of TV programming. Newcomb wrote that the "television formula requires that we use our contemporary historical concerns as subject matter . . . we [then] tak[e these] concern[s] and place [them], for very specific reasons, in an earlier time [when] values and issues are more clearly defined [and] certain modes of behavior . . . [are] more permissible."[9] Professional historians, in contrast, regularly take issue with TV's application of presentism as a guiding principle. What is lost, they argue, is the fuller historical picture, or that part of the past that is most unlike the present, but is nonetheless a vital component of the way things actually were.

Fifth, TV producers and audiences are similarly preoccupied with creating a "useable past," a longstanding tenet of popular history, where stories involving historical figures and events are used to clarify the present and discover the future. There is a method behind the societal self-absorption implied by presentism. Ken Burns's *The Civil War*, for example, attracted nearly forty million viewers during its initial telecast in September 1990 and has since been seen by an estimated seventy million Americans. Much of this documentary's success must be equated with the way in which Burns's version of this nineteenth-century conflict, stressing the personal ramifications of the hostilities, makes the war comprehensible to a vast contemporary audience.

Overall, *The Civil War* addresses a number of current controversies that reflect the shifting fault lines in the country's underlying sense of itself as a national culture, including the questions of slavery, race relations, and continuing discrimination; the rapidly changing roles of women and men in society; the place of federal versus local government in civic affairs; and the individual struggle for meaning and conviction in modern life. In this way, *The Civil War* as *useable past* is an artistic attempt to better understand these enduring public issues and form a new consensus around them, serving also as a validation for the members of its principal audience (which was older, white, male, and upscale in the ratings) of the importance of their past in an era of unprecedented multicultural redefinition.[10]

Sixth, collective memory is the site of mediation where professional history must ultimately share space with popular history. The mutual skepticism that sometimes surfaces between professional and popular historians is understandable and unfortunate. Each usually works with different media (although some scholars do produce historical TV programs, videos, and films); each tends to place a dissimilar stress on the respective roles of analysis versus storytelling in relaying history; and each tailors a version of the past that is designed for disparate—though overlapping—kinds of audiences. These distinctions are real enough. Still the scholar and the artist, the expert and the amateur, can complement each other more than is sometimes evident as they both make their own unique contributions to the *collective memory,* a term referring to *the full sweep of historical consciousness, understanding, and expression that a culture has to offer.*

Interdisciplinary work in memory studies now boasts adherents in American studies, anthropology, communication, cultural studies, English, history, psychology, and sociology.[11] The contemporary preoccupation with memory dates back to Freud, although recent scholarship focuses more on the shared, collective nature of remembering rather than the individual act of recalling the past, which is the traditional realm of psychological inquiry into this topic area. Researchers today make distinctions between the academic historical record and the rest of what is referred to as collective memory. Professional historians, in particular, "have traditionally been concerned above all else with the accuracy of a memory, with how correctly it describes what actually occurred at some point in the past."[12] "Less traditional historians have [recently] allowed for a more complex relationship, arguing that history and collective memory can be complimentary, identical, oppositional, or antithetical at different times."[13] According to this way of thinking, more popular uses of memory have less to do with accuracy per se than using the past as a kind of communal, mythic response to current controversies, issues, and challenges. The proponents of memory studies, therefore, are most concerned with how and why a remembered version is being constructed at a particular time, such as the aforementioned *The Civil War* in 1990, than whether a specific rendition of the past is historically correct and reliable above all else.

Rather than think of professional and popular history as diametrically opposed traditions (i.e., one more reliable and true; the other unsophisticated and false), it is more helpful, instead, to consider them as two ends of the same continuum. In his 1984 book, *Culture as History*, the late Warren Susman first championed this more sympathetic appreciation of the popular historical tradition. Susman noted that myth and history are intimately linked to each other. One supplies the drama; the other, the understanding. The popular heritage holds the potential to connect people passionately to their pasts; the scholarly camp maps out the processes for comprehending what actually happened with richness and depth. Susman's fundamental premise was that popular history and professional history need not always clash at cross-purposes. Together they enrich the historical enterprise of a culture, and the strengths of one can serve to check the excesses of the other.[14]

Many subsequent scholars from a wide variety of disciplines have concurred with Susman's basic thesis and continued to deepen his arguments since *Culture as History* first appeared. In his widely acclaimed book *The Noble Dream* (1988), Peter Novick has skillfully examined the controversies that have fundamentally affected history as a field of study over the last generation. Current debates continue in the literature and at conferences concerning the relative merits of narrative versus analytic history, synthetic versus fragmentary history, and consensus versus multicultural history.[15] Within this context, popular history and professional history are seen less as discrete traditions and more as overlapping parts of the same whole, despite the many tensions that still persist. For instance, popular histories can now be recognized for their analytical insights, while professional histories can similarly be valued for their expressive possibilities. Susman succinctly summed up this more inclusive vision with his often quoted affirmation: "History, I am convinced, is not just something to be left to historians."[16] He, of course, wrote this belief while also taking for granted that scholars were already essential to historical activity and would continue to be so in the future.

Seventh, the flip side of presentism is pastism (a term coined by historian Joseph Ellis), which refers to the "scholarly tendency to declare the past off limits to nonscholars."[17] Robert Sklar perfectly captured this longstanding bias in the context of "film and history" with his metaphor, "historian-cop," which alludes to the tone of policing that usually emerges whenever professional historians apply to motion pictures the standards they reserve for scholarly books and articles. In this specific instance, Sklar calls for a greater awareness of both the production and reception processes of filmmaking as a way of better appreciating how these more encompassing frameworks influence what audiences actually see and understand as history on the screen.[18]

"Television as historian" is an even more tempting and incendiary target than film and history for the proponents of *pastism,* especially since its impact and popularity with the general public far outstrips anything that can ever be achieved in theaters. As a result, histories on TV are sometimes rejected out of hand for either being too biographical or quasi-biographical in approach, or too stylized and unrealistic in their plot structures and imagery. Occasionally these criticisms are well-founded; historical programming certainly furnishes its share of honest "failures" or downright irresponsible and trashy depictions of the past. Other times, though, "television as historian" delivers ably on its potential as popular history, having even gained a degree of support in academe and increasing interest in the scholarly literature during the 1980s and 1990s, no doubt reflecting the growing desire among many professional and popular historians to finally reconcile each other's traditions in a mutually respectful, if cautious, working relationship.[19]

In retrospect, television and biography as branches of history have long shared company as second-class citizens in academic life. It goes without saying that television has only recently emerged as a focus of serious study within universities and colleges; one might even say that it has become a fashionable subject in a number of the humanities and social sciences. Biography, too, is making something of a comeback, although biographical scholarship certainly never resided as far out on the margins of academe as television studies.

The biographical approach probably reached its nadir in historical circles with the growing influence of the new social historians of the late 1960s and 1970s. This scholarly movement infused techniques primarily associated with the social and behavioral sciences into professional history, including a wide range of quantitative methodologies, which succeeded in more effectively delineating the social, economic, and demographic aspects of their subjects. The old-styled historical biographies appeared hopelessly unscientific and impressionistic in comparison, with their traditional reliance on narrative and their larger-than-life looks at "Great Men."

The most prominent and successful practitioners of the biographical approach to history during this era actually came from outside the academic world, led by best-selling writers such as Shelby Foote, with his three-volume *The Civil War: A Narrative* (1958–1974); David McCullough, with early works such as *The Great Bridge* (1972); and Michael Shaara, with his Pulitzer Prize–winning Civil War novel, *The Killer Angels* (1974).[20] Foote, McCullough, and Shaara, among others, were working within and renewing a much longer tradition of popular history, while also inspiring an even younger generation of nascent filmmakers who would initiate a minirevival in the historical documentary on television beginning just a decade later. Ken Burns, in particular, adapted McCullough's *The Great Bridge* as his first film, *Brooklyn Bridge*, in 1981 and decided to produce *The Civil War* after reading *The Killer Angels* in 1985, an experience he describes as "chang[ing his] life."[21]

The popular history tradition is actually as old as the historical impulse itself. The first historians, dating back to the ancient Hebrews and Greeks, were poets and storytellers, and their original approach to the past was to marshal whatever evidence and first-person stories they could into an all-inclusive historical epic. This master narrative was typically populated by heroes and villains, who allegorically personified certain virtues and vices in the national character that most members of the general population recognized and responded to immediately. Television as popular history still adopts facets of this strategy at its most rudimentary level, although our small-screen morality tales about the past are far more seamless and sophisticated in their construction, thus rendering these formulaic elements invisible to most viewers.

Popular history is essentially artistic and ceremonial in nature. In the case of "television as historian," the act of producing, telecasting, and viewing historical programming becomes a large-scale cultural ritual in and of itself. In turn, this process completes a number of important functions: it organizes together various viewing constituencies into a web of understandable relations, which are defined mostly by their differing identities and positions of power; it loosely affirms majoritarian standards, values, and beliefs; and it facilitates a society's ongoing negotiation with its useable past by portraying those parts of the collective memory that are most relevant at any given time to the producers of these programs as well as the millions of individuals who tune them in.

Professional history, in contrast, is resolutely scientific and empirical in orientation. It developed gradually over the second half of the nineteenth century, mainly in reaction to the twenty-five-hundred-year legacy of popular history. This new scholarly tradition recast the study of history inside the increasingly respectable and rigorous mold of science, with its principal attachments to systematic inquiry, objectivity, and the pursuit of new knowledge. In effect, professional history rejected the obvious mythmaking of popular history and adopted a more modern and disciplined method of gathering historical facts and then testing and cross-checking them for validity and reliability.

By the turn of the twentieth century, history had become institutionalized as a full-fledged occupation in colleges and universities. Professional historians pioneered a wide array of specialty areas, which they examined as impartially as they could, aspiring for a detached and truthful rendering of their subjects, independent of all personal tastes and biases. The ideal of objectivity has been modified considerably since the 1960s to take into account the inevitability that both scholars and their facts always come with very definite points of view. Moreover, from the vantage point of a new century the subjective excesses of popular history appear less like a difference in kind than a matter of degree, when compared against the ideological exuberance of contemporary scholarship.

Professional historians are also crossing over into the public sphere of popular history more than ever before. They are, for example, well represented as expert commentators on the increasingly popular History Channel. This network, another subsidiary of the aforementioned A&E, has already tripled its subscriber base to over eighty million households since its founding in early 1995. The experience of history on television is apparently alive and well for millions of viewers. The cooperation between professional and popular historians during numerous TV collaborations is similarly more active and vigorous than it has ever been.

The highly dynamic relationship between scholars and television producers these days features three principal patterns of interaction: First of all, TV as popular history is built upon the foundation of academic scholarship. It is essentially *synthetic* in nature and should not be judged on whether or not it generates new knowledge as much as it should on how creatively and responsibly it sheds additional light on the existing historical record. Secondly, professional historians are increasingly involved in the learning and production processes of popular historians, while still remaining tangential to the final results. In that way, scholars typically influence but do not control the end products of such teamwork. Lastly, popular history regularly provides professional historians with opportunities to introduce their scholarly ideas and insights to vastly wider audiences. "Television as historian" should never be feared as the "last word" on any given subject, but viewed as a means by which unprecedentedly large audiences can become increasingly aware of and captivated by the stories and figures of the past, spurring some viewers to pursue their newfound historical interests beyond the screen and into other forms of popular and professional history.

Any constructive evaluation of "television as historian" also needs to start with the assumption that it is an entirely new and different kind of history altogether. Unlike written discourse, the language of TV is highly stylized, elliptical (rather than linear) in structure, and associational or metaphoric in the ways in which it portrays images and ideas. A key goal of this collection of essays, in fact, is to better understand television as a popular art form, an evolving technology, a business and industry, and a social force of international proportions, all from a wide assortment of well-tried and effective historical-critical perspectives. This volume maps out the enormous repository that is "television as historian" into manageable and analytically useful categories—such as prime-time entertainment programming, the historical documentary, and TV news and public affairs—and seeks to establish quality criteria and levels of merit for television as "popular history" rather than judging it by the very different yardstick of professional history, or just dismissing the entire phenomenon as hopelessly flawed and ahistorical.

Part I addresses "Prime-Time Entertainment Programming as Historian." In the lead article, "History TV and Popular Memory," Steve Anderson considers the place of television in contemporary historiography. He outlines how TV has sustained an extremely active and nuanced engagement with the creation of collective memory, surveying a handful of different programs and concluding that television is both subversive of many of the implicit goals of professional history as well as an essential part of most contemporary Americans' cultural negotiation of the past. Mimi White then elucidates many of the historiographic tendencies described by Anderson in her close textual reading of two series from the early to mid-1990s, ABC's *The Young Indiana Jones Chronicles* and CBS's *Dr. Quinn, Medicine Woman*. In "Masculinity and Femininity in Television's Historical Fictions," White describes how current viewpoints on nationalism, internationalism, and multiculturalism are inserted into past events on these shows as an aesthetic means of "redressing the ills of the present" and, thus, finally "getting things right."

Robert Hanke's production history and textual analysis, "*Quantum Leap:* The Postmodern Challenge of Television as History," further builds upon Steven Anderson and Mimi White's chapters by depicting how this NBC series from the early 1990s can also be understood as part of the historical discourse that constitutes America's collective memory. He recounts in detail how the social histories of race relations, Vietnam, and the women's movement, in particular, consistently activate the plot lines of this program. In "*Profiles in Courage:* Televisual History in the New Frontier," Daniel Marcus concentrates on a more realistically styled fiction from 1964–1965. He distinguishes how this docudramatic series was situated squarely within the specific discourse of pragmatic moderate liberalism as well as the historiography of an American political leader, John F. Kennedy. Many of the episodes of *Profiles in Courage,* as a result, struggled with the same issues as JFK's New Frontier administration, such as the legacy of slavery and civil rights in the United States as a recurring narrative theme throughout the series.

Part II surveys "The Television Documentary as Historian." Peter Rollins begins by assessing the historiography of the hugely popular *"Victory at Sea"* as a "Cold War Epic." All told, the author reveals the interpretive limitations of this 1952 NBC series, especially in the way it glosses over the complex developments of naval operations during World War II in favor of sheer action and adventure, although he also acknowledges the skills and sincerity of the creators who produced this televisual history. Chris Vos provides a useful companion to Rollins's study by exploring his own country's public recollection of WWII hostilities in "Breaking the Mirror: The Development of Dutch Television History of the Second World War." Vos brings his special expertise as a filmmaker to bear on his close textual analyses of several widely seen historical documentaries about the war, which together contribute to his nation's process of "wrestling with" its memories of German occupation between 1940 and 1945.

Carolyn Anderson conducts a similar kind of investigation involving outside annexation and control in "Contested Public Memories: Hawaiian History as Hawaiian or American Experience." In this chapter, she pinpoints how the story of *Hawaii's Last Queen* (1997) is filtered through the common conventions of PBS's flagship series, *The American Experience,* depicting how a nationalist narrative can sometimes suppress a variety of alternative, localist perspectives when being designed for a much larger network audience. Gary Edgerton next hones in on the outlook of one historical documentarian in "Mediating *Thomas Jefferson*: Ken Burns as Popular Historian." He describes what Burns planned to accomplish by producing this particular television special and then judges the resulting program by these criteria. This inquiry ends with some concluding observations about the way in which Burns's *Thomas Jefferson* complements the admittedly different though reciprocal purposes of professional history.

Part III covers "TV News and Public Affairs Programming as Historian." Thomas Doherty looks back at the 1950s in constructing his traditional historical narrative, "Pixies: Homosexuality, Anticommunism, and the Army-McCarthy Hearings." He provides the cultural back story to this extensively viewed television event, focusing specifically on McCarthy, Cohn, and Schine and their violation of certain accepted codes of behavior at the time, especially "the duty to serve the United States military." Netta Ha-Ilan shifts attention directly to TV news coverage in "Images of History in Israel Television News: The Territorial Dimension of Collective Memories, 1987–1990." She specifically highlights how Israel Television news reported on the Palestinian uprising in the West Bank and Gaza during this three-year period, thus employing historical explanations of a ceremonial nature to imbue deeper meanings about the continuing conflict in the Middle East onto this one chronic incident.

David Culbert similarly analyzes how NBC, CBS, and ABC recast present-day impressions of the Berlin airlift and Kennedy's "Ich bin ein Berliner" speech for an American audience in "Memories of 1945 and 1963: American Television Coverage of the End of the Berlin Wall, November 9, 1989." The author describes the dramatic fall of the wall as a television news story, first and foremost, remembered mainly for its moving visual imagery of euphoric people celebrating this extraordinary event, which for most participants and viewers alike signified the symbolic end of the Cold War. Using videotaped copies and printed records from the Vanderbilt Television News Archives, Culbert investigates aspects of the TV reports, suggesting ways in which scholars might make historical sense of the various news coverage (and accompanying commercials) in hindsight. Philip Taylor completes this section by also considering the strengths and weaknesses of using television news as a primary archival source in "The First Flawed Rough Drafts of History: Television and War." In this historiographic think piece, he ruminates on the news reporting of several recent conflicts—most specifically the Gulf War and the Kosovo crisis—to insist that information conveyed by TV (and now the Internet) is essential to our understanding of contemporary events, particularly if these newer electronic news forms are carefully preserved in archives and properly evaluated by skilled historians and other capable analysts.

Lastly, Part IV locates "television as historian" within the overriding organizational contexts of TV production and reception. One of the more ironic aspects of history on TV is that television has long been identified by an assortment of scholars, such as the late cultural critic Christopher Lasch in his best-selling *The Culture of Narcissism* (1979), as one of the principal reasons why there is a "waning sense of historical time" in contemporary life.[22] According to this point of view, people in postindustrial societies live fully immersed in a mediated environment that ostensibly is invisible to them, even as they busily operate inside of it, habitually communicating and consuming electronic imagery and sound in an often wide-eyed present tense.

With the touch of a button, viewers around the world routinely summon into their homes the most extensive rendering of their own national culture and heritage, as well as aspects of many other cultures, and frankly, pay scant attention to the many clues that it has to tell them about their respective place within the historical flow of things. Proponents of media literacy, especially, advocate that we all should do more than just relax in this ephemeral stream of words and pictures; we should investigate more closely what these countless reflections suggest about who we are, where we came from, what we value, and where we might be headed in the future.

Many social theorists have likewise written about how Americans and members of other Western societies have radically transformed themselves and their cultures since World War II. They describe these various changes and the resulting new era by a number of fashionable terms, such as postindustrial, or postmodern, or the media age. Whatever we choose to call this period, America and other countries across the globe have profoundly changed since 1946, redefining the way people conduct their home life, work, and leisure time; participate as citizens and consumers; and preserve and value their relationship with the past as individuals and as members of mass-mediated societies throughout the planet. In 1964, Marshall McLuhan was the first media critic to describe TV as something more than just a medium, or an industry, or a social institution, or even a cultural force. He believed the sweep and impact of television was even larger and subtler than any of these four characteristics separately. In *Understanding Media,* he went so far as to claim that "TV is environmental and imperceptible, like all environments."[23] Part IV of this volume is similarly grounded on the assumption that analyzing the environmental components that to a large extent define and determine the TV content we see is vital to a fuller understanding of "television as historian."

In his role as founding coeditor of *Film & History* and in his subsequent publications, such as *American History/American Television* (1983) and *Image as Artifact* (1990), John E. O'Connor was particularly instrumental in encouraging critical attention to move beyond textual analyses alone to TV "production and reception [as] frameworks for historical inquiry."[24] In this spirit, Brian Taves evaluates the professional goals and programming output of the most prominent cable network specializing in historical content in "The History Channel and the Challenge of Historical Programming." Inaugurated in early 1995, this service has become an unqualified commercial success as a regular offering in most basic cable packages in the United States and Britain. Taves explains why The History Channel incorporates historical fiction into a mostly nonfictional format, delineating the types of popular history presented as well as the different styles that are utilized by the producers at this network. Douglas Gomery follows with a detailed examination of Washington, D.C., TV on January 21, 1957, the day of President Eisenhower's second inauguration, to illustrate the limits of using a mostly national perspective in "Rethinking Television History." The author, in contrast, constructs a "bottom up" view of how local TV developments eventually influenced programming and policy-making decisions on the network level by skillfully augmenting his research in media history with complementary findings gleaned from techniques more commonly used by social, demographic, and urban historians.

James Baughman then presents a production history of a single series in "Nice Guys Last Fifteen Seasons: Jack Benny on Television, 1950–1965," to reveal the larger industrial and institutional transformation of television during these critical early years of the medium. He continues to narrow the analytical focus to just one program, exemplifying how a behind-the-scenes history of *The Jack Benny Show* can greatly enhance our understanding of how generic formulas and a major star's appeal were adapted within an environment of rapid change, thus further clarifying the inside workings of TV culture at the time. Shifting the critical attention to reception, Michael Curtin also revisits America in the 1960s to investigate television's role as a facilitator in providing viewers with an historical awareness of their relative position within the scheme of things on the local, national, and international levels. In "Organizing Difference on Global TV: Television History and Cultural Geography," he closely explores two case studies from the New Frontier—special events programming on the networks and the development of local TV in Chicago—to argue that television is a highly efficient organizer of difference rather than a mere homogenizer of mass audiences, thus playing a crucial role in reorganizing spatial relations and transforming popular perceptions of place during the postwar era.

The first preliminary stage of this project began as a special issue of *Film & History: An Interdisciplinary Journal of Film and Television Studies*. Peter Rollins and I therefore acknowledge the help and assistance of Paul Fleming and Deborah Carmichael at Oklahoma State University (where *Film & History* is published) as well as the continuing interest of all the readers of this longstanding and important academic resource. I also want to thank Dean Karen Gould, College of Arts and Letters, and Old Dominion University, for supporting a research sabbatical during which I was able to bring this anthology to completion. We express our deepest thanks to our families for their love and understanding. Finally, we hope that one abiding result of this

effort is to encourage more scholarly work in this increasingly significant—
though often neglected—subject area.

Notes

1. See "Special Focus: The Gulf War and Television," *Film & History*, 22.1–2 (1992): 1–70; and "Special Focus: The Black Image in Film," *Film & History*, 25.1–2 (1995): 1–82.

2. Richard Katz, "Bio Format Spreads across Cable Webs," *Variety*, August 2–8, 1999, 23, 27; Richard Mahler, "Reality Sites," *The Hollywood Reporter*, Nonfiction Special Issue, April 8, 1997, N8–N9; and Ginia Bellafante, "These Are Their Lives," *Time*, March 17, 1997, 67.

3. James Poniewozik, *Time*, August 23, 1999, 62–66.

4. Horace Newcomb, *TV: The Most Popular Art* (New York: Anchor, 1974); John Fiske and John Hartley, *Reading Television* (New York: Methuen, 1978); Richard P. Adler, ed., *Understanding Television: Essays on Television as a Social and Cultural Force* (New York: Praeger, 1981); Robert C. Allen, ed., *Channels of Discourse: Television and Contemporary Criticism* (Chapel Hill: Univ. of North Carolina Press, 1987); David Bianculli, *Teleliteracy: Taking Television Seriously* (New York: Continuum, 1992); and Horace Newcomb, ed., *Television: The Critical View*, 5th ed. (New York: Oxford Univ. Press, 1994).

5. David Grubin, "Documentaries and Presidents" (ID#123826), C-SPAN 1, telecast on July 4, 1999; appearance recorded on April 6, 1999, 81 minutes.

6. Hayden White, *Metahistory: The Historical Imagination in Nineteenth-Century Europe* (Baltimore: Johns Hopkins Univ. Press, 1975).

7. See also Hayden White, *Tropics of Discourse: Essays in Cultural Criticism* (Baltimore: Johns Hopkins Univ. Press, 1985); Linda Hutcheon, *A Poetic of Postmodernism: History, Theory, Fiction* (New York: Routledge, 1988); and Elizabeth Deeds Ermarth, *Sequel to History: Postmodernism and the Crisis of Representational Time* (Princeton, N.J.: Princeton Univ. Press, 1992).

8. For a comprehensive overview of Native American stereotyping in a variety of popular media, including television, see S. Elizabeth Bird, *Dressing in Feathers: The Construction of the Indian in American Popular Culture* (Boulder, Colo.: Westview, 1996); and Peter C. Rollins and John E. O'Connor, eds., *Hollywood's Indian: The Portrayal of the Native American in Film* (Lexington: Univ. of Kentucky Press, 1998).

9. Newcomb, *TV: The Most Popular Art*, 258–59.

10. Statistical Research Incorporated (Westfield, N.J.), "1990 Public Television National Image Survey," Commissioned by the PBS Station Independence Program, September 28, 1990, 2.1–2.8; and "CBS, PBS Factors in Surprising Prime Time Start," *Broadcasting*, October 1, 1990, 28.

11. The literature encompassing memory studies is vast and found in many disciplines. A few well-known sources to start with are: Paul Fussell, *The Great War and Modern Memory* (New York: Oxford Univ. Press, 1989); Michael Kammen, *Mystic Chords of Memory: The Transformation of Tradition in American Culture* (New York: Vintage, 1993); Jacques Le Goff, *History and Memory*, European Perspectives (New York: Co-

lumbia Univ. Press, 1996); Bernard Lewis, *History: Remembered, Recovered, Invented* (Princeton, N.J.: Princeton Univ. Press, 1975; George Lipsitz, *Time Passages: Collective Memory and American Popular Culture* (Minneapolis: Univ. of Minnesota Press, 1990); Michael Schudson, *Watergate in American Memory: How We Remember, Forget and Reconstruct the Past* (New York: Basic Books, 1992); and Barbie Zelizer, *Covering the Body: The Kennedy Assassination, the Media, and the Shaping of Collective Memory* (Chicago: Univ. of Chicago Press, 1992).

12. David Thelen, "Memory and American History," *The Journal of American History* 75.4 (1989), 1119.

13. Barbie Zelizer, "Reading the Past Against the Grain: The Shape of Memory Studies," *Critical Studies in Mass Communication* 12.2 (1995), 216.

14. Warren Susman, *Culture as History: The Transformation of American Society in the Twentieth Century* (New York: Pantheon, 1984).

15. Peter Novick, *That Noble Dream: The "Objectivity Question" and the American Historical Profession* (Cambridge, U.K.: Cambridge Univ. Press, 1988).

16. Susman, 5.

17. Joseph J. Ellis, *American Sphinx: The Character of Thomas Jefferson* (New York: Knopf, 1997), 22.

18. Robert Sklar, "Historical Films: Scofflaws and the Historian-Cop," *Reviews in American History* 25.3 (1997): 346–50.

19. The scholarly literature on "television and history" is only a fraction of what it is for "film and history." Still, a number of key sources to begin with are Colin McArthur, *Television and History* (London: British Film Institute, 1978); John E. O'Connor, ed., *American History/American Television: Interpreting the Video Past* (New York: Ungar, 1983), which is also reprinted in Peter C. Rollins, John E. O'Connor, and Deborah H. Carmichael, eds., *The 1999 Film & History CD-ROM Annual* (Cleveland, Okla.: Ridgemont Press, 1999).; John E. O'Connor, *Image as Artifact: The Historical Analysis of Film and Television* (Malabar, Fla.: Krieger, 1990); John E. O'Connor, *Teaching History with Film and Television*, Rev. ed. (New York: American Historical Association, 1988); and Vivian Sobchack, ed., *The Persistence of History: Cinema, Television, and the Modern Event* (New York: Routledge, 1996).

20. Shelby Foote, *The Civil War: A Narrative (Fort Sumter to Perryville, Fredericksburg to Meridan, Red River to Appomattox)*, 3 volumes (New York: Random House, 1958–1974); David McCullough, *The Great Bridge* (New York: Touchstone, 1972); and Michael Shaara, *The Killer Angels* (New York: Ballantine, 1974).

21. Telephone interview with author, February 18, 1993.

22. Christopher Lasch, *The Culture of Narcissism: American Life in an Age of Diminishing Expectations* (New York: Norton, 1979), 5.

23. Marshall McLuhan, *Understanding Media: The Extensions of Man* (New York: New American Library, 1964), ix.

24. O'Connor, *Image as Artifact*, vii.

I | Prime-Time Entertainment Programming as Historian

1 | History TV and Popular Memory

Steve Anderson

A remarkable and misguided consensus exists among both historians and media critics regarding television's unsuitability for the construction of history. Notwithstanding The History Channel's promise to provide access to "All of History—All in One Place," Television viewers are often characterized as victims in an epidemic of cultural amnesia for which television is both disease and carrier. TV, so the argument goes, can produce no lasting sense of history; at worst, it actually impedes viewers' ability to receive, process, or remember information about the past. Raymond Williams's theorization of the "flow" of televisual discourse is invoked to argue that the contents of television simply rush by like answers on the *Jeopardy!* board without context or opportunity for retention. Film theorist Stephen Heath agrees, proposing that television "produces forgetfulness, not memory, flow, not history. If there is history, it is congealed, already past and distant and forgotten other than as television archive material, images that can be repeated to be forgotten again."[1] And according to Mary Ann Doane, "Television thrives on its own forgetability," relying upon "the annihilation of memory, and consequently of history, in its continual stress upon the 'nowness' of its own discourse."[2]

These arguments are rooted in Fredric Jameson's contention that in postmodern culture, TV and other visual media have fostered an increasingly "derealized" sense of presence, identity, and history. According to Jameson, history has been supplanted by a proliferation of stylistic pastiche and nostalgia symptomatic of a culture that still desires history, but is capable only of randomly cannibalizing styles and images from the past. Although Jameson rarely targets television as the cause of this affliction, its implication in the visual and industrial culture of late capitalism is unmistakable. Many theorists have characterized TV as a product of its own ideology of liveness and the culture of amnesia in which it exists.[3] In spite of the old-fashioned, TV-hating prejudices that still underpin much of the writing about television and the widespread persistence of suspicion toward visual media for the construction of history, it can be argued that TV has modeled highly stylized and creative modes of interaction with the past. Although these modes of interaction are subversive of many of the implicit goals of academic history, they play a significant role in cultural memory and the popular negotiation of the past.

With the erosion of confidence in scientific historiography in recent decades, it has become increasingly acceptable to view cultural relations to the past as overdetermined by the needs of the present, the desires of historians, and the ideological contexts of historical research. Once-solid borderlines separating empiricist history from the idiosyncratic realms of individual and cultural memory now appear dynamic and permeable. Arguments for the inclusion of visual media in historical discourse have developed a certain degree of credibility, even if the precise function and limitations of these media remain open for debate. Though still disparaged for its commercialism and reputed "banalization"[4] of significant events, television is likewise no longer simply dismissible as a bad object that is irrelevant to the development of historical consciousness. This essay proceeds from these conceptions of TV and history to argue that since its inception, American television has sustained an extremely active and nuanced engagement with the construction of history and has played a crucial role in the shaping of cultural memory.

Reconsidering Cultural Amnesia

Long a troublesome (or, more frequently, dismissed) concept for historians, memory—whether individual or collective—provides a key to theorizing the role of television in contemporary historiography. As theorists of popular memory have argued, history does not end with the production of documents, narratives, or analyses. People consume and process written, filmed, or televised histories within a web of individual and cultural forces that influence their reception and the uses to which they are put.[5] Further, historical meanings evolve over time, reflecting, among other things, the extent to which our relation to the past is conditioned by present circumstances. As *reception studies* of television have questioned assumptions about the passive spectatorship of TV viewers, *memory studies* provide a way of looking at historical reception, what people remember of history, and the ways it is made useful in their lives.

Like history, cultural memories are produced and must be understood in relation to an array of cultural and ideological forces. As Michael Bommes and Patrick Wright claim, "Memory has a texture which is both social and historic: it exists in the world rather than in people's heads, finding its basis in conversations, cultural forms, personal relations, the structure and appearance of places and, most fundamentally . . . in relation to ideologies which work to establish a consensus view of both the past and the forms of personal experience which are significant and memorable."[6] This notion of memory as a primarily social rather than individual phenomenon allows for exploration of the ways in which memories are rescripted in order to conform to existing historical narratives. Likewise, Maurice Halbwachs has argued that individual memories are always "interpenetrated" by collective influences, which fill in gaps and ascribe significance to lived experiences.[7] By situating memory within a complex and fragmentary social milieu, Halbwachs, Bommes, and Wright promote an idea of forgetting that is not merely the opposite of remembering. Indeed, the displacement and reconstruction of individual memories—termed "creative forgetting" by Friedrich Nietzsche and "active forgetting" by Andreas Huyssen—may be viewed as productive and inevitable components of cultural memory. How then can we describe television's role in the production and maintenance of these memories?

In the case of historical events such as the Challenger explosion or the first moon landing, television is widely regarded as an ideal facilitator of cultural memory, with its ritualistic, event-style coverage and capacity for endless repetition. Television is also recognized for its contribution to events that purport to bind the nation together in moments of remembrance and mourning, as seen in the televisual excess surrounding JFK's funeral and the proliferation of programming related to the fiftieth anniversary of World War II. For cultural theorist Marita Sturken, television and other constituents of popular culture are engaged in a relationship of mutual determination—or "entangledness"—with the flow of cultural memory.[8] Similarly, John Caldwell argues that television may provide viewers with "a great deal of textual and *historiographic power*, traits not normally associated with the medium in academic accounts that aim to define television's essential qualities—presentness, amnesia, and lack of context."[9] And in an important challenge to foundational television theory, Mimi White proposes a reconsideration of "liveness" as a structuring principle of TV, arguing that history, banality, and "attractions" offer equally compelling paradigms for understanding television's basic structure:

I want to insist that history, duration, and memory are as central to any theoretical understanding of television's discursive operations as liveness and concomitant ideas of presence, immediacy, and so forth. Indeed, liveness on television is routinely if variously imbricated with, and implicated in, history, momentous events, consumerism, and commodity circulation. Yet to make this claim flies in the face of certain influential theories of postmodernism which propose television as exemplifying, even propagating, the loss of history.[10]

Thus, for White, the privileging of liveness is not merely anachronous, but an active and semiarbitrary misconception that perpetuates TV's association with amnesia and ahistoricism. These recent examples notwithstanding, critical work that recognizes the contributions of television to historiography and memory remains a small countercurrent in contemporary scholarship. What is at stake in perpetuating the concept of television as an evanescent, ahistorical medium and memory as an imperfect tool in the service of individual recollection?

Politics of Memory

Memory, like history, is best understood as a site of discursive struggle. And like popular memory, part of the power and significance of televisual historiography lies in its flexibility and intangibility in comparison with "official" histories. Memories, which survive among individuals and communities, are frequently set in opposition to historical discourse, which is propagated from the top down via cultural and governmental institutions. This has proven to be an extremely effective strategy for oral history projects seeking to incorporate marginalized voices—especially those of colonized or disenfranchised peoples—into the official record. Even Michel Foucault argued that popular memory functions as a crucial site of resistance for oppressed groups: "Since memory is actually a very important factor in struggle, if one controls people's memory, one controls their dynamism. And one also controls their experience, their knowledge of previous struggles."[11] Foucault also warned that institutional mechanisms work tirelessly to influence the content and transmission of popular memory: "Now, a whole number of apparatuses have been set up to obstruct the flow of this popular memory . . . [Today there are] effective means like television and the cinema. I believe this is one way of reprogramming popular memory which existed but had no way of expressing itself."[12] Although widely quoted in support of the oppositional relationship between history and memory, these passages by Foucault demonstrate a surprisingly idealized view of preexisting social memories, untainted by the corrupting influence of mass media.

Ironically, nostalgia for authentic, prelapsarian social memories engaged in a David-and-Goliath struggle against official historical discourse implies the existence of precisely the sort of monolithic institutions and centralized apparatuses of social domination to which Foucault is elsewhere famously opposed. This view of popular memory also fails to account for memories that are formed through, rather than in spite of, interaction with "apparatuses" such as TV. A somewhat more modest approach is taken by Michael Frisch, who claims that the significance of popular memories lies not in their authenticity but their functionality: "What matters is not so much the history that is placed before us, but rather what we are able to remember and what role that knowledge plays in our lives."[13] Popular memory, thus conceived, highlights distinctions between the writing and the relevance of history, while simultaneously providing a crucial link between the two.

On both a personal and cultural level, memories acquire meaning in resonance with other historical constructs (images, narratives, politics, ideology, etc.). Sturken writes that unlike photographs, "Memory does not remain static through time—memories are reshaped and reconfigured, they fade and are rescripted. While an image may fix an event, the meaning of that image is constantly subject to contextual shifts."[14] Thus, the process of understanding how the past is transformed into memory—whether individual or collective—is best described as an archaeology in which the goal is not simply to uncover something that has been buried, but to discover how and why additional layers have been built on top of it. Viewed as a component of cultural memory, the past is less a sequence of events than a discursive surface, readable only through layers of subsequent meanings and contexts. The formation and function of popular memory is thus historically and contextually linked to the exigencies of a given community at a given time.

In a rare example of sociological research on the relationship between TV and cultural memory, Lynn Spigel interviewed a group of undergraduate women at the University of Southern California and discovered that students' belief in the progressive emancipation of women since the 1950s directly corresponded to the consensus view offered by television. Although her subjects claimed to be aware of the pitfalls inherent in basing their knowledge of women's lives during the 1950s on *I Love Lucy* reruns and nostalgia shows like *Happy Days*, Spigel concluded that these women's popular memories served to "discover a past that makes the present more tolerable."[15] Thus, even admittedly unreliable cultural texts such as TV sitcoms gained credibility by virtue of their use-value for women who still experience social discrimination. In considering the relationship between TV and cultural memory, Spigel's research suggests that it is necessary to include historical representa-

tions that make limited claims to authenticity but that may nonetheless profoundly affect people's understanding of the past.

Persistence of Suspicion

Whether or not film and television are fundamentally useful to the needs of
historical representation has been the subject of much controversy for historians. Under certain circumstances, film and TV are understood to make a
unique contribution to historical discourse because they allow viewers to
recover the "liveliness" and richness of the past—to see and feel what it must
have been like to be a part of history. On the other hand, film and television
are criticized because the stories they tell leave no room for critical interpretation and debate by historians. Each position is predicated upon certain
assumptions about what constitutes a work of history and for whom the
writing of history is most important. The first suggests that history is primarily the domain of individuals whose relation to the past is formed through
identification with naturalistic representations (e.g., period films like *Gandhi*
or historical programming like *Roots*). The second emphasizes the curator-
ship of historians over the past and expresses concern that filmed or televised
representations, whether documentary or narrative, are closed systems, which
resist the constant need for revision and debate.

This situation is further complicated by the enormous diversity of historical constructions that exist on film and TV, particularly at the extremes
of the high/low binary: popular culture and the avant-garde. In a rare attempt to address the significance of some of this work, Robert Rosenstone
identifies a mode of "postmodern" visual history that "tests the boundaries of
what we can say about the past and how we can say it, points to the limitations of conventional historical form, suggests new ways to envision the past,
and alters our sense of what it is."[16] However, Rosenstone limits his analysis
to films and videos that share the desire to "deal seriously with the relationship between past and present"[17] as it has been defined by more conventional
modes of history. The representational strategies mobilized by "postmodern
history" are "full of small fictions used, at best, to create larger historical
'truths,' truths that can be judged only by examining the extent to which
they engage the arguments and 'truths' of our existing historical knowledge
on any given topic."[18] Thus, Rosenstone essentially makes the argument that
certain films and videos may be considered works of history because they try
(with varying degrees of success) to do the same things that *real* historians
do. "Postmodern histories," though unorthodox, may be recuperated to the
extent that they point to histories that are verifiable through traditional means.

Thus, it is ironic that Rosenstone reinscribes these film and video texts, which he labels "postmodern," into a thoroughly modernist (rational, empirical) historical epistemology.

Since the late 1970s, theories of historiography have posed a much more basic challenge to historians whose work rests on the discovery or creation of "larger historical truths." Historiographers such as Hayden White have theorized that the work of the historian is not the transparent chronicling of a preexistent past, but the "emplotment" of historical information into recognizable narratives and literary tropes.[19] Among other things, these narratives obscure the "discontinuity, disruption and chaos"[20] of the past and enable the construction of histories which may be filtered, politicized, or influenced by their relation to systems of authority. Dominick La Capra has further argued that there is no historical "document" that may be considered naive or free of its own historical consciousness. No record of historical events, whether a personal diary or a documentary newsreel, may ever be considered neutral— it is "always textually processed before any given historian comes to it."[21] Simply put, the truth of history does not exist "out there" (as *The X-Files'* obsessive Fox Mulder maintains) where we can grasp it if we develop the right combination of representational tools and awareness of signifying practices. If we consider history to be constituted through discursive and cultural struggle, then we must look for meaning beyond the "footnotes, bibliography, and other scholarly apparatus" of professional historians to the way historical evidence is culturally processed, disseminated, and remembered.

Television's preoccupation with the past is not limited to overtly historical or nostalgia-oriented programming such as The History Channel, Ken Burns–style documentaries for PBS, or the cable station TV Land (which initially claimed to reproduce entire programming schedules from the 1960s and 1970s, complete with original commercials). History also repeats itself on television in more subtle ways, often in the form of playful or fantastic narratives that may not give the appearance of being "about" history at all. This is particularly evident in the science fiction and time-travel narratives employed by shows such as the various *Star Trek* series of the sixties, eighties, and nineties, *Quantum Leap* (NBC 1989–1993), *Dark Skies* (NBC 1996–1997), and *Timecop* (ABC 1997). A parallel trajectory may be seen in shows such as *You Are There* (CBS 1953–1957) and *Meeting of Minds* (PBS 1977–1981), which employ some of the same implicit historiographical strategies but aspire to explicitly pedagogical modes of address and more traditional standards of historical veracity.

Addressing some of the ways in which TV interacts with, and contributes to, the formation of popular memory, the remainder of this essay focuses on

Bizarre narrative contrivances, such as in the episode "Bread and Circuses," reveal Star Trek's obsession with the past, a critically neglected form of historical processing. Courtesy of NBC.

programs that raise questions of historical representation in unexpected ways. The characteristics that unite these shows, rather than their historical accuracy or sincerity of purpose, are such factors as irreverence, creativity, and the willingness to utilize—but also experiment with—historical conventions. Examples are drawn from each of the past five decades, though the threads of continuity connecting them are less dependent upon chronology or historical context than conceptual strategies and expression of shared desires.

Reporting Live from the Past: *You Are There*

In one of television's most remarkable products of the 1950s, the CBS television series *You Are There* offered a striking literalization of the link between TV liveness and history. Adapted from a highly successful radio program of the same name, *You Are There* simulated full-scale, network news reporting from the sidelines of notable historical events such as the Battle of Hastings, the execution of Joan of Arc, and Cortez's conquering of Mexico. The show featured CBS's lead news anchors and reporters (including Walter Cronkite and Mike Wallace) and closely mimicked the structure of a nightly news broadcast, complete with on-the-spot interviews and anchor desk commentary by Cronkite, who orchestrated the incoming reports and provided characteristically reserved commentary. During the broadcast, field reporters ingeniously qualified conflicting historical opinions and disputable facts as being uncorroborated due to the immediacy of the live, breaking event. The show thus merged conventions of historical speculation and investigative journalism, while bringing present sensibilities to bear on the experience of the past.

You Are There created a dynamic and compelling form of "living history" that made good use of the news format's commitment to fairness and objectivity, ostensibly without the benefit of hindsight. In an episode dealing with the assassination of Abraham Lincoln, for example, John Wilkes Booth agrees to do a live TV interview from the barn where he has barricaded himself after shooting the president, believing that television will allow him to tell his story to an "impartial witness." Booth speaks rationally of himself as a patriot of the Confederacy, whose actions were justified by a clearly articulated political goal. Supplementary interviews with family members and associates, however, emphasize personal motivations: jealousy of his brothers, desire for personal fame, desperation, or simple lunacy. The multiple perspectives offered by first-person interviews function as a surrogate form of historical analysis, offering precisely the kind of balanced presentation of the facts that links news reporting with more conventional modes of historiography.

Although *You Are There* models a brilliant form of strategic anachrony, the show is structurally configured to reinforce the idea that historical events unfold according to familiar narratives, complete with well-timed elements of drama and suspense. Although such factors undoubtedly contributed to the show's popularity, the opportunity to explore moments of "discontinuity, disruption and chaos" was thereby lost to a false sense of historical closure. From Cronkite's opening intonation that "All things are just as they were . . . except: *You Are There*," to the show's closing reassurance that "all the events reported and seen are based on historic fact and quotation," *You Are There* strove for accuracy and fairness within the limits of accepted historical knowledge and pedagogy.

The desire to see the past through contemporary eyes, evidenced by shows such as *You Are There*, is paralleled by instances in which historical figures travel forward in time in order to observe the present.[22] Perhaps the most eloquent example of this was the public television talk show *Meeting of Minds*. Hosted by Steve Allen, *Meeting of Minds* brought together groups of four actors portraying historical figures from various time periods and cultures to discuss contemporary topics and their relation to history. The historical personalities were selected to ensure controversy and debate, with Allen acting

Meeting of Minds, left to right, Irish Liberator Daniel O'Connell, Catherine the Great, Steve Allen, and Oliver Cromwell. Courtesy of PBS.

as moderator and provocateur. Interestingly, the guests on the show spoke not only from their own presumptive historical knowledge, but also as well-informed students of U.S. history, allowing them to make direct comparisons between their own age and the show's present. Thus, for example, the personages of Frederick Douglass and the Marquis de Sade discussed not only the relative merits of bondage and corporal punishment in their own times, but the debates over reform versus punishment in the American penal system of the 1970s. Likewise, when introducing Karl Marx, Steve Allen promised to hold him accountable for the atrocities committed in his name in the Soviet Union. While such transparently contrived and quasi-historical constructs have generally been excluded from discussions of television and history, when taken in combination with the other fantastic scenarios considered here, they indicate a cultural need to imagine a type of history that is productive rather than merely reproductive and, perhaps most importantly, open to interaction with the present.

In its most literal manifestations, this interplay of past and present includes situations in which fictional characters inaugurate "real" historical events. Perhaps the most celebrated cinematic example is Robert Zemeckis's *Forrest Gump*, in which a slow-witted character played by Tom Hanks is

According to *Quantum Leap*'s unique brand of "playful"
historical revisionism, Chubby Checker actually learned to
do the Twist by watching white time traveler Sam Beckett
(Scott Bakula, left). Courtesy of NBC.

digitally composited into archival film images as if he were present at or
responsible for historical events such as the desegregation of the University
of Alabama and teaching Elvis to dance. Nearly identical scenes occur in
another Zemeckis film, *Back to the Future,* including one in which a time-
traveling Michael J. Fox teaches Chuck Berry to play rock 'n' roll. And on
Quantum Leap, Scott Bakula helps to free Martin Luther King's grandfather
from slavery and teaches Chubby Checker to do the Twist. Although clearly
circumscribed by their fantasy constructs, the frequency with which these
fictional scenarios involve white characters taking responsibility for the his-

torical achievements of African Americans underlines only one aspect of the problematic nature of this type of "playful" historical revisionism.

Strange New Worlds, Same Old Sets: *Star Trek*

In the realm of fantastic or alternative histories, few genres open as many possibilities as science fiction. Narrative devices such as the time machine or passage through ruptures in the "space-time continuum" (a recurrent *Star Trek* phenomenon) offer endless opportunities for exploring the past. Other motifs include the scientific experiment that went awry (the pretense of *Quantum Leap)* and the flashback structure (utilized to extreme effect in both the Canadian police/vampire drama *Forever Knight,* and *Highlander: The Series,* in which immortal characters continually revisit events and figures from the distant past). On *Star Trek,* the historical periods reexperienced include such eclectic moments as the gunfight at the O.K. Corral; the outbreak of WWII; the alleged crash landing of an alien spacecraft at Roswell, New Mexico, in 1947; the first U.S. manned space launch; and the computer revolution of the 1980s. Similarly, *Quantum Leap* revisits events such as the U.S. Civil War, the Watts Riots, the Cuban Missile Crisis, the Francis Gary Powers U-2 spy incident, the death of Marilyn Monroe, the discovery of Elvis Presley, and the Ali-Foreman "Rumble in the Jungle" boxing match in Zaire.

The extreme diversity and idiosyncracy of these historical moments makes it difficult to define a single unifying characteristic or explanation behind them. However, it is possible to identify certain patterns and repetitions revolving around moments that lack historical closure. Whether due to the magnitude of the trauma or the sheer number of competing theories, an event such as the JFK assassination in November 1963, for example, provides fertile ground for the writing of alternative histories (in addition to Oliver Stone's *JFK,* both *The X-Files* and *Dark Skies* have recast the assassination in terms of government conspiracy and cover-up). However, the significance of such revisionism is not its contribution to a final or even most accurate "truth," but the elaboration and perpetuation of cultural mythologies. Although it is difficult to assess the extent to which this proliferation of counter-narratives affects the functioning of popular memory, the obsessive rewriting and fictionalizing of an historical episode has become part of the way history is written and remembered in contemporary American culture.

The persistent notion that history is open to interpretation and modification is also expressed in a more literal sense in shows that explore the narrative trope of time travel. The *Star Trek* series, for example, have avidly pursued

In the original series *Star Trek* episode "Patterns of Force," the show revisited the trauma of World War II and attempted to explain the logic of Nazism. Courtesy of NBC.

the logic of temporal causality and the possibility of multiple timelines, with deeply conflicted implications for the construction of historical agency.[23] On *Star Trek*, the idea that a single individual may cause dramatic social changes is axiomatic, though it often proves inadvisable. In "Bread and Circuses," for example, a rogue Star Fleet captain is responsible for transforming a planet into a culture of violence based on Ancient Rome, complete with televised gladiator matches. Likewise, in "Patterns of Force," a historian of "ancient" (twentieth century) earth becomes the ruler of a society that he models after Hitler's Germany, citing the efficiency and order of the Nazi regime. And in "City on the Edge of Forever," a lone political activist is responsible for delaying the United States' entry into World War II, the unintended result of which is Nazi domination of the planet. Perhaps as a result, later episodes in the series extend the "prime directive" against interference in developing cultures to include the proscription of actions that alter the past, so that time travel narratives invariably revolve around maintaining or reinstating the status quo.[24]

In contrast, the NBC television series *Quantum Leap* is more open about its moralistic approach to the rewriting of history. In each episode, the show's main character, Sam (Scott Bakula) "leaps" uncontrollably from one moment of history to the next, finding himself inside the bodies of various individuals (regardless of gender, age, race, etc.), "driven by an unknown force to change history for the better." Sam is accompanied on his adventures by a holographic companion (Dean Stockwell), who runs computer simulations in order to calculate which alterations to the historical timeline are necessary to "put right what once went wrong" and move on to the next leap/episode.[25] Unlike the typical *Star Trek* historical narrative, which operates on the level of geopolitical or eschatological conflict, *Quantum Leap* deals with more personal struggles (e.g., an African American doctor must survive the Watts riots to help rebuild his community; a boxer must win his last fight in order to finance a chapel for a group of nuns; etc.). On *Quantum Leap*, history is malleable, but only within the constraints of a preexisting master plan, the execution of which is governed by statistical probabilities and the good intentions of white, male scientists.

On repeated occasions, the writers of the original *Star Trek* series sidestep the inconvenience of the show's temporal "prime directive" by concocting scenarios in which the Enterprise crew encounters "strange new worlds" that bear uncanny resemblance to moments in the Earth's past. In various corners of the galaxy, for example, the *Enterprise* deploys its twenty-third-century military technology in the interests of a 1960s political agenda to reform a Chicago crime syndicate ("A Piece of the Action"), oust a corrupt Roman proconsul ("Bread and Circuses"), dethrone a despotic Greek emperor ("Plato's Stepchildren"), and overthrow a proto-Nazi regime ("Patterns of Force"). The frequency of this narrative device was undoubtedly motivated by the show's famously limited budgets and the availability of premade sets and costumes; but it may also be read as a revealing expression of desires to revisit or revise particular moments from the past. The compulsive replaying of Nazi scenarios twenty years after WWII, like the continual reworking of the Kennedy assassination, suggests that one of the roles for these fantastic histories may be therapeutic: the expression—and perhaps ultimate exorcism—of a collective trauma.

Our Future's Happening in Our Past: *Dark Skies*

Perhaps the most overt and self-conscious example of fantastic historiography on American television was the short-lived NBC sci-fi series *Dark Skies*, which reframed nearly every major news event of the post-WWII era in terms of a massive alien invasion. The series premiere of *Dark Skies*, for example, opens with a scene of a Cold War–era fighter pilot in pursuit of an unidentified flying object over Soviet air space. Shortly after making visual contact, the plane is blown out of the sky, forcing the pilot to eject while the U.F.O. disappears without a trace. A news report on television uses archival footage to reveal that the downed pilot was Francis Gary Powers, the U-2 pilot shot down over the Soviet Union in 1960. Later in the same episode, the aliens (who are linked to a central "hive," bringing super strength and vacant stares to their human host-bodies) are shown to be the cause of several other "real" historical events, including the Cuban missile crisis and the assassination of JFK.[26] Subsequent episodes deal with events such as the first U.S. manned space flight and the arrival of the Beatles in America, events that resonate powerfully in American cultural memory. The show seamlessly blends archival footage with recreations in creating an amalgam of historical fact and fiction.

Dark Skies' self-consciousness about its alternative historiography is made explicit in an opening credit sequence in which the series' main character intones ominously, "History as we know it is a lie." Promotional materials for the show similarly promise that *Dark Skies* reveals, "The American history you never knew." And according to the show's creators, Bryce Zabel and James Parriott: "This is being presented as alternative history. Everyone has their favorite conspiracies, but we will challenge and expand on those by building a framework that adds consistency to the alien-awareness theories. . . . The series premise is simply this: Our future's happening in our past."[27] But clearly this show is not about history in any conventional sense. Nor is *Dark Skies* adequately described as simply a show about memory or nostalgia (though it is both at times). The overriding tone of the show derives from contemporary paranoid and antigovernment conspiracy cultures, bearing an uncanny resemblance to both *The X-Files* and Oliver Stone's *JFK.* However, *Dark Skies'* creators misjudged the extent to which alternative history is rooted in resistant cultural positioning and a kind of homegrown anarchy that is not easily accommodated to network marketing strategies. The very consistency that the show's creators attempted to bring to "alien awareness theories" (still flourishing on the Internet and in subcultural communities) contributed to its downfall. In spite of a seemingly timely premise and NBC's strong commitment to the show, *Dark Skies* delivered consistently poor ratings and was canceled after only one season.

Although it would be possible simply to dismiss *Dark Skies* as a show about neither history nor popular memory, it may also be understood as a text that calls for a more mobile conceptual framework for dealing with the myriad ways in which historical information is culturally disseminated and processed. Although it never connected with the oppositional impulses of its prospective fan community, *Dark Skies* may be thought of as working with strategies of "creative forgetting."[28] Just as experimentation with language displays "the inherent oppressiveness of the symbolic order," histories that are "uncoupled from the instrumental need to signify" may reveal their own kind of creativity and anarchy.[29] TV shows such as *Dark Skies* and the historical impulses they manifest serve as indicators of the cultural processing and elaboration to which all types of history are subjected. As such, their significance may be more useful for the creation of a new paradigm of "popular" historical thinking in which once heretical concepts (e.g., that present and past are mutually interdetermined; that time and history are nonlinear and open to multiple interpretations; etc.) are all but taken for granted.

Historical criticism that engages only with those types of historical representation aspiring to conventions of academic historical writing is singularly ill-suited to theorizing many of the "historical" texts and practices that permeate American popular culture. Part of the power of these texts may lie precisely in their incomprehensibility and potential threat to more conventional historical forms, forcing—or allowing—viewers to choose their own path through the massively complex array of historical imagery and ideologies to which they are exposed.[30] Rather than simply learning new ways to forget, TV viewers may be acquiring a much more specialized and useful ability—to navigate and remember their own past with creativity and meaning, even when it goes against the design of historians.

Notes

1. Stephen Heath, "Representing Television," in *Logics of Television*, ed. Patricia Mellencamp (Bloomington: Indiana Univ. Press, 1990), 279.

2. Mary Ann Doane, "Information, Crisis, Catastrophe," in Mellencamp, 226–27.

3. Jane Feuer's 1983 article "The Concept of Live Television: Ontology as Ideology" formed the basis for much subsequent scholarship predicated on TV's essential liveness and subsequent ahistoricism. More recently, Anne Friedberg's *Window Shopping* (Berkeley: Univ. of California Press, 1993) and Lutz Niethammer's *Posthistoire* (London: Verso 1992) have offered symptomatic readings of the trivialized persistence of history in contemporary culture. For an excellent critique of prevailing assumptions about TV's ideology of liveness and its implications for historiography, see Mimi White's "Television Liveness: History, Banality, Attractions" in the fall 1999/winter 2000 issue of *Spectator*.

4. Doane, 228.

5. See for example, Stuart Hall, "Encoding, Decoding" in *The Cultural Studies Reader*, ed. Simon During (New York: Routledge, 1993), 90–103.

6. Michael Bommes and Patrick Wright, "The Charms of Residence: The Public and the Past," in *Making Histories*, eds., Richard Johnson, Gregor McLennan, Bill Schwarz, David Sutton (London: Anchor, 1982), 256.

7. Maurice Halbwachs, *The Collective Memory* (New York: Harper and Row), 44.

8. Marita Sturken, *Tangled Memories: The Vietnam War, the AIDS Epidemic, and the Politics of Remembering* (Berkeley: Univ. of California Press, 1997), 5.

9. John Caldwell, *Televisuality: Style Crisis and Authority in American Television* (New Brunswick, N.J.: Rutgers Univ. Press, 1995), 166.

10. Mimi White, "Television Liveness: History, Banality, Attractions" in *Spectator* 20, no. 1 (fall 1999/winter 2000), 37–56.

11. Michel Foucault, "Film and Popular Memory," *Edinburgh Magazine* 2 (1977), 22.

12. Foucault, 22.

13. Michael Frisch, *A Shared Authority* (Albany: State Univ. of New York Press, 1990), 16.

14. Sturken, 17.

15. Lynn Spigel, "From the Dark Ages to the Golden Age: Women's Memories and Television Reruns," *Screen* 36:1 (1995), 21.

16. Robert Rosenstone, *Revisioning History: Film and the Construction of a New Past* (Princeton, N.J.: Princeton Univ. Press, 1995), 12.

17. Rosenstone, 3.

18. Rosenstone, 209.

19. Hayden White, *Tropics of Discourse: Essays in Cultural Criticism* (Baltimore: Johns Hopkins Univ. Press, 1978).

20. Hayden White, 50.

21. Dominick La Capra, *History & Criticism* (Ithaca, N.Y.: Cornell Univ. Press, 1985), 34–35.

22. On *Star Trek* this has included a range of figures as diverse as Abraham Lincoln, Genghis Khan, Isaac Newton, Sigmund Freud, Amelia Earhart, Albert Einstein, and Mark Twain.

23. These episodes and many more on subsequent generations of the show may be situated within recent debates over film and history, postmodernism and the proliferation of counterfactual histories in popular culture, from *The X-Files* and *Forrest Gump* to the phenomenally popular literary genre variously known as Alternative History, Counterfactual History, Allohistory, Negative History, or Uchronia. These works may be further located within the context of a general cultural fascination with chaos theory and multiple-world scenarios found in recent movies such as *Sliding Doors* and *Run Lola Run*, each of which explore an alternate sequence of events triggered by a single, seemingly trivial variable.

However, by far the most sustained investigation of multiple-world phenomena has been articulated by the TV series *Sliders*, which originally aired on and was canceled by Fox only to be picked up by the Sci-Fi Channel following a massive letter-writing campaign by fans of alternate histories. *Sliders* is a science fiction genre show based on the adventures of a pompous professor, a boy genius, a rhythm and blues musician, and a sexy tomboy, all of whom are trapped in a state of interdimensional flux, careening wildly from one parallel universe to the next, trying in vain to return home like the characters on an interdimensional *Gilligan's Island*. Each world visited by this unlikely foursome is similar to our own, except for some more or less significant change in the historical timeline—ranging from a world in which dinosaurs still roam the earth to one in which J. Edgar Hoover executed a successful military coup following the Kennedy assassination, placing the United States under a perpetual state of martial law enforced by machine gun–toting, cross-dressing government troops known as "skirt-boys."

24. Another particularly overt example of the obsession with historical order within TV science fiction was the short-lived ABC series *Timecop* (1997), in which "temporal criminals" are pursued through history by members of a top-secret government agency known as the Time Enforcement Commission (TEC). The show opens with a warning that "history itself is at risk" from time-traveling villains who revisit notorious historical criminals such as Jack the Ripper and Al Capone. In response, the TEC is enlisted to maintain law and order (principally with regard to property relations) and restore the integrity of the "temporal stream." Apart from its connections to the 1994 movie of the same title, *Timecop* echoes the pursuit through time of Jack the Ripper in *Time After Time* (1979) as well as the long-running PBS children's game show *Where in Time Is Carmen San Diego?*, which pits junior historian-sleuths against a gang of thieves who rampage through time, stealing artifacts and changing history. In each of these cases, the possibility of time travel is conceived simultaneously as a threat to history's "natural" progression and an opportunity to go back and correct errors or transgressions of the past according to a contemporary, enlightened sensibility.

25. These quotations are drawn from the voice-over that accompanies the series' opening credit sequence.

26. According to *Dark Skies*, JFK was killed by a paragovernmental "Black Ops" team when he threatened to expose the alien invasion. Seemingly out of touch with its own irreverence at times, the show goes to extremes to preserve the Camelot mythos, offering repeated assurances that Kennedy was not part of the alien cover-up.

27. NBC *Dark Skies* website.

28. Andreas Huyssen, *Twilight Memories: Marking Time in a Culture of Amnesia* (New York: Routledge, 1995), 34.

29. Huyssen, 94.

30. This conception of historically resistant reading is drawn from Michel de Certeau's "Walking in the City," from *The Practice of Everyday Life* (Berkeley: Univ. of California Press, 1984), an essay that valorizes the navigation of urban spaces in ways that defy the intentions of urban planners. For de Certeau, this "misappropriation" of public spaces constituted a form of resistance to overly prescriptive urban planning.

2 Masculinity and Femininity in Television's Historical Fictions

Young Indiana Jones Chronicles and Dr. Quinn, Medicine Woman

Mimi White

For several months in 1993 on Saturday nights, *The Young Indiana Jones Chronicles* aired on ABC at the same time that *Dr. Quinn, Medicine Woman* was shown on CBS. *Dr. Quinn* was introduced mid-season, and its immediate ratings success secured its renewal for the following season, concomitant with the cancellation of the ratings-weak *Young Indiana Jones Chronicles*. Both programs project a sense of "quality family television," deploying a specific range of referential and aesthetic markers, while aiming to attract younger viewers along with their parents. More crucially, both programs are historical fictions offering revisionist histories and embedding a sense of progressive multiculturalism into their narrative constructions.

This conjunction of institutional placement and multicultural historical content presents an interesting case for comparative analysis. Both programs develop shifting perspectives on nationalism, internationalism, and multicultural understanding, engendering history for popular consumption. Reading these programs in relation to one another demonstrates how prime-time dramatic television series not only represent history, but also negotiate terms for historical understanding. Strategies introduced in this context include using the past as a site for investigating social-cultural concerns of the present, critiquing and revising the past from the perspective of the present, and even suggesting that the present is open to reexamination from the perspective of a revised past. To the extent that these operations occur simultaneously, even in contradiction, the programs enact the limits and possibilities of historical fiction in commercial prime-time television. A comparative analysis of the two programs discerns the manner in which television's multicultural historical fictions articulate gender with ideas of progressive enlightenment on the one hand and the containment of diversity on the other.

The Young Indiana Jones Chronicles (1991–1993)

Indy is the eponymous boy hero of *The Young Indiana Jones Chronicles*.[1] In the series two different actors portrayed Indy, embodying the character at different ages. The younger Indy (Corey Carrier), about ten years old, travels around the world with his parents as his Princeton professor father pursues lectures and research during a sabbatical. The older Indy (Sean Patrick Flanery), between seventeen and twenty, is an independent adventurer, who rebels against his father by joining the Belgian army under an assumed name. He ends up fighting in Africa and at Verdun, becoming a spy, and working as a translator after the war. Throughout the series Indy is placed in various global locales, where he comes upon famous historical figures, including: Sigmund Freud, Carl Jung, and Alfred Adler in Vienna (1908); T.E. Lawrence, first in Egypt (1908) and years later in Palestine (1917) and then in Paris (1919); Jiddu Krishnamurti in Benares, India (1910); Serge Diaghilev and Pablo Picasso in Barcelona (1917); Thomas Edison in New Jersey (1916); Kemal Ataturk in Istanbul (1918); Theodore Roosevelt in British East Africa (1909); and Mata Hari in Paris (1916), to name only a few.

Through the course of these encounters, Indiana Jones (who uses the self-selected nickname in lieu of his father's preference, Henry Jr.) is endowed with a distinctive historical vision and place. His relation to the past he inhabits is influenced by modes of historical understanding from the present in which the program is produced, as well as by the fictional adult he will become in the well-known Indiana Jones movies that circulated prior to his television incarnation. There is continuity in his fictional *persona*, as the historical situations he encounters in the TV series contribute to the global intelligence and expertise on which he draws in his fictional film future. From this perspective, the character scrutinizes his situation (and glimpses possibilities for the future) in terms of multicultural revision. This position is facilitated by Indy's status as a fictional character in an historical narrative, for the series can exploit present-day knowledge and awareness of the character's future fate to insert contemporary perspectives into the past. In the process it may hint at alternative possible, even counterfactual, futures.

The episode "Paris, May 1919"—and most of the episodes are named in this way, with a place and a date—is exemplary in this respect. Indy observes the postwar peace process as a confrontation between select Western imperial powers (France, England, and the United States) and more diverse national and ethnic interest groups from around the globe. Indy is working as a translator for the American delegation at the peace conference, with the possibility of long-term employment in the Foreign Service of the U.S. State Department. (This job suggests a sense of global mission, which is expanded considerably in the films.) As a result, he witnesses both the public proceedings led by French Premier Georges Clemenceau, British Prime Minister David Lloyd George, and U.S. President Woodrow Wilson, and private sessions where, for example, the future of the Middle East is discussed. Indy also runs into his good friend T.E. Lawrence, who is accompanying Prince Faisal of Arabia at the conference. He ends up spending a lot of time with Ned (Lawrence) and his friends, Middle East expert Gertrude Bell and historian Arnold Toynbee, who is also a member of the official British delegation. In addition, Indy makes the acquaintance of a young waiter from French Indochina, Nguyen That Thanh (who is later identified to Indy as a leader of the Vietnamese people, Ho Chi Minh), and helps him secure a hearing at the peace talks.

Indy is enthusiastic about the peace process, both in terms of watching world leaders and in terms of the promise for the global future the conference represents to him. When first discussing the situation with T.E. Lawrence, Indy declares, "I tell you, colonialism's dead. There must be dozens of countries competing to become free nations." It is clear that his heart lies with these nascent independence movements and that he believes they will be recognized as nation-states. He subsequently witnesses the official hearing for the Middle East delegation and the discrepant closed-door response thereto by Clemenceau and Lloyd George. He also observes the casual indifference encountered by Ho Chi Minh as the French delegate sleeps through the presentation of the Vietnamese petition. Indy comes to realize that the major European powers are going to ignore local concerns from around the globe and carve up the world in terms of their own interests. He is also sensitive to the situation of the German delegation and their humiliating treatment by the French hosts, as they are forced to accept nonnegotiable terms for peace.

Indy's disappointment in the peace process is all the more poignant because the effects of the specific decisions he witnesses can be clearly assessed from the vantage of the 1990s, beginning with Germany's situation after the war, Hitler's rise to power, and the eruption of World War II. Vietnam and the Middle East are also familiar as areas of prominent conflict, especially since World War II, from a western and U.S. perspective. These upheavals can be construed as the long-term "effects" of the decision-making processes witnessed by Indy, particularly for a television audience in the 1990s.[2] In this context, Indy's immediate support for both T.E. Lawrence with the Arab contingent and Ho Chi Minh endow him with a distinctive progressive vision. Indy is thereby aligned with the interests of marginal political and cultural "others." This support also evinces his sensitivity to the future—especially as it aims toward the late twentieth-century television viewer, whose life may have been affected (directly or otherwise) by conflicts in Vietnam and the Middle East.

Indeed, Indy's heroism in this episode is measured by the degree to which he supports diverse national interests. (In many other episodes his heroism is more closely aligned with conventional action, adventure, and suspense, as he battles at the front or engages in daring espionage activity.) Thus, it is Indy's personal intervention that enables the Vietnamese delegates to get to the peace conference floor in the first place, though their reception is gravely disappointing. The identification of heroism with Indy's idealistic, humanist support for a multicultural future is crucial. For it enables the program to sustain the interest of its central character, who interacts with history, but who can never be an agent of substantial historical transformation, because he is a fictional character dropped into a world of recognizable characters and events from the past.

While Indy's relationship to these events is that of a participant-observer, fueled by an idealistic passion, Arnold Toynbee is presented in this episode as the authoritative spokesman for "History," propounding rules about the events around him in the form of homilies. In his first encounter with Indy, at dinner with Lawrence and Bell, Toynbee notes that if the peace accord results in the destruction of Germany, there will be a predictable price to pay in the near future. In this regard he says of the conference conveners, "This lot are behaving like men with no memories. Those who forget the lessons of history are doomed to repeat it."[3] In the process, Toynbee not only establishes a moral for the episode (with explicitly forbidding implications when it comes to World War II, Vietnam, and the Middle East), but also offers a rationale for the series itself, as it offers world history lessons for family audiences. When the conditions of the peace agreements are finally settled and Wilson has largely capitulated to British and French interests (at least in the episode's interpretation of events), Toynbee reconfirms his position. He tells Indy and Lawrence that they fought for nothing and that the war will be fought over again "in ten or twenty years." This scene reflects general sentiments Toynbee did hold at the time, against harsh reparations for Germany. But the program implicitly attaches this to a specific future event, World War II, in ways that construe Toynbee's politics in terms of clairvoyance.

Yet even as the general logic of the episode seems to confirm Toynbee's

Young Indiana Jones (Sean Patrick Flanery) is fully involved in the forces of culture as a participant observer in historical events. Courtesy of Eddie Adams/ABC-Lucasfilm.

interpretive scheme regarding memory and historical repetition (especially with the inclusion of the Arab and Vietnamese subplots), a margin of doubt is sustained. When Toynbee first explains that "Those who forget the lessons of history are doomed to repeat it," there is a direct cut from the restaurant table to a close-up of Indy's journal, as Indy inscribes the phrase, followed by a large question mark. The transformative punctuation mark suggests the possibility for reconsideration of Toynbee's words. Whether Indy is challenging Toynbee's perspective or indicating his own lack of certainty about what it means is left open, an ambiguity that stands in for a host of potential alternative interpretations.

Moreover, the episode subsequently offers another partial mitigation of Toynbee's pessimism. It concludes with a parting scene between Lawrence and Indy at the train station. Indy has decided to return to the United States to study archeology (so he can grow up to become the Indiana Jones of the movie trilogy), and Lawrence is on his way to England. As Indy's train pulls out of the station, Lawrence shouts that after all, "It might have been worse." This could refer to the peace accord or to the war in which they have both just fought (or even to both). In either case, doubts or concerns about world history as it happened (and as it has been dramatized in the series) are at least potentially, partially assuaged. This affirmation also reconfirms the value of Indy's heroism in this and other episodes of the program, when he served as a Belgian soldier and spy defending Allied interests during the war.

A postmodern historical vision is carried in the variable narrative interests and perspectives that the program validates. The program clearly refuses a sense of definitive closure and the certainty of resolution in the past. The master narrative of Eurocentric history does not thereby collapse, but instead coexists with other interpretive positions that are fully integrated into the historical past. The hypothetical reversibility of the world's historical fate is thereby advanced as an implicit argument. These alternative interpretive positions embrace a multicultural vision, tacitly supporting the idea of self-determination for different people around the globe. The program's postmodern multiculturalism is equated with a heroic vision that emerges from the position of normative western white male privilege. The most forceful representatives of this vision are Indy, and in this episode, Lawrence and Toynbee. Along similar lines, it is Arnold Toynbee, an official British diplomat, who "predicts" the negative repercussions of the peace accord that his own nation had such a strong hand in designing.

Of course, identifying white western man as the representative of enlightened thought is not surprising per se. But in the case of the young Indiana Jones, the position of enlightened vision regularly entails speaking in support of the interests and autonomy of disenfranchised "others." On occasion, these sentiments are directly expressed by those whose interests are being articulated. In "Istanbul, September 1918," Kemal Ataturk rejects a secret French proposal brought to him by the older Indy, which ostensibly offers a quick resolution to the war in the Middle East. Ataturk explains that accepting the French treaty may secure his own power, but at the expense of extending self-determination to other Arabs leaders in the region. At another extreme, after a brief interlude with Pancho Villa, Indy encounters a Mexican peasant, who starkly contrasts the interests of ordinary people with those of the ruling classes and world historical leaders. In the view of this passing

A younger Indy (Corey Carrier) shares adventures in the wild and learns valuable life lessons from Teddy Roosevelt. Courtesy of Keith Hamshere/ABC-Lucasfilm.

anonymous peasant, none of the historical figures battling for control of Mexico offers anything to ordinary people whose lives are disrupted by revolutionary strife. As such, conventional history depicts struggles in which the interest of "the people" is ignored, and the peasants are always on the losing end. In the case of both Ataturk and this Mexican peasant, the "other" speaks, but this capacity is closely tied to Indy's presence, as he offers them an opportunity to articulate positions that are subsequently "lost" in the sweep of world historical events. In this sense, their effectiveness in speaking for themselves remains tied to the presence of an agent of white western culture who is willing to listen. Indy's capacity to listen to these alternative voices is clearly linked to his youth.

The program's progressive multicultural vision is not limited to explicitly "political" events or to the older Indy. In "British East Africa, September 1909," the ten-year-old Indy meets Theodore Roosevelt on safari.[4] Indy admires Roosevelt, both as a former U.S. president and for his spectacular public male heroics. He proves his own male mettle by emulation when he conspires with a young African boy to locate an oryx herd for Roosevelt. But he also expresses values more attuned to late twentieth-century versions of global ecology and animal rights. Thus, having proved his manhood by finding the animals that Roosevelt sought and that the professional hunters were unable to locate, he goes even further in his last-minute intervention to prevent Roosevelt from killing too many oryxes.[5]

At the same time, Indy's ultimate ineffectiveness in the past contributes to his ongoing "education," as he learns the truth of the power of white, western hegemony—a power into which he is progressively integrated as he comes of age. (The coming of age narrative is quite literally at stake in "Paris, 1916," in which Indy, on leave from the battlefields of Verdun, meets the exotic Mata Hari and has his first sexual experience.) Despite his restricted agency, Indy is persistently situated as a hero, through both his actions and his global vision and understanding perspectives, however naively formed. At times the program goes so far as to imply that world history would have been "better" had his youthful perspective prevailed.

Dr. Quinn, Medicine Woman (1993–1998)

Like Indy, Dr. Michaela Quinn, familiarly known as Dr. Mike, brings a range of recognizable contemporary values to the past—in this case set in the American West. The youngest of five daughters from a wealthy Boston family, Michaela (Jane Seymour) fulfilled her father's desire for a son by attending medical school and joining him in his medical practice. In the television movie that introduced the series ("Pilot"), Michaela's patients virtually disappear after her father's death, so she decides to pursue opportunities on the frontier. She responds to a newspaper ad for a doctor in Colorado Springs, is offered the job, and travels west only to learn that they were expecting Dr. Michael Quinn. The local telegraph clerk had assumed that the "a" at the end of her name was a middle initial, and elided it in the transcription of her telegram.[6]

Despite a cool reception, Dr. Quinn stays in town and after a predictable period of strained relations gradually wins professional acceptance and support in the community. In the introductory telefilm, Dr. Quinn's closest friend and supporter, the local midwife Charlotte Cooper, is bitten by a snake. Despite Dr. Mike's medical attention, Charlotte realizes she is dying and asks Dr. Mike to care for her three young children. Thus, by the end of the episode, Dr. Quinn is installed as a professional woman and a single parent struggling to adapt to the frontier and to unanticipated motherhood.

The process of establishing the character in a frontier setting reflects an ambivalent misfit status, in which she is initially "out of place" in both physical and ideological terms. When Dr. Mike first arrives in Colorado Springs, she is inappropriately dressed for the frontier town and ends up falling on her face in the muddy, unpaved road. She does not know how to ride a horse, but refuses to admit it; she is not particularly skilled at cleaning her own house, but Charlotte sends her children over to help out. Despite her lack of frontier skills and knowledge, which readily mark her as an "outsider," she immediately confronts the cultural and racial biases of the town. On her first evening at Charlotte Cooper's boarding house, she initiates a conversation with soldiers involved in land negotiations with the local Cheyenne. In her efforts to behave as a civilized, middle-class citizen, she immediately blunders by mistaking the colonel for a captain. And her polite inquiries about the treaty provoke brusque, racist complaints from the colonel, who would just as soon kill off what he calls the "red rebel." Dr. Quinn clearly opposes this crass bigotry.

The contours of her contradictory status in the community thus begin to emerge. On the one hand, her genteel eastern breeding make her ill fit for the frontier; initially she is literally unable to navigate the territory. Yet this same cultivation and education facilitate her ability to bring a progressive vision to the frontier community, especially when it comes to her attitudes towards gender and race. In the process, Dr. Quinn as an exceptional woman gets associated, even contaminated, with "other" forms of frontier life, specifically Native Americans and animals. Her contaminated status is apparent when she first goes to the general store to post a notice seeking housing and space for her medical practice. The owner of the store, Loren Bray (Orson Bean), has joined the community in initially rejecting the woman doctor and tells her there is no room for her notice. Dr. Quinn makes room by removing a sign that prohibits Indians and dogs on the premises and placing hers in its stead. The functional value of the sign she removes is undermined by the fact that the bulletin board is in a back corner of the store; it is the last thing one might see on entering, rather than the first. Yet this location reinforces its significance in terms of its symbolic value, expressing community values. The replacement of one sign by another affiliates Quinn with Indians and

Sully (Joe Lando), strong, silent, and wild, is immediately established as a potential love interest for Dr. Mike (Jane Seymour). Courtesy of the Museum of Modern Art/Film Stills Archive.

animals at the same time that it constitutes an act of defiance in relation to the town's conventional attitudes. It defines her at once as a social object and a social subject, a tension that characterizes her throughout the series.

Reinforcing the aggressive intent of her action, the removal of the sign occurs immediately after Sully enters the store, accompanied by his pet wolf and a member of the Cheyenne delegation. Sully is the series' "classic" Western and romantic hero, whose identity in between the wilderness and civilization is literalized in his appearance and by his role as a translator and part-time agent for transactions between the U.S. government and the Cheyenne. Strong, silent, and wild—with flowing tresses and frontier-style clothing—he is immediately established as a potential romantic interest for Dr. Mike. (His identity as a romantic hero is informed by the fact that the actor who portrays him, Joe Lando, came from daytime soap operas.) Sully provides Dr. Quinn with a place to live and introduces her to the Cheyenne, from whom she borrows some medical remedies, including one that ends up saving her mother's life, in a later episode. After a few seasons, Sully and Dr. Quinn marry.

The program's multicultural and revisionist impulses extend beyond its focus on a single professional woman in the West. Other regular characters include members of the Cheyenne tribe, two African Americans who run local businesses, and a prostitute under long-term contract to the bartender. From time to time the program also introduces other characters whose "minority" status is narratively explored (Chinese, Jews, etc.). Thus the program routinely presents an apparently diverse community, in line with revisionist understandings of the history of the American West in popular culture.[7] In this revisionist context, the white male characters who are familiar figures from the Western genre—Hank the bartender (William Shockley); Jake the barber (Jim Knobeloch); Loren, who runs the general store; Horace the postman (Frank Collison); and the Reverend Johnson (Geoffrey Lower)—are reconfigured. They wield privilege largely by virtue of being representatives of white patriarchal culture, but are more specifically characterized as boorish, bigoted, sexist, and/or small-minded, as well as embodying hyper and hypo masculinity in ways that often make the characters quite unappealing. Even in cases where they are sympathetic, they are largely ineffectual. The program nonetheless sustains sympathy for them as integral members of the larger, traditional Western community.

With this constellation of diverse individuals, and with Dr. Quinn at the center of its progressive impulses, the program begins to define a position that might be characterized as "communitarian postfeminism." In an array of issue-oriented plots, the program has addressed wife abuse ("Sanctuary"), corporal punishment ("Just One Lullaby"), environmental pollution ("Bad Water"), racism (against Swedish immigrants, Chinese laborers, Jews, African Americans, and native Americans), drug addiction ("Life and Death"), and so forth. These recognizably contemporary social concerns are historically interpolated. For example, the issue of drug addiction is explored in relation to a Civil War veteran hooked on morphine and alcohol, who is apparently the historical counterpart of the current media stereotype of the Vietnam veteran hooked on heroin. Or, the local water source is being poisoned by a local mining operation. Dr. Mike diagnoses the problem when the townspeople start to get sick, investigates and identifies the source of contamination, and goes after the mine owner to persuade him to change his mining process to assure a safe water supply.

The program represents its multicultural community of competing interests and beliefs by means of visual scenographies. At key moments in dramatic development the mise-en-scène explicitly displays the solidarity of community with its incommensurate and irreconcilable internal conflicts, or uses one character to condense these tensions. An episode dealing with black cavalry troops in the West offers a vivid example of this strategy ("Buffalo Soldiers"). Even before the main program titles, the episode introduces a series of conflicts. First, the white townspeople gape at and deride the cavalry troop as it rides into town, while Grace (Jonelle Allen) and Robert E. (Henry Sanders) look on with pride. The troop, seeking medical aid and lodging, at first rejects Dr. Quinn's assistance because she is a woman. But after the white male characters refuse to provide medical aid or lodging because the troops are black, they accept Quinn's aid. Then Sully shows up at the clinic with a wounded Cheyenne girl and questions her for helping the troops who killed the girl's family, while the African American sergeant wonders why Dr. Mike is diverting her attention from his wounded soldiers to help an Indian girl.

All of this occurs before the program's regular title sequence and is played out in a succession of medium and close shots, emphatically marking the visual distinctiveness of the characters whose shifting allegiances are at stake, as variable sexism and racism intersect. The scene culminates in a close shot of Dr. Quinn, caught in the middle of irreconcilable tensions of competing bigotry in which she has already been implicated as an object. The soldiers initially reject her services because she is a woman doctor, even though her son asserts her credentials by noting that she has even treated Custer's men. The culminating close-up reveals Dr. Mike's progressive humanitarianism as inadequate to the tensions thus generated.

Within the visual scenography, characters assume emblematic functions. These scenographic displays often constitute key moments of affective resonance, exposing the tensions and unities that constitute the community in explicitly visual terms. Along these lines, a Thanksgiving episode concludes with the Cheyenne and the townspeople sharing a meal during a drought ("Giving Thanks"). As they all sit together around a long table, a tracking shot exhibits the visual scenography of a diverse community provisionally able to overcome its differences (including explicit racism) for the sake of a celebratory ritual in a time of mutual need. (The immediate reward is signaled in a rainstorm that breaks during their outdoor communal meal.)

Another episode concludes by uniting the community (this time without the native Americans) after a particularly tense set of conflicts, instigated by fear of a typhoid epidemic ("The Offering"). In the course of the episode, Dr. Quinn's children are forced into quarantine because Matthew (Chad Allen) has typhoid fever. Dr. Mike and Sully are unable to help him because they are at the reservation helping the Cheyenne fight the disease. When a young girl in the "Swedish village" outside of town develops the fever, the townspeople immediately blame the infestation on this new immigrant population and destroy the immigrant settlement. (In fact, the source of the disease is the blankets brought to the Cheyenne by the U.S. Army. Matthew had taken a few of the provisions, including blankets, to his Swedish girlfriend.) Despite the destructive display of intolerance, differences are ultimately superseded and the community is brought together within the fiction and within the television frame to celebrate their common identity as Americans on George Washington's birthday. The annual celebration includes a dramatic performance of George Washington cutting down the cherry tree and the customary performance of Horace in the guise of Abraham Lincoln reading the Declaration of Independence. This iconic display of American freedom provides the context in which the community is symbolically reconstructed in shots that emphasize their common, communal spectatorship despite the events that have torn them apart.

As a progressive crusader, Dr. Quinn is effective within the confines of her community. Yet in the larger historical context of the program, with its revisionist version of frontier life, her interventions are *ultimately* as futile as the young Indiana Jones's efforts to eradicate colonialism around the globe in the television series that bears his name. Dr. Mike can extend her own humane sympathy to the Indians, but cannot change the fact that the United States implemented policies to systematically eradicate Native Americans. Indeed, despite her best sentiments, at times she cannot avoid being implicated in these policies. The same holds true for her perspectives on other forms of racism and sexism, the environment, the use of herbal remedies in medicine, the place of women in professional and social contexts, and so on. Even within the context of the Western community in which she does function her success is tempered, in particular by her extremely conventional femininity, evident not only in her physical appearance but also in her tender and morally balanced mothering and her artless romance behaviors.

The program promotes multicultural and communitarian impulses that are mutually supporting. According to its logic, cultural differences and individual beliefs can be recognized and maintained as long as they are ultimately unified by a larger community vision. In the case of the program, the community takes the form of the aggregate population of Colorado Springs, which in turn finds its meaning by reference to a common identity in U.S. citizenship. Thus, to function effectively, the community as a local entity props itself on the idea of the nation, as evidenced in "The Offering," discussed above, which culminates with the ritual celebration of George Washington's birthday. (This is the case even though the program is set in the Colorado territory.) In this context, Dr. Mike recognizes the Cheyenne population as having their own distinctive heritage and customs and as being deserving of human rights. But this does not necessarily include recognition as a distinctive national entity, with the rights of mainstream nation-states. In this way the program suggests that the question of human rights can be disentangled from the question of national identities.

Romancing History

Dr. Quinn develops these issues in conjunction with multiple romance subplots which involve different couples: Dr. Quinn and Sully, Robert E. and Grace, Loren and Dorothy, Jake and Dorothy, Horace and Myra, and Matthew (Dr. Quinn's oldest son) and Ingrid. Despite the circulation of these couples, whose amorous relations periodically become the narrative focus, the program maintains an equivocal stance when it comes to its most explicit romantic subplots. In fall 1993, one episode ("Saving Souls") was widely promoted as "the most romantic episode of the season." The network advertisements for the episode repeatedly showed Sully and Dr. Mike exchanging meaningful glances, but the episode itself was hardly concerned with their relationship. Instead, the episode's stories included a revivalist faith healer coming to Colorado Springs and drawing a following from some of Dr. Quinn's patients, a consumptive bounty hunter (Johnny Cash) bringing in a wounded horse thief, and the marriage of Grace and Robert E. While the wedding was certainly "romantic," it displaced the Sully-Quinn romance depicted in the promos for the episode. Moreover, the wedding also introduced the problem of racism, as the Reverend Johnson initially refuses to perform the ceremony in the local church, based on a church policy excluding blacks. (Needless to say, Dr. Quinn and Sully eventually persuade him to reverse his position.) There was a conspicuous slippage between the visual and verbal rhetoric of the program's promotion (which suggested over and over again that romance was going to blossom between Dr. Mike and Sully), and intertwined story lines concerned with racism, faith healing versus medicine, and a dying Western hero.

In this episode (and others) the program develops a strategy of ongoing displacements and alibis, whereby issues emerging from one place within its multicultural, postfeminist, Western, and romance interests are reversed or shifted to another site. In contrast to the episode just discussed, the very next episode aired was a special two-hour presentation in which Michaela returns to Boston to tend to her sick—and presumably dying—mother ("Where the Heart Is," Parts 1 & 2). She meets a young Boston physician who ends up proposing marriage. Sully follows her to Boston and is unable to comfortably fit into Boston culture, but finally declares his love for Michaela. In the context of its initial U.S. prime-time airing, this episode delivered on the promise of the promotional spots for the previous week—the "most romantic episode." This includes not only Sully's overt declaration of feelings, but also the possibility of Michaela's romance with another man, and her position in the Boston episode as a more conventional visual spectacle of feminine beauty, as more elaborate and fancy dress and behavior is required in the East than in Colorado Springs. In at least these significant ways—two subplots and overall mise-en-scène—this episode conforms to more traditional practices of romance fiction, but is not identified as such in advance. Indeed, the program's equivocation in this regard includes questioning the value of romance fiction, a genre that the program routinely engages.

"Heroes" directly explored the nature of popular romance literature and ended up as a critique of this genre, dramatizing a female reader who is overly affected by the fictions aimed at her. As it opens, Dr. Mike's adolescent daughter Colleen (Erika Flores) joins her friends, who are reading a recent installment of a serial romance in a weekly newspaper. Colleen is at the post office to pick up a present she has ordered for Dr. Mike, a modern stethoscope. But her excitement at its arrival is immediately forgotten when she hears the passionate tale of Colt and Caroline as her friends read aloud. This is clearly one of her first encounters with pulp romance literature, and she is instantly captivated. As she reads the previous week's episode, borrowed from her friends, she is nearly run over by a wild horse and wagon. But she is heroically saved at the last instant by Sully, who knocks the wind out of her when he pushes her out of the path of the oncoming wagon. As she regains her composure, she mistakes Sully for the fictional Colt, and is immediately convinced that she and Sully share a deep, mutual—but unspoken—passion. Her friends encourage her in this belief and interpret all interaction between Colleen and Sully in terms of the serial story they follow.

In other words, Colleen's very first exposure to weekly serial romance conforms to the widespread stereotype of women's responses to mass culture, characterized by overcloseness and persuadability, a relationship in which her friends also vicariously participate.[8] Predictably, when she tries imitating the fictional heroine's behavior in her own "real life," she ends up putting herself at risk, waiting for Sully in a mine during cold weather and nearly losing her hands to frostbite. Meanwhile, the stethoscope only gets to Dr. Mike at the end of the episode, confirming the deleterious effects of romance fiction, which intrudes into Colleen's life and delays the arrival and use of the new medical instrument. Modern medicine and scientific progress are hereby placed in opposition to the fantasies instigated by feminine mass culture. By virtue of this opposition the program aligns its central character with scientific progress and implicates progressive social scientific thought of the late nineteenth–early twentieth century. (This refers to the burgeoning field of "effects" research at University of Chicago and Hull House and their interest in scrutinizing the relation between working class and female publics and the popular culture they encountered.)

This opposition between mass culture and science is reinforced in a subplot that involves discovering the source of Hank's food poisoning with the use of a microscope introduced by Louis, an adolescent friend of Colleen. He visits Colleen during her recuperation and brings along his microscope to entertain her. They end up examining a meat sample that Myra left with Dr. Mike and determine that it is infested, a discovery later confirmed by Dr. Mike. This discovery proves that Hank is sick because of his own meat and not because of the food he ate at Grace's restaurant. In this way, scientific knowledge is affiliated with inquisitive boys, and the pursuit of scientific vision (literally through a microscope) coincides with the identification of a more appropriate boyfriend for Colleen, as she recovers from frostbite, from her crush on Sully and her encounter with pulp romance fiction.

The episode thus offers a pat critique of a mode of fiction in which the program itself routinely participates. Episodes regularly center on any number of developing romance relationships, especially the ongoing romance between Sully and Dr. Mike, culminating in their marriage in the season finale in spring 1995 ("For Better or Worse, Parts 1 & 2"). The program's equivocation about its own relationship to romance fiction results in a balancing act of Dr. Quinn as conventional romantic heroine on the one hand, and as an unconventional, progressive postfeminist crusader on the other. This refusal to place her solely or primarily in the realm of traditional romance facilitates her ability to intervene in the fictional history the program constructs. With its "knowing" critique of the most traditional forms of romance fiction, the program proposes that it offers a new form of female heroine, who is nonetheless never too unconventional when it comes to familiar modes of femininity.

Romance also emerges as an occasional concern in *Young Indiana Jones* and is even more clearly delineated as a distinctive sphere, apart from the world of male heroism. According to the logic of the program, affairs of the heart are by and large incompatible with international affairs and thus with Indy's heroic global activities. The global arena in which Indy circulates is represented as holding particular dangers for women and as a potential threat to conventional domestic stability. For women, the risk of encounters with history, especially in foreign locales, is suggested in "Florence, 1908," when young Indy's mother is aggressively and amorously pursued by the Italian composer Puccini while her husband is away on the lecture circuit.

The irreconcilability of romance and the world of male activity (which is integrally identified with history) is also developed in "Istanbul, September 1918." Indy is working as an agent for French Intelligence in Turkey, pretending to be a Swedish journalist. His specific mission involves bringing a secret French peace proposal to Mustafa Kemal (Ataturk). At the same time, Indy becomes engaged to an American woman, who is working with refugee children in Turkey. When she discovers that he is a spy and a fellow American who has not shared his true identity with her, she is disheartened and breaks their engagement. Later, she is mistaken for Indy when she borrows his raincoat and is fatally shot by someone trying to foil his mission. Based on this episode, it is clear that Indy's success as a spy depends on a level of discretion and subterfuge that is at odds with developing a meaningful relationship, and that the perils of his position extend to anyone close to him. In both of these ways at least, his heroism and adventure preclude romance. And any romance in which he is involved ends up being at the woman's expense.

Quality Family Television

While bringing elements of a progressive multicultural revision to the historical worlds they depict, these programs also participate in constructing quality family television, particularly, but not exclusively, in the U.S. context. The idea of quality television has most often been linked to the idea of a quality audience; that is, an audience in which the total size is less important than the purported buying power and habits of the regular viewers.[9] Quality programming also includes distinctive aesthetic practices, including self-reflexivity, innovative generic recombinations, or elements that affiliate television programs with the more prestigious theatrical film industry.

The quality cachet of *The Young Indiana Jones Chronicles* starts with its association with Lucasfilm and the highly successful theatrical movies featuring the adult Indiana Jones. Lucas's company produced the program and drew on the talents of writers and directors who are largely identified by their work in theater and film, including David Hare, Nicolas Roeg, Carrie Fisher, and even actor Harrison Ford (the film Indiana Jones) in one episode. The production incorporated careful attention to lighting and mise-en-scène, contributing to an "authentic" historical feel and also associating the program with the visual aesthetics of film rather than the conventional look of most prime-time series. Atmospheric mise-en-scène, including extensive night scenes, use of chiaroscuro lighting, and so on, were common on the show.[10] Quality also links technology and the Lucas association, insofar as the program was widely discussed for integrating cutting edge "high-tech" strategies as a way of cost containment.[11]

Dr. Quinn stars Jane Seymour, known especially for her participation in a number of television miniseries. As such, she brings a degree of prestige and glamour not routinely identified with weekly series television, especially when it comes to family viewing.[12] Yet her presence as a sign of quality also confounds the image of the national community purveyed by the narrative. For part of the Seymour cachet resides in her identity as a British actress. A curious tension arises as the British actress portrays a progressive U.S. citizen from Boston who carries her multicultural vision to the frontier. There are also signs of quality in the production itself. Notably in this vein, the program uses a masked title sequence, suggesting the cinemascope frame of theatrical Westerns. At the same time, without relying on details of historical accuracy, the program routinely references general knowledge of the West, including aspects of the popular genre and elements of revisionist history, as an integral part of its appeal. The very mix of characters is part of this "authenticity," which is extended in episodes such as those dealing with African American cavalry troops or typhoid-infested blankets. In all of these ways the program marks its distinction within the world of family television.

Dr. Quinn proved to be much more successful than *Indiana Jones* in the head-to-head Saturday evening network program schedule. Yet *Indiana Jones* has had significantly more diverse contexts of circulation. For beyond network episodes, the program also generated a number of book series for young readers. In addition, Lucasfilm created a formal *Series Study Guide* intended for teachers.[13] The guide offers a summary of each episode, along with information about the historical figures and a list of issues for discussion and research. Similarly, the novels based on the series often include book lists for further reading about the period and historical personages in question. Thus, the television program aggressively proposes itself as the focal point for a series of derivative texts and activities of educational value. Moreover, although the program was not successful enough to stay on network television, its exemplary status as quality family production led to its renewal on cable by The Family Channel (formerly the Christian Broadcast Network, then owned by televangelist Pat Robertson[14]), which subsequently televised a number of new two-hour episodes.

Gender, Nature, Culture, and World History

In "Is Female to Male as Nature Is to Culture?" Sherry Ortner theoretically accounts for women's secondary status by virtue of being seen as closer to nature, mediating nature and culture.[15] The figure of Dr. Michaela Quinn seems ideally modeled according to Ortner's delineation of women's ambiguous status between nature and culture. This status "may help account for the fact that, in specific cultural ideologies and symbolizations, woman can occasionally be aligned with culture, and in any event is often assigned polarized and contradictory meanings within a single symbolic system."[16] This status is even figured in the program's title, inscribing the mediation of culture and nature: *Dr. Quinn, Medicine Woman*. The first part signifies education and civilization, while the second name is conferred on the character by the Cheyenne chief, acknowledging her honorary, privileged status in relation to Native American culture, formulated in her case with a gender twist.

The relation to the West signaled in the program title is unstable, at once invoking tradition and a revision thereof. Dr. Quinn may be exceptional, but in ways which nonetheless conform to conventional expectations of woman's place in culture. Part of her exceptional nature is her ability to mediate so well, to embody heroism and singularity in a manner that binds her to the frontier community, which is also the site with the distinctive capacity to enable her to flourish as she does. (Boston, after all, rejected her medical expertise, as it later rejects her "crude" Western habits and behaviors.) In a crucial sense, she is brought into the mediating space between nature and culture by coming to the West and by immersing herself in a distinctive community culture (however much she struggles to transform it). Dr. Quinn's success and effectiveness is confined to this community, which itself functions in relation to the generic determinations of the West, however revised.

Indiana Jones is fully associated with the forces of tradition as he travels around the world with the full privileges of white western culture. However, because of his youth, he is still flexible and open-minded when it comes to learning from "others." But his experiences, even his romantic encounters, are designed as part of an educational process that progressively constructs him as a *man* of the world. While Indiana Jones cannot change the course of history, he is endowed with the capacity to travel around the world, both with his father and on his own, encountering well-known historical figures. In many of the episodes, an elderly Indiana Jones is the narrator of his own tales, a curmudgeonly figure who nonetheless serves as master of his own histories.

With their multicultural historical revisions, both *Dr. Quinn* and *Young Indiana Jones Chronicles* bring anachronistic perspectives to bear on the historical pasts that they depict. Yet the particular pasts they dramatize and the more modern perspectives they offer are overdetermined in divergent fantasies of "getting things right," redressing the ills of the present by revisiting the past. Moreover, their anachronistic visions are anchored in historical verisimilitude, representing two of the most significant ideological visions regarding their respective historical epochs. *Dr. Quinn* foreshadows a version of Frederick Jackson Turner's frontier thesis revised in terms of communitarianism in the Colorado territory, tacitly recognizing that the frontier is closed and working to cultivate the community in relation to a unified national identity. (In this vein, for example, she is an avid supporter of the railroad coming to Colorado, a familiar icon of "progress" in the Western genre.) The young Indiana Jones (in contrast to both Dr. Quinn and his own adult incarnation in feature theatrical films) expresses a version of Wilsonian liberalism rewritten in the terms of contemporary multiculturalism. He foresees countries coexisting as distinctive nation-states in harmonious, if competitive, balance.

Dr. Quinn is firmly enclosed in the Western past, an image figured in the weekly title sequence that places her in a wagon heading west (from right to left on the screen), crossing the U.S. landscape, traversing domestic, rather than global terrain. In the process she at least initially (mis)takes the many Native American tribes she sees as constituent communities within the United States, akin to the community she will join in Colorado Springs, and not as individual nations. Her forcefulness as a heroine is ultimately tied to this misrecognition. In this way, women in the West—even progressive postfeminists—are incorporated into a vision of manifest destiny and domestic unity, binding geographical territory to national identity. By contrast, boys in history hold forth the possibility of a renewed global imagination, especially as long as the women stay in their place in the family, in television, and in the world.

Notes

1. The 1991–1993 dates represent the first run of the weekly program on the network. The program was picked up by cable in 1994 and included the production of a number of made-for-cable movies between 1994 and 1996.

2. I am less interested here in particular viewers than I am in the probable age,

knowledge, and experience of the aggregate television audience when the program was initially produced and aired. Generally, they are likely to have little direct experience— or even much knowledge—of the period during which the program is set, whereas an awareness of Vietnam and the Middle East, as areas of more recent global conflict, is more likely.

3. In fact, this quote is from George Santayana, not Arnold Toynbee, but this is never made clear. However, the Santayana quote offers the general rule under which Toynbee can in some sense "predict" that the behavior of the negotiators will lead to World War II. Toynbee did serve as a diplomat at the Paris Peace Conferences.

4. Haraway, "Teddy Bear Patriarchy, " *Primate Visions*, (New York: Routledge, 1989), 26–58.

5. My discussion of this episode is based on the novelization as well as the episode that aired. *The Young Indiana Jones Chronicles: TV-3. Safari Sleuth*, adapted by A.L. Singer (New York: Random House, 1992). Based on the teleplay "British East Africa, September 1909," by Matthew Jacobs, story by George Lucas. There were a number of book series generated by the program, all versions of juvenile literature, demonstrating an interest and awareness on the part of producers in the child audience for the program.

6. In this and one other episode, discussed below, crucial dramatic moments hinge on letters that go astray. There is at least one additional episode in which a stray telegram (which can be considered a form of letter) is delayed in reaching its addressee, leading to narrative complications. Stray letters thus constitute a narrative strategy for significant moments in the program.

7. This multicultural revision of the West follows from a range of recent films and television programs (beginning, perhaps, with *McCabe and Mrs. Miller* and extending to *Dances with Wolves* and *Unforgiven* in film, and *The Young Riders* in television).

In *Prime Time Feminism: Television, Media Culture, and the Women's Movement Since 1970* (Philadelphia: Univ. of Pennsylvania Press, 1996), Bonnie Dow offers an extensive discussion of *Dr. Quinn* in relation to postfeminism, maternal feminism, and the revisionist Western. Her analysis details relationships between the program and contemporary trends in feminism, along with considerable discussion of the program's treatment in the popular press. She also discusses its status as a revisionist Western, although she sees the genre of the Western as constituting a mythic and nostalgic context for the program. The ways in which revisions of the West might be transformative are not addressed.

Other recent relevant sources on the Western and its revisions include Jane Tompkins, *West of Everything: The Inner Life of Westerns* (New York: Oxford Univ. Press, 1992) and Edward Buscombe and Roberta Pearson, eds., *Back in the Saddle Again* (London: BFI Publishing, 1998).

8. The association of women and romance/melodrama, especially the popular figuration of women readers/spectators as overly close to the texts they consume, is widely discussed by feminist theorists. Among others see: Mary Ann Doane, *The Desire to Desire*, (Bloomington: Indiana Univ. Press, 1987); Lynne Joyrich, "All That Television Allows: TV Melodrama, Postmodernism, and Consumer Culture," *Camerca Obscura*, no. 16 (1988): 129–54; Terry Lovell, *Consuming Fiction* (New York: Verso, 1987), 1–18; Tania Modleski, *Loving with a Vengeance* (New York: Methuen, 1982); Modleski, "Femi-

ninity as Mas(s)querade: A Feminist Approach to Mass Culture," in *High Theory/Low Culture*, ed. Colin McCabe (New York: St. Martin's Press, 1986), 37–52; and Mimi White, *Tele-Advising*, (Chapel Hill: Univ. of North Carolina Press, 1992), 14–18 and 89–92.

9. For more on the idea of quality television, see Jane Feuer, "The MTM Style," *MTM: Quality Television,* eds. Feuer et. al. (London: BFI, 1984), 32–60; and Mimi White, "What's the Difference? *Frank's Place* in Television," *Wide Angle* 13, nos. 3 and 4 (1991): 82–93.

10. John Caldwell discusses the program in these terms in *Televisuality* (New Brunswick, N.J.: Rutgers Univ. Press, 1995), 65 and 85.

11. To name just a few, these issues get raised in: Bernard Weinraub, "George Lucas on Issues, Ideas, and Indiana Jones," *New York Times,* January 27, 1992, sec. C, 17; Paula Parisi, "Digital Vid, 16mm Give 'Indy' Best of 2 Worlds," *The Hollywood Reporter,* August 17, 1992; and Paula Parisi, "Lucas Weaves Digital Web for Filmworks," *The Hollywood Reporter,* October 29, 1993.

12. For example, see Stewart Weiner, "Jane Stakes Her Claim," *TV Guide,* February 20–26, 1993, 8–12.

13. "*The Young Indiana Jones Chronicles:* Series Study Guide," Lucasfilm, Ltd., 1992.

14. For a more detailed discussion of CBN, especially how it defines itself as an alternative to and an extension of mainstream commercial television, see White, *Tele-Advising,* ch. 4, 119–22. In 1997, The Family Channel was purchased by Rupert Murdoch.

15. Ortner, "Is Female to Male as Nature Is to Culture?" *Women, Culture, and Society,* eds. Michelle Rosaldo and Louise Lamphere (Palo Alto, Calif.: Stanford Univ. Press, 1974), 67–88.

16. Ortner, 87.

3 Quantum Leap

The Postmodern Challenge of Television as History

Robert Hanke

She said: What is History?
And he said: History is an angel
Being blown backwards into the future
He said: History is a pile of debris
And the angel wants to go back and fix things
To repair the things that have been broken
But there is a storm blowing from paradise
And the storm keeps blowing the angel
Backwards into the future
And the storm, this storm
is called
Progress
        Laurie Anderson, "The Dream Before"

Theorizing that one could time travel within his own lifetime, Dr. Sam Beckett stepped into the Quantum Leap Accelerator, and vanished. . . . He awoke to find himself trapped in the past, facing mirror images that were not his own and driven by an unknown force to change history for the better. His only guide on this journey is Al, an observer from his own time, who appears in the form of a hologram that only Sam can see and hear. And so Dr. Beckett finds himself leaping from life to life, striving to put right what once went wrong, and hoping each time that his next leap will be the leap home.
        voice-over from the opening title sequence of *Quantum Leap*

Laurie Anderson's "The Dream Before," which recalls one of Walter Benjamin's theses on the philosophy of history, shall serve as a point of departure for this essay, just as the "Quantum Accelerator" serves as Dr. Sam Beckett's point of departure in the television series *Quantum Leap*.[1] This essay examines some possibilities for thinking about television as history. It considers what television studies could do to address television as remembered history and how the notion of popular memory works as a supplementary to the main arguments advanced by histories of television.

The agenda of this essay is three-fold. First, it describes the contours of the study of media history, Michel Foucault's remarks on popular memory, and the emergence of collective memory studies. Second, it suggests the usefulness of William Palmer's New Historicist holographic model of film history and criticism and applies it to *Quantum Leap*.[2] Moreover, it argues that this model needs to be revised in light of memory studies and the rise of cultural history as the "study of the construction of the subject."[3] Finally, it briefly presents some theses on the philosophy of television as history.

Before the advent of critical historiography in the 1970s, traditional approaches to media history were satisfied to look backward, like the angel in "The Dream Before," only to be blown into the future by visions of progress. Communication historians then began to take notice that traditional approaches produced a great (white, middle-class) man, top-down, press and artifact-centered version of U.S. media history.[4] Since then, a growing body of critical historiography has continued to challenge the traditional view and revise the practice of media history.[5]

In his critical history of the discipline, Hanno Hardt writes that communication studies must "recover its sense of history" and "recognize the relationship between history and theory."[6] Recovering our sense of history will entail more than assembling all of the necessary facts and getting the story of U.S. media right. For one thing, it will require us to recognize how standard historical accounts function as cultural myths about the past. James Schwoch, Mimi White, and Susan Reilly, for example, argue that television's view of its own "Golden Age" structures academic accounts of the "origins" of network television, valorizing "live" television production and severing television's development from economic, institutional, cultural, and technological factors.[7] For another, television has undergone massive technological and institutional changes since the 1980s, becoming part of the transnational media industry and a global mediascape. Consequently, "it has become impossible to treat [television] as a unitary phenomenon with a single line of history."[8]

Such acknowledgments, of course, resonate with the New Historicism, an intellectual challenge to antiquarianism that began in the 1960s and came to more widespread interdisciplinary recognition in the late 1970s and early 1980s. As Palmer aptly puts it, this "type of 'metahistory,' always aware of itself as text and of the interrelation between its texts, subtexts, contexts, intertexts, can elevate the past into the participatory position of being a layer in the holograph of present history."[9]

This intellectual development can, in turn, be treated as part of a longer-term history that would reveal how forms of historiography are articulated with media and (post)modernity. Following literary critic Richard Terdiman, George Lipsitz argues that the study of history took on a new meaning at the end of the nineteenth century in response to modernity.[10] Historians took it upon themselves to reconnect the present to the past at the very moment that new media—the telegraph and the daily newspaper—began to dissolve previous barriers of space and time. In the last decades of the twentieth century, we began to live within an accelerated modernity, represented by a new phase of time/space compression that began in the 1970s, and a shift from the mode of production to the "mode of information."[11] Rather than merely recapitulating the modernist crisis of memory, the New Historicism can be read as a response to the postmodern crisis of history. As Hayden White wrote in 1966, "We require a history that will educate us to discontinuity more than ever before; for discontinuity, disruption, and chaos is our lot."[12] If it is true that we have entered a "second media age" and a "post-television" culture, then it is important to reconsider how "time, history, and memory" are transformed in our shift to a "culture of real virtuality" and to "capitalist postmodernity as a chaotic system."[13]

As has also been pointed out, history is not only for historians, nor are historians the only producers of historical discourse and knowledge. Historical events, "which are inevitably susceptible to interpretation as texts, are expropriated, interpreted, and 'reworked' by mass culture mechanisms (books, the print media, television, films) to the point that new levels of the text become holographically overlaid atop the original text."[14] In this sense, television has the capacity to produce culturally salient knowledge of the past as a category of experience, even as television's production of history is "subsumed in an overwhelming 'present text' of television flow."[15] While television's representation of history may overlap with the knowledge and writing of historians (as in the public television series *Empire of the Air: The Men Who Made Radio*, or on The History Channel), live "media events," from President Kennedy's funeral to the fall of the Berlin Wall, "are in competition with the writing of history in defining the contents of collective memory."[16] In addition, ordinary, everyday television often blurs history and fiction, conflates historicity and contemporaneity, and is inseparable from popular memory, the active process of remembering and forgetting. Contemporary television culture is therefore a site of struggle over the meanings of historical experiences, in the shape of popular memory. Television, as a vehicle of popular memory, thus becomes an important site within which to examine the formation of contemporary historical consciousness and/or subjectivity.

What kind of historiographical practice can we develop to relate to and address television as history and popular memory? We might begin with Michel Foucault, whose attempt to construct a practice of "effective history" that would deconstruct "traditional history" has sparked some of the greatest controversies in contemporary historiography.[17] The relevance and importance of Foucault's philosophy of history for media studies has already been explored with particular attention to Foucault's archaeology of discourse and his genealogy of power.[18] His discussion of the panopticon, for example, has been deployed by communication scholars as a metaphor for understanding the function of the technological assemblage of computers, databases, and telecommunications networks.[19]

Also suggestive, however, are Foucault's remarks about popular memory. In an interview on the subject of "Film and Popular Memory," he discusses how popular print media as well as cinema and television have eroded the historical knowledge that the working classes once had of themselves. In the audiovisual media, he says, "people are shown not what they were, but what they must remember having been."[20] Furthermore, "memory is a very important factor in struggle."[21] Since contemporary popular media shape popular memory, and thus knowledge of past struggles, popular film and television are implicated in the dynamics of history making. Foucault teaches us that it is not only important to be critical of how the total story of history is told (how the past informs the present), but also how the present reads the past (how the media construct "history" as a category of popular memory).

Foucaultian history, as a practice of countermemory, would complement rather than displace histories of communication technologies, institutions, discourses, and practices by placing more of an emphasis on the historicity of history (and the form of time), the formation of subjectivity, and power/knowledge relations. Moreover, this formulation can also help us to avoid the impasse of skeptical postmodern views of the "end of history." It may also offer an alternative to a neo-Marxist, historical-materialist framework, such as Fredric Jameson's. In his effort to map postmodern cultural forms, informational media like television news are described as the "very agents and mechanisms for our historical amnesia."[22] This is a critique of television that reproduces much of the Frankfurt School's critique of the culture industry; at the same time, Jameson's analysis of postmodernism and television displays a high-modernist aesthetic sensibility in its privileging of avant-garde, experimental video over commercial broadcast or cable television—the source of many people's "pop images" of history. When Jameson does focus on the relationship between media and history, as in his discussion of the 1980s "nostalgia film," he contends that the "history of aesthetic styles displaces 'real' history."[23]

The notion of popular memory enables us to approach media as history in a way that is perhaps less dismissive of television's images of history. While historical materialist, or culturalist, perspectives enable us to grasp how televisual discourse may function to collapse history onto a perpetual present or misrepresent or abuse history, these positions presuppose an epistemological realism that usually leads to the conclusion that popular culture can only fail to represent "real" history.[24] This is the sort of "historiographical operation" that Michel de Certeau has opened up to criticism from a poststructuralist perspective.[25] In turn, the theory and politics of the "descent into discourse" have been examined and criticized from the perspective of historical materialism.[26]

The point is not to enter into that debate here, but only to acknowledge that the debates that emerged in the 1980s between social historians and the "new" cultural history signified a crisis in the field of history. The Chinese character for "crisis" represents both danger and opportunity. On the one hand, there are dangers in abandoning the distinction between the making of historical truth claims and regarding all such claims as an effect of discourse. On the other hand, the crisis presents an opportunity to examine how open television is to the memory of the struggles of diverse subjects of history, how television's historical pastiche "involves (re)historicization of the present as well as (re)presentations of the past."[27] It may be inadequate to analyze the dialectic of history's appearance/disappearance on television because, to quote Richard Dienst, "The issue turns on how a new technology of representation dissolves or betrays earlier figural devices in the process of inventing new ones. Although television seems simply to destroy history—through what might be called inaccuracies, indistinctions, and forgettings—it also constructs its own kind of historical material, precisely by projecting new lines of linkage and new speeds of reference."[28]

If the television apparatus constructs its own kind of history, then scholarly work on memory can also help us conceptualize how the order of history (forces and events) is transmitted into popular memory. In this regard, Barbie Zelizer has provided a comprehensive and very useful review that traces, from a humanistic, neofunctionalist perspective, a scholarly shift from "individual" to "collective" memory.[29] She contends that memory studies, even though sometimes perceived as a threat to the authority of traditional historians, may be "complementary, identical, oppositional, or antithetical at different times."[30] For Zelizer, "collective memory suggests a deepening of the historical consciousness that becomes wedged between the official markings of the past and ourselves in the present."[31] She goes on to identify eight premises of memory studies: 1) memory is a process, 2) memory is unpredictable, 3) remembering is dissociated from linear time, 4) memory is anchored in space, 5) memory is partial, 6) memory is useable, along social, political, and cultural trajectories, 7) memory is particular and universal, and 8) memory is material. While her review encompasses more than the memory work of media, it seems to me that many of these premises would apply to television, especially as it has taken on more of an archival function with cable channels like Nickelodeon and The History Channel and through convergence with the World Wide Web.

Zelizer also notes that representations of the past have become increasingly prominent in fictional television, appearing as a theme in *Homefront*, *Thirtysomething*, and *The Wonder Years*. Other programs, such as *I'll Fly Away*, also come to mind, but to go further with these exemplars requires greater attention to television's textuality. Palmer's New Historicist holographic model of film history and criticism is a useful starting point, for it enables us to conceptualize television's subtexts, intertexts, and contexts as well as the shifting relations of history to texts and texts to history. By appropriating his model, we can ask not only "how and in what shape media help—and hinder—the activity of remembering" but how television's present holograph of history interprets the past and fosters particular understandings of the present.[32] This approach would also attempt a "self-reflexive analysis of these different texts as a means of arriving at a metatext or metahistory."[33] Particular television shows, like some contemporary Hollywood films, have exhibited a "metaconsciousness of both past history and past films."[34] Moreover, television as a whole, with its increased flow of syndicated reruns, revivals, and remakes, has represented its own history in the "massive combination of texts that includes old and new, past and present, as equivalent choices."[35] To take just one example, consider Nirvana's music video for "In Bloom," MTV's number one video in January 1993. The Seattle-based grunge rock band's performance is framed and choreographed as a musical act on *The Ed Sullivan Show*, positioning the band within a remembered history of black-and-white television and rock 'n' roll. A holographic model would enable us to address this video's articulation of history and memory and its construction of historical sense.

Of course, within contemporary television or film, some texts will display this self-reflexive consciousness of history more than others. Palmer, for example, mentions 1980s "futuristic" films like *The Terminator* (1984), *Star Trek* (1986), *Back to the Future* (1985), and *Peggy Sue Got Married* (1986), which are premised on the notion "that in order for the future to exist and continue, the past must be understood and even revised."[36] This also aptly describes the premise of the science fiction, fantasy series *Quantum Leap* (NBC, March 26, 1989—May 5, 1993).[37]

A few questions are appropriate at this point: What is *Quantum Leap's* way of personifying and representing lived history, and how does this series implicate the viewer as a subject of postmodern historical consciousness? What sort of popular memory work does this series do?

Quantum Leap was conceived of as an anthology series that would allow its creator and executive producer, Donald Bellisario, to explore his interest in recent history.[38] The series' back story centers on two leading characters— Nobel prize–winning quantum physicist Sam Beckett and Admiral Al Calavicci—and an out-of-control time-travel experiment called Project Quantum Leap. As the opening voice-over suggests, Beckett "leaps" into the lives of people from the past, where he is observed and advised by Calavicci. One side effect of his time travels is that he has difficulty remembering who he is. However, he shares a technological link to the present through Ziggy, the bi-gendered computer with an "ego" that runs Project Quantum Leap. Through a "handlink" with this computer, Beckett and Calavicci can see each other as "neurological holograms," and Calavicci can retrieve information or project images. Beckett's time travel appears to have no destination, other than to create the possibility for his return to the present. However, this eventuality is linked to helping others avoid dire consequences (such as their own deaths) by altering the course or circumstances of their lives. From his first leap in the series' pilot episode (1995 to September 13, 1956) on, the time scale of Beckett's (heroic) action is his own lifetime (from 1953 to 1999).[39] For most of the series, he travels between the mid-1950s and the mid-1980s; in the final episode, "Mirror Image," he leaps to August 8, 1953, his birthday, walks into a bar, and sees his own reflection in a mirror, realizing that it's the actual day of his birth.

While this certainly suggests the time scale of autobiography, the relations between each episode's text (or plot) and history are multilayered. In the first place, once Beckett has leaped, the story remains within the time frame of the calendar date displayed at the beginning of each episode. Such dates, of course, measure time as linear; yet, from one episode to the next, time is treated as nonchronological. Differences in set and costume design, music, cultural artifacts and forms of expression, and social attitudes are imbued with historicity and evoke discontinuities between the past and the present.

In each episode's narrative, the past functions as more than a backdrop for the character's interactions and the dramatic situations. Some episodes, for example, contain what the story guidelines issued to prospective writers call the "kiss with history."[40] These are moments when historical events or persons appear as part of the fictional plot or as minor details. The majority of the ninety-five episodes, however, do not feature such representations of the "real" past. Most of the episodes take present dilemmas and vicissitudes of male friendship, romantic relationships, marriage, family, and career and displace them into a fictional past. At the same time, story guidelines advise writers to juxtapose contemporary information or attitudes with earlier times and places. In this way, the past is used to rehistoricize the present.

This being said, there are clusters of episodes where social, political, and cultural history appears as a subtext. To begin with, the series narrates a social history of race relations and racism in six episodes.[41] "The Color of Truth" (August 8, 1955) takes the Civil Rights movement as its backdrop. "So Help Me God" (July 29, 1957), "Justice" (May 11, 1955), and "Unchained" (November 2, 1956) address the issue of race and criminal justice, while "Black and White on Fire" (August 11, 1965) takes the Watts riots (using stock footage) as a backdrop to explore the issue of interracial love. In these episodes, Beckett leaps into the bodies of various subjects: a poor Southern black man, a white lawyer defending a black woman, a black medical student, a white chain gang member, and a member of the Ku Klux Klan (who has to prevent the lynching of a local black activist). However, recalling the "old racism" and popular struggles for Civil Rights, this narrative of racial inequality and injustice is contained within a 1950s–1960s time frame. While this may allow viewers to remember the justification for white liberal opposition to segregation and open discrimination, the elision of this issue from the stories told within the time frame of the 1970s–1980s also implies that racism is a thing of the past.

Both the antiwar movement and the women's movement make brief appearances in the series' remembrance of social history. In "Animal Frat" (October 19, 1967), Beckett has to prevent a fellow college student from dying in a bomb blast set up to protest the Vietnam War. In "Liberation" (October 16, 1968), Beckett leaps in as a middle-aged housewife turned "bra-burning" liberationist who has to keep her daughter from dying in a protest march that turns violent. In both cases, protests synecdochically represent social movements, and they are associated with violence rather than nonviolence. Such elliptical political memories can be understood as a "selective forgetting and reinscription" of the countercultural past that articulates with the conservative hegemony of the Reagan/Bush/Gingrich era.[42]

From a poststructuralist standpoint on gender difference and identity, the eight gender-crossing episodes are of particular interest.[43] In her analysis, J.P. Williams suggests that gender-crossing episodes "assert that gender is a malleable, socially constructed category, and that knowledge of one's own sexual identity is inherent and stable."[44] In this reading, the series plays with signs of gender at the same time it reaffirms masculinity and heterosexuality. In "Miss Deep South," Beckett leaps into a beauty pageant contestant and has to learn how to walk, talk, and dance like a Southern belle. In "A Song for the Soul," Beckett leaps in as a member of the Lovettes, a teenage female singing group, in order to prevent another member from being economically exploited. In her reading of episodes dated from 1955, 1961, and 1980, Williams argues that the series posits progress for women, but this position is contradicted by a masculine discourse that continues to define masculinity in relation to physical aggression and violence, and knowledge of being a man rooted, and thus naturalized, in the male body.

Two other episodes, which Williams does not discuss, represent the reconstruction of hegemonic (hetero)masculinity. In "Dr. Ruth," Beckett leaps into the celebrity sex therapist Dr. Ruth Westheimer and tries to help a couple having problems in their relationship, as well as a woman who is being sexually harassed in the workplace. Beckett's difficulties with Dr. Ruth's frank talk about sex is contrasted with the future, where he accepts some advice from the real Dr. Ruth. Here we see how the episode, originally broadcast in 1993, reads both the recent past and the near future, how "manmade" language and masculinist ideology is being challenged, and how hegemonic masculinity, caught in between the past and the future, attempts to modernize itself in response to liberal feminist gender politics. In "Running for Honor" (June 11, 1964), Beckett leaps into Cadet Lieutenant Commander Tommy York, a track star at a naval academy who is defending his ex-roommate's homosexuality. While this is not a gender-crossing episode, we can observe how an issue that surfaced in early 1990s news media reports is displaced onto a fictionalized and distant past. Initially, Calavicci embodies the military anti-gay standpoint that homosexuals are unfit for military service because they can be blackmailed or do not possess leadership qualities. For his part, Beckett never questions his roommate's sexual preference, and he tries to prevent anti-gay violence. In this case, the issue of gays in the U.S. military appears to have a longer history than it is presented as having in most news stories. In retrospect, this episode was the most controversial one aired, and even though it was threatened with advertiser defections, it expressed a more progressive impulse than President Clinton's "Don't ask, don't tell" policy. By the end of the episode, Calavicci's homophobia gives way to tolerance,

The memory of Vietnam activates the plot lines of several episodes of *Quantum Leap*, as in this example with Sam Beckett (Scott Bakula) as a commando and Al Calavicci (Dean Stockwell) as a Navy officer. Courtesy of NBC.

and he reveals that York's ex-roommate goes on to found the Gay Liberation Movement.

Thirdly, there is a cluster of episodes that articulate the Vietnam War subtext and that echo Jefford's thesis about Vietnam narratives and the "remasculinization" of American culture.[45] In "The Leap Home, Pt. II: Vietnam" (April 7, 1970), Beckett leaps to Vietnam and finds himself to be a member of his brother's SEAL unit the day before his brother's death. In "Nowhere to Run" (August 10, 1968), Beckett leaps in as a twenty-six-year-old Vietnam vet in a veterans' hospital who attempts to prevent the suicide of another veteran. Finally, in "The Beast Within" (November 6, 1972), Beckett leaps into a Vietnam veteran who lives with a friend suffering from seizures and hallucinations related to a war injury. These episodes indicate a shift in interest from the war experience to the "coming home" stories that centered on the problems faced by Vietnam veterans as they tried to assimilate into civilian life.

Fourthly, three episodes feature leaps into historical figures, or persons close to such figures. In "Lee Harvey Oswald," Beckett leaps in as Oswald on March 21, 1963; October 5–6, 1957; June 6, 1959; October 21, 1959; April 10, 1963; October 21, 1963; and the day of President Kennedy's assassination. This two-hour season premier was a rebuttal to Oliver Stone's *JFK* (1991), which challenged the official assassination story and provoked a national debate among journalists, critics, and historians over the "truth" of this

On *Quantum Leap*, Oswald didn't act alone. He had help from time traveler Sam Beckett (Scott Bakula) in this episode, which revisited an acutely traumatic moment in American history: the JFK assassination. Courtesy of NBC.

historical event and the role of popular film in representing and interpreting historical events.[46] In Bellisario's version, elements of Oswald's biography (his communist affiliations, his links to the KGB, etc.) are selected and arranged into a structure of interpretive possibilities that refutes Stone's version. Ziggy insists, and Calavicci agrees, that Beckett is leaping into Oswald to uncover the possible "conspiracy" that led to Kennedy's death. While Calavicci interrogates Oswald in the "Waiting Room," Beckett leaps into successive dates from Oswald's biography. Each time he leaps, he retains some residual knowledge of Oswald's "personality" and "soul," but these biographical glimpses confirm the official story. Sam's final leap is from Oswald in the Texas Schoolbook Depository to a CIA agent near the President's motor vehicle. While nothing stops Oswald from committing the crime of the century, Beckett does prevent Jacqueline Kennedy from being killed along with her husband.

Two episodes, both from the final season, center on the lives of living legends, thereby extending their posthumous careers and diffusing popular culture history. In "Goodbye Norma Jean" (April 4, 1960), Beckett leaps in as Marilyn Monroe's driver so she can live long enough to make *The Misfits*. In "Memphis Melody" (July 3, 1954), Beckett leaps in as Elvis Presley, two days before he is discovered by Colonel Parker and records with Sun Records. These two historical figures, by virtue of electronic reproduction, are emblematic of the baby boomers' cultural inheritance, and these episodes offer yet another opportunity to consume film and popular music stars as signs of their times. Of course, this begs further questions about whose stars are being remembered and how they articulate with cultural meanings and affective experiences in the past and the present.[47]

This brings us to a fifth cluster of reflexive episodes, which enables us to analyze the series' metatext and its implications for viewer's historical consciousness or subjectivity. The most self-reflexive episode in this cluster is "Future Boy" (October 6, 1957), in which Beckett leaps in as an actor in a children's television series about time travel called *Captain Galaxy*. Here, as in the other episodes in this cluster, "generic time" frames elements like character types and story patterns.[48] For example, some episodes recite "classics" of Hollywood film: "It's a Wonderful Leap" (May 10, 1958); "Play it Again, Seymore" (April, 14, 1953); "Rebel without a Clue" (September 1, 1958). "Double Identity" (November 8, 1965) cites *The Godfather*, while "Dreams" (February 28, 1979) cites *Dressed to Kill*. Other episodes draw upon television's generic traditions: "Moments to Live" (May 4, 1985) draws on soap opera; "Roberto!" (July 27, 1982) draws on tabloid-style talk shows; "Blood Moon" (March 10, 1975) crosses into the detective genre and the urban crime series.

Sam Beckett (Scott Bakula) even "leaps" back to the days of disco
dancing (with Tobi Redlich), complete with white pants and vest.
Courtesy of NBC.

In "The Boogieman" (October 31, 1964), Beckett leaps in as a horror novel-
ist, while "The Last Gunfighter" (November 28, 1957) revisits the Western.

At this level, the television series *Crime Story* (September 18, 1986—May
10, 1988) is something of a precursor to *Quantum Leap* because it treated
generic traits as "historical artifacts in their own right."[49] Like *Crime Story,*

Quantum Leap measures time not only in terms of calendar dates and historical periods but in terms of what Richard Dienst calls "multilayered generic time." In this time scale, history is a pastiche of popular film and television genres and this metagenericism functions to renegotiate the contract between media images and consciousness under contemporary conditions of media use and reception.

Following this line of thinking, *Quantum Leap's* metagenericism is not merely an extension of the 1980s television programming strategy of creating generic hybrids, but an indication of how popular narratives adapt, and even envision, what Jim Collins calls the vast "array" of media texts and technologies. *Quantum Leap* is "hyperconscious" not only about generic precedents but also about the conditions of watching cable television in the 1990s. In *Quantum Leap,* the anthology format of early broadcast television is used to channel cable television's own flow of heterogenous, multitemporal time into hi(s)tory. Moreover, Beckett is a figure for the television viewer him/herself, whose contemporary viewing practices include zapping through television channels with remote control units. As Richard Dienst summarizes, "A channel, once abandoned, is completely beyond recovery until turned to again. Even television sets capable of making a composite image from two channels at once cannot make the leap from the single visible to the many virtual images.... [Z]apping reintroduces a moment of circumscribed chance, making a transverse cut through the grid from one programmed zone to another until sense appears."[50] *Quantum Leap's* metagenericism offers an imaginary resolution to the viewing dilemma of our time and promises the pleasure of consuming an array of television's popular genres in a single series.

In memory of Walter Benjamin, four theses on the philosophy of television as history are:

I. "Effective history," Foucault tells us, should introduce "discontinuity into our very being."[51] By contending that *Quantum Leap* projects its own kind of history, this is not meant to suggest that television fiction produces effective history. But what if our critical reading of this series was guided by a sense of "effective history"? In such a reading, *Quantum Leap* is a fable in which the hero encounters the discontinuity of his own being, and past/present/future are folded into one another. The hero must apprehend possibilities so as to beat the odds—the certainties of "official" history as recorded and written. In this sense, history is a place of confrontation, where "official history" and the line of inevitability it traces between past and present may be disrupted not only by the angel of history, who cannot help but look backwards to the debris of the past, but also by chance events, randomness, and haphazard conflicts. In this fable, the sense of history is to be continued.

II. The purpose of "effective history," Foucault also tells us, is not "to discover the roots of our identity, but to commit itself to its dissipation."[52] History and subjectivity are related in the thesis of the dispersed or destabilized subject. In our fable, the hero leaves his body behind to inhabit the bodies of others, sometimes even marginalized or devalued others. As Jay Bolter and Richard Grusin note, when popular fictional plots turn on the empathetic occupation of another point of view, "the borders of the self dissolve, as it occupies the position and experiences the problems faced by other creatures."[53] If he does not become the Other, he is not quite the Same either. A leap in time makes a fissure appear, and the unified masculine subject falters into the future. Yet it is not only a question of masculinity, but also of technology and the boundaries of the humanist subject. The hero and his observer/guide appear only as holographic images for each other; indeed, it is the computer that makes their copresence possible. Does our fable not suggest that the subject once located within a dualistic structure of "Self/Other" is now dispersed beyond the limits of the body into multiple subject positions? The questions raised by the hero's time travels—Where am I? Who am I? And why am I here?—suggest that under conditions of time/space compression, the body is no longer coextensive with a single subject position. Within contemporary technoculture, new communication technologies are "altering the conditions under which the subject is constituted, indeed even the subject who writes history."[54] And if history is written from the "sedentary point of view," perhaps our fable's flow of multilayered, metageneric history, and its disrespect of the division between representation and the subject, can lay the basis for picking up speed and composing new allegories of nomadic subjects caught up in movements of de- and reterrorialization?[55]

III. "With acceleration," writes Virilio, "there is no more here and there, only the mental confusion of near and far, present and future, real and unreal—a mix of history, stories, and the hallucinatory utopia of communication technologies."[56] Laid over the historical subtext(s) of *Quantum Leap* is the metatextual concatenation of history and media memories that functions as a "techno-palimpsest."[57] What this series does—what television as a technology of representation does—is decelerate or accelerate the speed of historical reference. Our fable's representation of technology—the Quantum Accelerator, the Imaging Chamber, and the Waiting Room—can either be read backwards, as a representation of television as we have known it, or forwards, in anticipation of a post-television culture of virtual reality environments, computer-mediated communication, and cyberspace-time. What our fable transmits to our living rooms are lines of remembering and forgetting. Some lines are blocked or erased, and we can call those lines of historical elision. Some lines are redrawn, revealing what was/was not possible or emergent in a particular historical moment. Some lines—between private and public, past and present—are blurred. Other lines foster multilayered connections between texts, subtexts, and intertexts, evoking a reflexive sense of history. As popular culture, *Quantum Leap* departs from television's time-denying, present-minded flow of meanings and values so as to construct an impulse to interpret the past, adding "text-ure" to our historical sense of the present and our presence within it. This "text-ure" does not create a more inclusive account of the (dis)order of contradictory events and forces. Rather, the nondialectical, contingent dynamics of televisual popular memory reworks the past in order to postpone continuity, and with it, the unified historical subject that it brings into being.[58] *Quantum Leap* addresses its audience as agents of selective memory; it presumes to show seventy-eight million aging American baby boomers what they may remember having been. This does not mean, however, that televisual popular memory functions as a closed system of expression and repression (forget Freud) or that television as history is always already subsumed by a dialectic of appearance/disappearance (pace Jameson); it is more like a "rhizome rather than a tree," a "map, not a tracing."[59]

IV. In Michael Ondaatje's *The English Patient* (1996), the English patient and cartographer of the North African desert, who always carries with him Herodotus's *The Histories*, observes:

> I have seen editions of *The Histories* with a sculpted portrait on the cover. Some statue found in a French museum. But I never imagine Herodotus this way. I see him more as one of those spare men of the desert who travel from oasis to oasis, trading legends as if it is the exchange of seeds, consuming everything without suspicion, piecing together a mirage. "This history of mine," Herodotus says, "has from the beginning sought out the supplementary to the main argument." What you find in him are cul-de-sacs within the sweep of history—how people betray each other for the sake of nations, how people fall in love . . .[60]

Only as we begin to recognize television as an audiovisual vehicle for popular memory and popular memory as the illimitable supplementary to the main arguments inscribed in histories *of* television can we understand the dynamics of the perpetual (re)construction of television *as* history in motion, and so on.

Notes

Laurie Anderson, "The Dream Before," *Strange Angels* (Warner Brothers, 9 25900–4). I wish to thank Thomas Byers for intellectual support and editorial assistance, and Lynn Himmelman for her love and energy for life.

1. Walter Benjamin, "Theses on the Philosophy of History," in Hannah Arendt, ed., *Illuminations* (New York: Schocken Books, 1969), 263–64.

2. William Palmer, *The Films of the Eighties: A Social History* (Carbondale and Edwardsville: Southern Illinois Univ. Press, 1993).

3. Mark Poster, *Cultural History and Postmodernity: Disciplinary Readings and Challenges* (New York: Columbia Univ. Press, 1997), 10.

4. John Stevens and Hazel Dicken Garcia, *Communication History* (Beverly Hills, Calif.: Sage Publications, 1980); Carolyn Marvin, "Experts, Black Boxes, and Artifacts: New Allegories for the History of Electric Media" in Brenda Dervin, Lawrence Grossberg, Barbara O'Keefe, and Ellen Wartella, eds., *Rethinking Communication, Vol. 2: Paradigm Exemplars* (Newbury Park, Calif.: Sage, 1989), 188–98; Hanno Hardt, *Critical Communication Studies: Communication, History and Theory in America* (New York: Routledge, 1992).

5. To name only a few, see Paul Heyer, *Communications and History: Theories of Media, Knowledge, and Civilization* (New York: Greenwood Press, 1988); James Carey, *Communication as Culture: Essays on Media and Society* (Boston: Unwin Hyman, 1989); Carolyn Marvin, *When Old Technologies Were New: Thinking About Communications in the Late Nineteenth Century* (New York: Oxford Univ. Press, 1988); Lynn Spigel, *Make Room for TV: Television and the Family Ideal in Postwar America* (Chicago: Univ. of Chicago Press, 1992); William Solomon and Robert McChesney, eds., *Ruthless Criticism: New Perspectives in U.S. Communication History* (Minneapolis: Univ. of Minnesota Press, 1993); Janet Staiger, *Interpreting Films: Studies in the Historical Reception of American Cinema* (Princeton, N.J.: Princeton Univ. Press, 1992).

6. Hardt, *Critical Communication Studies: Communication, History and Theory in America* (New York: Routledge, 1992), 8.

7. James Schwoch, Mimi White, and Susan Reilly, "Television and its Historical Pastiche," in Schwoch et al., *Media Knowledge: Readings in Popular Culture, Pedagogy, and Critical Citizenship* (Albany: State Univ. of New York Press, 1992), 1–19.

8. Anthony Smith, ed., *Television: An International History* (New York: Oxford Univ. Press, 1995), 2.

9. Palmer, *The Films of the Eighties*, 3.

10. George Lipsitz, *Time Passages: Collective Memory and American Popular Culture* (Minneapolis: Univ. of Minnesota Press, 1990).

11. On time-space compression, see David Harvey, *The Condition of Postmodernity: An Enquiry into the Origins of Cultural Change* (Cambridge, Mass.: Basil Blackwell,

1990). On the "mode of information," see Mark Poster, *Foucault, Marxism and History: Mode of Production Versus Mode of Information* (Cambridge, Mass.: Polity Press, 1984) and *The Mode of Information: Poststructuralism and Social Context* (Chicago: Univ. of Chicago Press, 1990).

12. Hayden White, *Tropics of Discourse: Essays in Cultural Criticism* (Baltimore: Johns Hopkins Univ. Press, 1978).

13. See Mark Poster, *The Second Media Age* (Cambridge, Mass.: Polity Press, 1995); Peter d'Agostino and David Tafler, eds., *Transmission: Towards a Post-Television Culture* (Thousand Oaks, Calif.: Sage, 1995). On the "culture of real virtuality," see Manuel Castells, *The Rise of the Network Society* (Malden, Mass.: Blackwell, 1996); on communication theory and "capitalistic postmodernity," see Ian Ang, *Living Room Wars: Rethinking Media Audiences for a Postmodern World* (London: Routledge, 1996), 174.

14. Palmer, *The Films of the Eighties*, 7.

15. James Schwoch, Mimi White, and Susan Reilly, "Television and Its Historical Pastiche," 8.

16. Daniel Dayan and Elihu Katz, *Media Events: The Live Broadcasting of History* (Cambridge, Mass.: Harvard Univ. Press, 1992), 213.

17. For Foucault, "effective history" is a practice of countermemory and is directed against traditional modern historiography, and its will to knowledge, in three ways: it is directed against "reality"; it is directed against "identity"; and it is directed against the "truth." The first involves parodic subversions of "monumental" history by recovering "lost" or "forgotten" events of history; the second involves a "systematic disassociation of identity" by revealing the "heterogeneous systems that, masked by the self, inhibit the formation of any form of identity"; and the third involves the historical analysis of the "will to knowledge" that would reveal "that all knowledge rests upon injustice . . . and that the instinct for knowledge is malicious." Michel Foucault, "Nietzsche, Genealogy, History," in Donald Bouchard and Sherry Simon, trans., *Language, Counter-Memory, Practice* (Ithaca, N.Y.: Cornell Univ. Press, 1977), 163.

18. Poster, *Foucault, Marxism and History;* Heyer, *Communications and History,* chapter 10.

19. See Oscar Gandy, *The Panoptic Sort: A Political Economy of Personal Information* (Boulder, Colo.: Westview Press, 1993); Poster, *The Second Media Age,* chapter 5.

20. Michel Foucault, "Film and Popular Memory," in John Johnston, trans., *Foucault Live: Interviews, 1966–1984* (New York: Semiotext(e), 1989), 92.

21. Foucault, "Film and Popular Memory," 92.

22. Fredric Jameson, "Postmodernism and Consumer Society," in Hal Foster, ed., *The Anti-Aesthetic: Essays on Postmodern Culture* (Port Townsend, Wash.: Bay Press, 1983), 125.

23. Fredric Jameson, *Postmodernism, or, the Cultural Logic of Late Capitalism* (Durham, N.C.: Duke Univ. Press, 1992), 20.

24. On the collapse of history into a perpetual present, see Jameson, "Postmodernism and Consumer Society"; on the misrepresentation and abuse of history, see Robert Darnton, "Television: An Open Letter to a TV Producer," in Darnton, *The Kiss of Lamourette: Reflections in Cultural History* (New York: Norton, 1990), 53–59.

25. Michel de Certeau, "The Historiographical Operation," in T. Conley, trans., *The Writing of History* (New York: Columbia Univ. Press, 1988), 56–113.

26. Bryan Palmer, *Descent into Discourse: The Reification of Language and the Writing of Social History* (Philadelphia: Temple Univ. Press, 1990).

27. James Schwoch, Mimi White, and Susan Reilly, "Television and Its Historical Pastiche," 13.

28. Richard Dienst, *Still Life in Real Time: Theory After Television* (Durham, N.C.: Duke Univ. Press, 1994), 70.

29. Barbie Zelizer, "Reading the Past Against the Grain: The Shape of Memory Studies," *Critical Studies in Mass Communication* 12 (June 1995), 214–39.

30. Zelizer, "Reading the Past Against the Grain," 216.

31. Ibid., 218.

32. Ibid., 232.

33. Palmer, *The Films of the Eighties*, 11.

34. Ibid., 12.

35. Mimi White, "Television: A Narrative—A History," *Cultural Studies* 3 (summer 1987), 282–300.

36. Palmer, *The Films of the Eighties*, 13.

37. The series has also been distributed on the Sci-Fi cable channel and the Lifetime Network.

38. Bellisario's career as a television producer began with *Baa Baa Black Sheep*. He was a supervising producer on *Battlestar Galactica* and went on to create *Magnum, P.I.* as well as *Tales of the Gold Monkey* and *Airwolf.* These details, as well as others presented in this section, have been drawn from Louis Chunovic, *The Quantum Leap Book* (New York: Citadel Press, 1993), Julie Barrett, *Quantum Leap: A to Z* (New York: Boulevard Books, 1995), and my own (re)viewing of the series.

39. Two episodes are exceptions to this. In "Leap Between the States," Beckett leaps into his own great-grandfather during the Civil War in order to help with the Underground Railroad. In "The Leap Back," Beckett switches places in 1945 with Calavicci, who is a POW in the Second World War.

40. Chunovic, *The Quantum Leap Book*, 18.

41. One episode, titled "The Americanization of Machiko McKenzie" (August 4, 1953), dealt with racism against Japanese-Americans following the Second World War.

42. See Thomas Byers, "History Re-membered: *Forrest Gump*, Postfeminist Masculinity, and the Burial of the Counterculture," *Modern Fiction Studies* 42 (summer 1996), 419–44.

43. The eight episodes in chronological order are: "8 1/2 Months" (November 15, 1955), "Miss Deep South" (June 7, 1958), "What Price Gloria?" (October 16, 1961), "A Song for the Soul" (April 17, 1963), "Liberation" (October 16, 1968), "Raped" (June 20, 1980), "Another Mother" (September 30, 1981), and "Dr. Ruth" (April 25, 1985).

44. J.P. Williams, "Biology and Destiny: The Dynamics of Gender Crossing in *Quantum Leap*," *Women's Studies in Communication* 19 (1996), 289.

45. Susan Jeffords, *The Remasculinization of America: Gender and the Vietnam War* (Bloomington: Indiana Univ. Press, 1989).

46. See Barbie Zelizer, *Covering the Body: The Kennedy Assassination, the Media, and the Shaping of Collective Memory* (Chicago: Univ. of Chicago Press, 1992), and "Oliver Stone as Cinematic Historian," *Film & History: An Interdisciplinary Journal of Film and Television Studies* 28 (1998).

47. On Marilyn Monroe and 1950s sexual attitudes, see Richard Dyer, *Heavenly Bodies: Film Stars and Society* (New York: St. Martin's Press, 1986), chapter 1. On Elvis Presley's cultural afterlife, see Gilbert B. Rodman, *Elvis after Elvis: The Posthumous Career of a Living Legend* (New York: Routledge, 1996).

48. Dienst, *Still Life in Real Time*, 71.

49. Dienst, *Still Life in Real Time*, 72. Jim Collins makes a similar point when discussing the "genericity" of 1990s film. To quote: "The individual generic features then, are neither detritus nor reliquaries, but *artifacts* of another cultural moment that now circulate in different arenas, retaining vestiges of past significance reinscribed in the present." See his "Genericity in the Nineties: Eclectic Irony and the New Sincerity" in Jim Collins, Hillary Radner, and Eva Collins, eds., *Film Theory Goes to the Movies* (New York: Routledge, 1993), 256.

50. Dienst, *Still Life in Real Time*, 28–29.

51. Foucault, "Nietzsche, Genealogy, History," 154.

52. Ibid., 162.

53. Jay David Bolter and Richard Grusin, *Remediation: Understanding New Media* (Cambridge, Mass.: MIT Press, 1999), 247.

54. Poster, *Cultural History and Postmodernity*, 12.

55. On the "sedentary point of view" of historical writing, see Gilles Deleuze and Felix Guattari, *A Thousand Plateaus: Capitalism and Schizophrenia* (Minneapolis: Univ. of Minnesota Press, 1987), 23.

56. Paul Virilio, *The Art of the Motor* (Minneapolis: Univ. of Minnesota Press, 1995), 35.

57. Collins, "Genericity in the Nineties," 249.

58. Poster, *Foucault, Marxism and History*, 76.

59. It is worth quoting Deleuze and Guattari in full on this distinction: "What distinguishes the map from the tracing is that it is entirely oriented toward experimentation in contact with the real. The map does not reproduce the unconscious closed in upon itself; it constructs the unconscious. It fosters connections between fields. . . . The map is open and connectable in all of its dimensions; it is detachable, reversible, susceptible to constant modification. It can be torn, reversed, adapted to any kind of mounting, reworked by the individual, group, or social formation. It can be drawn on a wall, conceived of as a work of art, constructed as political action or as a meditation." Deleuze and Guattari, *A Thousand Plateaus*, 12.

60. Michael Ondaatje, *The English Patient* (Toronto: Vintage Books, 1996), 118–19.

4 Profiles in Courage

Televisual History on the New Frontier

Daniel Marcus

The presidential administration of John F. Kennedy is widely seen as having significantly expanded the interaction between White House politics and broadcast television. Kennedy's use of television—to convey his personal qualities and political stands—culminated in the television adaptation of his book *Profiles in Courage*, which ran on the National Broadcasting Company during 1964–1965. The docudrama series emerged in the context of the Kennedy administration's effort to resuscitate the tradition of "high-quality" television in the early 1960s, and corresponded to theories of history associated with Kennedy's New Frontier. The series shared with other New Frontier texts the themes of the importance of national unity, political moderation, and the public display of moral courage and personal strength. In keeping with a belief that domestic ideological dilemmas had been resolved by the triumph of a pragmatic, moderate liberalism, the political theory of Arthur Schlesinger Jr., Theodore Sorensen, and others called for a politics of charisma, constructing a notion of citizens as individuated but undifferentiated spectators of the images of strong leaders. Such a view of history was easily translatable into televisual terms. *Profiles in Courage* constructed a pantheon of American heroes who dramatically displayed the judgment and fortitude needed to sway the nation's populace.

The television version of *Profiles in Courage* varied at times from Kennedy's book in its examination of the nation's racial past. The gains of the civil rights movement in the early 1960s made Kennedy's 1956 approach to racial issues, which had downplayed questions of racial justice, seem increasingly out of step with liberalism's activist, integrationist thinking in 1964–1965.

NBC's *Profiles in Courage* (1964–1965) was situated within the discourse of prag-matic, moderate liberalism and the historiography of an American political leader, John F. Kennedy. Courtesy of the John F. Kennedy Library.

The political developments of the early 1960s made clear that not all do-mestic conflicts had been resolved, and the series producers struggled to come to grips with America's racial history while maintaining Kennedy's prefer-ence for moderate positions. Other areas of social conflict in American his-tory, such as class differences and gender inequalities, were more easily effaced from the series' narratives; indeed, gender relationships in the programs tended to bolster the authority of male political figures, even as racial prerogatives were being explicitly questioned and explored.

The Book (1956)

The original *Profiles in Courage* told the stories of eight United States senators who took principled political stands that threatened their careers, and gave shorter profiles to ten other politicians. Rumors circulated for many years that Theodore Sorensen had ghostwritten the book for Kennedy, which both men stoutly denied while Kennedy was alive. The book can be considered akin to Kennedy's speeches, written mostly by Sorensen, but reflecting Kennedy's own views and understandings.[1]

Five of the eight senators treated at length were profiled for their stands surrounding the issues of slavery, the Civil War, and Reconstruction. All five wanted to mute sectional conflict, to seek compromise that would unify the nation. Kennedy's position was that the importance of unity was paramount for the young nation, and that slavery was evil but could only be eradicated by and within the preservation of the Union. Once the Civil War was over, the North was obliged to rebuild the former Confederate states as full partners in America, and the Radical Republicans who wanted harsher treatment of Southern white society were destructive and dangerous.

The historical study was published in 1956, became a best-seller, and was awarded the Pulitzer Prize in History in 1957. *Profiles* gave Kennedy a veneer of intellectualism and seriousness that proved helpful to his 1960 campaign for the presidency. As a child of privilege and fame, Kennedy's demonstration of intellectual achievement served to strengthen his identity as an individual in his own right; as an Irish Catholic, his knowledge of American history placed his public persona more securely within what may have been considered by many voters as mainstream America.

New Frontier Historiography

The Kennedy administration included historians and political scientists in prominent positions. The treatment of history in both the print and television versions of *Profiles in Courage* shared several themes with other New Frontier historical texts, themes popular in the dominant historiography of the postwar era, and which also became prominent in the actions of the administration in its governance.

Warren Susman has identified a school of history writing in the postwar period that enjoyed scholarly status and wide popular acclaim. Politically moderate and featuring a strongly narrative approach, the works of historians such as Samuel Eliot Morison, Allan Nevins, and Arthur Schlesinger Jr., states Susman, "escape from ideology . . . by returning to the mythic and dramatic. . . . [W]e find a history that offers a reinforcement of current moral values and no effective challenge to the decision makers within the social order. . . ."[2] In an era that proclaimed the "end of ideology," in Daniel Bell's famous phrase, perceptions of ideological conflict were externalized into Cold War paradigms, and a technocratic pragmatism was put forward as an American consensus. American historiography drowned ideological questions in a sea of facts and stories. History that was strongly narrative and dramatic in approach was also proving to be easily translated into televisual terms, as the widespread success of NBC's World War II documentary series *Victory at Sea* (1952–1953) had shown.[3]

The Vital Center

Arthur Schlesinger Jr., as historian, polemicist, and political activist, was a key figure in the attempt to forge a moderately liberal domestic consensus in the post–World War II era. Before becoming a Special Assistant to Kennedy in 1961, Schlesinger had taught history at Harvard University and received the Pulitzer Prize for *The Age of Jackson* (1945). Active in the liberal lobbying group Americans for Democratic Action, he ventured into contemporary political writing with the publication of *The Vital Center* in 1949.[4] The book served as a manifesto for anticommunist liberals, defining an agenda that combined the social concerns of the New Deal with support for the Cold War policy of containment of Soviet power. Schlesinger created a tripartite schema to define domestic political forces. The "vital center" of society contains the New Deal liberals who have been in ascendancy since 1933. The liberals share a vision of the just society with the democratic left, and share an emphasis on individualism, pragmatism and accomplishment with the business right. The "politician-manager-intellectual" liberal is in the best position to introduce needed change without disrupting the basic social order.[5] Racial extremists on the right are regionally limited to the South, so the right contains no significant danger to the liberal agenda. Communists and fellow travelers on the left pose the primary opposition to American values from within and without.

In the aftermath of the Depression and World War II, a society marked by civil liberties and enlightened capitalism has answered the challenges of economic deprivation and competing military systems. What bedevils liberals in 1949, wrote Schlesinger, is a crisis of confidence. The reigning domestic problem is not material want or tyranny, but an anxiety stemming from a crisis of individual identity. Echoing the Progressive arguments of Walter

Lippmann and the existentialist critique of Erich Fromm, Schlesinger stated that modern individuals are free from ancient constraints, but feel abandoned and alone. "This freedom has brought with it frustration rather than fulfillment, isolation rather than integration. . . . Most men prefer to flee choice, to flee anxiety, to flee freedom," Schlesinger charged.[6]

Liberal leaders can prevent the collapse of democracy and triumph of Communism by offering themselves as public exemplars of the strength of the system, a strength that will comfort and earn the respect of the anxiety-ridden majority. "[T]he essential form of democratic education," Schlesinger stated, "is the taking of great decisions under the burden of civic responsibility."[7] Inspired by the presidency of Franklin Roosevelt, Schlesinger hoped that liberal leadership could continue to instill faith in the system in the easily swayed, vaguely identified, largely undifferentiated populace by public displays of vigor and courage. Schlesinger borrowed from Walt Whitman to close his book with a distinctly masculinist tone: "If democracy cannot produce the large resolute breed of men capable of the climactic effort, it will founder."[8]

Having anticipated the appeal of John Kennedy in 1949, Schlesinger worked on his presidential campaign in 1960 and returned to these themes in his writing. Schlesinger wanted the figure of the president in particular to symbolize the individual accomplishment that could answer the collectivist ethos and political determinism of Marxism and the anxiety-producing impersonality of modern industrialism. "A free society cannot get along without heroes, because they are the most vivid means of exhibiting the power of free men," he stated.[9] Schlesinger's emphasis on the personal can be seen as a displacement of more intractable social conflicts for which liberal ideology may provide no resolution. Schlesinger sensed a deep disquietude, but placed it at the level of the individual psyche, which could be answered by the public presentation of individual figures of charisma.

Schlesinger's work, along with political scientist Richard Neustadt's study of presidential power and works by other postwar consensus historians, played important roles in forming the New Frontier's initial outlook.[10] In *Profiles in Courage*, Kennedy's portrayal of exemplary behavior, stalwartness, and decisiveness among the political elite paralleled Schlesinger's concerns. Several of Kennedy's heroes were buffeted from opposing sides, and staked out middle positions that Kennedy praised as the products of reason and insight into the nation's long-range interests. The 1956 *Profiles in Courage* fit squarely into the tradition of strongly narrative works that posit that domestic ideological controversies had been resolved successfully, through the display of personal heroism and commitment to America as a whole.

Post-Regnum

The other major chronicler of contemporary events within the New Frontier did not publish his own major works until after Kennedy's assassination in 1963. Theodore Sorensen went to work for John F. Kennedy in 1953 as a speechwriter and general assistant and developed in time to be his closest political confidant, and his collaborator on *Profiles in Courage*. After Kennedy's election to the presidency, Sorensen ranked with Robert Kennedy and Robert McNamara as one of the president's closest advisors.[11] Only after the president's death did Sorensen come forward as an author in his own right, publishing a remembrance of Kennedy in 1965 and a look at the political impact of the Kennedy family in 1969.[12]

Sorensen's and Schlesinger's books about the Kennedys remain the major historical appraisals of the New Frontier from within its own circles. Both authors placed the administration's position of power within a tripartite structure, true to the constructs of *The Vital Center* and *Profiles in Courage*. On the right were Southern segregationists; on the left was the Soviet Union. For Schlesinger, Kennedy's prime importance was as the embodiment of strength, freedom, and virility the Republic needed to inspire public trust and participation. "His very role and personality, moreover—his individuality in a homogenized society, his wholeness in a specialized society, his freedom in a mechanized society—undermined the conviction of impotence.... [P]olitical action . . . no longer appeared so ludicrous or futile."[13] Kennedy was the politician-manager-intellectual hero Schlesinger had prophesied a dozen years before. At a time when society seemed to be breaking up in the throes of racial tension and Cold War, the role of the president was to instill reason, moderation, and a sense of security in a panicky public. Through demonstrations of his strength of will (as when he faced down Southern segregationists in the struggle to integrate the University of Mississippi, and did the same to Nikita Khrushchev during the Cuban Missile Crisis), Kennedy could reassure an existentially anxious nation that American society was still virtuous and vital.

Kennedy, Minow, and Television

John F. Kennedy's election to the presidency brought forth a new burst of activism from the Federal Communications Commission, with his appointment of Newton Minow to head the agency. As FCC Commissioner, Minow began a campaign to increase public service, children's, and educational programming on the three major networks.

One of Minow's favorite shows was *Omnibus,* a survey of cultural events and trends hosted by Alistair Cooke from 1952 to 1961.[14] The executive producer of *Omnibus* was Robert Saudek, who was outspoken about his belief that television was not living up to its potential: "I think the tragedy in television today lies in the fact that it sets a degrading, lazy and decadent tone for the citizens of the United States."[15] His equation of politics and broadcasting was in keeping with the New Frontier's: "The American people are capable of being inspired to world leadership fully as much by television as they have in earlier decades by statesmen, education and journalism." It was the responsibility of both political leaders and television producers to coax their public to support governmental aims for postwar America.[16]

Minow organized FCC hearings on television quality, at which Saudek joined other producers and writers to bemoan the decline in program quality since the late 1950s and offer their talents to reinvigorate the medium with cultural and educational programming.[17] One of Saudek's efforts, directed first to Minow and Sorensen soon after the 1960 election, was to approach Kennedy with the idea of adapting *Profiles in Courage* as a television series.[18]

The New Frontier on Screen

With his success in the 1960 debates with Richard Nixon, Kennedy had concluded that television could play a key role in garnering national support for his programs and conveying his personal strengths directly to the country. During the 1960 campaign, Robert Drew had produced *Primary,* a pioneering cinema verité look at Kennedy's and Hubert Humphrey's electoral efforts in Wisconsin. Kennedy had been pleased with the results, and allowed access to his staff for two ABC documentaries, *Adventures on the New Frontier* in 1961 and *Crisis: Behind a Presidential Commitment* in 1963.[19] Kennedy also organized the first live broadcasts of presidential press conferences and encouraged his staff to make themselves available to television journalists. Jacqueline Kennedy took viewers on a celebrated television tour of the White House in 1962. The president also gave his approval to the making of *PT-109* (1963), a feature film that dramatized his naval exploits during World War II.

Preproduction

Saudek persisted in his efforts to buy the rights to *Profiles* and in June 1963 announced his success.[20] The series was planned to be broadcast only after the 1964 election, to quell any charges of partisanship, and many of the heroes presented would be Republicans. Saudek persuaded Allan Nevins, professor emeritus at Columbia University and one of the country's best-known historians, to review all scripts for historical accuracy. Nevins had reviewed the original *Profiles* manuscript before publication and written a foreword to one of its editions.[21]

Since Kennedy had been particularly concerned that a production of the series not be seen as an electoral or public relations ploy, NBC agreed to air the premiere episode a few weeks after the start of the rest of its schedule, so as not to conflict with the presidential election in early November, 1964. By then, Kennedy presumably would be either a lame duck or leaving the presidency altogether, freeing the series to be appreciated for its commitment to quality rather than as a politician's aggrandizement. Still, if successful, the series would likely add to his prestige. After Kennedy's death, Saudek told Sorensen that he hoped the series would be a good answer to the politics of GOP presidential candidate Barry Goldwater.[22]

NBC provided the series with a budget equal to about 80 percent of budgets for established hour-long dramas, which reduced Saudek's hopes of attracting major stars and writers to the series, but he tried to maintain the production at a level above the norm.[23] He hired several writers who had worked on major films, as well as on *Playhouse 90* and other dramatic anthology shows of the 1950s, including Walter Bernstein, a former victim of the Hollywood blacklist. Instead of the usual industry practice of demanding a script within three or four weeks, Saudek gave his writers three to four months to polish drafts. In addition to Nevins's contribution, scripts were reviewed by Walter Kerr, drama critic of the *New York Herald Tribune*, who would later move to the *New York Times* as lead theater reviewer, the most powerful position in American drama criticism.

Kennedy and Sorensen were active in suggesting which figures from American history should be added to the series, which was projected to air for one season. All scripts went to Sorensen for approval of their political attitudes and historical characterizations. (Early scripts were delivered to the White House for Kennedy's personal inspection just after he had started his trip to Texas in November 1963.[24]) Sorensen had reviewed a number of scripts by the time he left the White House staff in February 1964 and continued the consultation as he began his biography of Kennedy, published in 1965. He rejected at least one script, a portrayal of Senator George Norris's opposition to American involvement in World War I (Sorensen's father had been a follower of Norris). In addition to claiming the script was "dull" and "confusing," Sorensen objected to a scene in which criticism of President Woodrow Wilson's policy toward the war was combined with considerations of an upcoming election.[25] Sorensen was still working at the White House, and

Lyndon Johnson was contemplating both the upcoming presidential campaign and escalating American involvement in Vietnam. The script was rewritten.[26] Robert Kennedy and Edward Kennedy also read some of the scripts before production started.[27]

In the book, John Kennedy had written that he admired moral courage more than physical courage, and he wanted the series to maintain the focus on hard decisions rather than on acts of physical bravery. Saudek restricted the focus to the direct experience of individuals, avoiding political conflicts involving large impersonal forces or multitudes of indirect actors; for example, he disallowed historical situations whose crucial battles were fought in the Supreme Court by lawyers, spokesmen who had little personal stake involved in the outcome of the cases.[28] The producer's decision led to a focus on personal commitment and charismatic display, rather than on the workings of organized groups within a context of institutionalized power. In planning the series, Saudek told one of his writers, "I think the *Profiles in Courage* plays are successful only when the hero does dominate the events and deliberately shape them."[29] This focus on individual action, so common in television narrative, corresponded to the narrative focus and drive of Kennedy's book and other historical works written in the postwar era.

The Network

Broadcasting *Profiles in Courage* could fulfill NBC's responsibility for educational programming, using a well-known source—*Profiles* had been on the best-seller list both when published and after Kennedy was elected. (It became a best-seller again after his death, along with a spate of other books related to Kennedy.) Robert Kintner, NBC's president, also hoped that the series would reinforce the "close relationship" the network enjoyed with the White House.[30] NBC scheduled the series for 6:30 P.M. Eastern time on Sundays, immediately after *Meet the Press* and before *Disney's Wonderful World of Color.* The show's scheduling function, then, was to keep a (usually adult male) public affairs audience, and add children, who could be directed toward the Disney program at 7:30. Against it, CBS offered a documentary series on World War I and the popular children's show *Lassie.* ABC gave its slot to local programming.

Profiles in Courage premiered nationally five days after the 1964 election, accompanied by a black-tie reception at the Senate Theater in Washington, hosted by Saudek and Senate Majority Leader Mike Mansfield. In attendance were Ethel Kennedy, Eunice Kennedy Shriver, fifteen senators, and the five most liberal members of the Supreme Court.[31]

The Series (1964–1965)

The televised version of *Profiles in Courage* consists of twenty-six episodes.[32] Each program opens with a voice recording of Kennedy, speaking on the value of courage, while the screen fills with images from the nation's historical legacy—an American eagle, the Liberty Bell, and the newest addition to national symbology, the Kennedy Dollar coin, minted in his memory. Each story concentrates on the moral courage of one individual. Most often this individual is situated as holding a principled middle ground between unreasonable, contending forces. The individual's struggle within the political triad comes to a climax at a public tribunal—a trial, session of Congress, or other forum, at which the hero(ine) attempts to sway opponents by logic, appeals to the Constitution, or sheer force of personality. Some succeed immediately; some in the long run; a few never do.

The conflicts portrayed in the series range across questions of racial inequality, freedom of speech and religion, and the proper spheres of governmental action. The list of central characters expanded from the book's ranks of senatorial heroes to include other political figures, judges, teachers, and social activists. The series frames the struggles of the individual heroes within a narrative of national progress that has led ultimately to a contemporary sense of civic-minded nationalism.

Slavery and the Union

Many of the episodes dramatize the issues surrounding the Civil War, which can be seen as particularly relevant to the early 1960s, a period that saw a resurgence in the visibility of racial issues in American society. The episodes on the conflicts leading up to the Civil War correspond to the message of Kennedy's book; the heroes span the ideological spectrum but hold the preservation of the Union to be crucial. As presented in two separate episodes, Daniel Webster has been a pro-abolitionist senator from Massachusetts, and Thomas Hart Benton a pro-slavery senator from Missouri, but both support the Compromise of 1850, which gives slave-owners new powers to reclaim runaway slaves while preventing the spread of slavery to new states. They support the Compromise because both fear the Southern states will secede without it. The book and series assert that the delay in secession strengthened the North's ability to win the Civil War and free the slaves, and thus the unpopular stand by Webster and Benton has been validated by history. In each case, the senator has to take on his constituents—Webster breaks with the inflexible abolitionists of New England, and Benton condemns the hotheaded pro-slavers of Missouri. Each searches for a middle ground and makes a public appeal—Webster orates in the Senate, while Benton regales a crowd in Missouri.

The producers were clearly uncomfortable about the compromise with slavery. Webster is shown confronting a slave trader and looking with sympathy at imprisoned slaves. While Benton is shown raging at almost everyone in sight, he is scrupulously polite to a black valet and a black waiter who serve him. The Northern abolitionists are not directly portrayed in this episode, leaving Benton the high ground in his visible opposition to Southern rejectionists. The program does not disclose that he was a slaveholder himself.

Henry Clay, the designer of the Compromise, condemns extremists on both sides and asks Webster to join him in the reasonable middle. It "takes more courage to compromise" than to take extremist positions, says Clay. He needs Webster on his side because he hopes Webster's abolitionist reputation will sway Northern liberals. Webster's "prestige and eloquence will command their attention." The abolitionists are the utopian leftists of their day—right in their principles but self-defeating in their impractical rigidity.

Sam Houston is also embroiled in the conflicts of the 1850s and 1860s. Another undeclared slaveholder, Houston opposes the drive to have Texas join the Confederacy, for he has sworn to uphold the Union. The need for national unity seems self-evident, since neither Houston nor anyone else in the episode actually gives any reason why it should be paramount. Houston's campaign for the end of regional conflict and his opposition to the wishes of a "transient local majority" in the South may have resonated with many Northern viewers at the end of 1964, the height of the Southern civil rights movement. In letters to Saudek, a number of fans in the South noted the importance of *national* values in the series; one Alabama teacher wrote that she appreciated the programs' emphasis on American democracy, "especially here where provincialism and state loyalty seem to outrank national patriotism."[33] The series harnessed the nationalism that pervaded Kennedy's book, in the service of the struggle for racial justice that the 1956 *Profiles* had barely recognized in its presentation of Civil War issues.

Another episode takes a very different angle from the senatorial programs, but arrives at some of the same conclusions. An episode on Frederick Douglass was created for the series; he was not featured in Kennedy's book. Once more, the producers used a tripartite construction to define political interests; Douglass speaks out against slavery, but also has differences with white abolitionists, who self-righteously support the dismantling of the Union because they do not want to associate with the institution of slavery in any way. Douglass supports keeping the Union together as the only way to eventually

J.D. Cannon as Sam Houston, who uses his iconic status as a
founder of Texas to argue against secession from the Union.
Courtesy of the Wisconsin Center for Film and Television.

free his race. When an abolitionist suggests repatriation of slaves and other
blacks to Africa as a possible solution, Douglass and other free blacks resent
and reject the proposal. His agenda is, as the New Frontier's was eventually
to become, integrationist—complete participation for blacks in American
life and prosperity.

Douglass wants to work within the system for change. Having first been
hesitant to speak publicly because he "felt [him]self still a slave," he goes on
to become a famous abolitionist speaker, providing personal testimony of life
under slavery. As a very articulate public figure, he comes to embody the
untapped potential of African Americans as human beings. He speaks so

Robert Hooks as Frederick Douglass, who must contend with both slavery and strained relations among abolitionists. Courtesy of the Wisconsin Center for Film and Television.

well, in fact, that his white allies suggest that he downplay his linguistic ability and erudition, because it makes audiences doubt his claim to have been a slave. Douglass rejects the suggestion. He now knows that to be truly free, he must fully be himself.

This episode, brought into *Profiles* in the mid-1960s and not 1956, displays a much more nuanced and troubled attitude toward race relations than the senatorial programs. Well-meaning whites refuse to touch Douglass physically; blacks resent their dependency on the well-organized and more socially free white activists. Douglass begins to condemn not only Southern slavery, but Northern racism as well; his white allies ask him to stop, saying it splits their movement and hurts the struggle against the greater evil. While Douglass shares the Kennedys' emphasis on integration and their techniques of public persuasion and personal moral embodiment, his conflicts exist in a more treacherous and confused moral environment than created in the book; Douglass lives in a world in which characters are constantly searching for and questioning the basis of their relations to each other.

Janice Rule as Prudence Crandall, bewildered by a campaign of terror when she opens her school to black students. Courtesy of the Wisconsin Center for Film and Television.

In an episode on Prudence Crandall's efforts to run an integrated school in 1830s Connecticut, racist resistance to educational opportunities for blacks is dramatized forcefully throughout. Crandall is subject to the poisoning of her water supply, ransacking of her school and home, and boycotting of her as a consumer by local merchants. While a local segregationist politician claims to be against violence, his opposition to Crandall's school only encourages other residents to terrorize the teacher. The program neatly parallels the segregationist response to the civil rights movement of the 1960s, as was the intention of the producers.[34] Even in this strongly antisegregationist episode, however, the moderate behavior of Crandall is contrasted not only to the racism of her neighbors, but also to the fanatical posturing of an abolitionist minister (despite preproduction objections by Allan Nevins[35]).

Elites and Others

Kennedy's book contained no presentations of class and gender issues; the producers introduced these subjects hesitantly and made no significant attempt to explore their conundrums as they occasionally did regarding race. Consequently, the heroes of the series never face challenges to their positions as members of political, social, economic, and gender elites as they seek to dramatize national ideals and values. Representations of women, in particular, tend to hew closely to the more traditional portrayals of the postwar era. A few strong-minded women act as heroines, but the remainder of the female characters serve to buttress the public prerogatives of the male heroes.

Emblematic of the series' position regarding nonracial conflicts was that no labor leaders are profiled in the series, but the producers did consider telling the story of "businessmen who pioneered in recognizing labor unions and collective bargaining."[36] Two shows also feature public officials sympathetic to early attempts to organize unions. Thus, progressive labor attitudes among elites could be portrayed, but depictions of active organizing among the working classes were avoided.

Walter Bernstein contributed a script about Richard T. Ely, a University of Wisconsin professor who won a victory for academic freedom after being hounded by authorities in the 1890s for his pro-union views. The early drafts of the script were very class conscious, with a narrator associating "workers" with "revolution" and "the right of working men," while associating "big business" and "bankers" with "savage repression."[37] Saudek removed these references[38] and told his script editor, "Narrator copy is totally wrong. It is both irrelevant to the issue of the story, and inflammatory. . . . In short, this is not the story of labor strife, suppression, strike-breakers and goon squads. It is the story of freedom to teach."[39] By removing the story from the historical context of violent capital-labor conflict, Saudek placed its meaning within a less incendiary frame of academic freedom.

Allan Nevins prodded the producers to include women as central figures in the programs, and to highlight the roles of first ladies in stories of their husbands.[40] The three heroines in the program are presented within the contexts of religion or education; only a small number of male heroes inhabit such contexts. The heroines, while sharing a strength of character with the men profiled, at times display less assertiveness and independence than their typical male counterparts. Prudence Crandall, while stalwart in her desire to teach, is often dependent on the support of her husband, clinging to him amid the racist violence aimed at her. She also is presented as less politically minded than the historical record indicates, in a very rare deviation of the producers from their usual obeisance to historical documentation. Religious rebel Anne Hutchinson, on the other hand, repeatedly stands up to male authorities in her struggles in Puritan Massachusetts.

The depictions of male heroes and their private relationships, however, follow a consistent pattern, maintaining a domestic sphere as a preserve of male authority and wisdom. Private, domestic scenes were absent from the print version of *Profiles in Courage,* and no woman was given more than a few lines of description or quotation. The inclusion of the domestic sphere and female characters in the television series—mainly wives and daughters of male heroes—serves to introduce domestic concerns into the narratives, humanizing and individuating the heroes. Depicting the heroes' domestic lives also dramatizes the disruptions in their lives that their principled stands entail. The public-minded heroes also live in a domestic world not unlike that of their audience, furthering the series project to make its truths relevant to the contemporary lives of its viewers.

Domestic scenes offer a break from the formal oratory and complex machinations of the public scenes in the series. They provide opportunities for explanatory dialogue, as the women characters assume nonexpert positions regarding public affairs, positions that parallel those of modern viewers not well versed in Constitutional law and nineteenth-century history. Wives of the heroes often initially object to their husbands' stands, but eventually come around and admire their spouses' courage and sense of civic duty.

Tellingly, Abigail Adams and Edith Wilson play very small roles in their husbands' dramas, although they were two of the best-known and most capable first ladies in American history. Abigail Adams was one of the most politically active first ladies, yet immediately upon her entrance into the program on her husband John (which takes place before the Revolution), she is situated within the spheres of domesticity, motherhood, and feminine beauty. In one of her two scenes, Abigail Adams cautions her husband against traveling through Boston during a period of bad weather and civil unrest. He indicates his coat and boots and says he is protected. Abigail replies, "Against Nature. Not against men." John states, "Men are part of Nature. That is why they have natural rights. You should listen to me argue in court more often." Conversation about the weather melds into explications of philosophy, making the principles of the American Revolution accessible and showing its participants capable of informal banter.

Edith Wilson ran the executive branch in her husband Woodrow's name during the last year of his term, after he was incapacitated by a stroke. The program takes place several years earlier, however, and her main function is to elicit sympathy for President Wilson, who must deal with several crises that intrude upon their new marriage. He never consults her on political matters, and she is relegated to serving coffee. The domestic sphere ultimately serves as an area of authority for the heroes, whose civic power is under constant challenge in public. Within the family sphere, the central characters enjoy masculinist prerogatives of knowledge and courage, buttressed by the admiring, if sometimes tardy, support of their wives.

Critical and Public Reception

NBC promoted *Profiles in Courage* as a high-quality drama, an expression of John F. Kennedy's spirit in the year after his death. In a *New York Times* ad for the premiere episode, a drawing of Kennedy looms over the text,[41] while the *Washington Post* gave the series the cover of its weekly TV magazine, featuring a silhouette drawing of Kennedy leading a small child (John-John?) by hand through the pages of a book, with the profiles of the Americans featured in the series lined up above them. The caption states, "Ask not what your country will do for you," conflating Kennedy's Inaugural Address with the book and series.[42]

With an industry-friendly Lyndon Johnson now in the White House and Congress restricting the domain of the FCC, the networks reduced their public affairs and adult drama programming in 1964, and critics bemoaned what they considered to be a horrible season. In *Profiles in Courage*, they found a throwback to the heyday of serious television drama, suitable for intelligent viewers and educable children, and relevant to contemporary issues. The program received rave reviews from many daily newspapers, *Time, Life, Newsweek,* and the *Saturday Review.*[43] Many agreed with a *Los Angeles Times* reviewer that "[T]he series unquestionably is commercial television's most distinguished weekly show—perhaps the only real program of stature this year."[44]

Ratings were in the high range for informational series, low for dramas. Out of ninety-six regular national series, *Profiles* ranked ninety-fourth, attracting a nineteen share of the viewing audience during its time slot.[45] The J. Walter Thompson Company, which had arranged the purchase of advertising time on the series, expressed its belief that the audience was demographically upscale; ratings were significantly higher in top metropolitan markets, particularly in the Washington, D.C., area.[46] The program was sold to at least thirty foreign markets, which made it a profitable venture for Saudek.[47]

Conclusion: Leadership, Display, and Public Affairs in New Frontier Television

Profiles in Courage was a rare occurrence—a commercial television series inspired by the specific perspectives and historiography of an American political leader. The series contained strong correspondences with New Frontier conceptions of leadership in politics and the civic importance of exemplary behavior. In its concentration on certain public conflicts and identities and neglect of others, the series articulated a dominant but increasingly challenged position of moderate liberalism. The series offered sporadic recognition of the conundrums of race in America, yet also displayed the New Frontier predilection for management of the social order by practical-minded elites bolstered by a renewed sense of masculinity.

Profiles in Courage can be seen also as a landmark in the conflation of politics and entertainment in the age of mass media. It contributed to an increasingly telecentric view of political leadership, an approach in keeping with the preferences of television producers for strong central characters and dramatic narratives. In the years since, American television often has presented the nation's political past through biographical docudramas, including a spate of specials and miniseries on the Kennedys themselves in the 1980s and 1990s.[48] *Profiles in Courage* also shared important characteristics with two television extravaganzas that had just preceded it: coverage of the Kennedy assassination and its attendant tributes to the fallen leader, and the presidential election of 1964. As *Variety* predicted, Lyndon Johnson and Barry Goldwater were "the leading, most talked about, most exposed tv personalities" of the fall of 1964.[49] *Profiles in Courage* ended its run in the summer of 1965, but the other show, with new casts and new titles, continues on.

Notes

The author thanks Julie D'Acci, Michele Hilmes, and Paul Boyer for their comments on early drafts of this essay, and the editors of *Film & History* for final suggestions.

1. John Kennedy, *Profiles in Courage* (New York: Harper & Row, 1956).

2. Warren Susman, *History as Culture* (New York: Pantheon, 1984), 24.

3. See Peter C. Rollins, "*Victory at Sea:* Cold War Epic," *Journal of Popular Culture* 6 (1972): 463–82. For the successor series to *Victory at Sea* and its historical treatments, see Daniel Marcus, "NBC's 'Project XX': television and American history at the end of ideology," *Historical Journal of Film, Radio and Television* 17 (1997): 347–66.

4. Arthur Schlesinger Jr., *The Vital Center* (Boston: Houghton Mifflin, 1949).

5. Ibid., 155.

6. Ibid., 52.

7. Ibid., 159.

8. Ibid., 256.

9. Arthur Schlesinger Jr., "The Decline of Greatness," in *The Politics of Hope* (Boston: Houghton Mifflin, 1962), 32.

10. Richard Neustadt, *Presidential Power: The Politics of Leadership* (New York: John Wiley & Sons, 1960).

11. Edwin Guthman and Jeffrey Shulman, eds., *Robert Kennedy: In His Own Words* (New York: Bantam, 1988), 421–22.

12. Theodore Sorensen, *Kennedy* (New York: Harper & Row, 1965); Theodore Sorensen, *The Kennedy Legacy* (New York: Macmillan, 1969).

13. Arthur Schlesinger Jr., *A Thousand Days* (Boston: Houghton Mifflin, 1965), 740.

14. James Baughman, *Television's Guardians: The FCC and the Politics of Programming, 1958–1967* (Knoxville: Univ. of Tennessee Press, 1985), 58.

15. Robert Saudek to Stanford Shaw, May 12, 1961, the Newton Minow Papers, Box 37, State Historical Society of Wisconsin, Madison. The other Saudek quote in this paragraph is from the same letter. All citations to the Minow Papers refer to the SHSW collection.

Saudek had worked for the Ford Foundation during his *Omnibus* years. He then produced a celebrated series of broadcasts featuring Leonard Bernstein and the New York Philharmonic and advised the Kennedy administration on the creation of what would become the Kennedy Center for the Performing Arts in Washington. His later career included serving as president of the Museum of Broadcasting (now the Museum of Television and Radio) in New York City (1975–1978), and leading the department of Motion Picture and Television in the Library of Congress (1983–1991). His papers regarding *Omnibus, Profiles in Courage,* and other projects are available at the Wesleyan Cinema Archive, Wesleyan University, Middletown, Connecticut.

16. For more on television network efforts during the Kennedy era to provide nationalist themes in their programming, see Michael Curtin, *Redeeming the Wasteland: television documentary and Cold War politics* (New Brunswick, N.J.: Rutgers Univ. Press, 1995).

17. Federal Communications Commission, "Activities and Attitudes of Creators of Live Television Programming," in *Memorandum for Commission, Consisting of Testimony, in brief, and Results to Date of Program Inquiry* (Washington, D.C.: GPO, 1962).

18. Robert Saudek to Newton Minow, February 6, 1961, and Robert Saudek to Theodore Sorensen, February 6, 1961, both in Minow Papers, Box 37.

19. Mary Ann Watson, *The Expanding Vista: American Television in the Kennedy Years,* (New York: Oxford Univ. Press, 1985) 146–51; Baughman, *Television's Guardians,* 60. For previous presidential efforts in using television, see Craig Allen, *Eisenhower and the Mass Media: Peace, Prosperity, and Prime-Time TV* (Chapel Hill: Univ. of North Carolina Press, 1993).

20. Val Adams, "Kennedy's 'Profiles' Sold for TV Series," *New York Times,* June 10, 1963, 1.

21. Richard F. Shepard, "Consulting Post to Nevins," *New York Times,* July 10, 1963, 71.

22. Robert Saudek to Theodore Sorensen, April 23, 1964, the Robert Saudek Papers, Box 310, Wesleyan Cinema Archive, Middletown, Conn. All citations to the Saudek Papers refer to the WCA collection.

23. Gordon Oliver, "Casting Suggestions," to Robert Saudek, December 11, 1963, Saudek Papers, Box 309. Oliver was in charge of production of the series in Los Angeles. Also see "Profiles in Courage—Principals," undated, unsigned production memorandum, from the Theodore Sorensen Papers, Box 37, John Fitzgerald Kennedy Library, Boston. All citations to the Sorensen Papers refer to the JFK Library collection.

24. Robert Saudek, "Producer's Letter," press release, October 26, 1964, Saudek Papers, Box 309.

25. Theodore Sorensen to Robert Saudek, January 10, 1964, Sorensen Papers, Box 38.

26. Mary Ahern to Walter Kerr, January 13, 1964, Walter Kerr and Jean Kerr Papers, Box 68, State Historical Society of Wisconsin, Madison. Ahern was a script editor working out of Saudek's office.

27. Robert Kennedy to Robert Saudek, April 27, 1964, Robert F. Kennedy Papers, Attorney General's General Correspondence, Box 52, John Fitzgerald Kennedy Library, Boston; Del Carnes, "First of 26 Courage Profiles, Quality TV Effort, Starts Today," *Denver Post*, November 8, 1964, p. 15 of "Round-Up" section.

28. Murray Schumach, "Episodes Added to TV 'Profiles': Series Based on Kennedy's Book Also Plans Deletions," *New York Times*, March 13, 1964, 41.

29. Robert Saudek to Andrew Lewis, April 21, 1964, Saudek Papers, Box 241.

30. Robert Kintner to Robert Saudek, August 8, 1963, Saudek Papers, Box 310.

31. "'Profiles in Courage' Gets a Black-Tie D.C. Screening & Reception," *Variety*, November 11, 1964, 39.

32. *Profiles in Courage,* produced by Robert Saudek Associates. Robert Saudek, Executive Producer; Gordon Oliver, Producer (National Broadcasting Company, 1964–1965). Individual episodes bear the name of their central character, e.g., "Daniel Webster." Copies of the series were distributed after broadcast by NBC and McGraw-Hill, and later by the Social Studies School Service of Culver City, California. Titles are no longer in distribution, but many can still be found in the audiovisual collections of schools and public libraries. The Library of Congress and the JFK Library in Boston also hold complete sets of the episodes, but have not made them publicly available.

33. Responses to Teachers' Guides, Saudek Papers, Box 203. The quoted writer was Sister Marie Danielle, of Mobile, Alabama.

34. Robert Saudek (?) to Andy Lewis, September 28, 1964, Saudek Papers, Box 241.

35. Allan Nevins to Robert Saudek and Mary Ahern, October 27, 1964, Saudek Papers, Box 241.

36. "Approved Subject List," unsigned production memo, August 7, 1963, Saudek Papers, Box 309.

37. Walter Bernstein, "Richard T. Ely," 2nd Draft, March 20, 1964, 1, Saudek Papers, Box 240.

38. Robert Saudek, "Notes on Richard T. Ely—First Draft," March 4, 1964, Saudek Papers, Box 240.

39. Robert Saudek, "Robert Saudek to Mary V. Ahern—re Ely Script," March 23, 1964, Saudek Papers, Box 240.

40. Allan Nevins to Robert Saudek, December 16, 1963; April 8, 1964; December 11, 1964, all in Saudek Papers, Box 240.

41. *New York Times*, November 8, 1964, sec. II, p. 14.

42. *Washington Post*, "TV Channels," November 8, 1964, cover.

43. "The Badge of Courage," *Time*, November 20, 1964, 72; "Lesson of History," *Newsweek*, February 15, 1965, 58; Richard Oulahan, "Profiles That Cast Long Shadows," *Life*, January 22, 1965, 8; Robert Lewis Shayon, "TV and Radio: Order vs. Lib-

erty," *Saturday Review*, December 26, 1964, 22. The *New York Times* also published an article about the filming of the series before it premiered: Paul Gardner, "Pulitzer 'Profiles' Get Video Face-Lifting," October 25, 1964, sec. X, p. 17.

44. Cecil Smith, "The TV Scene: Profiles Display Kennedy Spirit," *Los Angeles Times*, November 9, 1964, sec. V, p. 20.

45. "Hindsight 64/65," *Television*, March 1965, 34–35.

46. James H. Foster to T.E. Covel, March 31, 1965; J. Walter Thompson Company, "Profiles in Courage Post-Season Summary," May 28, 1965, both in Saudek Papers, Box 309.

47. Robert Saudek to Thomas Sherard, April 4, 1966, Saudek Papers, Box 310.

48. See Albert Auster, "All in the Family: The Kennedy Saga and Television," *Journal of Popular Film and Television* 19 (1991): 128–37. Recent biopics also include *Truman* (HBO, 1995) and *George Wallace* (TNT, 1997).

49. George Rosen, "Candidates Now Sold as 'Product,'" *Variety*, August 26, 1964, 1.

II | The Television Documentary as Historian

5

Victory at Sea

Cold War Epic

Peter C. Rollins

I have told my sons that they are not under any circumstances to take part in massacres, and that the news of massacres of enemies is not to fill them with satisfaction or glee.

Kurt Vonnegut Jr., *Slaughterhouse Five*

A television series like *Victory at Sea* may seem trivial as "history" when compared with the scholarly fifteen-volume dreadnought by Admiral Morison (on which it was based), but this academic judgment may miss the most important point for a media age. *Victory at Sea* received practically every major television award for which it was eligible: it won the Freedom Foundation's George Washington Medal; it was awarded an "Emmy" from the Academy of Television Arts and Sciences; it received "best documentary" awards from five major trade magazines; and it received a host of "outstanding achievement" awards. Its memorable, interpretive score, rendered by the NBC orchestra, became RCA's best-selling Gold Seal Album and is still available today on compact disc at major music outlets. The series has become a permanent part of America's popular culture.

Furthermore, the series has had an enduring popularity since it was first broadcast in 1952. As of 2000, *Victory at Sea* had been shown in excess of fourteen times in New York, twelve times in Los Angeles, and nine times in Milwaukee. This record is impressive, since the series consists of twenty-six half-hour programs. In 1961 when a ninety-minute compilation of the series was shown on television, Bob Williams of the *Philadelphia Bulletin* proclaimed that, "*Victory at Sea* is television's most prodigious achievement, and this distinction has not been surrendered." An advertising pamphlet, with an

The USS *North Carolina* steams toward victory. Courtesy of the U.S. Navy.

eye on the bottom line, underscored this eminence in terms of dollars and cents: *"Victory at Sea* has knocked *The Untouchables* off its perch as the hottest network show of the season." The research department of NBC (owner of the series) concludes, *"Victory at Sea* is a powerful attraction for men, women, and younger people in urban, suburban, and rural areas—in short, of every segment of the country's population." During the 1995 celebrations of the Allied victory in WWII, the series was rebroadcast on the Public Broadcasting Service (PBS) and made available for sale through PBS. Such an offer seemed calculated to attract older viewers during the annual fundraising drive. Later, Amazon.com advertised the entire series for sale at less than one hundred dollars. Unlike Admiral Morison's official history of naval operations during WWII, the series has never been retired to the mothball fleet.[1]

Any serious student of American culture in the twentieth century must wonder what makes *Victory at Sea* such an entertaining spectacle. Could it be that the series not only recorded the history of naval operations in World War II on film, but also supplied a convincing interpretation of the larger significance of the war? Admiral Morison's naval history may ultimately be the real history, but the reel messages of *Victory at Sea* continue to affect attitudes held by millions of Americans toward the character and utility of war, the place of the military in our society, and America's international mission.

Yet there are limitations to the image of war presented by *Victory at Sea*. The series certainly exhibited cinematic inventiveness and the many awards were deserved by the creators Henry Salomon (producer), M. Clay Adams (director), Richard Rodgers (musical themes), Robert Russell Bennett (musical score and direction), and Isaac Kleinerman (film editing). In 1953, when the U.S. Navy awarded Distinguished Service Medals to Henry Salomon, Richard Rodgers, and Robert W. Sarnoff, it was not because these men deserved to be rewarded for a successful publicity campaign. Such an interpretation of their efforts would be unimaginative and cynical. There is a more useful way to approach the limitations of this series: it can be examined as an historical document shaped by the currents of opinion in the era in which it was conceived and produced. Today, we see things differently because we are outside the dark penumbra that passed over the American landscape in the 1950s. What seemed so right then now strikes us as dangerously—even fatally—narrow. Yet while today's educators are trying to wipe the slate clean, a popular series like *Victory at Sea* continues to inscribe on the popular mind perspectives that most intelligent Americans are trying hard to forget. Indeed, we need to unlearn some of the lessons taught by *Victory at Sea*, a dangerously seductive epic of the Cold War era.

Production History

Henry Salomon, the originator of *Victory at Sea*, devoted much of his time as an undergraduate at Harvard to the dramatic arts. After graduating, he went to work for NBC's script division. When the war came, Salomon enlisted in the navy, where he was assigned to the public relations division. While with the navy, he produced a radio series entitled *The Victory Hour*.

In 1942, President Roosevelt commissioned Salomon's former tutor at Harvard, Samuel Eliot Morison, to commence work on a living history of naval operations, and Morison selected Salomon as his assistant. Roosevelt wanted his historians to be present while history was actually being made. He envisaged their "writing current history on the scene while events were happening for the first time since Thucydides accompanied troops in the Peloponnesian War." To carry out this presidential mandate, Salomon landed in six major Pacific invasions, where his only task was to observe history. After the war, he was dispatched by Naval Intelligence to Tokyo to interrogate Japanese naval leaders and to study their side of the operations.

From 1945 to 1948, Salomon continued to help with the fifteen-volume naval history. After leaving the navy in 1948, he approached Robert W. Sarnoff (a Harvard classmate) with the idea of a television series based on the research. Sarnoff was enthusiastic about the project. The general concept for the series was straightforward enough. On hand, due to Salomon's close contacts with the military, were about twelve hundred miles of film covering nearly every aspect of the most massive war the world had ever known. The propaganda films of Frank Capra's *Why We Fight* series had tapped only a few drops of this reservoir of film, and none of the wartime films had attempted a grand, sweeping panoramic perspective of the entire global struggle from both sides of the conflict.

As historian and dramatist, Salomon was bold enough to propose such an epical treatment. Furthermore, with the war over, Salomon believed that he was free to concentrate on the pure human drama on both sides of the conflict. The raw footage available could be used to portray the preparations, plans, and finally, the collisions of the antagonists. Here indeed was a marvelous opportunity to recreate, in the words of the NBC press kit, "the drama that's packed into history."[2]

Two weeks into the twenty-six-week series, *Time* enthusiastically proclaimed that the use of film depicting both sides of the action gave the new television series a "breathless" pace. The first episode ("Design for War") had successfully evoked the dangers of an Atlantic passage: "It leaps breathlessly back and forth between British film and captured German footage. The effect is to personalize the battle. The war becomes a stirring conflict between a Nazi submarine captain, gloating over a new kill as he downs periscope, and a half-drowned British mariner, hauled oil-covered from the wreckage of his torpedoed tanker."[3] The reviewer emphasized quite properly that this would be a continuing technique of the series, one that distinguished it from its documentary predecessors. His sense of involvement in the drama of the action identifies the compelling quality of the series—its capacity to drag the viewer willy-nilly into the fighting spirit of the war: "This Week, *Victory's* second chapter, 'The Pacific Boils Over,' had TV critics cheering again. The Pearl Harbor attack is pictured—from a conference of Japanese naval brass all the way through the fateful Sunday morning when the carrier-based Japanese squadrons flew in low over Oahu's mountains. Televiewers are able to watch from enemy planes as the bombs are released. Then, from harbor vantage points, the film recreates the American feeling of dazed disbelief as the U.S. fleet is crippled. In terms of our later discussion, it is significant that the reviewer emphasized the power of the music to draw the viewer into the "mood" of the scene: "The entire sequence runs without spoken narration or sound effects; the Rodgers score comments on the situation far more effectively than the words could."[4]

Like Arthur Knight of the *Saturday Review*, many found the series "a stirring and dramatic demonstration of the power of the film medium to mold raw fact into artistic, meaningful, even memorable statement." All of the reviewers agreed that "*Victory at Sea* is supposed to stir up the emotions, and it does."[5]

Unfortunately, none of the contemporary reviewers found it necessary to define precisely *what* emotions were excited or toward what end. The creators of *Victory at Sea* wished to involve their television audience in the drama of war. They were successful in arousing their audience—perhaps too successful. *Scholastic Magazine* interviewed Henry Salomon shortly after *Victory at Sea* first appeared on television. The reporter concluded that Salomon was a teacher of history with a very special student body: "Salomon's classes will be conducted not at the school blackboard, but right in the family parlor."[6]

Many friends have recounted their childhood memories of the hushed atmosphere of these parlor-classrooms: no laughing, no random noises were allowed on those somber Sunday afternoons during the fall and spring of 1952 and 1953. Even Bernard DeVoto (who was editor of *Harpers*) confessed proudly that his house was a tightly rigged ship when *Victory at Sea* was on the air: "For twenty-six Sundays last year neither the telephone nor the doorbell was answered at my house between 3 and 3:30 P.M." As mainland China and Russian-occupied territories of Eastern Europe were being swallowed by the Communist behemoth, what DeVoto saw on these reverential Sunday afternoons provided him with consolation and inspiration about the role of America in international affairs.

As a result of his involvement in *Victory at Sea*'s theme of liberation (including, it should be noted, the liberation of French Colonialists in North Africa), DeVoto arrived at a conclusion that is consonant with the message of the series. Americans have a duty to carry forward the spirit of Liberty: "We forget too easily; everyone should see the whole series every year. It will be all right with me if Congress sees it twice a year."[7]

Other journalists recognized that the organizing theme of the series was "the preservation of freedom and the overthrow of despotism," and quoted approvingly DeVoto's remarks about "liberation." But some critics, who were closer to their TV audience than the prestigious editor of *Harpers*, saw a more relevant contemporary application for these lessons. As Jack O'Brian concluded (not without a little chauvinism), the series proved that it wasn't "ever safe to push the U.S. too far. It might even be a good idea to show *Victory at Sea* to Nikita Khrushchev. A very good idea." Here was a viewer who had learned his lessons well![8]

Indeed, it would be extremely difficult not to sympathize with the Allied cause in *Victory at Sea*. "Japs" may want rubber, oil, copper, and other strategic goods. On the other side of the globe, German "hordes" may swarm into defenseless nations for purposes of exploiting resources and enslaving populations, but the Allies are above such worldly interests. The series elevates the argument beyond the level of power politics to the ethereal regions of "moralism" and "legalism" from where it makes many such ideological points, with the unfortunate effect of driving home into the consciousness of the audience precisely what George Kennan in his *American Diplomacy, 1900–1950*, had warned must be *unlearned* by Americans in the 1950s.[9] In the Pacific, for example, we are not inching toward a military objective. Our efforts have a more transcendental meaning: "From island to island, continent to continent, the children of free peoples move the forces of tyranny from the face of the earth . . . it is, it will be so, until the forces of tyranny are no more." As a viewer absorbs this rhetoric of liberation, he is forced to survey the wreckage of machines and men. How will the viewer act on some future occasion because he has internalized such a summation of the war experience? If he has been totally uncritical, he will believe that it was not only the stern duty, but also the quasi-religious honor of our military men to fight and die on the Pacific beachheads. If they were strong men in battle then, we must be so in the future when our turn comes to defend the cause of freedom. Thus, while scholars in the 1950s were attempting to show that the myth of American innocence was a real obstacle to creative thinking, *Victory at Sea* was exploiting the myth for all the innocence it could carry.

A Consensus View of History

According to *Victory at Sea*, America has no pressing social problems and thus no real need for internal politics. The madness of political zealots and bigots is strictly a European and Japanese specialty. As an innocent nation, these greedy and rapacious antagonists coerce us into the global war. (Not a word is mentioned about America's desire for "normalcy" in the 1920s, or that our isolated innocence may have been purchased at the price of a second, larger war.) As an "arsenal of democracy," America manufactures arms, bandages, ships, and disciplined men. Since an isolated, innocent nation cannot assist unless its "goods" are delivered to the front, the U.S. Navy enters the story not so much as an arm of the military machine designed to kill as a guardian for the conveyors of goods.

A person who holds to an ideal of political consensus will inevitably interpret dissent as an alien intrusion. At the time that *Victory at Sea* was being broadcast, such people were the willing tools of demagogues like Joseph McCarthy. The prescription for dissent in such a perspective is that we must cauterize the body politic of its unhealthy elements. The makers of *Victory at Sea* would reprehend such paranoia, yet their celebration of America's innocence provided fuel for such a crusade.

In addition to reassessing the myth of national innocence, Americans in the 1950s should have been reassessing the uniqueness of America's revolutionary experience. *Victory at Sea's* lesson on our role as a democracy is as anachronistic as its statement about American innocence. We are told that the American experience has created a free society that is different in degree from other societies, but that our highly developed, free enterprise, capitalist nation is in no way different in kind. We may be freer, happier, richer than the rest of the world, but this is not because we have been so lavished with special privileges; as a result, it is our mission to transform the rest of the world into our image. If we become frustrated in our attempts, we are justified in using any power necessary, for we represent the cause of freedom.

Pearl Harbor pushed the United States into the global struggle. We certainly would not have gone to war to preserve the British Empire. Yet, in the Mediterranean episode of *Victory at Sea*, the British naval campaign to keep the lifelines of empire open is reported with reverence and enthusiasm. Great Britain was fighting desperately to retain its colonies. Yet many Americans at the time, including FDR, believed that the British had no right to an empire to start with. The viewer of *Victory at Sea* does not have time to make such cynical judgments. The orchestra interweaves the storm theme with the victory theme. We viewers quickly become too emotionally involved to do anything more than absorb the spectacle and admire the courage of the British Navy. Other imperial designs are not so sympathetically treated. *Victory at Sea's* contempt for Italy's relatively smaller (although more recent) efforts in the colonial field provides a good contrast. During the march on Rome by the U.S. Army, Leonard Graves explains that Italy is receiving (as Germany and Japan will eventually receive) a deserved punishment for toying with dreams of Empire.

Episode number seventeen ("The Turkey Shoot") conveys a similar judgment. The program first shows how the Japanese forcibly established themselves on Guam, which, since the Versailles Treaty of 1919, had been an American protectorate. The Japanese cruelly impose their language and customs upon the inhabitants. Next comes a savage battle to retake Guam. Finally, the program elicits admiration as the Americans develop the island as an *entrepot* for U.S. Pacific operations. Once the benevolent Americans have regained control from the Japanese, it seems only proper that we should teach the natives English in the public schools and that George Washington's birthday should become an obligatory island festival. After all, we represent liberty, not strategic self-interest. Our customs will enlighten and liberate, whereas Japanese customs have been designed only to enslave. (In the year 2001, Guam has become an even more crucial strategic site for U.S. Naval and Air Force bases.)

The unselfconscious acceptance of "the white man's burden" approach to Empire is best captured in a single image in episode number eight, "Mare Nostrum." We see a heavily clad Arab barely moving ahead of his obstinate donkey in the foreground of this visual portrait. Towering over him in the background is a sleek but threatening British cruiser that is gliding through the Suez Canal. The implicit message here is that Western man's technical superiority justifies his control of strategic isthmuses and natural resources.

Film Language: Framing the Violence of War

Victory at Sea has very little to say about the individual participant's perspective of the war. Instead, viewers are flooded with sublime scenes of machines in action: we see flaming broadsides fired at enemy targets; we see the sky filled with squadrons of fighters; we watch hundreds of bombs fall in retribution toward enemy cities. Because it is obsessed with these technological elements, the series neglects to report as dramatically on the human costs. The reality of this human dimension—which might truly threaten the viewer and perhaps elicit sympathy or fear—is muffled by a number of framing devices.

Superior editing provides the most significant framing device. For example, the military operations in *Victory at Sea* are always perfectly planned and conducted. In the first stage of any operation, a group of planners are working at their desks, or sitting (in dress uniform) around a large table discussing "the big picture." This is the "think tank" from which plans trickle down to lower echelons. While the orchestra plays the "communications theme," we "see" the attack order sent by wireless to ships at anchor or on station in the high seas.

We are now at stage two: here we see a facial close-up of the admiral or general in command of the operation. The impression given is very important—we are subtly told by the sequence of images and sounds that battle orders are not impersonal, not based on scanty information, but are as personalized as the chain of command we are following. We are certainly *not* living in the world of alienation and depersonalization to which Joseph Heller exposes readers of *Catch-22*. In *Victory at Sea*, the chain of command always has a human face and always cares.

Undeniably "dramatic" battle scenes follow the preparations for battle.

Yet here again the camera is more interested in the machines of war and the visual excitement of the scene than with the less photogenic effects upon human bodies. The series does not attempt to portray the individual's frustration, his sense of being an expendable cog in the gigantic machine of war—even under the best conditions. Both narration and music promote deep involvement with the scene, assuring viewers that the great naval juggernaut has a broader purpose, and that the participant in the actual battle is as conscious of this purpose as the television viewer.

Some distinctions seem necessary at this point. A man immersed as a living (and potentially dead) human being in an actual battle is a "participant." A man watching a film about a battle on a movie or television screen and caught up in the emotional drama of what he sees may be called a "participant-observer." Finally, we may call the student of the overall causes and cost of war an "observer."

A "participant" in battle is concerned first and foremost with one thing—staying alive. Obviously, at least while he is firing his rifle, he is not in the mood to watch a TV documentary about war. On the other hand, the "observer" does not want to surrender his faculties to the seductive drama of the media. He wants his sources of information to speak to his real and pressing questions, to give him hard data rather than nostalgia or vicarious excitement. *Victory at Sea* has nothing to say to either the "participant" or the "observer."

Viewers as Participant-Observers

The real target for *Victory at Sea* drama of battle is the "participant-observer." For the participant-observer, World War II becomes a masculine conflict unlike the Super Bowl only in the sense that a certain amount of social relevance has been added to the contest. The ambiguous aspect of this participant-observer's relationship to the drama is that he often thinks of himself as an actual participant, when the only combat he has seen has taken place within the confines of his thirty-five-inch television screen. Even if he has once been a "participant" in the battles portrayed by the series, he will most likely jettison what terror and distress have clung to his memories in favor of the more reassuring "top brass" perspective that *Victory at Sea* gives him as a "participant-observer." The danger, therefore, of Isaac Kleinerman's superb film editing and the arousing orchestrations by Robert Russell Bennett is that they will convince even the veteran that the war was not an unmitigated horror.

The experience of death in combat is always framed; in addition, death in

Victory at Sea is always public and dramatic. Men do not appear to die accidentally or senselessly—for example, we never see an infantryman blown up by a land mine, or a flight deck crewman of an aircraft carrier sliced in two by a propeller, or a resting soldier accidentally shot by his foxhole neighbor. These were common events in war, but they have no place in an epic. When we are watching whole armadas of ships and planes cruising on toward victory, it is distracting to stop for consideration of the individual casualties.

The music supplies a unifying emotion that makes the disparate parts of the scene cohere for the participant-observer. Even if we do see members of our fighting team "wasted" en route toward the objective, the music tells us that something larger than these individual lives is succeeding—indeed, living. We are told on countless occasions that what lives on is the spirit of freedom, but what we actually see on the screen is the survival of naval vessels, planes, and guns.

The music has other important effects on the participant-observer. The battle scenes always call for the most strenuous efforts of the orchestra. Yet an approach less fascinated with machines might pay more attention to the pain inflicted by the participants upon one another. For a participant, the sinking of a single ship (if he is on it); the wounds of a solitary individual (if they are his wounds); the loss of a single loved one (a husband or father) *could* be seen as a climax of not only a single battle, but the entire war.

Narrator commentary muffles full recognition of the merciless beating imposed upon the First Marine Division in "Guadalcanal." Musical and editing effects are also used in the Guadalcanal episode to frame the true violence of war experienced by a participant. First, the orchestra introduces the "Guadalcanal March," a melody around which viewers order their visual perceptions. The fighting on Guadalcanal is going badly for the Americans, but with this rousing tune in his ears, the participant-observer is flown back to the States for a heartening tour of the domestic mobilization. The theme grows louder, is developed by a rich orchestration as we survey the massive industrial muscles of America start to flex. As the episode progresses through a number of impressive production sequences—steel mills flaming in the night, riveters and welders by the dozen putting the finishing touches on planes, tanks, and ships—the participant-observer grows increasingly confident that however poor America's showing may be in the early rounds of the war, we will eventually drown the enemy in the torrent of our material wealth. With our confidence thus fortified, we return to Guadalcanal. The impression upon the participant-observer is one of immediate danger—but also of long-term reassurance. While it may in fact be true that the "nation" as an abstraction, the "campaign" as a large-scale effort over a number of years

USS *Yorktown* takes a direct hit. Courtesy of the U.S. Navy.

here started on an upward climb, it is also important to note that the viewer is relieved of the responsibility of absorbing the full intensity of the terror and pain incurred in this particular battle by the marines of the First Division. As a result of his protected position, the participant-observer carries away a pseudorealistic rather than a true picture of what war has been—and therefore, will be.

In episode fifteen ("D-Day") there is an interesting twist. The narrator tells about the confusions and miscalculations that characterized the invasion of Europe: "Few casualties occur where expected. Sometimes no casualties occur where the most are expected . . . but all men are doomed to experience their own end." There is an admirable candor in this description, but visual or musical materials do not reinforce it. Such an examination of the confusion and chaos of war would detract from the impression of the inexorable momentum of the Allied assault on Fortress Europe.

Because *Victory at Sea* is organized around an official perspective of the war, it has neither the time nor the desire to tell of the human cost of advancing the struggle. The result is indeed paradoxical: although the series is composed almost entirely of actual footage, it does not give a truly realistic picture of battle. Through superior editing, through the reassurances provided by music and narration, the viewer as participant-observer is kept far enough away from the heart of darkness to see its lights and shades as romantic and alluring.

Neither the thoughts nor the voices of participants are allowed to thrust their way into our midst. Early in the *Victory at Sea* project, Henry Salomon established a rule that actual sounds should be used as little as possible. Instead of the actual voices of participants, we hear the authoritative voice of Leonard Graves speaking about broad-sweeping generalizations such as "freedom" and "democracy." Rather than the actual sounds of supporting guns and exploding shells, or even the high whine of a ship's engine, we are treated to the evocative orchestration of Robert Russell Bennett. Because these effects establish a distance between viewers and the visual images, no one is forced to confront the face of war. Indeed, the creators of *Victory at Sea* have succeeded in insulating us from the experience of war to such an extent that we can think of the explosions and the carnage before us as entertaining TV drama.

Some Especially Egregious Scenes

There are a few moments—unforgivable moments—in *Victory at Sea* that deserve special attention, since they exhibit a lapse of taste that could have passed unnoticed only in an atmosphere like that provided by the Cold War. We have talked about the sequence showing domestic mobilization in the "Guadalcanal" episode. One portion of this sequence shows African Americans bent over cotton rows, contributing their might to the national effort. We have noted that the war was in part a tragedy because it diverted America's attention from needed domestic reforms. The use of this particular footage of cotton pickers is doubly ironic because it was lifted from a crusading *March of Time* documentary on the plight of tenant farmers in the South. One wonders what the responsible individual thought about as he extracted shots for this sequence. In a wartime documentary, we might be more tolerant of such callousness, but in a documentary assembled in 1952, we are shocked by this kind of misuse of archival footage.

In episode number eight ("Mare Nostrum"), our ears are caressed with a romantic lullaby as we watch an Italian cruiser plunging to the bottom of the Mediterranean. In episode number nine ("Sand and Sea"), we fly over the captured enemy to the peppy strains of a Broadway finale. The music and the triumph raise our spirits—after all, we won the battle for North Africa, and the thirty thousand German prisoners we see stumbling along below on the desert deserve their humiliation. Even a tendentious German propaganda film such as *Baptism of Fire* (1940) never goes so far as to ridicule an enemy who has suffered a severe defeat.

Episode number eleven ("Magnetic North") offers perhaps one of the truly unforgivable sequences of the series. In this dramatization of the Allied effort to convoy goods through the North Sea, we are shown a number of shots of merchant marine vessels being sunk. In one case, after we see a ship go down, we suddenly find ourselves closing in on a dory filled with survivors. The camera acquaints us with the strained faces of the six crewmen who are rowing the lifeboat. At the helm is an elderly man in a flowing beard, obviously the venerable captain. As he looks up, we follow his line of sight to a German light bomber flying overhead. (By this time, we realize that we are not watching actual footage at all, but a slice of venom from a fiction film). The camera closes to within a yard of the cockpit, from where we can see a diabolical gleam in the eye of the flying Hun. He pushes the stick forward and begins strafing, moving his shot pattern on line with the lifeboat, cutting into flesh and wood as the mechanically perfect pinpoints of parallel fifty-caliber bullets sweep across their target. After the plane passes over, we focus in again on the lifeboat—it is now sinking and most of the crew is now dead. Those who are still living are wounded so badly that they probably will not be able to keep themselves afloat for very long.

Such sequences could be understandable in wartime propaganda films, but they are inexcusable in a documentary assembled in 1952. Why should we need to personalize the hatred of Germans seven years after the war? The historically useful emotion to encourage in 1952 was a hatred of war. Hatred of another unit of mankind can find its expression only in polarization and conflict.

The two worst cases of *Victory at Sea* moral lapses are both in episode number thirteen ("Malanesian Nightmare"). The first involves a desperate, last-ditch attempt by the Japanese to reinforce their flagging defense of Rabaul. The scene itself is pathetic—the Japanese hoped that they could race an unprotected troop transport containing three thousand infantrymen across the Bismarck Sea without being discovered. Unfortunately for the three thousand troops on that ill-fated ship, an American observer plane spotted the lumbering transport.

For some reason, the creators felt that this was an exciting moment worthy of dramatic reconstruction. However, in disagreement it can be noted that in this segment there is the same ironic contrast between the pathos of the situation and the exultation of the hunt that was evident in the episode ("The Killers and the Killed") that reported the capture of a German submarine. First, an observer plane spots the Japanese ship. The pilot radios his information back to an operations center where the course of the enemy transport is plotted. Then pilots are briefed and bombers loaded with their deadly cargo. (All footage for these stages of preparation was lifted from navy training films.) As the planes make an initial pass over their defenseless target, the music reaches a heroic crescendo. Finally, the bombs and torpedoes do their work. Again, we do not question the necessity of the participants to go through with their bloody drama, but in 1952 why give the whole performance an air of sport? Why should we cheer because we have been allowed to be in at the death?

A second tasteless scene from "Malanesian Nightmare" explains that the significance of death depends upon whether or not one is on the winning side. For the dead Americans, there is a promise of afterlife and a deep tenderness from the voice of Leonard Graves as he reflects over the coffins: "Death . . . these brave men know thy sting . . . God grant they know thy victory." While the viewer may not realize this immediately, the death of Christ is subtly identified with the death of American soldiers for their nation's cause. In isolation, such a statement would be harmless, but clear contrasts are established with the fate of our adversary in the Pacific.

Japanese servicemen do not die with the same prospects before them, because their personal sacrifice has been for a losing cause. Footage from Japanese films shows grief-stricken families claiming urns filled with ashes of their sons, fathers, and husbands. The narrator explains that there is little consolation for the survivors and absolutely no spiritual reward to be expected by the men who sacrificed their lives. Speaking in ironic cadences, Leonard Graves addresses the dead Japanese: "Welcome home, young man. . . . You are home, but you will never know anything but a long, endless night." This moral is reinforced by the visual contrast of American dead being shipped back

USS *Yorktown* abandoned. Courtesy of the U.S. Navy.

home in full-size coffins versus the Japanese delivery of ashes in little metal tubs. These images, plus the narrator's subtle sarcasm about the Buddhist denial of an afterlife, are perniciously effective. They communicate a message that American deaths are better, more glorious deaths than Japanese deaths.

This kind of moralism is dangerous. Winning the contest should not be a payoff for the deaths of our friends and loved ones. Death strikes us all as human beings, not as members of nations. If in no other way, a recognition of the democracy of death could be the beginning of an insight into the democracy of the living. We have a duty to respect men above and beyond their group association or intellectual beliefs. To lose this universal perspective, to be thrilled by the bombing of a helpless target or to mock the tragic loss of husbands and sons is to degrade both the series and the audience.

The purpose of *Victory at Sea* was to bring back into focus what was gradually slipping out of memory. But there are dangers of remembering the so-called "lessons of history" too well: a drama of commemoration may possess a dangerous beauty that will mislead us. As the thirteen-hour series progresses, we become ever more deeply involved with the military tactics and machines that are needed for our crusade to liberate enslaved peoples. We are assured that our cause is just, because America has been designated by nature as a land of liberty and plenty. By the time the entire twenty-six-week cycle has come to a close, we have become inextricably meshed in a psychology of self-righteous moralism—what some have called "the Cold War mentality." We automatically associate any sympathy for fallen peoples with a military response. Furthermore, we probably feel that it is useless for an individual to oppose this militaristic reflex, because the drama of a unified, innocent people in a complex, fallen world has convinced us that personal protest would not only be ineffectual, but profoundly un-American.

In short, we become trapped by our reverence for World War II as a crusade for freedom. As George Kennan and others were trying to explain in the 1950s, Americans should have been learning entirely new lessons. But *Victory at Sea* did not encourage its viewers to look for complexity or irony in history. Instead, by exploiting the old myths of American innocence and the ideology of freedom, it actually impeded the audience's ability to take a fresh look at the American situation.

An Alternative Approach: Leo Hurwitz's *Strange Victory*

There were other ways to use the raw stuff of World War II history. *Strange Victory*, an excellent documentary made in the 1950s by Leo Hurwitz, used one of these alternative approaches.[10] It serves as an excellent foil to *Victory at Sea* because it was released at about the same time *Victory at Sea* began its first run on television. It is also a fascinating contrast because, unlike *Victory at Sea*, *Strange Victory* was almost entirely ignored.

Strange Victory is as concerned with remembrance as *Victory at Sea*, but there is a vast disagreement in these films about what is commemorated: *Victory at Sea* celebrates the efforts of "men called 'sailors,' 'marines,' 'soldiers.'" The Hurwitz film also does justice to the national war effort, but *not as a good in itself.* The nation's unity in time of war is considered in terms of our ability *after* the war to live up to the principles we so self-righteously packed aboard our naval vessels. Hurwitz, in effect, reversed the dramatic perspective of *Victory at Sea:* rather than emphasizing what happened when America throws off "the lethargies of peace," Hurwitz explores the tragedy of our inability to throw off the lethargies of war. He is especially disappointed by our inability to make the Four Freedoms a domestic reality. Looking abroad, he drives home the irony of our self-sacrifice in the Allied cooperative effort to destroy the enemy as it contrasts with our pettiness when similar occasions arise for unified action at home.

The titles of both films proclaim their different perspectives: *Victory at*

Sea encourages viewers to live through the epic effort of war. By the end of the series, we are given the impression that most of the work to establish a just society in the United States has already been accomplished. After all, America had no internal problems to begin with, and since we have established democratic governments ("men, not dictators; men, not generals") in Japan and Germany, future harmony and freedom are guaranteed. In contrast, Hurwitz's *Strange Victory* takes precisely the opposite approach. After it critically examines the moralism of our wartime rhetoric, it asks with embarrassing plainness: if we were so idealistic in our aims, why do we have inequality and racial prejudice in our own country once the war is over? Combat footage is used, but not to celebrate the drama of war. These scenes of battle serve as reference points for the ironic question: if we could mete out such brutal punishment on the Axis powers for their violation of freedom, how can we tolerate assaults upon freedom at home? Hurwitz shows men by the hundreds diving out of planes or advancing by fire and maneuver. The narrator forces a special relationship upon viewers of these scenes: "This was yesterday; this was how it was, remember? This is what Joe has put away in the album . . . pictures . . . momentoes. . . . We paid, everybody paid. . . . This country fought for the four freedoms, world unity—remember? In the name of the four freedoms, we unleashed more force that has ever been seen before."

The film, then, presents a series of contrasts between our sacrifice during the war in the name of the ideology of free peoples, followed by a return to the postwar America where indifference is allowing the country to fall back into acceptance of inequality based on race, origin, religion. The narrator muses over these ironic contrasts: "Strange Victory indeed—the values of the defeated being adopted by the victors."

Rather than dramatizing the excitement of war, Hurwitz gives the center stage to the promise of a fulfilling life for the individual under ideal social conditions. We see a pregnant woman daydreaming about the future of her child. Next, we see newborn infants in a hospital nursery. The camera closes in on the first prehensile movement of a hand. Hurwitz then expands the meaning of this first distinctly human act—the child's grasp, after all, is an earnest of his tool-using ability. A long segment on tools and industrial production follows. It serves as a fitting contrast to the production and mobilization sequence in the "Guadalcanal" episode of *Victory at Sea*. The images commence with the simplest tools and then progress to the most intricate electronic equipment of the day. We flash back to a child taking his first steps, from which the ideal of physical dexterity is expanded by images until we see a high jumper clearing a bar at six feet. The hunger of a child for the breast is articulated as a metaphor of nourishment, which includes the need to absorb culture. Creativity is the mark of the entire sequence. The child is shown as having an infinite set of possibilities: throughout these sequences the machines do not dominate man, they are never pointed toward his destruction; all of the forms at man's disposal in the arts and sciences are seen as means toward his self-expression.

Having given us a hope for the creative use of the tools and forms of the world, *Strange Victory* then steps back to the moment of the child's birth. As we watch a newborn infant being delivered, whispers intrude onto the sound track, violating our sense of wonder and life: "Nigger, Kike, Greaser." With the shock effect still on the audience, we return to the war scenes and a discussion of the mass movements at the roots of the world war. We are reminded how easily societies (including American society) are brought to treat men as things.

In sum, *Strange Victory* agrees with *Victory at Sea* that the experience of the war may be slipping out of focus, but it disagrees about the significance of the "experience of war." By his visual presentation, Hurwitz has demonstrated the pain and brutality of war, but he has continuously related the experience to relevant, contemporary issues. We are to remember the war not for itself, not for the drama and excitement of the battle, not for the epic moments when intelligent armies collided by night. Instead, to invoke the title of Frank Capra's series of films, we need to remember *why* we fought. We can commemorate the price paid by our soldiers, sailors, and marines only by carrying those idealistic principles into our own lives. Surveying contemporary America, *Strange Victory* is not optimistic about the prospects of renewed dedication: "Nobody seems to know where the victory is—lost, strayed, stolen—it isn't here. If we won [i.e., our value system triumphed with the armies and navies] why does it look as if we lost?" *Strange Victory* concludes with the moving explanation: "If we want Victory, we'll still have to get it." The point is telling: we cannot assume that America's efforts in the war against an outside enemy have solved the problems within. Hurwitz's cinematic essay may be faulted for overpersonalizing the forces of racism in America, but ultimately, his short film fulfills a powerful documentary function. He helps us to understand and feel intensely about real problems in our own time, problems that carry on their virulent life below the official rhetoric of freedom and self-righteousness, which *Victory at Sea* is only too willing to accept at face value.

Conclusions

Ultimately, *Victory at Sea* failed as a documentary because it succeeded as a massive spectacle. The makers were too absorbed in the war experience for its own sake. They surrendered their true documentary role of informing and moving their audience to humane social action. The war may have had its drama, but we betray our real duty to the men who died by allowing the causes of war to remain unexamined and uncondemned—especially if one of the causes of war is tacit public acceptance of military action as dangerous, but thrilling, manly sport. *Victory at Sea* draws our attention away from reality, it bestows upon us a national pat on the back; but it does not give us what we really needed in 1952 and what we need all the more today—an insight into our real duties as Americans and as human beings in a world of suprapersonal organizations, monstrous weapons, and a penchant for violence.[11]

Notes

1. *Victory at Sea,* Producer Henry Salomon, NBC, 1952. Purchase: <www.amazon.com>.
2. Much of the encomia can be found in the standard press kit distributed by NBC to prospective clients for *Victory at Sea.* Most of this collection of reviews, statistics, and plot summaries will be quoted but not cited. This press kit has been placed in the Special Collections Division of the Oklahoma State University Library, Stillwater, Okla. 74078.
3. "Victory by Installments," *Time,* November 19, 1952, 105.
4. "Victory by Installments," 105.
5. Arthur Knight, "Victory at Sea," *Saturday Review* (1954), 26.
6. Larry Sims, "History Is Fun—on TV," *Scholastic Magazine,* August 1952, 4.
7. Bernard DeVoto, "The Easy Chair," *Harper's,* January 1954, 8.
8. Jack O'Brian, "TV's 'Victory at Sea' Might be Shown to Mr. K," *Victory at Sea* Press Kit.
9. A cluster of books were being written as *Victory at Sea* was being produced and broadcast, all of them directed toward a reconsideration of such important issues as American innocence, American uniqueness, and the American mission. None of these fine works—or their precursors in journals in magazines—were touched, as were none of the suggestions by George Kennan. Kennan's famous diatribe against "legalism" and "moralism" in the history of American foreign policy became standard reading for college students in the 1950s and 1960s, although it seems clear that Kennan's views were not shared with the makers of the NBC series—indeed, Salomon and his writers pushed "legalism" and "moralism" as far as they could for dramatic purposes.
  The Virgin Land: The American West as Symbol and Myth by Henry Nash Smith (New York: Vintage, 1950) provided an entirely new spin on the limitations of America's self-identification as Nature's nation, a land absolved from the evils of European politics and conflict. Two other works to achieve universal recognition—if not agreement—in academic circles attempted to redefine and to reinterpret the origin and significance of American political ideas. Daniel Boorstin's *The Genius of American Politics* (Chicago: Univ. of Chicago Press, 1953) concluded that the United States is actually a conservative country in the tradition of Edmund Burke, despite our claims about a "revolution-

ary" heritage. *The Liberal Tradition in America* by Louis Hartz (New York: Harcourt, Brace, and World, 1955) examined the "irrational Lockeanism" of American political thought and further redefined our self-styled revolutionary origins.

10. *Strange Victory,* Director Leo Hurwitz, Frontier Films, 1952. Purchase: Museum of Modern Art.

11. For related analyses, see Peter J. Matthiesen, "Persuasive History: A Critical Comparison of Television's *Victory at Sea* and *The World at War,*" *The History Teacher* 25.2 (1992), 240–52; Peter C. Rollins, "*Victory at Sea:* Cold War Epic," *Journal of Popular Culture* 6.4 (1972), 463–82; and Peter C. Rollins, "*Nightmare in Red:* A Cold War View of the Communist Revolution," in *American History/American Television: Interpreting the Video Past.* John O'Connor, ed. (New York: Ungar, 1983), 134–58. (This book is out of print, but the text has been reprinted in the *Film & History 1999 CD-ROM Annual,* eds. Peter C. Rollins, John O'Connor, and Deborah Carmichael (Cleveland, Okla.: Ridgemont Press, 1999).

6 Breaking the Mirror

Dutch Television and the History of the Second World War

Chris Vos

The public memory of the Second World War certainly stays alive. In the United States, the fiftieth anniversary of the ending of the war was marked by a controversy about an exhibition on the *Enola Gay;* in France, there was and is a bitter dispute about the "Vichy Republic"; and in Germany, the publication of Daniel Goldhagen's study *Hitler's Willing Executioners* provoked a public uproar about the alleged participation of common German citizens in the Holocaust. Indeed, especially in countries that were occupied by the Germans, the memory of the war seems to be a continuing focal point for public discussion.

It is hardly surprising that in the Netherlands, occupied by the Germans between 1940 and 1945, there has also been an ongoing concern with the Second World War. The "Occupation," as this period simply is called, is the subject of many books, plays, public discussions, films, and television programs. Many of these reflections can be looked upon as a form of "wrestling" with the past, attempting to reconcile a dark period with the centrist liberal traditions that are honored by Dutch society. Television seems to be especially dominant in this process: literally hundreds of television documentaries were dedicated to the war, and many evoked strong discussions in Dutch society.

This essay analyzes the role of Dutch television in the remembrance of the war, with an emphasis on the first twenty-five years of the medium. In this period, the public image of the war was subjected to fundamental changes, and these are both reflected *and* stimulated by the way television treated the war. This analysis principally concentrates on three important television documentaries, which will serve as examples of the shifting trends that can be seen in the audiovisual history of the Second World War on Dutch television.

Historical documentary production in the Netherlands has been strongly dominated by the war. For instance, between 1951 and 1990 more than 1,100 documentaries were produced on Dutch history. One-third of them (about 330) address the Occupation, making the war the number one subject—a clear sign of the traumatic nature of the war experience. Another phenomenon is also striking at first sight: as the war recedes into the past, historical interest in it is clearly growing, reflected in a sharply rising number of these documentaries over the years.[1]

Dutch television started in 1951, six years after the end of the war, in a time that was characterized by a minimal interest in the war. Immediately after the war there was a strong upsurge of plays, books, film documentaries, and even feature films about the war, but this interest soon subsided. By 1951, the dominant issues of the day were the beginnings of the Cold War, the rebuilding of the devastated country, and the colonial conflict in Indonesia.

Within this atmosphere there was not much room to look back at the war. Survivors of the camps had noticed that there was not much interest in their stories. For instance, it was hard to find a publisher for Anne Frank's diary. When at last it was published, it remained obscure until late in the 1950s, becoming a success only after a Broadway stage hit and an American movie release in the Netherlands.

Television shared this silence. In the fifties, very few documentaries were produced about the war. These documentaries, usually aired on memorial days (which in the Netherlands take place in early May), for the most part borrowed their terminology and atmosphere from the rituals of the memorial service: a strong emphasis on the heroism of the Resistance, on the martyrs fallen for their country, and on the lessons for today's society.

One aspect of these early documentaries is particularly intriguing in the Dutch context. In the Netherlands, broadcasting was managed not by a national network but by special interest groups rooted in the so-called "pillars" of Dutch society.[2] There were—and to some extent still are—for instance, Catholic, Protestant, and socialist broadcasting networks. These networks needed to proclaim their identities, and for this reason the documentary became one of the more important and prestigious categories of Dutch television. It formed the "voice" of the pillar, a focal point for its identity. Television as a whole was strongly felt to be a medium that could function as a carrier for the ideology of the pillar, which could be used to enlighten people, interpreting (historical) events within the framework of the movement.

The host and presenter of *The Occupation* is historian Dr. L. De Jong. Courtesy of the Dutch Television Archives.

But these ideological differences were conspicuously absent when the war was an issue. The Occupation was seen as a *national* cause, an issue clearly above partisan struggle. One may say that in these early postwar years, re-membering the war *united* the nation; there were certainly no dividing cracks visible as there were, for instance, in Belgium and in France. In Belgium there existed controversy about the position of the king during the war, and in France there was—and is—the issue of the collaborating Vichy govern-ment, leading to what Henry Rousso has called a "Vichy-syndrome."[3] Nothing similar was visible in the Netherlands in those early years.

It must be one of the reasons why the first serious audiovisual history of the war, broadcast between 1960 and 1965, was experienced as a national happening. This series, simply called *The Occupation (De Bezetting)*, con-sisted of twenty-one parts and took five years to complete.[4] The series gave an overview of the complete history of the war in the Netherlands. Orga-nized in such themes as the persecution of the Jews and the role of the Resis-tance, and with detailed accounts of the battles fought on Dutch territory, it

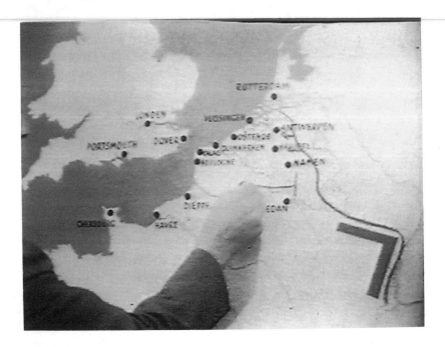

The Occupation was produced in an educational style. The presenter, for example, explains the German invasion of The Netherlands. Courtesy of the Dutch Television Archives.

contained all the "highlights" of the history of this period. *The Occupation* adhered closely to the narrative principles of television production at the time: a central role for a TV moderator, long interviews, and a limited use of film clips. The TV moderator in this case was a well-known historian specialized in the Occupation, Dr. Louis de Jong, and he was backed by the academic expertise of the war research institute he headed.

In line with the documentary style of this period, the program was very slow moving: statements were long and the number of shots limited. But a more important characteristic can be found in the highly educational overtones of the program. The series centered on the presence of the moderator, who acted like an old-fashioned schoolteacher. He led the story, presented the interviews, and introduced the film clips. A very peculiar narrative strategy was visible in the interviews: the people interviewed *looked straight into the camera*, in clear violation of the principle that only the moderator may look directly into the camera. In this case it seemed to signify a transfer of authority from the presenter to the witnesses. Indeed, throughout the series, *their* views of what happened in the war were presented on an equal footing

Witnesses are treated as equals to the host/presenter in *The Occupation*. Here a socialist statesman makes a statement, looking directly at the camera. Courtesy of the Dutch Television Archives.

with those of the anchorman. In fact, most of the people interviewed in this program represented the elite: politicians, industrialists, and magistrates. Because of their equal standing and the time allotted to them, they could in effect evaluate their own functioning during the war.

There is another aspect of the narrative strategy that was striking: the interviews were highly constructed, rehearsed statements, and the interviewees' reading from paper was sometimes visible. And there was no use of *crosscutting*, contrasting different statements by placing fragments from separate interviews together. One must note, however, that crosscutting was seldom used in those years, because in Dutch television circles it was considered "impolite" to crosscut in interviews.

Thus, *The Occupation* presented a view very much in line with the official consensus. It contained strong elements of chauvinism, stressing the stories of heroes and martyrs and placing great emphasis on the heroic role of the Dutch Resistance. The conclusion of the first part was exemplary in this respect. It ended in patriotic style, with images—taken from a fiction film made after the war—of sabotage actions by the Resistance, accompanied on the sound track by the playing of the national anthem. *The Occupation* thus offered a very comforting evaluation of the war: its central message was that the Dutch people had—with the exception of a few criminals—bravely resisted the Germans. In its tone and content, the program became a tribute, an audiovisual monument to the "brave" Dutch people (so reminiscent of the American *Victory at Sea* series). There is no doubt that by doing this, the series painted a strong black-and-white picture in which there was little room for the issue of compromise and collaboration among the population as a whole.

It is striking that within this context the *victims of the war* were only present at a distance. In the program that treated the extermination of the Dutch Jews, many authorities were interviewed, but not a single survivor of the concentration camps. The dominating impression conveyed in the program was one of the solidarity of the Dutch population with the hunted Jews.[5]

That fit, of course, nicely into the rhetoric that could be heard on memorial days. But it ignored the fact—known at the time within the circle of professional historians (and the series was made by a professional historian) that the Netherlands had the highest number of volunteers for the Nazi SS and the highest percentage of Jewish victims of all occupied countries in Western Europe. Seventy-five percent of the Jewish population was killed, which was in striking contrast with, for instance, France (25 percent), neighboring Belgium (40 percent), and especially Denmark (2 percent killed—the majority of the Danish Jews were smuggled out to Sweden).[6] There are good reasons for the difference between the nations—geographical factors in a flat country with few escape routes, the harshness of the SS regime—but certainly the rather meek and passive attitude of the Dutch population also contributed. None of this was discussed in the program.

But it would be unfair to consider *The Occupation* only as another example of memorial day rhetoric. It was much more. It was an attempt by professional historians to produce a comprehensive *audiovisual* history and as such formed the very first reconstruction of the war—however slanted—to use the new medium of television. Public response to the series was enormous: widespread praise at first, later followed by criticism, especially from the younger generation. In many ways the series was exemplary. It led to the first psychological reworking of the war experience. It stimulated public interest in the war and initiated many debates on war-related issues. Other programs copied its format and, at a time when audiovisual archives were not easy to get into, borrowed its footage. This last aspect is of some importance, because the recycling of footage meant *The Occupation* often formed the first link in a chain that eventually led to many of televisions "iconic clichés" of

This shot of a girl looking out of the door of a train leaving for Auschwitz was first used in *The Occupation*. It became a symbol of the Holocaust in the Netherlands and was used in many later documentaries. Recent research has shown the girl to be a gypsy. Courtesy of the Dutch Television Archives.

the war—that is to say, images that are frequently repeated and grow into well-known symbols of the war. For instance, in the (German) film about the Dutch concentration camp Westerbork, the famous image of a Jewish girl looking out between the doors of a wagon of a train leaving for Auschwitz has become an international symbol for the suffering of the Jews, and it reappears in almost every documentary on the camps. In the Dutch context, that footage was first used in *The Occupation* and later widely copied. The widespread use of this image of a Jewish girl "between the doors" brings to the attention another problem of audiovisual history: the difficulties in ascertaining the original context of images. In this particular case, later research disclosed that the Jewish girl was not in fact Jewish, but a gypsy.[7]

By the 1970s, other approaches became visible in the way Dutch television looked at the war. These changes were in part related to the rise of a new generation that was knocking, not always very politely, on the doors of the establishment. Although the generation conflict in the Netherlands was never as severe as elsewhere—as seen for instance in the May 1968 revolt in France—there certainly was societal turmoil. And one of the central issues that came to be debated between the generations was the war.

There are two central shifts in attention to be seen within this changing atmosphere. One is the challenging of the established audiovisual history of the war, as exemplified in *The Occupation*. Critical questions were asked: why had Dutch authorities been so passive toward the extermination of the Jews during the war? What happened to the common man or woman? But another shift was even more pronounced: a growing attention to the victims of the concentration camps and the atrocities of the Nazis that would eventually dominate all other themes in the memory of the war. For television this last shift came quite suddenly in a 1972 parliamentary debate (with an enormous public response) about a general pardon for still-imprisoned war criminals. Television played an important role in this debate. Within two weeks, more than twenty hours of television were spent on interviews with victims, psychological experts, politicians, and even the families of war criminals. A climax in this television coverage was the broadcasting of the documentary *Begrijpt u nu waarom ik huil?* (Do you now understand why I'm crying?), a recording of a therapeutic session with a concentration camp victim, retelling his experience under the influence of LSD. The program attracted, not least because of the therapeutic use of this drug, wide publicity and a large audience.[8] The televised discussions and the documentary placed the victim "on the map," so to say, both in society and in politics. Polls showed strong effects: within a fortnight, the majority that had existed for a general pardon evaporated.[9]

These changes in the character of public memory were not an isolated phenomenon for the Netherlands; similar trends were visible in other countries in Europe. One way in which these international trends influenced the Dutch situation was the regular programming on television of foreign historical documentaries. The famous documentary by Marcel Ophüls and André Harris, *Le chagrin et la pitié* (The Sorrow and the Pity), shown on Dutch television in the same year of the discussion about the releasing of war criminals, 1972, especially created a lasting impression. *Le chagrin* was more than four hours long and differed from other documentaries in both content and form. By means of interviews and archival footage, it traced the history of the small French city of Clermont-Ferrand during the war, presenting a picture of daily life under the Occupation that certainly incorporated less heroic aspects. In this way the program revealed—as Henry Rousso has said—"vast areas of amnesia"[10]: like the existence of French anti-Semitism and collaboration. And it was clear that in France not everyone was ready to fill in these

Influenced by direct cinema techniques, the interviews in *Vastberaden, maar soepel en met mate* were held in an informal style with a constantly moving camera in the home of each witness. Here a witness is shown with his wife. Courtesy of the Dutch Television Archives.

gaps in the national memory: for ten years French television refused to air the program.

But in the Netherlands the documentary was broadcast, and it provided an inspiring model for a new kind of audiovisual history that would take issue with series like *The Occupation*.[11] Several projects were set up to do "*chagrin*-type" programs concerning the Dutch Occupation. The most successful of these was a very long documentary, made in 1974 with the mystifying and untranslatable title: *Vastberaden, maar soepel en met mate* (approximately: "Determined, but reasonably tolerant").[12] In contrast to *The Occupation*, with its lavish use of authorities and prominent role for the historical expert, *Vastberaden* tried to tell the story from the viewpoint of the common man and woman, without the interference of a moderator or compelling narrative. In more than three hours, twenty-two witnesses—from collaborators to resistance fighters—told about their war, "not as it should have been, but as it was," as the advertisement for the program claimed.

Their interwoven stories gave a view that stressed the continuity of the period: the war had just been an interruption, and fundamentally not much in Dutch society had changed. Even the same elite was still in power; they had only built a bridge over these troubled waters, and tellingly enough, this Simon and Garfunkel music was used under the end titles.

In its form, *Vastberaden* was heavily influenced—as was *Le chagrin et la pitié* to some extent—by the *direct cinema*, the American counterpart of *cinéma vérité*. Direct cinema was inspired by technological innovations, especially the development of portable sound cameras and improved light-sensitive film. It revolutionized television and filmmaking: it was now possible to move around on a location, even indoors, without problems with light and sound. It led to a new documentary style that quickly developed an ideology of its own.[13] Famous examples of the direct cinema style were soon broadcast on Dutch television, including documentaries by Frederick Wiseman and Richard Leacock.

In *Vastberaden*, the direct cinema principles were adapted and crystallized in a very particular style. As in regular direct cinema, there was little interference with the happenings before the camera, and narration was kept to a minimum. There was ample room for interviews, but they were held in a much more casual style than in the older documentaries. The "common" man or woman figured prominently in the interviews, and they were filmed in their "natural" environment, in a spontaneous context. Rather than authoritative and rehearsed statements, as in *The Occupation*, here hesitations and the like were allowed to stand. The naturalism of the situation was furthermore strengthened by a casual camera, actively looking for striking personal details, often in large close-ups. This naturalism could also be seen in the long takes and in the frequent use of the camera on the shoulder, allowing the cameraman to keep moving around his subject. The witnesses were interviewed in a domestic setting, and the long takes gave more than enough room for observation of this context of family life. And the lavish use of music and sound effects (that certainly differed from the direct cinema documentaries from abroad) provided a very purposeful guidance for the viewer.

The use of archival footage in *Vastberaden* is also interesting. More than half of the program consisted of old images—taken from propaganda films, feature films, and home movies—beautifully edited, but also misleading. In one sequence on the 1938 Munich conference, for instance, the images of Hitler were taken from *Triumph des Willens*, the infamous propaganda film by Leni Riefenstahl, and so were actually shot in Nuremberg in 1934, and not in Munich in 1938. The liberties taken by the producers with the editing of the archival material also led in some other cases to historical inaccuracy.

The narrative of *Vastberaden, maar soepel en met mate* locates this over-the-shoulder shot of Hitler as being in Munich in 1938. In reality the shot came from *Triumph of the Will* and so depicts Nuremberg in 1934. Courtesy of the Dutch Television Archives.

They presented, for instance, a sequence from Eisenstein's *October*—showing the storming of the Winter Palace—as documentary footage. They changed the narrative—and thus the context—of a newsreel on the Allied bombardment of the Philips factory in Eindhoven. Many of the images of German atrocities were taken from feature films made *after* the war. This procedure certainly made visible one of the basic dilemmas of audiovisual history. Using footage from the archives gives an innocent public the sensation of looking through a *time machine* at real historical events, but the manipulation inherent in the editing and reworking of this material, in fact, often destroys its historical authenticity.

Another difference may be noted here. Television documentary in this period began to incorporate journalistic principles. Instead of the old, rather one-sided propagandistic or educational film documentary, the convention of putting together opposing viewpoints became the norm. Crosscutting was often used to underscore the conflicts within the narration. One would expect *Vastberaden* to follow this journalistic convention of uniting the opposites, but in fact the documentary used another mode of narration, without doubt inspired by the principles of *direct cinema*. Because the producers did not interfere with the happenings before the camera, the "truth" is what witnesses recount: *no one is doubted or confronted with different views.* The Nazi collaborator interviewed in the program enjoys the same status as everybody else, and his statements are given at face value. The effect of this narrative strategy cannot be underestimated: because "the good and the bad" were shown simultaneously, it constituted a new way of looking at the Occupation, giving plenty of allowance for nuances. And it soon became clear this mixture could also evoke strong emotions. The Nazi collaborator, for instance, though already edited into the program, at the last moment didn't agree to the broadcast, fearing public revenge. In the end he was made unrecognizable by the manipulation of image and sound, and in the reruns of the program his role was taken by one of the producers, who read his statements before the camera.

If you look closely at the program, more can be seen. There is a clear perspective, visible in the selection of witnesses and in the narrative itself, that nothing much had changed since the war: the same elite was still in power. Even a mayor who—as the program showed—collaborated with the Germans during the war still enjoyed a comfortable governing position. In effect, the war is used here as a *touchstone* for contemporary society, with a rising awareness of the dubious roles played by some public figures during the conflict. Whereas in the 1950s a politician could get away with a dubious war record, this became unthinkable in the second half of the 1970s. Thus, the program forms a clear example of the use of history to criticize contemporary society.

Vastberaden was the forerunner of a "wave" of critical documentaries, although the program remained an exception at first. The basic dilemmas of the Netherlands under the Occupation, those of collaboration and compromise, were one year later tackled in a series made by Thames Television: *The World at War*.[14] In one of the programs, dedicated to the German occupation of the Netherlands and broadcast in 1975, the issues of guilt and collaboration were openly addressed, including interviews with prominent collaborators. At that time, only *Vastberaden* and a much smaller documentary, on the life of the Dutch Nazi leader Anton Mussert, had done this so openly. And that latter documentary, a thirty-five-minute TV-biography of the Dutch *Führer* Mussert, was surrounded by difficulties: it had at first been postponed and was broadcast only after an extensive re-editing, which had softened the tone of the program.[15] But the floodgates were now opening, and in the following years dissenting voices could soon be heard all over the screen. More and more critical documentaries appeared, often related to trials of war criminals at home and abroad. One incident in 1976, for instance, concerning the businessman and Nazi collaborator Pieter Menten, sparked a whole series of documentaries by the current affairs program *Aktua*, taking issue with the political protection of Menten after the war. Other current affairs programs also produced documentaries searching for dubious war records of public persons and institutions, often concluding that not individuals but "the system" was to blame.[16] These critical documentaries shattered the consensus on the war that had once united the nation—the television-mirror that had presented such a positive view of the role of the Dutch people in the war cracked. All kinds of controversies were now fought out on the television screen, and there was hardly a societal dilemma (for instance, the rising racism towards ethnic minorities) that was not "measured" by the benchmark of the war. Thus, television certainly fueled public debate on the war, augmenting the split in a complete reversal of its role in earlier decades.

As noted before, another phenomenon can be seen in the 1970s: *the rise of the victim*. This was especially reflected in the establishment of a new television genre—that of the *concentration camp documentary*. This decade shows a strong and growing interest in the victims of the war, culminating in a rising number of documentaries about the death camps. By the end of the 1970s this trend had grown so strong that stories of concentration camps, war crimes, and the Holocaust had formed the prime category within the war documentary—in effect, replacing the heroism of the Resistance by the suffering of the victims. Many of these camp documentaries used the narrative form of a *quest*, a personal search based on the oral history of witnesses, with a rich use of first-person documents (like diaries) and historical locations—a long-term trend still visible today. Two foreign programs played an especially important role in this "resurrection of the victim": the American drama series *Holocaust*, aired in the Netherlands in 1978, and the documentary *Shoah*, by Claude Lanzmann, broadcast eight years later. Both programs were widely discussed and created deep impressions, but were certainly no exceptions in the Dutch stream of documentaries about the camps.

Interesting in this respect is a Dutch counterpart for *Shoah*, produced years before, in 1978. *History of a Location* (*Geschiedenis van een plek*) is a long documentary (more than three hours) about the history of the concentration camp Amersfoort, using a narrative technique that could be called "emotional archaeology."[17] Central in this program is a wandering camera, which "digs" almost literally at the surface of the location, sometimes for minutes

In very long takes, the camera is searching in *History of a Location*, sometimes in extreme close-ups. Courtesy of the Dutch Television Archives.

searching around, looking silently for traces of the past, without any narration. The historical location of the camp is now the site of a police academy; in the first sequence of the film, cadets are shown during a shooting exercise. In this manner, current events and historical truth, present and past, are mixed. But there is another layer: that of sound and music. The dark tones of a Mahler symphony and, later in the program, singing Nazis add to the significance of the location: it is a "guilty landscape," as one of the producers put it.

In a way, the program makers had no choice; there existed no archival footage of the camp. The program itself relied heavily on interviews, made in the now-established informal style. But again and again these interviews were interrupted by the camera, searching for the place where it all happened. This style reminds one of an early film documentary of the camps: *Nuit et Brouillard* (Night and Fog), by Alain Resnais (1955), but the earlier French film included archival footage and was backed by a strong narrative. In *History of a Location*, the "archaeological" aspect, the use of the actual historical location, is developed much further. The searching camera in all

The "guilty landscape" of a Dutch concentration camp in *History of a Location*. Courtesy of the Dutch Television Archives.

its silence is in effect telling a separate story that not only illustrates the interviews, but is so dominant and compelling that it strongly reinforces the "historical feeling" of the program. Thus, it foreshadows Lanzmann's documentary, which also eschewed archival footage and leaned heavily (apart from its interviews) on very long takes of landscapes in and around the camps. But for all its impressiveness there is one significant omission in the program. Right after the war the Amersfoort camp was used to detain Nazi collaborators, and they were treated so badly that a number of them did not survive. *That* aspect of the history of this "guilty landscape" was not mentioned, although everyone else was interviewed—even the man who demolished the camp and remarked that the barracks had "a good quality wood."

The example of *History of a Location* shows us that the camp documentary is of a different category than the critical documentary. In its quest form, it provides a participant observation, focusing more on the emotions of the witnesses than on the historical context of the story. Their suffering is at all times central in the narrative, and there is hardly room for authorities and the like. The historical expert is replaced by the personal and subjective view of the witness—or that of the documentary maker. But still the camp documentary indirectly contributed to the rising critical mood. These documentaries often made deep impressions, stimulating public discussions about the magnitude of the Holocaust and how it could have occurred. They gave the memory of the war an emotional charge that sparked many a critical documentary, as for instance in 1976 *Een Schijn van Twijfel* (A Shadow of a Doubt), a documentary beginning with the demolition of the camp Westerbork but soon changing into a personal quest for the Nazi murderers in today's society.[18]

What conclusions can we draw about the role of television in the memory of the war in these first decades? First of all, it is easy to criticize the quality of this audiovisual history. Many productions look superficial to a professional historian: they appeal to cheap emotions, are made by nonexperts asking overly simple questions and sometimes getting the wrong answers. But audiovisual history has its own set of rules, which cannot easily be compared with the rules of written history. It borrows its narrative system from film and television—and this means that *dramatization* and *personalization* dominate. The camp documentaries constitute a fine example of both trends: history is reduced to the experience and testimony of a single individual, whose story is cast in a dramatic mold in which every means of dramatic expression available to television—music, sound effects, iconic clichés—is used to intensify the emotions. Often there is also a strong emphasis on conflict; it is used as the driving force in the story. This means, for instance, that less interesting features and witnesses that do not fit into the "conflict scheme" are left out. Thus, in *The Occupation* the grey-toned nuance of a majority of the population easily adapting to the regime of the Germans is simply outside focus; a story on the struggle between the good and the bad doesn't leave much room for other interpretations of the wartime experience.

Vastberaden does not use a "good and bad scheme," but paints with its oral history and *direct cinema* techniques a strong picture of everyday life during the war, leaving more than enough opportunities for nuances. But it also has its limitations. The selection of the witnesses, for instance, is guided by the exceptional. All had abnormal, out-of-the-ordinary experiences—a waitress in whose bed landed a (nonexploding) bomb, the trumpet player who was forced to play at the executions in Auschwitz. And it was not the history of the common man or woman, as the producers had intended, but of people who represented particular groups, like Resistance fighters and camp victims, groups that played a special role in the war. These selection criteria led more generally to a process in which—in the words of Robert Rosenstone—history becomes memory: memory is presented as history, and collective movements are reduced to persons.[19] This bias is clearly evident in the Dutch audiovisual history of the war, and it holds true for all the documentaries mentioned here.

But within these boundaries, audiovisual history has proven itself—at least in the Dutch situation—to be surprisingly strong, and this study underlines the role television can play in societal debate. The Dutch war documentary challenged and thus changed—sometimes in a sudden upheaval—the image of the past, although in that process it also broke the unity of that image and cracked the mirror. The war documentaries stimulated extensive public discussion about the past and seem to have had a stronger effect on historical awareness than that achieved by professional historians. Both *The Occupation* and *Vastberaden*, for instance, were followed by heated debates about the war in the press and on television. When *The Occupation* was repeated in 1966, it was even accompanied by a separate series discussing the content of the original series.[20] So at first sight, television certainly played an important role as "magnifier" or "accelerator" in public discussions on the Occupation, and at the very least kept interest in the war alive.

Yet there also seems to be a kind of "inertia." If one looks closely, television is no forerunner, no avant-garde, in societal change. All the changes in the approach to the war, as discussed above, were usually visible first in public debate in society and only later followed by television. The discussion about the causes of the high percentage of Dutch Jews killed during the war is a case in point. Here television followed years after the printed discourse. As early as 1965 the Dutch historian Presser published an in-depth study about the persecution of the Jews, and the publication had, according to one observer, a "shattering" impact on the public mind.[21] In the 1970s, other professional historians had done further research on the subject.[22] But not until the middle of the 1980s did one begin to see a fundamental treatment of this issue on television—first in a series broadcast by one of the "pillars," the liberal AVRO, under the name of *Forty Years After (Veertig jaar na dato)*.[23] In that program there was no attention for heroism of the Resistance or solidarity with the Jews; instead, there was the story of the administrator who had registered the Jews for deportation, the trains that kept running punctually to and from the camps, the futility of many a Resistance action, and the way the entertainment industry had let itself be used for German propaganda. Later, in 1990, one can see a further eroding of the rather positive image of Dutch society during the war in a twenty-one-part remake of *The Occupation*. This remake eminently reflected the changes in perception in the previous thirty years. Although much of the material used (especially interviews) was taken from the original series, there was a much more critical view of the role of civil servants and industry, especially compared with the old series. And, finally, the issue of the high percentage of Jewish victims was here treated very thoroughly.

Why is there such a time lag between the development of audiovisual history and societal and scientific debate? Three factors could help to explain this inertia. Certainly in the earlier years there was a restraint in handling difficult issues on which no societal consensus existed. These restraints were not due to commercial pressure (in those days the Dutch system was non-commercial), but to a widely felt fear of the alleged influence of the medium. Television was seen by the broadcasting organizations as a dangerous instrument, which should be handled with care and could easily get out of hand. The result was that during the first two decades of television, in fact, a prohibitive code functioned that blocked dissenting views of the war—so helping in "uniting" the nation. Secondly, the planning and production of documentaries took a considerable amount of time. It was no exception that between conception and transmission there was a period of several years. And thirdly, one can—anyway in the Dutch situation—see an augmenting division between the professional filmmaker and the professional historian. *The Occupation* was produced by a professional historian, but in later years the professional historian became marginal to the production of historical documentaries, both on and behind the screen. This meant that developments in the professional historical debate were picked up only when they had reached a much wider public sphere.

There is considerable ambivalence in the role of television as it has been sketched here. It is obvious that the medium can initiate, strengthen, and structure debates; all the documentaries here analyzed had such short-term effects, and other examples can easily be documented. Still, as has been indicated, it is hard to find an *autonomous* change initiated by television in this respect, and one should be cautious in giving television too prominent a role in changing historical awareness. Seen over time—at least in this study and in the Dutch context—its main effect on the historical image of the war seems to lie in two areas. Firstly, it strengthened existing tendencies for change by "cracking the mirror," thereby further weakening an already failing consensus on the war. And secondly, by the creation of "iconic clichés," the medium influenced the *form* of the historical image. In this last sense, the historical imagination is indeed quite literally shaped by television.

Notes

This chapter is based on the author's study: *Televisie en Bezetting, een onderzoek naar de documentaire verbeelding van de Tweede Wereldoorlog in Nederland* (Television and the

Occupation: A study of television documentaries on the Second World War in the Netherlands) (Hilversum, The Netherlands: Verloren, 1995).

1. This could be a misleading figure, because the total production of historical documentaries also rises yearly. But indeed even the share in the total production over the years is growing. See Vos, 30–39.

2. In the Netherlands, no single political group has the majority, so governing is characterized by cooperation among the different groups. But the societal organizations used to be "pillarized"; for instance, in sports, school, and youth organizations there existed for every pillar a separate organization.

3. Henry Rousso, *The Vichy Syndrome: History and Memory in France Since 1944*, (Cambridge, Mass.: Harvard Univ. Press), 1991.

4. *The Occupation* was broadcast by the NTS between 1960 and 1965 and repeated in 1966–1968. In 1990, a remake was produced and aired by the same maker.

5. For another analysis of this program, which reaches similar conclusions, see: Frank van Vree, *In de schaduw van Auschwitz, herinneringen, beelden, geschiedenis* (In the shadow of Auschwitz, memories, images, history), (Groningen, The Netherlands: Historische Uitgeverij, 1995), 57–89.

6. R. Hilberg, *Die Vernichtung der europäischen Juden* (The extermination of the European Jews), Band 2, (Frankfurt am Main, Germany: Fischer Verlag 1982), 598.

7. This was discovered by a Dutch journalist. A television documentary (*Gezicht van het verleden* (Face of the past), VPRO, 1994) was made about his search for the girl.

8. *Begrijpt u nu waarom ik huil?* (Do you now understand why I'm crying?), VARA, February, 26, 1972.

9. Data from the viewing polls indicate a dwindling from 51 percent to 39 percent in fourteen days. See *Kijken en Luisteren 1972–1974*, Jaarboek NOS Kijk-en Luisteronderzoek, (Hilversum, The Netherlands: NOS, 1975), 30.

10. Rousso, 104.

11. As for instance in the leading newspaper *Het Parool*, September 30, 1972.

12. *Vastberaden, maar soepel en met mate* was produced by the VPRO, broadcast on May 4, 1974, and repeated in 1978 and 1989.

13. See for instance Richard Meran Barsam, *Nonfiction Film: A Critical History*, rev. ed. (Bloomington: Indiana Univ. Press 1992), 300–309.

14. *De wereld in oorlog* (The world at war), part 18, Nederland in de oorlog (The Netherlands at war), Thames Television/KRO, May 3, 1975.

15. *Portret van Anton Adriaan Mussert* (Portrait of Anton Adriaan Mussert) was produced and directed by Paul Verhoeven (now famous as a Hollywood director) in 1968. The broadcasting organization VPRO, after a considerable delay and extensive revision by the later director of *Vastberaden*, Hans Keller, who was then a member of the editorial staff of the VPRO, transmitted the program on April 16, 1970, in a less popular slot later in the evening.

16. See for instance the current affairs specials *Nuremberg 1946–Düsseldorf 1974*, VARA, May 4, 1976, and *De beul van Sobibor* (The hangman of Sobibor), NCRV, June 1, 1978.

17. In a statement of one of the editors, Hans Keller, during a congress at the Erasmus University Rotterdam, *Televisie en de verbeelding van de geschiedenis* (Television and the

imagination of history), June 3, 1994. *Geschiedenis van een plek* (History of a location) was broadcast by the VPRO in May 1978 and repeated in May 1980.

18. *Een Schijn van Twijfel* (A Shadow of a doubt), VARA, September 6, 1976.

19. Rosenstone states this mechanism is not necessarily linked to the medium: you can look at Eisenstein—and, I may add, even Riefenstahl—to see examples where a history of collective movements is presented. The same is obviously true for many compilation documentaries (like *Victory at Sea*). But still one may say the bulk of television documentaries concentrate in their narratives on individuals. See R. Rosenstone, *Visions of the Past: The Challenge of Film to Our Idea of History*, (Cambridge, Mass.: Harvard Univ. Press, 1995), 22, 30. For another discussion of this phenomenon, see Chris Vos, *Het Verleden in Bewegend Beeld* (The past in moving images), (Houten, The Netherlands: De Haan, 1991), 145–56.

20. *De bezetting ter discussie* (The occupation under discussion), a six-part series broadcast by the NOS, 1966–1967.

21. The historian Jan Bank in his inaugural lecture: *Oorlogsverleden in Nederland* (The memory of the war in the Netherlands), (Baarn, The Netherlands: Ambo, 1983), 22–23. The publication he is referring to is: J.Presser, *Ondergang, De vervolging en verdelging van het nederlandse Jodendom 1940–1945*, (Downfall: The persecution and extermination of Dutch Jewry, 1940–1945), (Den Haag, The Netherlands: Staatsuitgeverij, 1965).

22. Dutch historian Blom, for instance, states in an overview that at the end of the 1970s this subject became central in historical debate, years before television attended to this issue thoroughly. See J.C.H. Blom, "The Persecution of the Jews in the Netherlands in a Comparative International Perspective," in J. Michman, ed., *Dutch Jewish History*, (Assen/Maastricht, The Netherlands: Van Gorcum, 1989), 273–89.

23. *Veertig jaar na dato* (Forty years after), four-part documentary, AVRO, May 1985.

7 Contested Public Memories

Hawaiian History as Hawaiian or American Experience

Carolyn Anderson

On January 27, 1997, in his introduction of *Hawaii's Last Queen* to a national PBS audience of nearly seven million viewers, historian David McCullough, host of *The American Experience,* labeled the 1893 overthrow of the hereditary monarchy of Hawai'i as "an unfamiliar story to most Americans today."[1] Then McCullough acknowledged another audience of people not only familiar with, but invested in, this story: "In Hawaii, however, the subject is anything but old hat, and interpretations of what actually happened differ sharply, depending on who's telling the story." McCullough recognized—but located elsewhere—the production of history as an essentially political project; he linked an environment of contestation to local politics and familiarity with "the story." His allusion to the current political environment in Hawai'i was oblique, yet nevertheless a reminder of the situated nature of public memory, of the importance of not only who's telling the story, but who's hearing it, and where.

This essay considers how historical stories are told on public television through an examination of *Hawaii's Last Queen* and five recent productions from the island state that share a focus on 1890s Hawai'i. It follows the lead of public historians who recognize the significance of the local in the creation of public memory and of Cultural Studies scholars who emphasize the centrality of the acts of formation and dissemination of cultural products.[2] It is thus assumed that general contexts and the particulars of the production and use of historical products shape understandings of those texts. At the beginning of the twenty-first century, Hawai'i shares, and seriously extends, nationwide challenges to notions of a homogenized present cultural identity and a unified sense of America's past. Michael Roth's simple but penetrating questions are relevant: "What is the point of having a past, and why try to recollect it? What desires are satisfied by this recollection?"[3] Two crucial flashpoints in Hawaiian history—the overthrow of Queen Lili'uokalani and the Hawaiian nation in 1893, and the U.S. annexation of Hawai'i in 1898— function as symbols of, and necessity for, a growing movement for native sovereignty in Hawai'i, a movement that deeply complicates the concept of nationhood. Where the story of the overthrow and annexation fits in a Hawaiian centennial narrative or in an ongoing American narrative of expansionism, imperialism, and treatment of native peoples is a matter of contestation.

National History: *Hawaii's Last Queen* for *The American Experience* (1997)

The American Experience, produced at WGBH in Boston, is the only regularly scheduled prime-time television historical documentary series in the United States; it is arguably the most influential and certainly the most awarded series. Created in 1987 by Peter McGee, who "wanted to do for American History what *Nova* is for science,"[4] the series takes an aggressive stance in (re)organizing the discourse of national memory and in presenting itself as sensitive to the multicultural diversity contained within what is nonetheless a metanarrative labeled "*the* American experience."

In 1991, with an eye on the 1993 centennial of the overthrow of the Hawaiian monarchy, independent producer Vivian Ducat submitted a proposal to *The American Experience* for a project that would consider the overthrow as a factor in the debates around "what it meant to be imperial" that took place in America at the end of the century.[5] Ducat had become interested in Hawai'i while on location there as writer-director of the final segment of an eight-part BBC documentary series, *Nippon*. After returning to her home in New York, Ducat read the work of historian Merze Tate, who introduced her to "this incredible story of the overthrow" and inspired her proposal. Ducat met with executive producer Judy Crichton and senior producer Margaret Drain, who expressed concerns about the expense of such a project and encouraged Ducat to seek additional funding. Ducat contacted possible backers, including Hawai'i Public Television, but was unsuccessful. Unable to devote herself to fund-raising, Ducat moved to other projects. Several years passed; then in 1994, Ducat was contacted by Crichton, who indicated interest in "the Hawaiian idea," but cautioned that *The American Experience* thinks in terms of characters an audience could relate to, and suggested that the story be told through the life of the Queen. Ducat was interested, but hesitant to get involved in such a time-consuming project, since she was pregnant; Crichton was flexible regarding a start-up time, which became May 1995.

Because of (what was perceived as) the confined setting of this story and the importance of developing relationships with the local community, *The American Experience* front office encouraged Ducat to go to Hawai'i early on and urged her to select a native Hawaiian associate producer (Nicole Ebeo). On her first scouting trip to Hawai'i, and later when she returned to film, Ducat's association with a well-known, well-funded national series operated as both access and obstacle.[6] Ducat later described the situation: "People had their backs up. I was an outsider getting national funds to make a film about their story. . . . I had to gain their trust, and I did that by doing my home-work."[7] That homework was partially assigned by the academic advisors the producer/writer/director chose: Davianna Pomaika'i McGregor (University of Hawai'i, Mānoa) and Tennant McWilliams (University of Alabama, Birmingham). *The American Experience* urges producers to employ both a specialist and generalist and to consult them, especially on matters of historical accuracy, at all stages of the process. Ducat discovered that few generalists in late-nineteenth-century American history know much about the overthrow. McWilliams, who has published on the (Congressional) Blount Report (which urged the United States to restore the monarchy), was a fortunate exception. Ducat relied on her advisors on-screen and off, with McGregor becoming an important link to the Hawaiian community. Throughout the process, Ducat struggled with the expectations and suspicions of a community that has often been misrepresented and whose "judgment [she] felt on [her] shoulders the entire time" and, simultaneously, her contractual obligations to produce a film that would be understandable and interesting to "people in Nebraska, and the people in Miami, and the people in Seattle, and the people on farms, and people who live in big cities."[8]

Ducat's solution to this dilemma is a biographical piece deeply admiring of the last Hawaiian queen. McCullough introduces Lili'uokalani's story as part of a narrative of turn-of-the-century American expansionism. Nevertheless, Ducat's emphasis is on Hawaiian loss, rather than American conquest; on Hawaiian isolation, rather than American intervention. *Hawaii's Last Queen* begins with a prologue, which swiftly accomplishes several narrative and conceptual moves. The narrator opens with, "Just a century ago, there was an isolated kingdom . . . a beloved queen . . . removed from her throne. . . . It was a great loss to her people." An elderly Hawaiian woman, Thelma Bugbee, appears first, saying, "If you can imagine something within

Queen Lili'uokalani, circa 1881. Courtesy of Hawai'i State Archives.

your own culture that is tremendously important to you . . . totally ripped out and gone. If you can imagine yourself relating to something like that, that's what we went through." The narrator mentions Lili'uokalani's background and training: "But nothing had prepared her for the crisis she would face as queen." Aaron Mahi, conductor of the Royal Hawaiian Band, comments, "Liliu . . . knew the values of both sides. Knew the inevitable of what was going to happen to Hawaii." The series title then appears on the screen.

The prologue promises a story of a great woman whose life was filled with accomplishment, drama, and intrigue. A sympathetic elder, operating as witness at a personal, experiential level, invites an audience of presumed outsiders to "relate to" a wrenching loss. A respected member of the Hawaiian community refers to the last queen familiarly, while describing "what happened to Hawaii" as "inevitable." The rest of the documentary elaborates on and verifies a theme of tragic inevitability. An off-screen narrator (Anna Deavere Smith) and nine on-screen storytellers collaborate, with one notable exception, to present the biography of an honorable and wise leader, whose commitment to peace was used against her and her people in an immoral and illegal overthrow, orchestrated by greedy local businessmen. Strongly opposing this interpretation is Honolulu newspaper publisher Thurston Twigg-Smith, grandson of Lorrin Thurston. The narrator provides a telling context: "Leading the opposition [against King Kalākaua, Lili'uokalani's brother, who preceded her on the throne] was a young, hotheaded lawyer and journalist named Lorrin Thurston. He formed a secret society of white businessmen." Twigg-Smith describes Kalākaua as a man aching for absolute power, then offers these motives: "He [Thurston] wanted, as did the other members of that group, to do what the colonists had done in 1776, which was to throw off the yoke of monarchy and take on the civil rights and other things of a democracy. And they believed that was in the best interests of the Hawaiians and I believe so, too." Twigg-Smith's rhetorical strategy is clear as he invokes associations to American democracy in an attempt to seize the moral high ground as heir to and (in this film singular) apologist for his grandfather's actions. Twigg-Smith's position—a view that dominated written history for most of the last century—seems included as a gesture toward "objectivity," which is an abiding goal of *The American Experience*, according to executive producer Margaret Drain.

By personal preference and following series guidelines, Ducat eschewed historical reenactments, but she employed a moving camera perspective through various historical locations (which *The American Experience* encourages for its experiential possibilities). In setting up one of these location shoots, Ducat ran into a difficulty that illustrates the resonance of history, and the intensity of loyalties, in contemporary Hawai'i: owners of Victorian homes were unwilling to have their residences photographed as the meeting place where the overthrow was planned, since they presumed a visual association would be obvious and mark them as sympathetic to the overthrow. Ducat did not need to find local actors to express unpopular opinions, for she shunned the radio-drama style of voicing historical sources to add liveliness and emotional texture. Lili'uokalani is quoted on eleven occasions, usually from her autobiography and her diaries and, poignantly, from the quilt the dethroned queen embroidered while under house arrest, but the quotations are presented *as* quotations. Ducat directed narrator Anna Deavere Smith not to change her speaking voice to impersonate the queen; rather, Smith continues in an understated style that characterizes the narration. This strategy simultaneously draws listeners into Liliʻuokalani's thoughts, yet maintains a sense of historical distance.

The biography builds to the climax of the Queen's abdication, then moves swiftly to annexation. The last on-camera speaker recalls the first in displaying the emotional, experiential dimensions of public memory. Identified as a cultural specialist, Malcolm Naea Chun (an expert in Hawaiian medicine) has spoken before, with conviction and from a nationalist perspective, but with restraint. In this final appearance, while recounting the events of annexation day, Chun describes the lowering of the Hawaiian flag and the insult of its being cut into small ribbons, given to the sons and daughters of missionary families as "tokens of remembrance . . . of their great victory over the Hawaiian kingdom and the end of the tyranny of the Hawaiian monarchy." While speaking, Chun lowers his eyes, and his voice cracks; then as he concludes, he suddenly looks up in sadness and proud resolution.

In conclusion, the narrator briefly recalls Liliʻuokalani's last years—as an American citizen—and her death. The film ends with the sounds of chanting, images of the Hawaiian shore, and these words: "For weeks after her funeral, strange events were recorded in the islands. Volcanoes erupted and the seas turned an odd hue, from the sudden appearance of a multitude of red fish. It was as if the elements recognized that the kingdom was no more."

Hawaii's Last Queen premiered at the Hawaiʻi International Film Festival in Honolulu in October 1996, with a special "Governor's screening" at the recently restored Hawaiʻi Theatre. Ducat spoke briefly after the film and answered questions. Local reviews and responses were generally favorable—some strongly so; others were tempered in their praise, with two recurring complaints: the absence of discussion of the contemporary sovereignty movement, and the mispronunciation of Hawaiian words by the narrator. Since *The American Experience* policy is to focus only on the past, Ducat had followed the template of the series (and most historical documentaries). The second criticism struck a nerve, although here, too, Ducat had followed a series practice: utilizing a "box office" narrator. After considering local performers—it seemed a given that the narrator would be a woman—Ducat chose Anna Deavere Smith because of her vocal skills and her national reputation, partially based on those skills. Audiotapes of all Hawaiian words in the narration were prepared by a Hawaiian speaker for Smith's tutoring. Yet good intentions, hard work, and professional skill are not enough sometimes. Ducat recalled, "I felt a sense of shame that, in the end, with all this effort, we didn't get it perfectly, because I thought we could have. It comes down to me, because I am directing the narration . . . but not being Hawaiian, I couldn't hear the phonetic nuance between what was right and what wasn't."

Others from the resident community found quite different faults. Thurston Twigg-Smith, in a letter published in a local newspaper, considered the documentary "biased and one-sided," distorting "major elements of Hawaiian history"; an anonymous review written by "The MAN" posted this warning: "Viewers should look with a critical eye to see how much of this program is truth and how much is misleading propaganda designed to influence local politics."[9]

Several months later, in January 1997, PBS broadcast *Hawaii's Last Queen* nationwide.[10] Almost seven million viewers—more than typical for the series and far more than *American Experience* executives anticipated—saw the documentary. Reviews were positive and especially responsive to the freshness of an unfamiliar historical tale; there were no challenges to accuracy. With an array of headlines, literally hundreds of newspapers ran a complimentary Associated Press piece written by Honolulu-based Ron Staton, which begins with a clear demarcation of audience expectations: "Beyond Hawaii, Queen Lili'uokalani, the islands' last monarch, probably is best known as the composer of '*Aloha O'e.*' But to native Hawaiians, Lili'uokalani is the revered symbol of their loss of sovereignty." Staton later quotes Ducat as saying, "This is not a film about sovereignty. I tried to stay out of local politics."[11]

In March 1998, *The American Experience* programmed a national rebroadcast of *Hawaii's Last Queen*—many stations had already utilized their option of three plays in four years—and cleared the documentary for foreign broadcast and satellite transmission. The documentary is marketed vigorously, through PBS video catalogs (first in the "Heroes" section, later under "Visionaries") in three formats (home use, audiovisual instructional use, and an indexed audiovisual edition). PBS handles video sales, with the series receiving 50 percent of the profits. *The American Experience* maintains an extensive website on *Hawaii's Last Queen*, providing a transcript, bibliography, information on some of Lili'uokalani's musical compositions, and a teacher's guide organized around "themes" of "cultural values, expansionism, politics, racism, [and] exploitation."[12]

Local History: The Overthrow of 1893

For a decade before the 1997 broadcast of *Hawaii's Last Queen* to a nationwide audience, producers in Hawai'i, operating from a variety of funding bases and political agendas, had told the story of Queen Lili'uokalani and the overthrow of 1893. Three examples of Hawai'i-based productions demonstrate the uses of history for local (and marginalized) populations.

1. Hawai'i Public Television Production: Hawaiians (1987)

Like many public television stations, KHET in Honolulu carries a small permanent staff and often recruits from the local production community for specific projects. That was the case for an ambitious three-part history of Hawai'i produced by the Hawai'i Public Broadcasting Authority (with corporate backing from Bank of Hawai'i) in 1987. *Hawaiians* was produced by Lynn Waters of the KHET staff, who also cowrote the series with Ellen Pelissero. It was directed by Roland Yamamoto. By the mid-1980s, the Islands had experienced a full decade of what is known locally as the "Hawaiian Renaissance," a period of renewed interest in and admiration for Hawaiian language and culture. *Hawaiians* taps and extends such interest and admiration in a sweeping, three-hour series, promoted as "the definitive historical account of the native people of the most famous islands in the world."

Part Two, "Innocence Betrayed," presents the 1800s as a century of loss, dramatized as a tragedy in three acts as the losses accumulate and deepen: first, of a uniquely Hawaiian culture, then, of the people's land, and finally, of the Hawaiian kingdom. A typical disembodied narrator—here the voice of "she-who-knows"—guides understandings of the visual material, displayed as evidence. Also typically, a chain of "experts" appear and reappear, their comments linked, sometimes one to another but more commonly to a narration presented as conclusive. The nine commentators are all Island residents, most of them are Hawaiian.[13] They selected their own self-labels; Kekuni Blaisdell, who has the most speaking turns, presents himself as "M.D., Citizen of the Hawaiian Nation." Many locals would recognize Blaisdell, a founder of *Ka Pakaukau*, a coalition of sovereignty groups, and a University of Hawai'i Medical School professor instrumental in establishing clinics for Hawaiians. But for all viewers, Blaisdell introduces a subtext of contemporary political activity with his forceful self-description.

What is atypical stylistically in "Innocence Betrayed" is the use of actors impersonating historical personages, literary characters, and historical types, quoting from written sources in direct address. Here the editing strategy is often one of juxtaposition, whereby the writings/words of a historical person (especially Captain James Cook and missionary Hiram Bingham) will be challenged and discredited by the comments that follow, sometimes from another "historical person," at other times from a contemporary expert, thereby creating a rhetoric of rebuttal against the words and actions of the colonizers and by implication, the once-standard histories of Hawai'i. This representational style drives the first two acts; then, when the chronicle reaches the 1870s (and thus historical photographic materials exist) the reenactments disappear, with one notable exception: Lili'uokalani, the last monarch, who speaks in direct address to the camera three times. These appearances—ghostly, and visually jarring—have an intriguing performative quality. Although the referents in her speech span the period from 1887 to 1893, her dress and physical appearance do not change. The result suggests memory embodied—her personal memory (through her words of recollection) and also a public memory (formed partly in response to these quotations). First, she describes her 1887 return to Hawai'i from England (where she had been invited to attend Queen Victoria's Fiftieth Jubilee) and her subsequent realization of "a conspiracy against the peace of the Hawaiian kingdom"; then she recounts the circumstances by which she was "compelled to take the oath to the Constitution which had led to the death of [her] brother"; and finally, she reads the letter in which, under protest, and to avoid bloodshed, with the hope of reinstatement by the United States government, she yielded her authority as the constitutional sovereign of the Hawaiian islands.

The narrator's omniscient voice resumes, providing more historical information paired with a series of early twentieth-century moving images, made all the more bittersweet, since, at the point when the photographed Lili'uokalani finally comes to life through movement, the narration recalls the relative powerlessness of her last years. The narrator sadly concludes: "Lili'uokalani, a singular woman, on whom the tragedy of the Hawaiian race fell, lived 77 years. On her death in 1917, 139 years after the arrival of Cook, fewer than 40,000 Hawaiians survived. The people were gone; the heroes were gone; the religion was gone; the land was gone; the spoken history of 2,000 years was gone; and, with her passing, the last Hawaiian hope was gone, too."

According to historical researcher and cowriter, Ellen Pelissero, a central goal of the series was to educate young Hawaiians about their own history and to make them proud of it; the producers wanted *Hawaiians* "to definitely be from the Hawaiian perspective."[14] Consequently, Waters, Yamamoto, and Pelissero—all from Hawai'i, but not Hawaiian—approached their task with considerable trepidation and consultation. Many applauded their work. Pelissero tells a story of a young Hawaiian man who, after watching the television series, told Yamamoto, "My aunties and my grandmother told me I should be proud I'm Hawaiian, but until last night, I didn't know why."

Queen Lili'uokalani (Marlene Sai) is arrested by Captain Robert Parker (Jake Ho'opai) in a scene from *Betrayal*, a television docudrama about the final days of the Hawaiian monarchy. Courtesy of Hawai'i Public Television.

Some challenged the limits of empathy, criticizing the series for not having been written by a Hawaiian or a person fluent in the Hawaiian language.[15]

Although in 1987 producers of *Hawaiians* expected to broadcast (and rebroadcast) only in the Islands, the series has enjoyed a far wider reach over a considerably longer period of time than anticipated. KHET has broadcast the three-part series annually for over a decade, and public television stations on the continent continue to rebroadcast it. Video rental copies are available at commercial outlets in the Islands; the series is sold as a boxed video set at national chain stores. The Mountain Apple Company, owned by local composer-performer Jon de Mello, distributes the series. Because de Mello already had a distribution system in place—handling mostly musical material—*Hawaiians* has a commercial life that is rare, but probably not unique, for a local public television series. Frequent classroom use and community access cable casting in the Islands extend the series' reach and credibility.

2. Hawai'i Public Television Coproduction: Betrayal (1993)

Even before the series *Hawaiians* was produced, Marlene Sai, who portrays Lili'uokalani in Part Two, "Innocence Betrayed," had been linked in the local imagination with the Queen.[16] In the 1960s, Sai, a popular local singer, recorded some of Lili'uokalani's compositions. She appeared as the Queen in *Hear Me, Oh My People*, a one-person play written by Don Berrigan, presented in Hawai'i in 1984 and in Washington, D.C., in 1987. Sai's two successful performances in Washington added momentum to a growing interest in Hawaiian history. In 1988 the recently elected (and first native Hawaiian) governor, John Waihee, encouraged Sai to film her performance.[17] With this goal in mind, Sai formed the Kukui Foundation. For reasons that ranged from the stylistic (the one-person format was seen as too constrictive), to the personal (Sai and the playwright had a falling out), to the academic (Pelissero, who would write the screenplay for the new production, had found the earlier play "grossly inaccurate" historically), the Kukui Foundation decided to produce an original docudrama with a large cast.

To create dramatic situations and dialogue for *Betrayal*, Pelissero depended on the Queen's autobiography and diaries. Likewise, she turned to the published memoirs of Lorrin Thurston and Sanford Dole, two key historical figures in the overthrow of the queen. Thurston and Dole became central antagonists in the docudrama. But there were limits to the elasticity of this technique; consequently, dialogue and composite characters had to be created. To add action, location shooting, and some levity to what was essentially a drawing-room revolution—and from the producers' perspective, a tragic one—a subplot about the failed counterrevolution of 1895 was added. Especially for the scenes that dramatize, with some humor, the situation of the last counterrevolutionaries to be captured by the Provisional Government, local comedy writer Tremaine Tamyose joined Pelissero as cowriter and Joy Chong as codirector.

A $350,000 grant for the production of *Betrayal* was secured from the Hawai'i Legislature in 1991, but a series of complications caused delays; nevertheless, the production moved ahead slowly, then, in 1992, with velocity. The Kukui Foundation negotiated generous agreements with KHET for its sound stages and the services of its union crew; local actors worked for scale. The shooting schedule was tight—only twenty-eight days—and began with a traditional Hawaiian blessing of the set. The state legislature appropriated a $100,000 completion grant, and several local foundations, which had refused earlier, provided financial support for postproduction costs. What had been a minority historical perspective in the Islands re-

Soldiers of the Army of the Provisional Government of the Republic of Hawaii in front of the former 'Iolani Palace, renamed the Executive Building, 1894. Courtesy of the Bishop Museum.

garding the overthrow only several years before was becoming a mainstream local perspective.

By the time *Betrayal* was ready for broadcast, it was summer of 1992. Kukui and KHET decided to delay airing the piece until January 1993 to position *Betrayal* as an important part of the observance of the centennial of the overthrow. According to Pelissero, Kukui imagined a local audience of three subgroups: 1) native Hawaiians, eager to know "their own" history; 2) all students in the state (attending schools where the producers assumed they were incorrectly taught that Hawaiians had supported annexation); and 3) the local non-Hawaiian audience, especially the *haole kama'aina* (white, longtime resident) culture who "have their view of history" (which needs correcting). Certainly *Betrayal* takes the historical view that the Queen was betrayed and her subjects were wronged, but the docudrama ends in 1917— the last year of Lili'uokalani's life—on a note of optimism regarding the possibilities of justice in America. In the final dramatized scene, she tells her loyal assistant that she has flown the American flag, an unexpected act provoked by her wish to honor the "Hawaiian boys" who died representing America in World War I. She speaks with hope, speculating that since Ha-

waiians have the vote, they may someday "be able to vote our lands back."
And, in contrast to her male friend, who cannot, a feminist Lili'uokalani can
imagine that women, too, will someday vote in America.

Since the Kukui Foundation had been turned down, quite unequivocally,
for funding from national organizations, there was little to no expectation of
broadcast outside the Islands. However, once *Betrayal* was completed, Kukui
successfully negotiated with the American Program Service of PBS. Although
only Alaska Public Television broadcast *Betrayal* on the actual centennial,
many PBS stations showed the docudrama in 1993, as well as in later years.
The western region of public stations awarded Marlene Sai an honorable
mention for her memorable performance as Lili'uokalani. *Betrayal* is not
distributed commercially, but like *Hawaiians,* it moved easily and deeply into
the state educational system. In "The Making of *Betrayal,*" a short film aired
with the docudrama, Sai spoke of another important and easily underestimated use: as the most ambitious local television production ever mounted
in Hawai'i, and one that employed "99% local people." In this way, *Betrayal*
functioned as creative outlet and training ground for the production of local
history.

3. Hawai'i Independent Production: Act of War: The Overthrow of the Hawaiian Nation (1993)

Nā Maka o ka 'Āina (Eyes of the Land) is a two-person video production
company established and operated by Puhipau and Joan Lander.[18] Puhipau
(also known as Abraham Ahmad Jr.) was born of a Hawaiian mother and
Palestinian father in Hawai'i and has lived in the Islands most of his life.
Lander came to Hawai'i in 1970 and soon after became involved in public
access video. In 1980 Puhipau and Lander formed a political, personal, and
professional alliance. Since 1981 *Nā Maka o ka 'Āina* has produced almost
one hundred videos, including a series on "history, sovereignty, and independence." In some respects, *Nā Maka* operates as guerrilla television—but *Nā
Maka's* crucial links to various types of state and federal support mark it as a
successful grassroots production company with considerable influence in its
own community and an impressive reach beyond it.

Made with extremely modest budgets, sometimes in Hawaiian, often supported by the Hawai'i Department of Education, *Nā Maka* productions were
regularly screened on public access channels throughout the 1980s. In 1991,
realizing that the centennial of the overthrow was approaching and provoked by learning that a non-Hawaiian documentarian had plans (which
never materialized) for a film about the events of 1893, *Nā Maka* and col-

Producers Joan Lander and Puhipau of *Act of War*. Courtesy of Bruce Lum.

leagues from the Center for Hawaiian Studies at the University of Hawai'i decided they had "better do one that has the Hawaiians' point of view." They submitted a proposal for a documentary on the overthrow to the recently formed Independent Television Service (ITVS).[19] Their $290,000 proposal was approved; later they received $20,000 from the Native American Public Broadcasting Consortium. For the first—and, as of this writing, only—time, *Nā Maka* had an operating budget that allowed production flexibility, as well as the opportunity to repay a decade of favors. Also for the first time, they had a contractual obligation to create a documentary for a national audience.

Act of War was a joint project, with Professors Haunani-Kay Trask and Lilikalā Kame'eleihiwa controlling the script and Puhipau and Lander making production decisions. The documentary opens with a bold prologue of striking contrasts: a narrator begins with a Hawaiian creation legend. Her voice and that story of idyllic island life are ruptured by images and synchronized

A scene from the independently produced *Act of War: The Overthrow of the Hawaiian Nation*. Courtesy of Bruce Lum.

sound from news footage of protests. Hawaiian land and sea and Hawaiian activism are juxtaposed with the song "Blue Hawaii." This musical sign of Hollywood Hawaii then pairs with visuals of tourism and (sub)urban sprawl. Under footage of a march, the narrator summarizes Hawaiian history and announces the perspective of the documentary: "We are the Hawaiian people. These islands have always been our home. We were sovereign over this land before there was an England, long before there was a United States. By the nineteenth century, our independent nation was recognized by the dominant powers of the world. And in 1893, in an act of war, in an armed invasion, and in violation of international law, our nation was taken. And we have been compelled, against our right to self-determination, to become United States citizens."

The news footage continues; a woman in traditional Hawaiian clothing tells a cheering crowd: "We are not American. We are not American. We are not American. We will die as Hawaiians. We will never be American." Cut to title: *Act of War: The Overthrow of the Hawaiian Nation.*

Most viewers from Hawai'i would recognize the events and individuals pictured in the news clips from January 1993; the images of fifteen thousand marchers and of spokesperson Haunani-Kay Trask would operate as familiar reminders of the challenge to public memory mounted by Hawaiian activists. Viewers completely unfamiliar with Hawaiian history and contemporary politics could still recognize the iconography of protest and the documentary's unambiguous rhetorical position. The film's task is then persuasion through historical elaboration. Four scholars—Trask, Kameʻeleihiwa, Kekuni Blaisdell, and Jon Kamakawiwoʻole Osorio—all Hawaiians, all identified with their academic credentials, join the off-screen narrator in telling the story of the overthrow of the Hawaiian nation. Trask is the primary storyteller, with almost fifty turns. Blaisdell is not identified as "Citizen of the Hawaiian Nation" as he had been in *Hawaiians*, but that citizenship is implied through an attitude of righteous indignation that characterizes the comments of all four speakers.

According to Osorio, *Act of War* is "Native history, revisionist history." When the historian joined the project, Puhipau told him that it would be important to Hawaiians, and Osorio thinks it has been.[20] J. Kēhaulani Kauanui argues that *Act of War* "recreates an indigenous genealogy . . . and offers a new way [for Hawaiians] to make sense of the loss."[21] But the producers also had an obligation to make *Act of War* accessible to a broad audience, and partly for this reason the hour-long documentary is packed with details of Hawaiian history from pre-Western contact to annexation. Periods are punctuated with grim statistics of catastrophic declines in the native Hawaiian population. More than one hundred quotations—some from Hawaiians, but predominantly from British and American explorers, missionaries, and their descendants—are incorporated into the audio track. Authors' names (or publications) and dates appear on screen, but the historical figures are not "enacted." Instead, drawings, archival photographs, political cartoons, and contemporary photography of historic locations present a visual equivalent of the historicity of the quotations. The commentators extend, analyze, and sometimes contradict these fragments of a historical record (and public memory) that is presented as often untrustworthy or incomplete.

Approximately a third of the documentary focuses on four days—January 14–17, 1893—which are recalled by Trask, Kameʻeleihiwa (both wearing *pareo*, traditional native dress) and Osorio (in a contemporary "aloha shirt"). Each speaks directly into the camera, often in the present tense. As elsewhere, quotations are voiced, here edited in an especially rapid tempo. The most obvious rupture in presentational style and mode of argument comes when the source of the title is revealed to be President Grover Cleveland, who said: "By an act of war, the government of a friendly and confiding people has been overthrown. A substantial wrong has thus been done, which we should endeavor to repair."[22] The film then shifts to a *mele*, or traditional Hawaiian song, on the sound track and archival footage of turn-of-the-century life in Hawaiʻi on the visual track. Superimposed on these vintage moving images is an English translation of the Hawaiian song lyrics, alternating with captions describing historical events of 1894–1896, including the declaration of the Republic of Hawaii in 1894, the failed counterrevolution of 1895, and the imprisonment and subsequent pardoning of the Queen. Here, in an imaginative and dramatic gesture, English narration is silenced and the emotional and experiential qualities of Hawaiian memory, and history, are evoked.

After a short section on annexation, which considers "the taking of the Hawaiian Islands" as pivotal in the dawning of the United States as a global military power, the narrator concludes with recognizing the tragedy of postannexation Hawaiian life, not as something that happened in the past to "them," but as a present, lived experience for "us." *Act of War* ends, not with resignation, but with a call to action:

> And what has been the result of becoming part of America? Our children were punished for speaking our native language; taught to be ashamed of our culture, our names, our skin. Our home became America's playground, their battleground, their 50th state, their real estate. And in our own homeland, we are the homeless, we are the poor, we have the shortest life expectancy, we are the uneducated, we fill the prisons. But, after more than a century of dispossession, we are still here. Today we are discovering our history, learning our language, and asserting our right to the land and to self-determination. The time has come for us, the *Kānaka Maoli*, to once again take our place among the family of nations.

In May 1993, public screenings of *Act of War* began in Honolulu; in June it was broadcast on Hawai'i Public Television with little publicity; in September with far more. In 1994, it screened broadly in the international festival circuit and began to air on public television stations on the U.S. continent through the Pacific Mountain Network Satellite feed.[23] Reviews, locally and globally, were mainly positive, many strongly so; most reviewers considered the documentary historically credible, politically persuasive, and morally necessary.[24] In June 1993, while visiting a Hawaiian health clinic, Hillary Rodham Clinton met a friend of the producers of *Act of War*, who gave her a copy of the documentary and asked her to show it to the president. By the end of the year *Nā Maka* was able to add a postscript to *Act of War* announcing that President Bill Clinton had signed a congressional joint resolution that acknowledged the illegal overthrow of the Kingdom of Hawai'i and apologized to Native Hawaiians on behalf of the people of the United States.[25] In 1994, Lander and Puhipau received an official commendation from the Hawai'i House of Representatives in recognition of their work, with particular mention of the international success of *Act of War*.

Nā Maka distributes all its videos; they have sold over one thousand copies of *Act of War*, mostly to American universities (splitting profits with ITVS), and have donated an equal number of copies. The documentary continues to be shown on public television in Hawai'i and elsewhere and is used in many classrooms, often in combination with other *Nā Maka* productions. For Hawaiians living off-islands, *Act of War* has functioned as an important organizing tool for the sovereignty movement.[26]

Local History: The Annexation of 1898

In anticipation of the August 12, 1998, centennial observance of the U.S. annexation of Hawai'i and propelled by recent archival findings by a Hawaiian researcher of massive native petitions against annexation, *Nā Maka o ka 'Āina* and Hawai'i Public Television both coproduced historical documentaries that extended and deepened the revisionism of earlier productions.

1. Hawai'i Independent Production: We Are Who We Were: From Resistance to Affirmation (1998)

Coproduced by The Hawaiian Patriotic League and *Nā Maka*, this fifteen-minute video makes a startling claim: there was no annexation of Hawai'i. Through a combination of narration and voiced quotations of historical figures (Queen Lili'uokalani, President Grover Cleveland, American journalists, and a member of the 1898 Hawaiian Patriotic League), the documentary summarizes the recent findings of Noenoe Silva that demonstrate widespread resistance to annexation. It outlines the requisites for a legal treaty and then argues that Joint Resolution 55, passed by a simple congressional majority in 1898, did not have the effect of a treaty and, thus, American sovereignty has never existed in the Islands. The documentary addresses a Hawaiian constituency with its assertion that "It is an illusion that we went from being Hawaiian subjects to American citizens." Before the centennial, the video mobilized this constituency with its mention, after the credit roll, of a planned anti-annexation march for August 12, 1998. The copyright indicates rights reserved under "Hawaiian Kingdom Law."[27]

During the summer of 1998, *Nā Maka* distributed copies of *We Are Who We Were* to all the Hawaiian organizations that comprised the Annexation Centennial Committee.[28] It played repeatedly on public access channels in July and August; the Hawaiian Patriotic League purchased air time for its broadcast several days before the centennial on the local Fox affiliate. Predictably, the video provoked strong feelings. "The annexation that never was" became a debate topic on local talk radio, as did the documentary's presentation of a controversial legal claim that by July of 1998 had resulted in a United Nations Report recommending that Hawai'i be included in a U.N. list of "non self-governing territories" and thus become eligible for decolonization and a U.N.-sponsored plebiscite.

2. Hawai'i Public Television Coproduction: Nation Within: The Story of America's Annexation of the Nation of Hawai'i (1998)

In early 1997, Tom Coffman, a former chief political reporter for the *Honolulu Star Bulletin* and the producer of several historical documentaries, began to write a documentary treatment and a book-length manuscript on the annexation period. Coffman, who has lived in Hawai'i for over thirty years—his entire career as a journalist—was committed to taking the concept of Hawaiian nationhood seriously while simultaneously understanding annexation as an American event.[29] He obtained funding support from a variety of local foundations—some with national affiliations, and also from a "Pacific facing" foundation—and formed a crucial collaboration with KHET, which provided staff, facilities, and broadcast potential. KHET producer-director Joy Chong-Stannard, whose credits include codirection of *Betrayal* and numerous historical documentaries and whose family has lived in the Islands for five generations, joined the project as director. Early on, a broadcast target date of the August 1998 centennial of annexation was set.

Throughout *Nation Within*, Coffman and Chong-Stannard blend national and local perspectives. Their documentary begins and ends in Washington, D.C., grounding its history in that site of American decision-making, but the figures within that ground are two Hawaiian researchers (at the National Archives, in the opening scene) and a statue of King Kamehameha (in the statuary hall of the Capital, in the final scene). *Nation Within* is reflexive about the historical project; the work of historical research is shown (hands on microfilm readers, researchers in archives) and the issue of historical revisionism is recognized in references (usually in the narration) to events and people labeled as either forgotten or misrepresented. This rhetorical strategy culminates in naming two influential—and, to the documentarians, disreputable—publications: Belle M. Brain's 1898 book *The Transformation of Hawaii* is labeled "the first volume of what became a vast literature of denial," and Lorrin Thurston's 1936 memoirs are characterized as "setting the tone for the written history of Hawai'i in the twentieth century."

Nation Within seeks to end a century of denial of the widespread, organized, and sustained resistance by Hawaiians to American intervention in, and control of, their nation. The first words heard in *Nation Within* are in Hawaiian (then translated into English); they quote a petition against annexation, which, along with another, carried the signatures of almost the entire Hawaiian population. Six historians and writers collaborate on-screen to tell an American story of expansionism, personified in the figure of Theodore Roosevelt. They also tell a story of Hawaiian resolve that pictures Queen Lili'uokalani as a steadfast champion of the Hawaiian nation, but not alone in her courage. The Hawaiian nationalist leader Joseph Nawahi, who advocated a Hawaiian republic, emerges as a central figure; both male and female members of the Hawaiian Patriotic Leagues appear as staunch opponents to an American destiny whose inevitability was—and through the on-screen comments, continues to be—challenged. Much of the documentary tracks the complicated relationships of American politicians and businessmen with the missionary descendants who orchestrated the overthrow and then controlled the territorial government of Hawai'i. This fact-driven, eighty-five-minute documentary also explores the global politics of the 1890s, building on Coffman's original research to demonstrate how pro-annexationists in Hawai'i exploited American fears of a Japanese empire.

By opening with the quotation "To understand today, you have to search yesterday," *Nation Within* positions itself as concerned with current political realities, but the sovereignty movement is never mentioned on the audio track. It is certainly referenced visually (for a local audience) when footage of a 1993 mass demonstration pairs with the narrator's recognition that the centennial of the overthrow was an occasion for retelling stories of Hawai'i's last queen; by implication, the 1998 centennial of the annexation (with its anticipated atmosphere of protest) occasions "unearthing the strange five years" between the overthrow and the annexation. And, of course, the title announces support for the contention that a Hawaiian nation exists *within* America. The two Hawaiian scholars, Noenoe Silva (whose work with Hawaiian-language archives is seminal in recent revisionist history) and Jon Kamakawiwo'ole Osorio (pictured in the National Archives in the opening scene) are pivotal in telling the story of native protest. Silva and Osorio speak with force, conviction, even outrage, but always as scholars, never using the first person to claim personal identification. It is to voiced quotations that the documentary turns for past experiences and attitudes, as expressed by Hawaiian, American, and Japanese writers/speakers (sometimes voiced in Hawaiian or Japanese, accompanied by English subtitles). Three narrators of various gender, age, and racial permutations bring different perspectives to a point of joint agreement: this annexation story is a tale of injustice. One of the narrators notes that treaties "should have" a two-thirds vote of the

Senate and implies that moving to a joint resolution (passed by a simple majority vote) was dishonorable, but the legality of annexation is not challenged. With annexation, "A small band of white men, supported by the government of the United States, had given away the national heritage of a 2,000-year-old society." The documentary ends with Hawai'i's part, as a U.S. territory, in setting the stage for America's emergence as a great naval power in what became known as "the American century."

Public television stations KHET and KHEB broadcast *Nation Within* twice in the week preceding the August 12, 1998, centennial of the annexation and again on October 19 (as part of a "Life Pledge Drive" that raised a near-record amount for Hawai'i Public Broadcasting). The day after the first broadcast, producer Tom Coffman responded to Thurston Twigg-Smith (who subsequently published his version of annexation) and others on a special "Price of Paradise" live radio show; local newspapers featured debate on the documentary during the centennial week.[30] Although Coffman was able to include a sixty-minute version of *Nation Within* in the broadcast schedules of seventy-six public television stations in 1999, his early attempt to place *Nation Within* with *The American Experience* was unsuccessful. He was told that the series had already covered a related topic with *Hawaii's Last Queen;* moreover, Coffman's use of multiple narrators would not be acceptable, since "we [at *The American Experience*] have one narrative voice of history."[31]

Conclusion

What might be learned about how public television operates as historian from these six abbreviated production histories? First and foremost, local productions demonstrate a variety, a vitality, and an impact that should not be overlooked in a full discussion of the role of television in the creation of public memory. At both local and national levels, funding sources anticipate, influence, and reinforce production agendas. *The American Experience* operates with a considerable budget of both public funds and corporate underwriting. In many respects, local public television in Hawai'i operates as a mirror, on different economies of scale, of the national public television agenda to appeal to and represent diverse but ultimately united communities. These examples remind us that local constituencies are not monolithic; there are ongoing challenges to the notion that any minority population and its viewpoint(s) can be fairly represented by skilled and sympathetic professionals, even if that group's representatives are included in some participatory capacities. General resentments often find expression in specifics, presumed emblematic of ignorance, disregard, or bias. Special funding sources seem necessary to break the loop and put underrepresented groups in control of their own representations; yet there remains another power struggle for credibility that extends beyond the confines of "point of view."[32] Assumptions of a unified perspective (of history, of public memory, of current political agenda) based on race, ethnicity, or cultural identification are as problematic at the local level as they are at the national level. In many discourses surrounding these productions, "the Hawaiian perspective" is an unstable referent, clearer in its rejection of historical writing and attitudes that had celebrated the overthrow of Liliʻuokalani and annexation than in its embrace of a current political agenda.

Second, although national funds rarely flow to local projects, distribution patterns are increasingly flexible, while remaining tied to resources and sponsorship. The international festival circuit, desktop publishing, Internet connections, and links to various distribution sites facilitate the ability for local productions to reach national and even global audiences—and to reach beyond the television screen through home and educational video markets. Nevertheless, access to broad-reaching, well-established, and well-maintained distribution channels is neither guaranteed nor easily available to local productions. Local history usually remains local; still, projects designed for local audiences (partially, and perhaps ironically) often measure their success by the breadth of audience reach.

Third, context counts in shaping expectations and understandings of audiences. Viewers obviously respond to texts but also to the conditions of production. Local projects have pride of place to local audiences. In contemporary Hawaiʻi, the debates about sovereignty are so intense—and the consequences so great—that any production dealing with the overthrow of 1893 or the annexation of 1898 automatically becomes "political" and part of a recognized experience of struggle over historical representation and public memory. The work of Nā Maka o ka ʻĀina has been at the center of that struggle. In just a decade, historical opinions about the overthrow and annexation and ways of "doing history" (such as reliance on Hawaiian-language archives and the use of the Hawaiian language) have changed drastically in Hawaiʻi. Many attitudes and methods considered radical a decade ago have become mainstream—i.e., supported by Hawaiʻi Public Television—but contestation remains on both sides of the stream.

At the national level, the contextual shifts are less drastic and more diffuse but still impacted by a spirit of revisionism. For many Americans, Vivian Ducat's admiring portrait of Hawaii's Last Queen (which now has the endorsement of an honorable mention for the 1998 Erik Barnouw Award from the Organization of American Historians) has become the official and complete history of the overthrow and its (peripheral) place in the American experience; it may occupy that position for some time. Ironically, the documentary most determined to see the overthrow and annexation as a not-at-all-peripheral part of American history—*Nation Within*—was produced in Hawai'i. For many citizens of the state, or nation, of Hawai'i these six televised productions comprise only a part, albeit an important one, of a complicated public memory, based on an *experience* of Hawai'i's past that is fluid and in constant negotiation with a sense of Hawai'i's present. And future.

Notes

1. Hawai'i is the traditional Hawaiian language form of the word. Native activists began using Hawaiian pronunciation markings a generation ago. By the 1990s, the state was incorporating traditional accents and diacritical marks in all Hawaiian words printed at state offices. In 2000, such usage is widespread—although not universal—in the Islands. I adopt traditional usage in this essay; however, in the title *Hawaii's Last Queen* and in the transcript provided by *The American Experience* the American English formation "Hawaii" is employed, so I replicate that form in quotations from the documentary. The resulting inconsistency in these "contested" markings/spellings reminds us that history is written—and revised—through language.

2. See David Glassberg, "Public History and the Study of Memory," *The Public Historian* 18: 2 (spring 1996): 7–23, and Raymond Williams, "The Future of Cultural Studies," 151–62, in Tony Pinkney, ed., *The Politics of Modernism* (London: Verso, 1989).

3. Michael S. Roth, "*Hiroshima, Mon Amour:* You Must Remember This," 91. In *Revisioning History: Film and the Construction of a New Past,* ed. Robert A. Rosenstone. (Princeton, N.J.: Princeton Univ. Press, 1995).

4. Interview with Margaret Drain, February 17, 1998, Boston. McGee recruited Judy Crichton from CBS News, who in turn recruited colleague Margaret Drain. In 1997, Crichton left WGBH and Drain became executive producer of the series.

5. Information on Ducat and *Hawaii's Last Queen* was obtained from an interview with Ducat, March 7, 1998, New York; her participation in the panel "The Television Biography as Popular History," National Communication Association Annual Meeting, November 1998, New York; and from personal correspondence.

6. According to Drain, a producer receives between $8,000 and $15,000 for research and development, which is then deducted from the production budget. Drain took exception to the average cost per hour for fiscal year 1997—$740,500—that Daniel Golden claimed in his four-part series on WGBH; she put costs between $400,000 and $500,000. See "Local Programming Doesn't Rate," *Boston Globe,* June 23, 1997, p. A9. Golden's estimate includes station overhead and educational outreach; he lists his source as WGBH.

7. Ducat, as quoted by Tim Ryan, "Portraits of the Past," *Honolulu Star Bulletin,* November 2, 1994, D1.

8. This description of the audience is from Drain, personal interview. Drain was surprised at the "heat" surrounding Queen Lili'uokalani and said she did not think the

series had "done [any other] film that has so many current-day political ramifications as *Hawaii's Last Queen.*"

9. Twigg-Smith, "Overthrow Documentary Left Out Important Details," *Honolulu Star Bulletin,* January 29, 1997, p. A1; *"The American Experience: Hawaii's Last Queen* Needs Critical View," *Molokai Advertiser-News,* January 15, 1997.

10. The Hawai'i Public Television broadcast of *Hawaii's Last Queen* was preceded by a KHET coproduction, *First Ladies of Washington Place,* and followed by a 1981 documentary, *Her Majesty Lili'uokalani,* in which seven elderly Hawaiians recall their memories of the queen.

11. For example, "Last Hawaiian Monarch Still Revered," *Rocky Mountain News* (Denver), January 27, 1997.

12. See <http://www.pbs.org/wgbh/pages/amex/hawaii>.

13. In its most common use in the seven-island chain, "Hawaiian" is a classification of indigeneity, *not* residency. See J. Kēhaulani Kauanui, "Off-island Hawaiians 'Making' Ourselves at 'Home': A (Gendered) Contradiction in Terms?" *Women's Studies International Forum* 21:6 (1998): 681–93 on the complications of identification. Until fairly recently, the term "local" was a nonproblematic term for those, especially non-Caucasians, born and raised in Hawai'i. The Hawaiian words *kama'aina* (old resident) and *malahini* (newcomer) also indicate residency distinctions. Hawai'i state and U.S. federal definitions of "native Hawaiian" impose a 50 percent plus blood quantum rule. This rule is resented and in daily practice is often ignored by many *Kānaka Maoli* who identify as "Hawaiian." Yet, as Blaisdell and Makuau report, this rule simultaneously leads 96 percent of Hawaiians to describe themselves as "racially mixed," Kekuni Blaisdell and Noreen Mokuau, *"Kānaka Maoli,* Indigenous Hawaiians," in *Hawai'i Return to Nationhood,* 49–67, ed., Jonathan Friedman and Ulla Hasager, IWGIA Document 75. (Copenhagen: The International Working Group for Indigenous Affairs, 1993).

14. Telephone interview with Ellen Pelissero, March 8, 1998. All subsequent quotations from Pelissero are based on this interview and personal correspondence.

15. For example, Haunani-Kay Trask, who in 1987 had recently become the first full-time faculty member in what was then called the Hawaiian Studies Program at the University of Hawai'i-Mānoa; that year she and her sister, attorney Miliani Trask, had founded *Kā Lahui Hawai'i,* a native Hawaiian initiative for self-government. See *From a Native Daughter: Colonialism and Sovereignty in Hawai'i* (Monroe, Maine: Common Courage Press, 1993; rev. ed. Honolulu: Univ. of Hawai'i Press, 1999), 147–59, for Trask's critique of published histories of Hawai'i. Pelissero has studied Hawaiian but does not consider herself fluent.

16. Another local actress/entertainer, Leo[nelle] Anderson Akana, portrayed the Queen in *Lili'uokalani,* a two-person play written by Aldyth Morris and produced by the Mānoa Valley Theater in 1992. Akana plays the voice of Liliu and narrates *Act of War;* she also appeared as Lili'uokalani at the *'Onipa'a* ceremonies, January 13–17, 1993, when historical reenactments were performed on the grounds of 'Iolani Palace. On a much smaller scale, various local groups routinely present public reenactments of historical events to mark key dates in Hawaiian history, activities similar to local "living history" practices on the continent.

17. See Jeff Nicolay, *"Betrayal," Honolulu Star Bulletin and Advertiser, TV Week,* January

17–23, 1993, 1, and Stu Glauberman, "Overthrow Documentary Funded by the State," *Honolulu Advertiser,* August 17, 1992, A4. Nicolay quotes Sai as saying "sovereignty is inevitable. I think [*Betrayal*] will only help direct the people of Hawai'i with a positive understanding of the basis for sovereignty. This can only come about if we all understand what happened in history and why." Background information on *Betrayal* and related projects was also provided by Ellen Pelissero.

18. Information on *Nā Maka* comes from a personal interview with the producers, July 27, 1997, Na'alehu, Hawai'i; their visit to an NEH Seminar at the East-West Center, Honolulu, June 19, 1997, and various profiles in the *Act of War* press kit, including Catherine Kekoa Enomoto, "The Fallen Reign," *Honolulu Star Bulletin,* March 22, 1992, F1. For current information, access <http://www.namaka.com>.

19. ITVS was created by U.S. Congressional action in 1988 obligating the Corporation for Public Broadcasting (CPB) to set aside monies for productions of independent producers with the stated purpose of increasing diversity of programming and addressing the needs of unserved and underserved audiences. See "Friends of Public Television," *Wall Street Journal,* February 7, 1992, p. A14, for complaints lodged in Congress by Senator Robert Dole, and by the editorial writer, regarding the "radical" productions funded by ITVS, among them *Act of War.* Between 1974 and 1981, five minority consortia—including the Native American Public Broadcasting Consortium and the Pacific Islander Educational Network—were established to add diversity to public television. Hawaiians are inconsistently included in various federal mandates that address Native American concerns.

20. Interview with Jon Kamakawiwo'ole Osorio, July 22, 1997, Honolulu, and subsequent personal correspondence. See Osorio's dissertation, "Determining Self: Identity, Nationhood and Constitutional Government in Hawai'i: 1842–1887" (University of Hawai'i, 1996) for an account of the period directly prior to the overthrow and annexation. For a developed history of the Hawaiian nation from traditional times until the 1848 *Mahele* (land division), see Lilikalā Kame'eleihiwa, *Native Land and Foreign Desires* (Honolulu: Bishop Museum Press, 1992).

21. J. Kēhaulani Kauanui, "Images of Struggle/Imagining Nations: *An Act of War* for Off-Island Education on Hawaiian Sovereignty." Unpublished manuscript, presented at the ASAO Meeting, February 1997.

22. Grover Cleveland, "Message to the Senate and House of Representatives," December 18, 1893, *Affairs in Hawaii, Foreign Relations of the United States, 1894,* p. 456.

23. An ITVS report issued July 3, 1997, indicated that out of three hundred public television stations, ninety-three had broadcast *Act of War,* some stations multiple times. Not all stations responded.

24. The day of a local rebroadcast of *Act of War* on KHET, Vicki Viotti wrote, "The video's view of history is open to criticism. Critics from various schools could argue . . ." (but she did not make any argument herself). *The Honolulu Advertiser,* September 17, 1993. Reviewers outside of Hawai'i often linked the documentary to other native rights struggles.

25. Joint Resolution Senate Resolution, #19 of the 103rd Congress, introduced by Senator Daniel K. Akaka of Hawai'i, was signed on November 23, 1993. United States Public Law 103–150, 1993, states that "the indigenous *Hawaiian* people never directly

relinquished their claims to their inherent sovereignty as a people or over their national lands to the United States, either through their monarchy or through plebiscite or referendum."

26. Kauanui, *passim*. At the symposium "Native Pacific Cultural Studies: On the Edge," University of California at Santa Cruz, February 11–12, 2000, several participants noted the importance of *Act of War* and other historical videos in both teaching and organizing.

27. According to Joan Lander, as of April 2000, the most comprehensive websites containing current information on these issues are: <http://www.Hawaii-nation.org>; <http://www.hookele.com/kuhikuhi/ea.html>; <http://www.Hawaii-nation.org/links.html>; and <http://www.AlohaQuest.com>.

28. The video has also been shown in many Pacific locales. Information provided by Joan Lander, private correspondence, August and September 1998.

29. Information from telephone interview with Tom Coffman, October 12, 1998, and subsequent personal correspondence. Additional information on *Nation Within* came from telephone conversations and personal correspondence with Joy Chong-Stannard, March, April, and October 1998. Video and book versions of *Nation Within* are available through Epicenter, 44–114 Bayview Haven Place, Kēneʻohe, Hawaiʻi, 96744; KHET; Ingrams; and Amazon.com.

30. Twigg-Smith, *Hawaiian Sovereignty: Do the Facts Matter?* (Honolulu: Goodale Publishing, 1998).

31. The account is from Coffman, of his meeting with senior producer Mark Samels, WGBH, Boston.

32. The first publicity materials carried the subtitle: "Hawaiian History through Hawaiian eyes." Before its premiere festival screening, Puhipau said, "*Act of War* is a historical account of what went down 100 years ago. It's not merely a point of view" (Gary C.W. Chun, "Reely Big Show," *Honolulu Advertiser*, November 7, 1993, G1).

8

Mediating
Thomas Jefferson
Ken Burns as Popular Historian

Gary R. Edgerton

You set out with a desire to learn about Thomas Jefferson and in the course
of things you enrich yourself by that process of discovery. . . . I go at it
looking for Thomas Jefferson and the Thomas Jefferson that I found is not
THE Thomas Jefferson, but my Thomas Jefferson.

Ken Burns, 1997

Ken Burns's career defies all conceivable expectations. He became one of
public television's busiest and most celebrated producers during the 1980s, a
decade when the historical documentary held little interest for most American TV viewers. He operates his own independent company, Florentine Films,
in a small New England village more than four hours north of New York
City, hardly a crossroads in the highly competitive and often insular world of
corporately funded, PBS (Public Broadcasting System) sponsored productions. His fifteen major specials so far are also strikingly out of step with the
special effects and frenetic pacing of most nonfiction television, relying mainly
on filmic techniques that were introduced literally decades ago.[1] And at forty-
seven, he has already won virtually every major professional and scholarly
award that is relevant for him to win, including Emmys, Grammys, Golden
Globes, Academy Award nominations, "Producer of the Year" from the Producers Guild of America, and over two dozen honorary doctorates from
various colleges and universities nationwide.

Burns is best known, of course, for his eleven-hour documentary series
The Civil War (1990), which achieved public television's highest ratings ever
based on national Nielsen data, when 38.9 million people tuned in to at least

one episode of the five-night telecast between September 23 and 27, 1990, averaging 12 million viewers at any given moment.[2] *The Civil War* was an unlikely popular success, even holding its own against the major network competition, and established this documentary miniseries as PBS's prototype of "event TV." The program was mentioned on episodes of *Twin Peaks, Thirtysomething,* and *Saturday Night Live* during the 1990–1991 television season. Ken Burns appeared on *The Tonight Show,* and he was selected by the editors of *People* magazine as one of their "25 most intriguing people of 1990." The series also grew into a marketing sensation as the companion volume by Knopf, *The Civil War: An Illustrated History,* became a runaway bestseller, as did the accompanying Warner sound track and the nine-episode videotaped version from Time-Life. Burns reminisced during a February 1993 interview, saying, "I was flabbergasted! I still sort of pinch myself about it."[3] He would again be surprised just two months later by his own mixed reception at a scholarly conference in Boston, when the largely complimentary relations that he had typically enjoyed with the academy up to that point were now becoming far more complicated as a result of his own heightened profile and success as well as that of the historical documentary in general.

The two-day conference entitled "Telling the Story: The Media, the Public, and American History," was hosted by the New England Foundation for the Humanities (NEFH) on April 23 and 24, 1993. The impetus for initiating such an event came from "the phenomenal public response to Ken Burns's public television series, '*The Civil War,*'" according to JoAnna Baldwin Mallory, the then-executive director of NEFH, and the "truly astonishing work, a fluorescence of documentary filmmaking and historical programming that has come to national attention . . . in a mere decade."[4] Clearly this wellspring of new made-for-TV histories was not only attracting large audiences, but also the notice of the professional historical establishment. In a recent article in *The Public Historian,* Gerald Herman, a history professor at Northeastern University with extensive media production experience, recalled how "most historians for a long time insisted on the marginality of [film and television] presentations to their concerns, to their training, to their individualized methods of work."[5] He added that, "respected historians didn't bother to list their work with media-based presentations on their curriculum vitae for fear of having their reputations as serious scholars diminished by the association."[6]

In contrast to this attitude, a small but committed group of scholars, led by John O'Connor and Martin Jackson, formed the Historians Film Committee at the 1970 American Historical Association annual conference, publishing its first issue of *Film & History* the following year. Still, a majority interest in "film and television as historian" never reached a critical mass among professional historians until the mid-1980s, largely in response to the marked rise in popular mediated productions on historical subjects, emanating from both inside and, most surprisingly, outside the academy. As a result of the unprecedented success of *The Civil War*, as well as the widespread attention and accolades accorded his other work—most particularly *Brooklyn Bridge* (PBS, 1982), *The Shakers: Hands to Work, Hearts to God* (PBS, 1985), *The Statue of Liberty* (PBS, 1985), and *Huey Long* (PBS, 1986)—Ken Burns emerged as the signature figure for this nascent historical documentary movement. "Seven years after Ken Burns's *The Civil War* proved that history on TV could be engaging—and attract millions of viewers," announced *TV Guide* in 1997, "documentaries are all over the dial."[7] Burns likewise became a lightning rod for scholars to express a spectrum of pro and con reactions about the growing popularity of films and television programs about the past, especially with the general public, overshadowing the one-time preeminence of written histories alone.

The historic transformations from orality to writing to printing to filming and televising are generally understood today as producing concurrent shifts in the way in which societies privilege certain forms of expression and knowledge over others. Some historians, for example, have admonished Burns for emphasizing the empathetic and experiential aspects of history in *The Civil War* more than detailed analysis.[8] What such criticisms overlook, however, is that the visual media's codes of historical representation are far different from, though often complementary to, those of print. The present image-based histories of Burns and other producer-directors feature the simulated experience of engulfing viewers in a sense of immediacy or "being there," in contrast to the printed word's propensity toward logic, detachment, and reasoned discourse. In Ken Burns's own words, "For nearly two centuries, we were animated entirely by the book, and what we knew about our past came from books, and we're going to need to restate the old heroes . . . [and] the old dramas, and we'll have to do it in a new visual way. And that's what I'm trying to do."[9]

Professional history typically rejects the mythmaking of popular history. This tradition, which dates back to the second half of the nineteenth century, recasts the study of history inside the larger framework of scientific inquiry with an allegiance to objectivity (albeit modified these days), a systematic and detached method of investigation, and the pursuit of new knowledge. In contrast, the much older legacy of popular history is far more artistic and ceremonial in approach. It is usually consensus-oriented, narrative and biographical in structure, and intended to link producers and audiences in a mainly affirming relationship based on the immediate experience they are sharing together around the characters and events of their cultural past. The most prominent and influential examples of popular history in America are now surprisingly found on prime-time television, and Ken Burns has come to symbolize this phenomenon in many people's minds, mostly on account of the unprecedented impact and reception garnered by *The Civil War*.

Criticisms of *The Civil War* and other historical documentaries also rest on differences of interpretation, of course, although a more fundamental struggle over authority and control of historical activity in general is never too far from the surface of these present-day debates between professional historians and their popular counterparts. Valuable critiques of *The Civil War* concerning its cursory portrayal of Reconstruction, for instance, or the need for a fuller representation of the role played by African Americans in bringing about the social transformations now associated with the conflict, were both raised at the 1993 NEFH Conference and later published in Ken Burns's *The Civil War: Historians Respond*, along with five other responses to the series, ranging from complimentary to ambivalent to condemning.[10] Occasionally, though, spoken remarks or written passages also slip through alongside the actual analyses, remarks that disclose as much about the deeper concerns of some academic critics as they do about Burns and *The Civil War*:

> This documentary *Wunderkind* [italics in original text] has rejuvenated serious interest in history—from networks, corporations, and perhaps, even the viewing public. Burns's historical influence has brought people back to reading (or at least buying!) more books, created a vogue in Civil War scholarship (especially for the new media darling, Shelby Foote), and launched numerous projects at libraries and state humanities commissions across the country. Our students, our readership, and the entire enterprise of bringing history to the people have profited. This very volume symbolizes his impact. We must salute him, even as some may seek to bury him.[11]

A recent article in *The Chronicle of Higher Education* was similarly entitled "Taking Aim at the 'Ken Burns' View of the Civil War."[12] The scholar interviewed provides a revised interpretation that rejects the "established narrative" imbuing the war with "an overarching moral purpose it lacked at the time." The piece continues, "since the dawn of the civil-rights movement . . . historians have oversimplified the war," as James M. McPherson, author of the best-selling *Battle Cry of Freedom*, is singled out as a prime example.[13] Most tellingly, however, a generation of accepted historical thinking is not characterized as the "McPherson [but the Ken Burns] View of the Civil War," reflecting both the de rigueur dismissal of an outlook that has now been turned into popular televisual history, as well as the unstated though implied recognition that *The Civil War* is built upon the foundation of academic scholarship, however conventional that historical record may be from this new revisionist point of view.

All of Burns's historical documentaries, in fact, are modeled on existing research and designed to build a bridge between public interest in the subjects he chooses and the findings of the scholarly community. *Thomas Jefferson*, for example, incorporates roughly a quarter century of professional historical thinking on its subject, while also attracting a reported seventeen million viewers when it debuted on public television on February 18 and 19, 1997.[14] On the more than one thousand–page interactive website created to accompany the miniseries, Burns discusses his role as a popularizer of academic ideas: "We are in the business of helping to disseminate ideas—challenging ideas, contradictory ideas, tragic ideas, powerful ideas. And Jefferson is of course a master at all of those things. So we're looking for those scholars who can help us set into vibration the facts of his life with the ideas of his life."[15]

The rest of this chapter examines Ken Burns as a popular historian, using *Thomas Jefferson* as an illustrative example. It hones in on the "Ken Burns" view of history, delineating it first and foremost from the filmmaker's perspective. The goal is to describe what Burns planned to accomplish by producing this particular television special, and then to judge the resulting program by these criteria. This inquiry ends with some concluding observations about the ways in which Burns's *Thomas Jefferson* complements the admittedly different though reciprocal purposes of professional history.

Mediating Past and Present

Several years ago, I argued in *Film & History* that Ken Burns is an "ideal filmmaker for this period of transition between generations, bridging the sensibilities of the people who came of age during World War II along with his own frame of reference as a baby boomer."[16] I still very much view his work this way. Burns explores America's heritage in the subjects he selects, responding to those aspects of the past that he and his colleagues find most relevant and compelling, while leaving behind that which is nonessential to present-day concerns. "All of the contradictions in Thomas Jefferson's life and times," he says, "are played out again in our late 20th century national life."[17] According to Burns, Jefferson "helps define the issues which will animate our national discourse right up to the present."[18] This artistic reintegration of the past into the present is one of the major functions of popular history. It is a process of reevaluating the country's historical legacy and re-confirming it from a new generational perspective. As Burns reveals:

> I now think that these subjects choose me. I have been saying for a very long time that I was interested in a very simple question, which is "Who are we?" That is to say, what does an investigation of the past tell us, Americans, about who we are . . . I now begin to think that I am very much tied up in the asking of that question—that these films are also a way of saying, "Who am I?" And that gets a little bit more confusing and harder to nail down. Suffice to say, I think that these projects are chosen because they are compelling dramatic stories. They are chosen because they have as a central feature an element of biography. . . . They are driven by the notion that people can change events—that people do change events for the better and for worse.[19]

In the case of *Thomas Jefferson*, Burns engages a subject who is much more a figure of words and ideas than physical action. The filmmaker dramatizes the themes associated with Jefferson by the narrative choices he makes, as well as his usual strategy of employing expert commentators to personalize the concepts being presented. In assembling his plot structure, Burns uses the chronological events of Jefferson's life as the fundamental story line on which to anchor the narrative. In part 1, especially, Jefferson's family history is used to humanize Thomas Jefferson, the icon; and family history similarly becomes another bridge to national history and the discussion of Jefferson and race, Jefferson and the role of government, and Jefferson and the meaning of freedom—the three most important issues in the series.

Burns and chief writer Geoffrey Ward construct the plot, for example, around the three most celebrated concepts in the Declaration of Independence, "Life," "Liberty," and the "Pursuit of Happiness." Part 1, which is eighty-seven minutes long, introduces Jefferson as a young son and bookish student in "Life," and as a husband and rising political star in "Liberty: Our Sacred Honor." This portion of the miniseries contains a far greater number of viewer involvement strategies than does part 2, such as the many opportunities to identify with Jefferson falling in love, honeymooning at Monticello, and becoming a father. These intimate moments heighten the accumulated effect of the historically significant scenes; for instance, the first-person camera point of view when the audience is literally placed inside Jefferson's room with him in Philadelphia during the writing of the Declaration of Independence.

The most arresting personal vignette occurs approximately one hour into the program, as Sam Waterston and Blythe Danner read passages from Laurence Sterne's *Tristram Shandy* in voice-over to simulate the loving interaction between Jefferson and his wife, Martha, nicknamed "Patty," who is

Filmmaker Ken Burns in front of Monticello, the home of
Thomas Jefferson. Courtesy of Lisa Berg/General Motors.

dying after a difficult childbirth. As this exchange intensifies, the rhythms of
the actors and the pacing of the interior live shots inside their bedroom at
Monticello almost function like a traditional dramatic scene. Later, toward
the end of part 1, there is another five-minute scene involving the love affair
between Jefferson and Maria Cosway in Paris, where Burns noticeably begins to shift dramatic gears. Waterston performs an affecting reading of
Jefferson's famous "Head and Heart" letter, but, significantly, his first-person
monologue stands in stark contrast to the two-person interplay of the previous *Tristram Shandy* scene, since Maria Cosway has now returned to her
home in England. The camera holds for a long take on a lovely painting of

Maria, but Jefferson is basically left to himself, trying to sort out his thoughts and feelings alone. The effect is to intimate that Thomas Jefferson, the character, is emotionally withdrawing, just as on-screen commentator Clay Jenkinson concludes that this affair "produced a crisis for Jefferson . . . [who] reasserted the head . . . fe[eling] that human relations were too painful and that it was simply better to live in a world of abstraction and ideas and architecture," prefiguring the more conceptual agenda of part 2.

The second half of *Thomas Jefferson*, lasting eighty-nine minutes, is far less personal and more contemplative than part 1. There are a few emotional flourishes, such as the exchange of letters between Jefferson and John Adams, although even this sequence, "The Pursuit of Happiness," is much more discursive in structure than the earlier dramatic portions of the program. Ken Burns is far more interested in words than most filmmakers, and he purposely slows down the pace of part 2 to more fully explore the principal themes that he introduced earlier in the series. Burns's handling of the Sally Hemings controversy is a case in point. This scene takes place during "Liberty: The Age of Experiment" in part 2, a sequence that examines Jefferson's terms as secretary of state, vice president, and president. Hemings is introduced in a Federalist broadside in 1802, claiming that this young slave of Jefferson's is also his longtime mistress and the mother of his mulatto son, Tom. Burns investigates this charge and the related issues of race, slavery, and freedom by constructing an *editing cluster*, which involves cutting together images of his subjects with a montage of commentators, who typically present both corroborating and conflicting opinions, creating a collage of multiple viewpoints.

In this five-minute-and-forty-five-second scene, shots of Jefferson (i.e., Rembrandt Peale's 1800 painting) and Monticello (i.e., both interior and exterior photographs) are intercut with five differing reactions to the controversy: Clay Jenkinson ("We don't know. The evidence is slender"); Natalie Bober ("a moral impossibility"); Robert Cooley, Hemings descendant ("I have the benefit of 200 years of consistent, solid, oral history . . . Sally, was without a doubt, his mistress, lover, and substitute wife for 38 years"); Joseph Ellis ("If it were a legal case . . . the evidence would now be such that Jefferson would be found not guilty"); and John Hope Franklin ("It doesn't really matter whether he slept with her or not. He could have. After all he owned her. She was subject to his exploitation in every conceivable way"). Burns's own position is readily apparent by the editing choices he makes, which lead inevitably and inexorably to Franklin, who forcefully articulates the broader context and implications of the controversy during the final minute and fifteen seconds of the scene (i.e., Thomas Jefferson owned many slaves, provid-

Thomas Jefferson as painted by Rembrandt Peale in 1800. Courtesy of the White House Historical Society.

ing him with a privileged existence at their expense. He is, therefore, guilty of profiting by and supporting an institution that allowed other white masters all over the South to sleep with their slaves, whether or not he himself was ever intimately involved with Sally Hemings.).

Ken Burns, moreover, follows the example found in much of the historical literature by identifying Jefferson with an assortment of current issues of national interest, especially in part 2. Joseph Ellis traces this tendency back to nineteenth-century historian James Parton, who is quoted in *American Sphinx: The Character of Thomas Jefferson*: "If Jefferson was wrong, America is wrong. If America is right, Jefferson was right."[20] Ellis underscores in his book how many eminent professional historians from the past, including

Ken Burns (pictured) had an exact replica of Thomas Jefferson's garden pavilion built next to his home in Walpole, New Hampshire. Courtesy of Owen Comora/General Motors.

Jefferson biographers Dumas Malone and Merrill Peterson as well as scores of current citizens from all walks of life, still evoke Jefferson as a way of discussing American culture and society.[21] Burns's approach in *Thomas Jefferson* is to similarly envision Jefferson as "a kind of Rosetta Stone of the American experience."[22] He explains:

> When we talk about the separation of church and state, prayer in the classroom, school funding for parochial education, Thomas Jefferson is there looking over our shoulders. When we debate states rights versus big government and think about the tension between home-grown militias on the one hand and a monolithic federal government on the other . . . When we think about the intractable problems in our country born of race . . . Thomas Jefferson and his agonizing internal contradictions are looking over our shoulder, making us who we are for better or worse.[23]

As a way of better integrating these issues into the plot, Burns employs Clay Jenkinson almost as a second surrogate narrator to complement Ossie Davis throughout part 2. The filmmaker utilizes him twenty times, or more than half of the thirty-eight total commentaries used in this entire final half of *Thomas Jefferson*. Jenkinson, a National Humanities Medal–winning Jefferson impersonator and professor at the University of Nevada at Reno, provides plenty of anecdotes to animate part 2's emphasis on "abstraction and ideas and architecture." He, too, is a skilled popular historian, contributing a rich human-interest dimension to the miniseries, even though he never assumes the character of Jefferson in the film. Jenkinson, instead, offers many background stories, which link Jefferson's private life to his cultural interests and his political ideas. The camera even enters into Thomas Jefferson's inner sanctum in part 2, dissolving through a montage of ethereal black-and-white interior shots of hallways, rooms, and furnishings, as Jenkinson suggests onscreen that "Monticello is most of all a metaphor for Jefferson's soul." Ken Burns always pays close attention to the narrative possibilities of his subjects. In selecting a biographical approach above all others, he also directs his undivided attention onto a single individual of consequence from the past, striving to stimulate for himself and his audience the kind of intense connection with an historical character that is usually only achieved in fiction filmmaking.

Mediating Objective and Subjective Stylistics

The documentary narrative is a particular mode of knowledge and means of relaying history, and Ken Burns uses the inherent characteristics of photography, film, and television to create his popular histories. He explains that "a documentary has as much artistic possibility as a fiction film . . . history is just the medium, like a painter choosing oil as opposed to watercolors, that's what I work in, but, first and foremost, I am a filmmaker trying to learn my craft."[24] As a result, Burns, like many other producer-directors of his generation, is often preoccupied with traversing the stylistic border between fact and fiction. The pre-photographic nature of *Thomas Jefferson* actually induced him to experiment much more with the documentary form than he usually does, given his largely traditional approach to media form and aesthetics. For example, Burns commissioned architectural photographer Robert C. Lautman to take hundreds of platinum Palladium prints with a nineteenth-century view camera inside and outside Monticello and throughout the accompanying slave quarters, so he could approximate the look of old archival images, which of course do not exist as far back as Jefferson's lifetime.[25] The filmmaker's intention was to rephotograph Lautman's stills, thus realizing one of his main strategies in this documentary of portraying Monticello as a visual analogy for Jefferson himself, while also continuing one of his trademark techniques.

Burns typically reshoots photographs as if they were moving pictures, panning and zooming within the frame, shifting between long shots, medium shots, and close-ups, turning these single images into scenes rather than just shots. In the final twenty minutes of *Thomas Jefferson*, for example, there is a brief but bittersweet forty-five-second scene composed entirely of one of Robert Lautman's antique-looking stills, rephotographed from three varying vantage points. As Sam Waterston reads a portion of one of Jefferson's last correspondences to John Adams, the camera shows his writing table situated near his alcove bed; there follows a cut-in of the table top as Waterston's voice-over "recollect[s] . . . when youth and health made happiness out of everything"; and, finally, the vignette climaxes with a close-up of the seat where Jefferson once sat, as his spoken words intimately share with Adams the calm realization that they are both close to "the friendly hand of death."

Burns also recruited Peter Hutton to produce time-lapsed black-and-white motion picture footage of the interior of Monticello to intercut with his rephotographed images.[26] Hutton's camerawork is featured prominently in the many montages of Monticello throughout part 2, along with the aforementioned *Tristram Shandy* scene involving Patty Jefferson's death in part 1. Ken Burns characteristically intercuts the highly active rephotographed footage with Hutton's live shots, which are framed more like still photographs, thus simulating the mood and pre-filmic vocabulary of the late eighteenth and early nineteenth centuries of the subject under review. Burns describes this expansion of his technical and grammatical repertoire as "18th century virtual reality."[27] In point of fact, his stylistic approach to documenting reality is far less subjective than many of his contemporaries. In a recent roundtable discussion on the state of the documentary, thirteen of Burns's peers generally agreed that the line between nonfiction and fiction "is an illusory distinction."[28] Ken Burns, too, mediates the stylistic distinctions between fact and fiction, although he relies mostly on techniques introduced decades ago, such as rephotographing and time-lapsed cinematography, which are both a half-century old. In this way, he characterizes: "poetic license [as] the razor's edge between fraud and art that we ride all the time. You have to shorten, you have to take shortcuts, you have to abbreviate, you have to sort of make do with, you have to sometimes go with something that is less critically truthful imagery-wise because it ultimately does a better job of telling the larger truth, but who is deciding and under what system becomes the operative question."[29]

Even Burns's inclusion of visual reenactments for the first time in his career in *Thomas Jefferson* was similarly understated in its application. These three shots, lasting less than thirty seconds each, take the form of either a horse-drawn coach or a man alone on horseback, silhouetted against the pink twilight. They occur during the introduction, following the death of Patty Jefferson, and on Jefferson's return to Monticello after the completion of his presidency. They are all intended to lyrically suggest the presence of the protagonist, thereby, once again expanding the available imagery. Despite the controversial nature of reenactments these days, Burns has aurally employed this strategy since the beginning of his career by his "chorus of voices" technique, referring to his use of actors and actresses to deliver dramatic readings from diaries, letters, personal papers, and other printed recollections of various kinds. Burns regularly integrates live and historical source material, putting each on an equal footing in the present tense, thus rendering these subjects from the past more accessible and immediate to modern audiences. The aesthetic effect he is striving for is to "bring the past back alive onscreen."[30]

All told, Ken Burns's historical documentary style is a kind of poetic realism, capitalizing on the inherent ability of photography, film, and television to suggest analogies (e.g., the many sides of Jefferson are intimated by the architecture, furnishings, and grounds at Monticello; the self-divisions in Jefferson's personality are reflective of the nation as a whole, etc.), moreso than to assert precise meanings (which, of course, is a basic strength of written discourse). As a result, Burns's made-for-TV history of Jefferson portrays the contradictions in his character, debates them, but never provides any final resolutions. The ambiguities that reside in *Thomas Jefferson* and all of his other television histories, moreover, afford audiences of tens of millions some interpretive space on which to explore differing ideas and opinions, and most essentially, engage with figures like Jefferson and his times in the present, which is the penultimate goal of popular history. In Burns's own words, "we're not here to debate as much as we are to cohere."[31] His documentary style, in turn, expresses his liberal pluralist leanings, offering a view of the United States that is basically fixed on agreement and unity, even as it struggles with its heritage of race and slavery and the place of Thomas Jefferson in contemporary life.

Mediating Ideological Differences

Most of Ken Burns's subjects are majoritarian rather than marginalized—for example *The Statue of Liberty, The Congress, The Civil War, Baseball,* and, of course, *Thomas Jefferson*—although he does incorporate multicultural issues and outlooks into the broader panorama of his nationalist narratives. John Hope Franklin, for example, asserts on-screen that "Thomas Jefferson personifies the United States and its history. He was a man who claimed to be a man of the Enlightenment. He was a scientist, a humanist. He knew what he was saying when he said that all men are created equal. And it simply can't be reconciled with the institution of slavery."[32] As mentioned earlier, Burns furthermore contends that by making these documentaries he is "asking one deceptively simple question: who are we? That is to say, who are we Americans as a people?"[33] This preoccupation with the elemental question "Who are we as Americans?" could not be more relevant in an era when multiculturalism has become the source of sweeping and fundamental reappraisals of almost every aspect of national life. *Thomas Jefferson* is designed as such a reexamination. Jefferson's image is clearly in transition today, and his racial legacy is the major reason why he now occupies such a problematic place in American history and culture.

   Burns's most effective tool in reexamining Jefferson's meaning in the present is, once again, his editing clusters, or his linking together of Jefferson-related imagery with a montage of assorted commentaries. In the coda, for example, paintings of Jefferson by Rembrandt Peale (1800), Charles Wilson Peale (1791), and Gilbert Stuart (1805) are interspersed with seven separate opinions of Jefferson's accomplishments, his shortcomings, and his current significance: Joseph Ellis ("There is a simple but extraordinarily resonant message that Jefferson somehow symbolizes, namely the future is going to be better than the past"); Gary Wills ("I think the thing to remember from Jefferson is the power of the word—that ideas matter"); a shot of the Declaration of Independence next pans across the phrase, "life, liberty, and the pursuit of happiness"; Clay Jenkinson ("It is Jefferson who is indispensable because he is mysterious, idealistic, pragmatic, misunderstood, complicated, paradoxical, hypocritical. He is the stuff of America and that is who we are and that is why Jefferson has to be the center of our national discourse"); a shot of a slave; John Hope Franklin ("The legacy of Jefferson is both a gift and a curse . . . he cursed us with a practice of inequality and slavery and a denial of justice that scarcely can be erased by anything we can think of").

Burns, then, allows the audience to rest for a moment and absorb what's been said as he intercuts an old photograph of Monticello, the Capitol building in Washington, D.C., at mid-century, another image of several slaves, and a live shot of the Jefferson Memorial before Andrew Burstein prefigures the Civil War in the next statement ("I don't think he was convinced that America would be able to advance without fits and seizures and numerous torments. He didn't know how to hold the union together, but in the end I'm sure he felt he had done his best—that he had lived up to his dreams"); Gore Vidal ("With all his faults and contradictions . . . if there is such a thing as an American spirit, then he is it"); Clay Jenkinson returns off-screen over various portraits of Jefferson:

> Jefferson essentially tells us that we cannot be complacent until two conditions are met. Every human being born on this continent has a right to equal, indeed, identical treatment in the machine of the law, irrespective of race, gender, creed, or class of origin. And, secondly, everyone born on this continent has a right to roughly equal opportunity at modest prosperity, and until these conditions are met, we cannot rest. When those conditions are met, we may say as Jefferson said he would, *nunc dimittis*, you may dismiss me, my work is done.

In summary, therefore, individual speakers differ on the exact meaning of Jefferson's legacy throughout this editing cluster, but disagreement ultimately takes places within the broader framework of agreement on underlying principle. The scene ends with a dramatic time-lapsed shot of the sun setting, with the words of Thomas Jefferson spoken by Sam Waterston about the enduring nature of representative government and "this country['s aim] to preserve and restore life and liberty."

Ken Burns, overall, articulates a version of the country's past that conveys his own perspective as a popular historian, intermingling many widespread assumptions about the character of America and its liberal pluralist aspirations. Like other documentarians of his generation, he too addresses matters of diversity, but unlike many of his contemporaries, he presents an image of the United States pulling together despite its chronic differences rather than a society coming apart at the seams. In his own words, "I know I've said it before, but I see myself as an emotional archaeologist, trying to excavate what there is in our history that speaks to the *unum* and not the *pluribus*."[34] Exploring the past is also his way of reassembling a future from a fragmented present. Clay Jenkinson's final commentary, in particular, reminds viewers that much work still needs to be done before Americans more fully enact the essential ideals that Jefferson professed.

Finding a Place for Popular History Alongside Professional History

During the six-week promotional tour preceding the debut telecast of *Thomas Jefferson*, Ken Burns gave literally hundreds of interviews, delivered dozens of variations of his prepared speech, "Searching for Thomas Jefferson," and screened portions of a selected clip from the series whenever the opportunity arose. The brief segment Burns selected to show in this context was the writing of the Declaration of Independence scene from part 1. This entire eight-minute-and-thirty-second set piece is skillfully executed, beginning with the activities at the Continental Congress where Jefferson is assigned the job and culminating inside the small room in Philadelphia where he actually completed the submitted draft of the famous document. One minute into the scene, Clay Jenkinson tellingly portrays the personality of Thomas Jefferson as "bland and careful and aphoristic and high flown, his rhetoric always soared toward aspiration and human dignity." This characterization also suggests a certain similarity to Ken Burns's poetic stylistics and his empathetic (and sometimes romantic) approach to his material, indicating in part why this producer-director identified so closely with his particular subject in this instance, even claiming that, "*Thomas Jefferson* is the most intensely personal film I've made."[35]

All of Burns's work demonstrates certain ideological, narrative, and biographical imperatives that support one another, together forming an image of America that is primarily liberal pluralist in outlook, dramatic in structure, and intimate in portrayal (i.e., "his goal, he says, was to explore the 'inner Jefferson.'").[36] The nature of the historical biography is yet another reason why Burns and a viewership of millions responded so personally to the Thomas Jefferson who emerged in this miniseries. Ken Burns formed a

Artist John Trumbull's painting of the signing of the Declaration of Independence. Courtesy of Owen Comora Associates.

strong attachment to his subject over a seven-year period, while shepherding this project from initial concept to finished three-hour documentary as its executive producer-director.[37] Audience members, too, make their own kind of individual commitment during two ninety-minute viewing sessions, which simulate powerful feelings of intimacy for them as they watch and relate to the featured character's life story on TV. This interlocking ritual of producing, telecasting, and watching *Thomas Jefferson* becomes a shared ceremonial experience for both the filmmakers as well as the vast numbers of Americans who tune in to see this newly adapted screen version of the historical Jefferson. Monticello is again an apt analogy: "There is no denying that Monticello has become a Jefferson museum-shrine, but most examples of restored domestic architecture are museums that lift the past out of context and place it on display. An inhabited house, unlike a museum, bears the imprint of its owners: the ashes in the hearth, the fingerprints on the walls, the scuffs, knocks, scrapes, and rubbings of human contact—the detritus of everyday life. All of these vanish beneath the cosmetic touch of the restorer's art."[38]

Ken Burns's art involves similar slights of hand. The stylistic features of photography, film, and television strongly influence and embellish the kinds of historical representations that he and his colleagues portray. Camera reality in *Thomas Jefferson* is comparably revivifying and pristine, much like the condition of the living preserve at Monticello; it is also a highly decorative, visual tribute to Jefferson, only this time shot on film. Burns and his crew employ their considerable formal talents as artist-popular historians to raise up a semblance of Jefferson from the past and insert him into the present tense of television, offering a prime-time special event for literally millions to see, hear, and, most importantly, identify with in the comfort and privacy of their own homes.

Made-for-TV histories are, thus, never conceived according to the standards of professional history. They are not intended chiefly to debate issues, challenge the conventional wisdom, and create new knowledge and perspectives. *Thomas Jefferson,* specifically, is designed for the far less contentious environment of public television, supported largely by the continuing patronage of well-established governmental and corporate sponsors.[39] Burns's popular history, in turn, is artfully serious and respectful, warmly and sumptuously photographed, and occasionally rhapsodic in tone. Part 2 of *Thomas Jefferson,* for instance, begins with George Will's reverential appraisal: "Jefferson was, I think, the man of this millennium. The story of this millennium is the gradual expansion of freedom and an expanding inclusion of variously excluded groups. He exemplified in his life what a free person ought to look like. That is someone restless and questing his whole life under the rigorous discipline of freedom."

As a corrective to such grandiloquent remarks, Burns also interjects more critical assessments, fashioning a more useable and realistic Jefferson for a contemporary America struggling anew with the challenges of race and diversity. Paul Finkleman's counterpoint is a case in point:

> One of the defenses of Jefferson is "well, he was just a Virginia planter and we can't expect anything else from him. He was just like his neighbors." And I think the point to be made is that he's not just like his neighbors. We don't build monuments to people who are just like their neighbors. We don't put them on the nickel. We don't make them icons. Jefferson was a very special man and we expect more from him. So we compare him to the best of his generation, not merely average. We compare him to Washington who freed his slaves, to his cousin John Randolph of Roanoke who freed his slaves, to his neighbor Edward Coles, to the thousands of individual small Virginians who freed their slaves. The free black population of Virginia grows from 2,000 to 30,000 in a space of about 30 years. A lot of Virginians were freeing their slaves. Where's the master of Monticello? Why isn't he there?

The Jefferson of *Thomas Jefferson* is, therefore, a more complicated and conflicted figure than is evident in the nearly three dozen previous filmic and televisual depictions—such as *1776* (1972), *The Adams Chronicles* (1976), *The Rebels* (1979), *Jefferson in Paris* (1995), and *Liberty! The American Revolution* (1997), just to name the most prominent post-1970 examples—although Burns's documentary never approximates the comprehensiveness and precision of the existing academic literature. *Thomas Jefferson* incorporates commentaries by professional historians and subsequently aids in the popularization of their scholarly work (e.g., Joseph Ellis's *American Sphinx* became a best-seller after being strategically released by Knopf the same week as the television series).[40] However, like other expressions of popular history, Burns's documentary on Jefferson is only a partial reflection of the published record. *Thomas Jefferson* and its producer-director never pretend to present all there is to know on the subject; that is not the strength or the purpose of photography, film, and television as history. This historical documentary, instead, is far more significant because of its ceremonial ability to connect unprecedentedly large television audiences in the present with a shared sense of their common past.

Above all else, then, Burns's popular history is an intermediary site bridging the findings of professional historians with the interests of the general public. *Thomas Jefferson* functions, first and foremost, as the focal point of a large-scale cultural ritual based on fusing the stories of the past with the concerns of the present for a vast contemporary viewership. The current controversies over Jefferson reflect the internal divisions that now exist over the very definition of America's national identity. Ceremonial historical narratives, such as Ken Burns's *Thomas Jefferson*, are artistic attempts to reconstitute the cracks and fissures of that identity at a new point of agreement and consensus. Burns's work as a whole is an artistic reimagining of the national sense of self from a new generational perspective (i.e., "Who are we Americans as a people?").

Scholars, too, can seize this opportunity to reach beyond the academy and engage the outside community more with their own increasingly original and detailed accounts of past events, figures, and issues. The widespread popularity of historical documentaries on TV is indeed a reminder that history is for everyone. Some histories can mediate differences and reawaken what people take for granted in their collective past. Other more revisionist and unconventional approaches to history can also challenge established values—provoking, interrogating, unsettling. *Thomas Jefferson* falls into the former category; and no one has drawn more Americans to history of every kind through the power and reach of prime-time television than Ken Burns.

Notes

The opening epigraph appeared in "Special with Ken Burns on the Making of *Thomas Jefferson*," *Virginia Currents*, WHRO TV-15, Hampton Roads Public Television (30 minutes), April 2, 1997.

1. Ken Burns's fifteen public television specials are *Brooklyn Bridge* (PBS, 1982), *The Shakers: Hands to Work, Hearts to God* (PBS, 1985), *The Statue of Liberty* (PBS, 1985), *Huey Long* (PBS, 1986), *Thomas Hart Benton* (PBS, 1989), *The Congress* (PBS, 1989), *The Civil War* (PBS, 1990), *Empire of the Air* (PBS, 1992), *Baseball* (PBS, 1994), *The West* (PBS, 1996), *Thomas Jefferson* (PBS, 1997), *Lewis & Clark: The Journey of the Corps of Discovery* (PBS, 1997), *Frank Lloyd Wright* (PBS, 1998), *Not for Ourselves Alone: The Story of Elizabeth Cady Stanton and Susan B. Anthony* (PBS, 1999), and *Jazz* (PBS, 2001).

2. Statistical Research Incorporated (Westfield, N.J.), "1990 Public Television National Image Survey," Commissioned by the PBS Station Independence Program, September 28, 1990, 2.1–2.8.

3. Telephone interview with the author, February 18, 1993.

4. JoAnna Baldwin Mallory, "Introduction" to *Telling the Story: The Media, The Public, and American History,* Sean B. Dolan, ed., (Boston: New England Foundation for the Humanities, 1994), vii, ix.

5. Gerald Herman, "Chemical and Electronic Media in the Public History Movement," *The Public Historian: A Journal of Public History* 21.3 (summer 1999), 113.

6. Herman, 125.

7. Neal Gabler, "History's Prime Time," *TV Guide,* August 23, 1997, 18.

8. See Gary Edgerton, "Ken Burns's Rebirth of a Nation: Television, Narrative, and Popular History," *Film & History* 22.4 (1992): 118–33.

9. Ken Burns quoted in "A Filmmaking Career" on the *Thomas Jefferson* (1997) website at <http://www.pbs.org/jefferson/making/KB_03.htm>.

10. See Robert Brent Toplin, ed., *Ken Burns's* The Civil War: *Historians Respond* (New York: Oxford, 1996). The seven responses to the series actually cover a spectrum of opinion ranging from complimentary (Woodward and Toplin) to ambivalent (Boritt and Gallagher) to condemning (Foner and Litwack) and even dismissive (Clinton). Also, the collection ends with chief writer Geoffrey Ward and Ken Burns offering their own sides of the story, as well as their impressions about the chasm that all too often exists between themselves, the general public, and professional historians.

11. Catherine Clinton, "Noble Women as Well," in *Ken Burns's* The Civil War: *Historians Respond,* 66. Clinton later explains on page 189: "I regret it is so self-serving and ironic for me to trash Burns on the topic of his egregious and blatant neglect of women, as two of my last three books are shaped to deal with the topic of women and the Civil War. . . . But after being drafted, it is *not* [italics in original text] a tough job, and somebody's got to do it."

12. Christopher Shea, "Taking Aim at the 'Ken Burns' View of the Civil War," *The Chronicle of Higher Education,* March 20, 1998, A16.

13. See James M. McPherson, *Battle Cry of Freedom* (New York: Oxford Univ. Press, 1988).

14. "Primetime TV Rate Race," *Hollywood Reporter* 366.4 (February 26, 1997), 37; Larry Bonko, "Ken Burns Series Reveals Virginia Roots of Famous Trek," *The Virginian-Pilot*, November 4, 1997, E2.

15. Ken Burns quoted in "Process + Production" on the *Thomas Jefferson* (1997) website at <http://www.pbs.org/jefferson/making/KB_01.htm>.

16. Edgerton, 130.

17. "*Thomas Jefferson*, a New Film by Ken Burns About One of Our Nation's Most Eloquent Presidents, Will Be Broadcast on PBS Feb. 18 and 19, 1997," *Thomas Jefferson Press Kit* (New York: Owen Comora Associates, a Division of Serino Coyne Public Relations, 1996), 1.

18. Ibid.

19. "Ken Burns and the Historical Narrative on Television," The Museum of Television and Radio University Satellite Seminar Series (90 minutes), November 19, 1996.

20. Joseph J. Ellis, *American Sphinx: The Character of Thomas Jefferson* (New York: Knopf, 1997), 3.

21. See Dumas Malone, *Thomas Jefferson and His Times*, 6 Volumes (Boston: Little, Brown, 1948–1981); and Merrill D. Peterson, *The Jefferson Image in the American Mind* (New York: Oxford Univ. Press, 1960).

22. Ken Burns in speech, "Searching for Thomas Jefferson."

23. Ibid.

24. "Special with Ken Burns on the Making of *Thomas Jefferson*," *Virginia Currents*.

25. "Ken Burns Creates '18th Century Virtual Reality' in His Cinematic Portrait of Thomas Jefferson," *Thomas Jefferson Press Kit*. (New York: Owen Comora Associates, a Division of Serino Coyne Public Relations, 1996), 2.

26. Eric Rudolph, "*Thomas Jefferson* Evokes Era of Enlightenment," *American Cinematographer* 78:1 (January 1997), 84.

27. "Ken Burns Creates '18th Century Virtual Reality'", 2.

28. B. Ruby Rich, "Documentarians: State of Documentary," *National Forum: The Phi Kappa Phi Journal* 77.4 (fall 1997), 23. The producer-directors taking part in the roundtable were St. Clair Bourne, Arthur Dong, Rob Epstein, Su Friedrich, Deborah Hoffmann, Steve James, Ross McElwee, Errol Morris, Michel Negroponte, Lourdes Portillo, Renee Tajima-Pena, Jessica Yu, and Terry Zwigoff.

29. Telephone interview with the author, February 18, 1993.

30. Interview with the author, February 27, 1996.

31. Ken Burns quoted in "Process + Production."

32. The transcription of Burns's entire interview with Franklin can be found on the *Thomas Jefferson* (1997) website at <http://www.pbs.org/jefferson/archives/interviews/frame.htm>.

33. Ken Burns in speech, "Sharing the American Experience," Norfolk Forum, Norfolk, Virginia, February 27, 1996.

34. Interview with the author, February 27, 1996.

35. Conversation between Ken Burns and the author prior to the Historians Film Committee panel, "Television and History: Ken Burns's *Thomas Jefferson*," at the 112th Annual Meeting of the American Historical Association, January 10, 1998, Seattle, Washington.

36. "Ken Burns: Exploring the Complexities and Inner Turmoil of Thomas Jefferson," *Thomas Jefferson Press Kit* (New York: Owen Comora Associates, a Division of Serino Coyne Public Relations, 1996), 1.

37. The timeline under "The Process" delineates that preparation began in spring 1990 and assembly ended during the fall of 1996 on the *Thomas Jefferson* (1997) website at <http://www.pbs.org/jefferson/section 3.htm>.

38. Jack McLaughlin, *Jefferson and Monticello: The Biography of a Builder* (New York: Henry Holt, 1988), 383.

39. *Thomas Jefferson* was a production of Florentine Films in association with WETA-TV, Washington, D.C. Corporate funding was provided by General Motors Corporation. Additional funding was furnished by the Pew Charitable Trusts, the Corporation for Public Broadcasting, the Public Broadcasting Service, Virginia Department of Tourism, and the Arthur Vining Davis Foundations.

40. Joseph J. Ellis, "Whose Thomas Jefferson Is He Anyway?" *The New York Times,* Sunday, February 16, 1997, H35.

III

TV News and Public Affairs Programming as Historian

9 Pixies

Homosexuality, Anti-Communism, and the Army-McCarthy Hearings

Thomas Doherty

During the Army-McCarthy hearings, broadcast live on television from April 22 to June 17, 1954, a risqué exchange provoked gales of laughter from the unruly gallery packed into Senate Caucus Room 310. While examining a doctored photograph offered into evidence by the McCarthy staff, Joseph N. Welch, attorney for the U.S. Army, made the sardonic suggestion that perhaps "pixies" were the culprits responsible for the alterations. McCarthy snidely asked Welch to define "pixie" because "I think [you] might be an expert on that." "A pixie," the lawyer snapped back, eyeing McCarthy's side of the table, "is a close relative of a fairy."[1]

The testy banter made oblique reference to an unspoken suspicion hovering over the official charges and countercharges between the army and McCarthy: that a homosexual liaison between Roy Cohn, special counsel for the McCarthy subcommittee, and G. David Schine, former unpaid consultant for the subcommittee and current private in the U.S. Army, was at the root of Cohn's obsession with Schine's welfare in uniform. After all, upon Schine's induction into the army in the fall of 1953, Cohn had pressured, badgered, and abused army officials, from the Secretary of the Army on down to Schine's company commander, to provide Schine with special privileges and choice assignments. His irrational outbursts and vituperative language were the catalyst for the Army-McCarthy hearings, America's first nationally televised political spectacle—and the stage, ultimately, for the downfall of Joseph R. McCarthy.[2]

In an age when sexuality of all kinds is not just a fit but an incessant subject for televisual discourse, when sitcoms and soap operas showcase gay

Joseph N. Welch was the attorney for the Army during the Army-McCarthy Hearings, which were telecast live from April 22 to June 17, 1954. Author's collection.

characters and talk shows chatter frankly about sexual orientations of gymnastic variety, the discretion and ignorance over matters of non-missionary position sexuality in America in the 1950s may be difficult to credit. For many Americans, an awareness of the existence, much less the mechanics, of homosexual activity was beyond the scope of imagination. To read back a homosexual subtext onto the Army-McCarthy hearings is thus an act of interpretation that drifts perilously near the shoals of historical presentism, the logical fallacy of seeing the past through the lens of the present. The methodological risks are underscored by the fact that pioneering televiewers who witnessed the hearings characteristically aver that it simply never entered their minds, that the very notion of homosexuality—so quick to bubble to the service in any discussion of close male friendship today—was seldom a thought that reached conscious awareness in 1954.

The postwar cultural context militated against homosexual insinuations in other ways. During World War II, close male friendships forged in combat served as survival mechanism and emotional sustenance. Whether in *Yank* magazine's cartoon buddies Willie and Joe or real-life duos like Guadalcanal heroes Al Schmid and Lee Diamond, intimate male bonding

The Army-McCarthy Hearings set the stage for the eventual downfall of Sen. Joseph R. McCarthy from Wisconsin. Author's collection.

was seldom fraught with suggestive undertones. The recent findings of the Kinsey Report in 1949—that one in three American men had engaged in some kind of homosexual activity—gave the psychologists pause, but virile commingling between adult males was more apt to be configured as a normal refuge from intrusive females than an aberrant desire for same-sex contact.

At the same time, a gender contract written in concrete seemed to be cracking around the edges. The immutability of sexuality was being challenged by medical science (in the case of the pioneering transsexual Christine Jorgensen) and in television programming. Concurrent with the Army-McCarthy hearings was the strange and meteoric rise of Liberace, the "telepianist marvel" who became a sensation brandishing the fashion trademarks of a raging queen: flamboyant outfits, Louis XIV decor, candelabra, and lisping. "When will Liberace marry?" queried a 1954 cover story in *TV Guide*, as if the effeminate mama's boy was a hot marriage prospect for white-gloved coeds.[3]

Certainly the sexual politics of the day situated homosexuality as doubly beyond the pale. The link between homosexuality and communism—of perversion and subversion, fag baiting and red baiting—was overt in American law and culture in the 1950s. Like domestic communists, homosexuals met in secret cells, possessed a preternatural ability to detect one another, and threatened the moral fiber of the nation. In 1950, the Senate Permanent Subcommittee on Investigations issued a "Report on Employment of Homosexuals and Other Sex Perverts in Government" that concluded:

[The homosexual has a] tendency to gather other perverts about him. Eminent psychiatrists have informed the subcommittee that the homosexual is likely to seek his own kind because the pressures of society are such that he feels uncomfortable unless he is with his own kind. Due to this situation, the homosexual tends to surround himself with other homosexuals, not only in his social life but in his business life. Under these circumstances if a homosexual attains a position in government where he can influence the hiring of personnel, it is almost inevitable that he will attempt to place other homosexuals in government jobs.[4]

As a potential threat to national security, however, a homosexual was more likely to be deemed a "security risk" rather than a "loyalty risk," a distinction crucial to the calculus of Cold War patriotism. An individual was designated as a loyalty risk if he or she had actually expressed anti-American or pro-communist beliefs or joined like-minded organizations. Membership in the Communist Party USA or one of its many alleged "front" groups was prima facie evidence of being a loyalty risk. Such sentiments or affiliations were legitimate reasons for termination of employment from sensitive government jobs and for precautionary surveillance by government agents. By contrast, the "security risk" label was applied to an individual who, although not anti-American or pro-communist in opinion or association, might be subject to blackmail because of personal habits. An alcoholic, an immigrant with relatives in Eastern Europe, or a homosexual might be unquestionably loyal to the United States, but as a potential target of pressure from communist agents might be unfit for sensitive positions in government or private industry.

On April 27, 1953, President Eisenhower issued Executive Order 10450, which recalibrated the bipolar distinction established under President Truman. Henceforth, security rather than loyalty would be the decisive standard. "It is important to realize that many loyal Americans, by reason of instability, alcoholism, homosexuality, or previous tendency to associate with Communist-front groups are unintentional security risks," Eisenhower explained in his memoirs. "In some instances, because of moral lapses, they become subjected to the threat of blackmail by enemy agents. I emphasized that working for the government must be regarded as a privilege, not a constitutional right."[5]

Obviously, the regulations promulgated under the Truman and Eisenhower administrations tended to conflate the essence of patriotism with the habits of personal life. Like the distinctions between loyalty and security, the differences between communist activities and homosexual practices might blur and overlap. No wonder the imputation of homosexual entanglements colors so much of the backdrop of the political and media culture of the Cold War. The most famous homosexually charged, communist-affiliated couple was Alger Hiss and Whittaker Chambers. When in August 1948 Chambers accused Hiss of engaging in espionage for the Soviet Union in the 1930s, Hiss and his defenders rallied by characterizing Chambers's accusations as the vengeful retaliation of a jilted homosexual cruiser.[6]

One legacy of the Hiss-Chambers contretemps was that Hiss's bureaucratic berth, the State Department, was configured as a seething hotbed of homo-communist activity, an enclave of effete patricians by day doubling as perverted espionage agents by night. The nation's premiere purveyors of stereotypes, Hollywood motion pictures and television, cultivated the caricatures. In Leo McCarey's anticommunist melodrama *My Son John* (1952), actor Robert Walker portrays the title subversive as a mincing mama's boy. Fresh from his homoerotic turn as the murderer in Alfred Hitchcock's *Strangers on a Train* (1951), Walker's inflections and gestures exude an aberrant sexuality that seems an apt index of his subversive politics.[7] Likewise, in the syndicated series *I Led 3 Lives* (1953–1956), the Communist Party cell leaders encountered on a weekly basis by triple agent Herbert A. Philbrick (citizen/"communist"/counterspy) tend to be prissy intellectuals who wilt before the virile Americanism of actor Richard Carlson.

McCarthy himself evinced a steady interest in the correlation between communism and homosexuality. "One reason why sex deviates are considered security risks is that they are subject to blackmail," McCarthy wrote. "It is a known fact that espionage agents often have been successful in extorting information from them by threatening to expose their abnormal habits."[8]

Despite limits on the explicit discussion of matters of sexuality in the early 1950s, the question of the relationship between loyalty and security, communism and homosexuality, was aired in public—even televised—forums, albeit mainly by way of oblique references and between-the-lines shadings. For example, on the December 13, 1953, episode of *Meet the Press* ("a program of national significance"), broadcast soon after President Eisenhower had reportedly fired 1,427 government employees under the authority of Executive Order 10450, a suggestive dialogue occurred between Senator McCarthy and reporters John Madigan and Lawrence Spivak:

"Do you know how many of those [1,427 fired employees] were actually loyalty risks and how much involved human frailty?" Madigan inquired of McCarthy, choosing his words carefully.

McCarthy shuffled somewhat. "The number who were discharged on the grounds of communist convictions is extremely high . . . it varies . . . but it's extremely high. You take those discharged for communist connections and perversion, add the two together, it runs over 90 percent."

"90 percent for what?" injected Spivak.

"90 percent of the total of 1,427."

Spivak pressed on. "90 percent for perversion and 90 percent for loyalty?"

"The combination of communist activities and perversion?"

"Yeh," Spivak replied patiently. "But what part of that is communist activity? Do you know?"

"I couldn't break that down for you, Larry."

John Madigan jumped in. "Do you think they should be made public by the administration as protection against those that maybe—were just—had bad companions?"

McCarthy: "Do you mean should the administration tell who was discharged because he had bad companions—"

Madigan completed the thought: "—and those that were loyalty risks because of treasonable potentiality?"

"I doubt that anything would be gained by that," McCarthy finally responded.[9]

Yet on McCarthy's own subcommittee two men who may well have fit the contemporaneous definition of "security risks" occupied very sensitive positions. Like Alger Hiss and Whittaker Chambers, Roy M. Cohn and G. David Schine were an odd couple. Cohn had joined McCarthy's staff as chief counsel in January 1953 after a meteoric career as a precocious and ruthlessly ambitious twenty-three-year-old prosecutor, fresh from the U.S. Attorney's office in New York, where he had helped obtain the conviction for espionage of Julius and Ethel Rosenberg.

By contrast, G. David Schine was a rich layabout. Born in Gloversville, New York, the second of four children, Schine was the scion of wealthy hotelier J. Meyer Schine. The senior Schine and his brother Louis had made a fortune in motion picture exhibition during the Great Depression, and in the postwar era had expanded their operations to hotel ownership. By the early 1950s, the Schine family was wintering at their hotel in Boca Raton, Florida, and holding parties for the Duke and Duchess of Windsor. Schine's theatrical holdings were widespread enough to run afoul of federal antitrust laws. While the Senate was investigating the son, the father was being sued by the Justice Department for failing to comply with the Paramount Decree of 1948, the Supreme Court decision that required the major studios to divorce themselves of their exhibition chains. In 1952, he composed a six-page

Roy M. Cohn was chief counsel of Sen. Joseph R. McCarthy's staff during the Army-McCarthy Hearings. Author's collection.

pamphlet entitled *Definition of Communism,* copies of which were placed in every room of his father's hotel chain.[10] The pamphlet (or its author) caught Cohn's eye, and on February 6, 1953, Schine began work as the sole unpaid consultant for the McCarthy Committee.

Cohn and Schine were first linked during a widely publicized tour of European USIA offices in April 1953. For two and a half weeks, the duo descended on overseas libraries, examined book stacks, gave press interviews, and in general behaved like innocents abroad. The trip was lambasted on both sides of the Atlantic. They were called "Laurel and Hardy" and "Abbott and Costello," but the label that stuck was bestowed by Theodore Kaghan, a State Department official in Germany, who ridiculed the pair as "junketeering gumshoes." (When Cohn in retaliation accused Kaghan of communist sympathies for a play he had written twenty years earlier, Kaghan resigned his post.)

The shoulder-to-shoulder association of the two single young men in their twenties did not go unnoticed by McCarthy's enemies. Foremost among them was investigative journalist Drew Pearson, whose syndicated column, "The Washington Merry-Go-Round," was relentlessly anti-McCarthy. "The two McCarthy gumshoes seemed unusually preoccupied with investigating alleged homosexuals, including one very prominent United States official," Pearson reported. "The pair also made a show of registering for separate hotel rooms, remarking loudly that they didn't work for the State Department." Smirking, Pearson described Schine as a "handsome, haughty twenty-five-year-old kid with a dreamy look in his eye, and who sometimes slaps Cohn around as if they were dormitory roommates."[11]

While in Frankfurt, Germany, a quarrel flared up between Schine and Cohn. United Press reporter Bill Long filed the story with UP, but the syndicate opted not to print it, whereupon Long turned it over to the *Frankfurt Abenpost,* which did. According to Long's report, Schine misplaced a notebook and dispatched his driver back to the hotel to search for it in his other trousers. When the driver came back empty-handed, Schine forced Cohn to return with him to the hotel. For some reason, Schine accused Cohn of stealing the notebook. "The spat got so heated in the hotel corridor that Schine smacked Cohn over the head with a rolled-up magazine. Schine also demanded a search of Cohn's luggage, then suddenly remembered he had left the bothersome notebook in California. Later their room was found in disarray."[12]

A more sympathetic reporter, in a kind of overcompensation, portrayed Cohn and Schine as dashing and attractive ladies' men-about-town. Walter Winchell regularly mentioned the pair, or Cohn singly, squiring about some beautiful socialite or would-be actress in the Stork Club.[13] The alleged heterosexual prowess of G. David Schine reached the level of articulation on the first day of the Army-McCarthy hearings. During his testimony, Secretary of the Army Robert T. Stevens, a gray-flannel-suit-type devoid of humor, recalled that Cohn phoned him to obtain a weekend pass to New York for Schine "perhaps for the purpose of taking care of Dave's girlfriend." A reaction shot to McCarthy's side of the table shows the senator cracking up, followed a beat later by Cohn and the gallery.

Pearson may have been responsible for Schine's induction into the United States Army. In 1945, the final year of the war, Schine entered Harvard and procured a draft-exempt job in the Army Transport Service. With the outbreak of hostilities in Korea in June 1950, the peacetime draft geared up for the police action. In 1951, when Schine's legal residence was in Pasadena, the California Selective Service had classified him as 1–A. At Schine's request, his case was transferred to New York, where after a second examination on Governors Island, he was classified 4–F for a combination of physical and psychic dislocations: a "heightened disc L4–5 [left vertebrae Nos. 4 and 5] with schizoid personality."

Two years later, the Pasadena Draft Board requested a reclassification, which was done in New York. The reason for the Pasadena Board's renewed interest in Schine may have been a Drew Pearson column on July 17, 1953, questioning Schine's fitness to stand in judgment of the military given his own lack of uniformed service. "Schine is delighted to discuss his career—except when you get to the touchy question of his military service," wrote Pearson. "Then he becomes as evasive as a McCarthy witness."[14] This time the New York Draft Board classified Schine as 1–A. Schine appealed the reclassification, but the appeals board sustained the 1–A classification. On November 10, 1953, Schine was drafted into the United States Army.

By all accounts except his own, Roy Cohn then went ballistic. After withstanding five months of Cohn's intrusions into Schine's military career, the army on March 11, 1954, released a chronology documenting Cohn's many phone calls badgering army officials on Schine's behalf. Almost immediately, G. David Schine "without firing a shot in anger," became "America's most public private."[15]

On March 14, 1954, Cohn faced a quartet of reporters on NBC's *Meet the Press.* Prefiguring a strategy he would take in the televised hearings, Cohn countercharged that the army had actually held out to him the possibility of exposing a homosexual ring on an air force base if Cohn would "get off the Army's back" about security failings at its post at Fort Monmouth, New Jersey. Cohn alleged that, "a specific proposal was made to us [by army counsellor John G. Adams] that we go after an Air Force base wherein, Mr. Adams told us, that there were a number of sex de-vi-ates and that that would make excellent hearings for us."[16] (The countercharge inspired some lighthearted banter during the hearings. In mock defense of the honor of their home states, senators on the subcommittee each sought assurance from an army witness that the alleged homosexual ring was not located in Tennessee, or Arkansas, or South Dakota . . .)

The question of what a member of the *Meet the Press* panel called Cohn's "extravagant concern for your friend Dave Schine" arose as did the perhaps more curious question of McCarthy's own attachment to Cohn. Cohn's actions had exposed and endangered McCarthy in a way the Senator's own irresponsible behavior never had. The obvious course for the Senator, the politically expedient course, was for McCarthy to deny foreknowledge of the actions of his chief counsel on behalf of Schine, to denounce them, and to fire Cohn. McCarthy could credibly claim that his own role in the whole fandango was minuscule. In fact, from the moment Schine came aboard the subcommittee as an unpaid staffer, Cohn's obsession with him had tried McCarthy's patience. "Roy thinks that Dave ought to be a general and operate from a penthouse at the Waldorf Astoria," the senator told Secretary of the Army Stevens. And later, tellingly: "[Schine's induction] was one of the few things I have seen [Cohn] completely unreasonable about."[17]

That McCarthy failed to fire Cohn and thereby left himself open to attack raised suspicions that the relation between the senator and his chief counsel was not merely professional. On *Meet the Press*, Mae Craig, a feisty reporter for the *Press Herald* of Portland, Maine, pointedly asked Cohn about demands by Senator Ralph Flanders, Republican of Vermont, for an investigation "to find out whether you have any hold on Senator McCarthy which would induce him to keep you on." Cohn bristled and shot back, "I have no other hold on Senator McCarthy and I resent the suggestion." Cohn explained the senator's loyalty as simple reciprocity, invoking the military dictum that loyalty flows both ways. "No chairman ever had a more loyal staff than Senator McCarthy has on that committee and I think no staff ever had a more loyal chairman than we have in Senator McCarthy." Such virtue was hard to credit as the sole motive, though. In a report on Roy Cohn's appearance on *Meet the Press*, *Variety* commented elliptically: "The questioning of the panel of reporters was sharp and sometimes hostile in tone, but definitely not exceeding the allowable bounds for newspapermen. Certainly no nasty rumors, which even an immediate denial cannot erase, were let loose by any of the questioners."[18]

However, more blatant insinuations were being voiced from the floor of the United States Senate. On June 1, 1954, Senator Flanders delivered his third anti-McCarthy speech in as many months. As his fellow senators sat in tense silence, Flanders accused McCarthy of driving "a blundering ax" into his church, his country, and his party by tactics of "division and confusion." He compared the senator to the temperamental cartoon character Dennis the Menace. "Were the Junior Senator from Wisconsin in the pay of the communists, he could not have done a better job for them," Flanders thundered. Calling upon the Senate Permanent Investigations Subcommittee to investigate the "personal relationship" between Cohn, Schine, and McCarthy, he asked why Cohn "seems to have an almost *passionate*"—he caressed the word—"anxiety to retain Schine as a staff collaborator." Flanders continued: "And then there is the Senator himself. At times he seems anxious to rid himself of the whole mess, and then again, at least in the presence of his assistant, he strongly supports the latter's efforts to keep the army private's services available. Does the assistant have some hold on the Senator? Can it be that our Dennis, so effective in making trouble for his elders, has at last gotten into trouble himself?"[19]

Perhaps the most explicit evidence of the sexual subsurface is an article in *Rave*, a monthly scandal magazine sold for twenty-five cents. Billing itself as "the magazine that's not for idiots," *Rave* was a ripe version of that peculiar 1950s newsstand genre, the scandal sheet. The most notorious example is *Confidential* magazine, which specialized in innuendoes about the sex lives of the stars, such as Liberace's penchant for the companionship of husky young men and Lizbeth Scott's lesbian barhopping. The June 1954 issue of *Rave* published an article entitled "The Secret Lives of Joe McCarthy" by Hank Greenspun, editor and publisher of the *Las Vegas Sun*, where the piece had originally appeared the previous February. "Although it is unquestionably the most startling and explosive story to come out of Washington in twenty-five years, no magazine or newspaper has yet dared to reprint it," raved the editors. The article implied—actually it reported—that if not a card-carrying homosexual himself, then McCarthy was at least a fellow traveler.

Despite its sensationalistic venue, Greenspun's article is a sharply written piece of reporting. Practicing the virulent Freudianism that was far more epidemic than Marxism in Cold War America, the reporter psychoanalyzed the senator in doctrinal terms: "McCarthy has been operating through a defense mechanism caused by a guilt complex. When McCarthy started on his first large publicity campaign, he uttered a charge that the State Department was honeycombed with homosexuals. According to the senator from Wisconsin, perverts were security risks because of their susceptibility to blackmail through fear of exposure." Greenspun speculated:

> I always thought that McCarthy "protesteth too much" and a search of his past disclosed that he, too, had often surrounded himself with known homosexuals. His tactics became clear. By leading a supposed fight against perverts in government, he could avert suspicions from himself. For anyone to say that McCarthy is a sex deviate, would bring an instant retort: "ridiculous, he is the foremost fighter against perverts." . . . And yet the plain unvarnished truth is that McCarthy, judged by the very standards by which he judges others, is a security risk on the grounds of homosexual associations.[20]

In launching a series of charges that could only be called McCarthyite, Greenspun and Senator Flanders both took a perverse delight in turning the senator's modus operandi back at him. Nonetheless, there is some justice in Roy Cohn's observation that "if Senator McCarthy had said or implied something like this without any basis in fact, he would have been pilloried by the same liberals who propped up Flanders to do their below-the-belt dirty work."[21]

Though such accusations came in just under the radar of widespread public awareness in 1954, the sexual subtext was very much in the air during the Army-McCarthy hearings. In hindsight, of course, the animating role of homosexuality in McCarthy's fateful confrontation with the army is unmistakable. Drawing upon FBI files obtained through the Freedom of Information Act and memoirs and biographies that see no percentage in discretion, revisionist histories place the sexual politics of the McCarthy era in heightened relief.

More than any other factor, however, it was Roy Cohn's death from AIDS in 1986 that acted as a sort of ex post facto confirmation to what was only insinuated in 1954. According to popular entertainment set in the McCarthy era, such as the TV movie *Citizen Cohn* (1993) or the Broadway play *Angels in America* (1993), the homosexual orientation of at least one of the principals is an established fact.

Still, no matter how irresistible the irony that it should be sex, not politics, that initiated McCarthy's downfall, viewing the hearings through a sexual prism may obscure an appreciation of the other code of conduct violated by McCarthy, Cohn, and Schine; namely, the duty to serve in the U.S. military. Though one should not be too naive about the willingness of the rich and powerful to undertake military service, one should not to be too cynical either. During the Cold War, the obligation to perform military service when called upon was an article of faith in the democratic catechism that crossed class lines. Every able-bodied adult male was expected to serve in uniform and, if not endure actual combat, to at least experience the crucible of basic training, military discipline, and the rough egalitarianism of barracks life. More often than not, the sons of the wealthy and the influential did their hitch. Secretary of the Army Stevens, a patrician millionaire, had himself served in both world wars and tried, with evident sincerity, to persuade Cohn and Schine that a passage in the service was a character builder, an experience to treasure in later life. The chamber of the U.S. Senate itself offered a poignant example. In 1942, the son of Democratic senator John McClellan of Arkansas was serving quietly in the U.S. Army. When he went on sick call with an undiagnosed illness, he wrote his father and urged him to refrain from using senatorial influence to obtain for him any special treatment. The same day Senator McClellan unsealed his son's letter he received the news that his son had died of spinal meningitis.[22]

Another father-son relationship in the Senate sheds harsher light on the sexual politics of the Cold War era. On the morning of June 19, 1954, two days after the conclusion of the Army-McCarthy hearings, Senator Lester C. Hunt (D) of Wyoming closed the door to his office and committed suicide by putting a rifle to his head. "I am not sure whether it had to do with the threat Senator McCarthy made yesterday that he was going to investigate a Democratic Senator who had fixed a case, or whether it was Hunt's concerns over his son's homosexual troubles," speculated Drew Pearson in his private diaries. Hunt had earlier announced his retirement from the Senate for health reasons. "Personally I think he just didn't want to face the innuendo and rumors regarding his boy during the election campaign." Abiding by a journalistic ethos unimaginable today, Pearson observes: "I was on the verge of writing a story about this last December, but got a call from Tracy McCracken of the Wyoming newspapers, who pleaded with me not to. Hunt also told Jack Anderson at the time that if the story was written, his wife would die."[23] Neither Pearson's column nor the reports about the senator's sensational suicide made even veiled reference to his son's homosexuality and trial for sodomy.

In the end, however, it was the political overtones, not the sexual undertones, that rang out most clearly from the Army-McCarthy hearings. Few areas were as culturally freighted in postwar America as service in the military, a duty that affirmed the citizen's compliance with America's egalitarian ethos. In violating this contract, the McCarthy Committee was transgressing against a taboo far more sensitive than First Amendment rights and engaging in conduct nearly as disreputable as homosexuality. Five years later, an army draftee whose fame surpassed even Schine's would realize—or his manager would realize—that to protest or sidestep military service might destroy his career. But unlike Elvis Presley, G. David Schine did not possess management as coldly detached and savvy as Colonel Tom Parker, a man concerned only with protecting a meal ticket. The hot-blooded Roy Cohn, whose interest in Schine, whatever its true source may have been, was never purely mercenary.

Notes

1. All quotes from the televised hearings are taken from the extant kinescopes, screened at the Motion Picture Division of the Library of Congress.

2. Of course, scholarship on McCarthy and his "-ism" is an academic growth industry. See Thomas C. Reeves, *The Life and Times of Joe McCarthy* (New York: Stein and Day, 1982); David M. Oshinsky, *A Conspiracy So Immense: The World of Joseph McCarthy* (New York: Free Press, 1983); and William Bragg Ewald Jr., *Who Killed Joe McCarthy?* (New York: Simon and Schuster, 1984). For a revisionist view, see Arthur Herman, *Joseph McCarthy: Re-Examining the Life of America's Most Hated Senator* (New York: Free Press, 1999).

3. "When Will Liberace Marry?" *TV Guide*, September 18, 1954.

4. Joe McCarthy, *McCarthyism: The Fight for America* (New York: Devin-Adair, 1952), 14–15.

5. Dwight D. Eisenhower, *Mandate for Change, 1953–1956* (New York: New American Library, 1963), 376.

6. Alan Weinstein, *Perjury: The Hiss-Chambers Case* (New York: Random House, 1979), 67–68.

7. For an extended discussion of the trope in Hollywood cinema, see Robert J. Corber, *In the Name of National Security: Hitchcock, Homophobia, and the Political Construction of Gender in Postwar America* (Durham, N.C.: Duke Univ. Press, 1993).

8. Joe McCarthy, 15.

9. *Meet the Press*, December 13, 1953, screened at the Motion Picture Division of the Library of Congress.

10. "G. David Schine—Authority on Communism," in James Rorty and Moshe Decter, *McCarthy and the Communists* (Boston: Beacon, 1954), 154.

11. Drew Pearson, "Cohn, Schine Also Disturb Sedate GOP," *The Washington Post*, July 17, 1953, 51.

12. Drew Pearson, "More on Cohn-Schine Jaunt," *The Washington Post*, June 5, 1954, 13.

13. Neal Gabler, *Winchell: Gossip, Power, and the Culture of Celebrity* (New York: Knopf, 1994), 455–59.

14. Drew Pearson, "Cohn, Schine Also Disturb Sedate GOP," *The Washington Post*, July 17, 1953, 51.

15. Saul Pett, "Army's Best Known Private Wanted to Be Someone Special," *The Washington Post*, May 3, 1954, 3; Drew Pearson, "Schine 'Studied' Via Secretary," *The Washington Post*, May 4, 1954, 39.

16. *Meet the Press*, March 14, 1954, screened at the Motion Picture Division of the Library of Congress.

17. Reeves, 598.

18. "Television Follow Up Comment," *Variety*, March 17, 1954, 26.

19. Robert C. Albright, "McCarthy Is Hit as Menace by Flanders," *The Washington Post*, June 2, 1954, 1, 2.

20. Hank Greenspun, "The Secret Lives of Joe McCarthy," *Rave* (June 1954), 58–72.

21. Roy Cohn, *McCarthy* (New York: New American Library, 1968), 244.

22. Drew Pearson, "The Washington Merry-Go-Round," *Washington Post*, June 10, 1954, 59.

23. Drew Pearson, *Diaries*, edited by Tyler Abell (New York: Holt, Rinehart, and Winston), 323.

10 Images of History in Israel Television News

The Territorial Dimensions of Collective Memories, 1987–1990

Netta Ha-Ilan

Television news tells the story of the key events of the last hours. Behind this apparently simple definition there are a number of theoretical questions dealing with the modes through which television news imposes some order upon the chaotic nature of the "real" and grants meaning to current events. In this process, television news selects, categorizes, combines, and narrates by means of sights and sounds. It attempts to represent the real world using culturally understandable signs and symbols. It is argued here that the latter are often linked to definitions of a collective past and the demarcation of social boundaries. Thus, television news often deals with the issue of collective identity by using historical narrative.

News has been described as discourse. It includes codes, styles, and conventions, together with professional practices and textual devices. As discourse, "news strives to control and limit the meaning of the events it conveys."[1] This essay stresses the importance of historical narrative in television news discourse and its definition of collective identity. The collective past is used to define a common history and shared destiny. Eric Hobsbawm's remark about historical writing is fully applicable to the news discourse. It creates, dismantles, and restructures the images of the past.[2] The latter belongs not only to world of specialist investigation, but to people as political beings.

Historical narrative in television news appears either in common or ceremonial modes. The former applies when the past is enlisted to interpret an event that is not directly linked to the issue of social boundaries. It has no special form or pattern. Television news places certain events in historical perspective by using descriptions such as "the worst weather in fifty years," "the largest fall in share prices since 1983," or "old-timers in the House cannot recall such a stormy debate."

The ceremonial mode appears to commemorate social cohesiveness. The argument here is that ceremonial historical narratives act as an affirmation of collective boundaries through well-defined patterns of newsreel items. Focusing on the case study of the Israel Television news, the paper describes the characteristics of the ceremonial mode and explains when it is used. The example of the Israel Television news clarifies the circumstances under which collective memories are enlisted to grant meaning to current events. For Israel Television news, these attempts are made under conditions of acute internal divisions over the very definitions of national identity. Clearly, the dispute is bound to have a marked impact on social discourse. Thus, the changes over time in the presentation of social boundaries in television news reflect the reconstitution of collective identity. Television news is an arena in which the struggle over meanings and signification takes place.

This essay is based on news items broadcast by Israel Television, a public broadcasting service, between December 1987 and January 1990. Broadcasting by Israel Television started in May 1968, less than a year after the occupation of the West Bank and Gaza began. Therefore, the challenge posed by the occupation to Israeli society and politics was already present. During the following years, the news staff was forced to respond to the development of the issue as it grew from something relatively nonproblematic (in the early seventies) to an issue with the status of a central problem (during the eighties). At the end of the period examined here, a new era was ushered in due to the transformation effected by the Gulf crisis and the nascent peace process between Israel and the Palestinians.[3]

The Israel Broadcasting Authority (IBA) is based on the BBC model. Since 1965, the IBA has operated as a statutory authority governed by a board appointed by political parties according to their relative parliamentary strength. Until 1993, the IBA had a monopoly on broadcasting television news in Israel. During this period, television news was the most popular program in the state. At the peak of its popularity, 70 percent of Israelis watched the nine o'clock evening news. Television news was the most prestigious, and almost the only, original domestic program.

The Political Context

The State of Israel was formed in 1948. In 1967, Israeli troops captured the

Sinai Peninsula, the Gaza Strip, the West Bank of the Jordan River, and the Golan Heights. As a result of the occupation there has been a lack of congruity between territorial and social boundaries—Israel rules territories, but the Palestinian inhabitants are considered foreigners. Formally, Israel never annexed the territories except for East Jerusalem (1967) and the Golan Heights (1981).

The occupation rekindled the pre-1948 debate inside the Jewish population of Israel about the desirable borders of the state. Unlike the earlier period, the debate has practical political implications marked by religious, strategic, and military arguments. The different positions reflect, to a great extent, contradictory definitions of collective identity. The primordial definition stresses the connection between nation and religion and puts these considerations at the center of its view of social boundaries. According to this view, the occupied territories, particularly the West Bank and East Jerusalem, are integral parts of Israel. On the other hand, the secular-liberal concept of collective identity regarded the occupied territories as negotiable in the framework of future peace talks.[4] Since 1968, Jewish settlements have been established in the occupied territories, the number of settlers rising to 5,000 in 1977, 53,000 in 1985,[5] and about 100,000 in the early 1990s.[6]

The controversy inside Israel about the occupation has grown in intensity over time and has overlapped different stages in its political development. These periods have differed in the relations between territory, symbolic order, and key institutional features.[7] In the first years after the occupation, the scale and content of struggles over the annexation or separation of new territories did not challenge the structure of state institutions, or the underlying beliefs and identities of the population.[8] However, since the mid-seventies, particularly after Sinai was returned to Egypt as part of a peace accord in 1982, the internal confrontation has concerned the rules of the political game and the symbolic order.[9]

The Palestinian uprising of 1987–1990 fueled the internal controversy, focused attention on the daily practices of the occupation, and brought about an increase in television news coverage of the West Bank and Gaza. Israel Television news was forced to develop an appropriate imagery for the situation and grant meaning to developments that challenged the collective self-perception. The response of Israel Television news to this challenge offers an opportunity to study the modes through which it made sense of events and created images of "us" under the internal dispute.[10] Here, the aim is to outline when and how television news enlisted collective memories for this purpose and what limitations there are to the use of historical narrative.

Ceremonial Historical Narrative

Four examples, three of them relating to salient events at their time, were chosen to illustrate the use of ceremonial historical narrative in Israel Television news. The coverage of a fire in the Carmel Forest in September 1989 offers an excellent example of the use of ceremonial historiography to celebrate unity in the face of an apparent external threat. Despite the fact that there were no casualties during the fire, television news used a ritualistic and historical framework to grant meaning to the events. Collective memories were enlisted for this purpose.

Israel Television news covered the fire in five different items over four consecutive days. The area affected was a widely known spot within the pre-1967 borders. There were no human casualties, but a number of animals in the nature and wildlife reserve were killed. During that summer there had been several forest fires that were later proved to be arsons connected to the Intifada (the Palestinian uprising). Reports on the first two days followed this pattern: responsibility was attributed to arson, damages were enumerated, and the measures taken to cope with the situation were shown. Thus, despite the fact that the fire did not take place in the occupied territories, it was presented as connected to the Intifada and to the issue of social boundaries.[11]

An historical explanation first appeared on the third day during a regular news item, and was fully elaborated on the next day in a report appearing on the weekly news "magazine." The tone that dominated the coverage was one of grief, almost mourning, over the damage to nature. On the third day, images of burnt trees and small flames accompanied the implicit historical interpretation given by the reporter. "A few evil hands," he said, had succeeded where Ottoman rule (of Palestine), which had "erased the forests of the land on behalf of its army," had not. The connection to a collective perception of the past was strengthened by enumerating the kinds of trees destroyed by the fire as listed in the Bible: "terebinth, oak and carob." The reporter, creating continuity over time thus linked past and present.

It is this kind of continuity over historical time that grants meaning to the categories of "us/we" and "them/they." Destructive forces are identified with "them," while "we" are linked to constructive efforts. "They" are always dangerous outsiders who abuse and destroy the land, while "we" are allied and identified with nature. The linkage between nature, history, and collective identity is rooted in Zionist master historical narrative, which in turn was influenced by nineteenth-century European Romanticism.[12]

A similar linkage to the biblical past appeared on the fourth day on the weekly news magazine, again decrying the destruction of nature, with em-

A detail from the report on the fire at the Carmel forest in September 1989. The story represented animals as "victims of evil forces." Courtesy of the Israel Broadcasting Authority.

phasis placed on the damage the fire caused to the animals in the wildlife reserve. The reporter speaks about "biblical animals which were returned to the land of Canaan" to live as "their forefathers did." By anthropomorphizing the animals, the report presented them as a symbol of "us." Moreover, they were exhibited as innocent victims of evil forces, a pattern that clearly fits with Zionist martyrology. In the same way, the wildlife reserve came to represent the bond between the land and Israeli society. In this framework, the fire became an extension of harmful outsiders, who threatened collective existence.

The different threads of meaning present in the fire coverage were brought together and summarized in the last part of the weekly news item. A deputy director general from the Nature Reserves Authority effectively delivered a speech in the formal framework of an interview; he spoke without interruption; no questions were heard. The speech was composed of a series of expressions widely used in Israeli political discourse. Its skeleton was the basic opposition between "us" and "them," with a number of additional dichoto-

An official from the Nature Reserves Authority summarized the fire in the Carmel forest as an historical clash between forces of construction and destruction. Courtesy of the Israel Broadcasting Authority.

mies accompanying the prime conflict, granting meaning to the entire structure. The interviewee said:

> We invested our souls here for almost seventeen years, just to make a better and prettier Land of Israel, [to raise] animals that once lived here and vanished. A super-human effort to bring them back. [We only wanted] that the Land of Israel of our children and grandchildren should be the same Land of Israel in which our forefathers, who wrote the Bible, lived. Suddenly comes a hand and destroys the work of years. It destroys it in such a brutal way that there is no way to repair it but by working more years then already spent, and you stand powerless before such a manifestation of unequaled evil that only destroys what is pure and beautiful in the human soul.

In this way "we" (Israelis or Jews) are described as a constructive force, while "they" (Arabs) are destructive and threatening. "We" are the embodiment of goodness and purity, while "they" are the representatives of evil. "We" are a perennial factor, bringing past, present, and future together by working for posterity, while "they" are an ephemeral element not rooted in history. "We" are the victims, while "they" are the offenders. "We" are rational, acting according to a well-devised plan, working today for the sake of tomorrow, while "they" are impulsive, following the whims of the moment.

As a summary of the fire coverage, this speech can be seen as spanned by two axes: historical and ceremonial. The former is clearly evident in the connection repeatedly made between present and past and the recurrent references to "our forefathers." The fire is a metaphor of the evil forces that connect the isolated event of the fire to a long and painful history of outsiders who strive to harm "us." The ceremonial axis is apparent in the form of grief over a collective tragedy that may be termed civic grief. The notion of victimization is condensed into the suffering of the animals. Moreover, salient elements in the tone and the structure of the coverage are analogous to those usually found in civic memorial ceremonies in Israel. This can be seen by the use of music and in the reference to a sudden catastrophe that put an end to harmony and life. All these elements can be found in ceremonies performed during memorial days.[13]

The coverage of the fire is a prominent example of historical narrative in television news. Its structure and contents are connected to a master commemorative narrative that is largely undisputed and stresses a preferred periodization of Israeli history, marked by symbolic links between antiquity and the modern nationhood. Within this periodization some events are emphasized, like the Holocaust and the 1948 War of Independence.[14] Therefore, it is possible to state that collective memories are employed as an interpretative scheme when the available past is undisputed and well-known by the potential audiences and news staff.

A report on the Golan Heights, broadcast on May 19, 1989, on the weekly news magazine,[15] serves to illustrate this argument. Like the West Bank and Gaza, the Golan was occupied in 1967. The Syrian non-Druze population was expelled, and Israeli settlements, linked to the Israeli Labor Party, were established at an early stage. The Golan was unilaterally annexed in 1981. At the time the report was made, there was minimal opposition to this annexation within the Jewish population of Israel.

The manifest topic of the report was the work of a group of sculptors, who use basalt rock that is typical of the region. It soon developed, however, into a commemoration of the annexation, symbolically extending social boundaries to the area. The link to the Jewish past of the Golan was established by sequences of the archeological remnants of an ancient Jewish home, and the reporter said: "Some 1500 years ago, the basalt rocks were used to build tens of synagogues in twenty-seven Jewish settlements in the Golan." Later he added that a Jewish community flourished in the area. This was

A detail from the report on sculptors at the Golan Heights. The story represents the link between the sculptures and archeological remnants as "an arch between times." Courtesy of the Israel Broadcasting Authority.

reinforced by several of the sculptors, who described their work. They claimed that they were a part of the continuity of "our culture." The reporter then commented that the Golan rocks were "an arch between times," namely, a link between ancient Israeli-Jewish history and the future of Israel. The rocks were thus turned into representatives of the collective entity. No mention whatsoever was made of the period in which there was no Jewish presence in the Golan Heights. Moreover, the legitimacy of the occupation was underscored by the appearance of Druze men and women willingly helping the sculptors.

The sculptors represented "us" and "our culture"; they were working for posterity, in apparent harmony with nature and the local population. The images and verbal messages presented them with empathy; they could not be reduced to cognitive factors only. The organizer of the sculptors' work explained, "Look, we are all the time searching for a link: a link to the roots, a link to the culture, a link to the place. It is not enough just to study this link; one must feel it, experience it, and even more should create and contribute to it. Each one in his own way must add his own small stone to the

The news anchorman introduces a May 1989 story about sculptors at the Golan Heights. The report developed into a commemorating of annexation and extended boundaries. Courtesy of the Israel Broadcasting Authority.

large string that forms our culture." The report leads to recognition and identification, not only to a cognition of the sculptors' practices.

Ceremonial historical narrative is characterized by dramatization, style, and tone linking the verbal and visual contents of news to affirmation of social cohesiveness. This connection is given by connotation, which is defined as an order of signification in which a sign stands for a value system.[16] Connotation relates images and sounds to a second and third order of meaning and turns them into something that is culturally understandable. As the example illustrates, connotation enables television news to produce a definition of "us" based on cognitive and affective shades of meaning; therefore, the appearance of ceremonial historical narrative is related to a second component, namely, a prior challenge to social boundaries or to self-perception of "us." This is accompanied by an element of identification with the images of some of the people appearing in the item.

One example that illustrates these points is a weekly magazine item broadcast on March 4, 1988, some days after a report of a foreign television net-

An image of a guarding post at a kibbutz village at the pre-1967 border. The reporter links present to past by stressing that "People of this kibbutz stopped the Iraqi invaders in 1948." Courtesy of the Israel Broadcasting Authority.

work showed Israeli soldiers in the West Bank hitting and kicking two captured Palestinians. The original report stressed that the Palestinian youngsters were arrested after throwing stones during disturbances. The event generated a public debate in Israel, since it exposed a behavior that is considered to be unnormative, opposed to the army's ethos, and contrary to self-image of "us." The central issue in this magazine story was the television coverage of the Palestinian uprising in the West Bank. The debate laid open the internal dispute among Israelis about the occupation of the West Bank and Gaza.

The piece opened with the complaints of Israeli settlers in the West Bank about alleged pro-Palestinian bias of news coverage. One of them appealed for "at least objectivity." A foreign reporter reacted to this accusation, stressing the professional criteria of his job. At this point there was a sudden shift in the story's basic narrative line as viewers were taken into the pre-1967 border. The camera concentrated on the gate and the guarding position of a kibbutz village, symbolizing its role in defending the frontier. The reporter

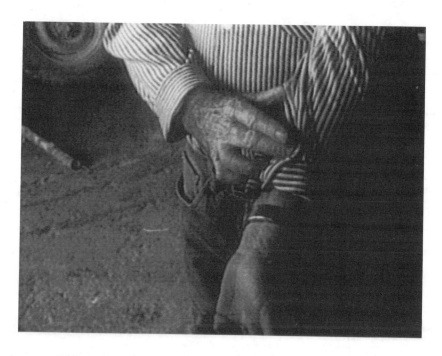

A veteran kibbutz member presents himself as a Holocaust survivor. The story turns him into a representation of collective identity. Courtesy of the Israel Broadcasting Authority.

then said that the people of this kibbutz stopped the Iraqi invaders in the 1948 War of Independence and added that its name was never stained. One of the soldiers shown hitting the Palestinians was born and educated there.

The image of the fence and the guarding position stood in stark contrast to the houses of the settlers in the West Bank, which the reporter hinted were subsidized by the government. Furthermore, the image of the kibbutz village served as vehicle of memory to a period marked by stronger internal agreement. It tied the item's contents to the accepted narrative of the 1948 War of Independence. Vehicles of memories are images (and objects) that are culturally turned into links, through which collective remembrance is created and sustained. In this matter the image of the fence and the gate of the kibbutz were also symbolic and tangible lines of demarcation that sustain and safeguard the moral definition of "us."

The use of the vehicle of memory was further developed in an interview with a veteran kibbutz member and his son. Asked about the incident, the veteran replied, "It hurt me more" (than the Palestinian hit by the soldiers).

An image of the Jordan Valley. The landscape symbolizes a bygone harmony. Courtesy of the Israel Broadcasting Authority.

He then remarked that the Palestinians had burned Israel's flag. By rolling his sleeve and hinting about a tattooed number on his arm, he presented himself as a Holocaust survivor, adding that the national symbols were extremely important for him. He was presented on the one hand as a personification of high moral standards and on the other as the embodiment of the link to the narrative of Holocaust and national revival, a salient component of the Zionist master narrative. His son also deplored the soldiers' conduct in hitting the Palestinians, and his answers served to illustrate the continuity of moral standards over generations. The interview highlighted the element of recognition and identification referred to in the previous example. The veteran's image was not only a vehicle of memory, a Holocaust survivor, he was also "one of us."

The third stage in the historical narrative opened with a long-shot sequence of the landscape of the valley surrounding the kibbutz village. The reporter then noted that the cameraman who shot the hitting incident for the foreign television network, the hitting soldier, and the commander in charge all resided in neighboring kibbutz villages in the same valley (the Jordan Valley). This particular area is of significance in the history of Israel in modern times—communities were set up there at the beginning of the century, and the foundation of Zionist presence in Palestine was established.

Of crucial importance was the use of a poetic-biblical style by the reporter. He chose words from the Book of Lamentations to indicate the tragedy involved in the situation: "How does destiny fool us . . . a photographer of birds chases soldiers and films his neighbor." The tone was one of grief over the lost unity and internal accord of the "good old days." The report expressed sorrow by turning the particular landscape of the Jordan Valley into a condensed symbol of acute internal conflict and bygone harmony.

It is possible to summarize the news item as an attempt to exorcise the shadow of the severe internal dispute. The report achieved this by identifying the conflict itself, deploring it, and building the image of "old Israel" as an anchor that helps to recover the lost cohesiveness.

The mode in which physical space is portrayed is a salient property of the previous example. The historical and geographical perspectives were depicted by the combination of the images of the Jordan Valley and the kibbutz village fence, loaded with symbols of collective memories, with verbal references to the 1948 War of Independence. They were also connected to the present by the references to the soldier, the photographer, and the commander, who represent the current rift in Israeli society. The transformation of a defined space into a symbol of the entire society is not particular to this example. The wildlife reserve at the Carmel Forest fulfilled the same purpose in the item examined above.

On another occasion, the view from a bus traveling from Tel-Aviv to Jerusalem served in the same capacity. This report appeared on July 7, 1989, a day after a Palestinian caused a bus of the same line to fall into an abyss, killing fourteen persons. The report opened with the presentation of passengers and drivers, who expressed opposed political views about the Israeli–Palestinian conflict. Again, the people images appeared to express a shared destiny. These images were then combined with collective memories to create an historical narrative and stress continuity over time. One of the interviewed drivers mentioned that he used to drive in military convoys to Mount Scopus before 1967, when it was an enclave in Jordanian-ruled East Jerusalem. Another driver told about his father, who drove in the convoys to besieged Jerusalem during the 1948 war: "My father is Haim Valinsky . . . I am Yoram Valinsky. Why should I be afraid?" He even added a reference to a well-known documentary that presented the accepted tale of Zionist history. A professional witness, the bus company's psychologist, reinforced the theme of continuity over time. She said that drivers never stopped driving, in spite of tragedy and fears, and she added "this [brave behavior] passes from one generation [of drivers] to another."

Travelers in the bus to Jerusalem in July 1989. The story presents the trip as a re-enactment of 1948 convoys to besieged Jerusalem. Courtesy of the Israel Broadcasting Authority.

In the second part of the item, the motif of the 1948 War of Independence emerged as the underlying framework of the report. The trip from Tel-Aviv to Jerusalem became a symbolic reenactment of the 1948 convoys to Jerusalem. This was done by verbal references to the remnants of armored cars from the convoys, which had been left along the route in order to serve as monuments. Thus, collective memories were linked to the physical landscape of the road to Jerusalem and the "historical landscape" attached to the "physical landscape." Two completely different situations, separated by decades, were symbolically united by means of the news narrative.

One effect of using the past as an interpretative scheme is to create a symbolic continuity over time. In this way, television news is instrumental in portraying the collective as remaining the same across the years, in spite of the changes it may have undergone. When television news uses the historic explanation, it performs a mediation over time. It is important to stress the implications of this feature of television news. Not only does the past become relevant to explain present developments, but also collective memories are reconstructed in light of present meanings.

A woman traveling to Jerusalem a day after a terror attack against a bus in the same line. The report constructs people images as a symbol of shared destiny. Courtesy of the Israel Broadcasting Authority.

Thus, past and present dwell together in television news, coexisting in the images and meanings it conveys. This description is related to the symbolic continuity over time of the collective entity, the sense of ontological security for individuals, and the existence of affective elements, which are turned into collective sentiments in the same process of mediation. This mediation over time can be summarized as creating a kind of "historical landscape," which integrates cognitive and affective elements.

Television news also performs a mediation over space, linking individuals' immediate surroundings to a "collective space," and thus delineating the geographical boundaries of the group. This mediation is achieved by loading a physical and geographical space with cognitive and affective elements. In this way, television news symbolically constructs a geographical landscape, which in turn becomes a symbol of the bond between members of the collective. However, these two types of landscape, the historical and the geographical, do not exhaust what television does by way of mediation.

There is a third important feature of mediation as a routinized practice of television news. In the process of mediation between individual and group, television news suggests who should be considered "one of us." This classification is carried out by means of images that symbolically define certain traits as common to members of society. At the same time, these images stress the difference from outsiders.

Television news is superbly suited to carry out this type of mediation, since it specializes in the visual presentation of people. The key term here is human faces, the frequent use of close-ups and medium shots, which eliminate the distances between the viewers and the images. In this way, television news fills the abstract notion of social boundaries with content. By means of identification, it constructs a human landscape that presents the category of "us."

Thus, granting meaning to events in television news through ceremonial historical narratives entails structuring these three landscapes: historical, geographical, and human. It is clear that each side of this signification triangle relies on the other two. Collective memories are often embodied in the geographical landscape. Geographical boundaries are sustained by the historical landscape. Both history and geography are seen as an extension of the attributes of the group.

Limitations to Historical Narrative

The preceding analysis highlights the construction of frames of remembrance combining social, geographical, and historical elements.[17] The signs and symbols used in television news are those that can produce an emotional attachment; therefore, identification is of key importance in the construction of this frame. The news viewers are expected to recognize the places shown in the news as testimonies of heritage and continuity of the collective over time; consequently, collective memories must be attached to a physical space and turned into "lived space."[18]

Obviously, these components limit the use of ceremonial historical narrative in Israel Television news, and other frames must be adopted to grant meaning to the concept of "us." The internal dispute in Israel over the occupied territories restricts the application of the ceremonial historical narrative frame to occasions in which collective memories are sufficiently shared. It is evident that when Israel Television news deals directly with an event taking place in the West Bank and Gaza, it cannot apply historical narrative, since these regions are at the very focus of the internal dispute; the situation dictates the use of a different frame to grant meaning to developments in those areas. This section concentrates on how that frame is built by examining the coverage of confrontations between Israeli soldiers and Palestinians during the Palestinian uprisings.

An Israeli soldier in Nablus at the West Bank during the first days of the Intifada, December 1987. Courtesy of the Israel Broadcasting Authority.

A most relevant example of this type of imagery can be found in five consecutive news items, broadcast during the first week of the Palestinian uprising between December 12 and 15, 1987. At this stage, a large part of the coverage of the uprising dealt with Israeli soldiers and their actions. The five reports showed soldiers patrolling empty streets, guarding, inspecting Palestinians at checkpoints, dealing with road blockades, or preparing to break up demonstrations. It should be noted that this way of coverage characterized the reports from the Intifada by Israel Television news.[19] Israel Television news constructed the images of soldiers by presenting and reporting the situation from the soldiers' perspective; the shots were always from their point of view. Thus, the news viewers could look at empty streets, burning tires, or rioting Palestinians apparently as the soldiers saw them.

The reports also included several interviews and close-up shots of soldiers. As a consequence, the soldiers and their conduct became closer and more understandable to the news viewers. In an outstanding sequence, the unseen reporter asked a long-haired soldier: "'Is it quiet here?' He replied: 'What do you mean quiet? It is never quiet here.'"[20] He then proceeded to don his helmet in front of the camera, an act that symbolically transforms him from an average Israeli youngster into a soldier on duty. This resembles an actor changing costumes on stage and assuming another character in front of the audience. The stress on the soldiers' perspective and their affinity to the news viewers turned their image into a human landscape and allowed identification and recognition based on a strong affective element, the images of the soldiers represented "us."

While the human landscape was present in these reports, there was no attempt to put the soldier's action in an historical perspective; there was no historical landscape of the type described above. In numerous news items, confrontations between soldiers and Palestinians in the occupied territories were referred to as jobs or missions. This left the television news to report every event in relative isolation. While there was an awareness that the event stemmed from the Israeli–Palestinian conflict, it was presented as a local episode. The conflict became routinized and reduced to a chronicle of endless incidents. This argument can be illustrated by the verbal explanation of the reporter seconds before a military unit confronted rioting Palestinians. In the December 15 item, the situation was referred to as a riot and great emphasis was put on the technical means at the disposal of the soldiers. No explanation was given for the riot during the entire report.

The lack of historical landscape was accounted for by the place of event; these were the streets of Palestinians' towns and refugee camps. Their inhabitants were located outside the social boundaries, and they were geographically placed in disputed areas from the Israeli point of view. Such circumstances precluded the attachment of collective memories to the places shown in these news items. At a cognitive level, Israel Television news offered an account of the space where the patrols, the guarding, the inspection, and the antiriot actions were taking place. The territory thereby became a site of daily occupation practices, but the space was not structured as a site of remembrance. At least part of the potential viewers would not recognize it as such, and there would be no affective attachment to the physical surroundings of the soldiers. Hence, all the streets shown in news items from the West Bank and Gaza looked alike. For the news viewers there was no sense of place, besides the general notion of the occupied territories.

The definition of the collective in these instances was based solely on the human landscape, without framing of historical or geographical landscapes. The image of the confrontation between "us" (Israelis) and "them" (Palestinians) transformed the soldiers' representation on Israel Television news into an anchor of collective identity. It must be noted here that general recruitment and the reserve system make the army in Israel an inclusive organization that provides an almost ready-made definition of the collective without the need to draw territorial frontiers.

The mode in which the images of soldiers were used as an anchor of collective identity was produced as a combination of two poles: professionalism and humanity. The former was composed of elements that symbolized the character of the army as a well-equipped, efficient, and organized body, whose members were performing a task in a disciplined and professional manner. The humanity pole stressed the aspects that underlined the similarity of the soldier to the potential Israeli news viewer. A special feature of this pole was the emphasis on the unpleasantness the confrontation with the Palestinians caused the soldiers, their suffering, and their lack of choices.

The union of the two poles was clear in the items referred to above. On the one hand, soldiers, often reservists, could be heard complaining about how they lacked training to cope with a civilian uprising. On the other hand, they were shown as a disciplined and well-equipped body. The argument can also be illustrated by means of a news item broadcast on February 6, 1988. This was a routine report. It did not deal with any exceptional events, nor was its mode of presentation in any way unusual. It was representative of a large number of items on the West Bank and Gaza broadcast from 1987 to 1990.

The piece dealt with reservists in Gaza. The reporter said that they had been enlisted ten days before, thus informing the viewers that they had already completed about one-third of their reserve duty. This remark contained two messages: the viewer was reminded that the soldiers perform a job limited in time, and also that in everyday life these were ordinary Israeli civilians. The story opened with a long shot of a soldier walking and a jeep patrolling an empty street. Thus, both the visual and the vocal messages placed these soldiers in the context of carrying out a mission, without sense of place, while the content of the report was consistent with the two-pole characterization.

The same pattern of "a job or mission" in a two-pole framework can be found in the second part of the news item. A group of reservists, some of them middle aged and wearing civilian clothes, was shown meeting the head of the army's Southern Command, to whom they expressed their opinions about the need to avoid clashes with civilians. The commander answered that the soldiers should exercise full determination when their presence was required, but at the same time they should display maximum sensitivity to human life. He stressed that bloodshed would not solve any problems. It is important to note that the two-pole theme appeared twice in this short and ordinary item, first via the voice of the reporter, and second in the general's statement. Therefore, the reporter's voice and the officer's statement mutually reinforced the two-pole concept with emphasis on the mission or job.

Granting meaning to events is achieved by encoding messages using signs

Reservists soldiers at Gaza meet the head of the army's Southern Command. Courtesy of the Israel Broadcasting Authority.

and symbols; however, in circumstances of acute internal dispute among potential viewers, news staff must be aware of the possibility of oppositional decoding. This limits one to the use of historical narrative based on collective memories. As already noted, when those memories are contested, news staff must enlist frames of reference that render their reports acceptable.

The quest for such a frame leads to the use of the soldiers as an anchor, a symbolic object to which identity can be attached. The anchor obviates the need to lean on contested collective memories or disputed spaces to define social boundaries. Historic and nonhistoric narratives coexist in this presentation of the collective. Consequently, when discourse is looked upon as whole, it emerges that the use of historical narrative and anchoring are complementary devices in delineating social boundaries.

Conclusions

The feeling of belonging to a community seems immediate and basic in daily life. There is an awareness of shared history, traits, or destiny that defines the collective, making it different from other groups and setting its social boundaries. This feeling is so prevalent that collective identity has become obvious. The idea that the group's shared history is invented, and that communities are imagined, has gained certain acceptance during the last decade.[21]

Inventing social memories and imagining a community are ongoing processes in the production of collective identity. Yet, memories can become social only through the production of knowledge, whether institutionalized or not, which mediates between the intimate experience of individuals and the abstract notion of a group. Thus, the dimensions of time and space grant meaning to the categories of "us" and "them."[22] Indeed, social knowledge defines the collective entity in relation to a territory and establishes a shared past, present, and future.

Ceremonial historical narratives are part of social knowledge, and they involve affective, and not just cognitive, components; therefore, historical narrative is not only the reflection of ideology. In terms of the previous analysis, ceremonial historical narrative enlists collective memories and arouses collective emotions. However, memories and sentiments cannot lead an objective existence; they reside only in the minds of individuals. Collective entities cannot think, remember, or feel; people can. Sentiments and memories cannot be shared unless there is a mediation between the private, or individual, experience and the public sphere. Ceremonial historical narrative, when applied by cultural mediators, is one way of making this connection.

Television news uses ceremonial historical narrative to produce versions of collective identity for dissemination among its audiences. In Eric Hobsbawm's words, "the history which became part of the fund of knowledge, or ideology, of the nation-state, or movement, is not what has actually been preserved in popular memory, but what has been selected, written, pictured, popularized and institutionalized by those whose function is to do so."[23]

Certain components of the above analysis must be highlighted. Ceremonial historical narratives are very much concerned with inclusion and exclusion from the social boundaries. Internal tensions within the collective are symbolically abolished. In television news performance, historical narrative affirms the group's cohesiveness and unity.[24] The only possible acknowledged threat comes from the outside. In the case of Israel Television news, the Palestinians are often portrayed as the embodiment of this external threat.

The construction of collective identity seems to be a straightforward task when there is a high degree of social consensus. However, it is a much more difficult and complex process in the face of acute internal conflicts. Segments within the collective may hold opposing definitions of territorial boundaries and invent opposing collective memories. The community is still imagined as an inclusive one, but memories and boundaries are contested. Unless one perception of the collective is hegemonic, mediating public institutions (national television or radio, the state educational system, national museums) must devise ways of coping with internal division and display shape, a common definition of the community.

This essay raises the possibility of problems in the relationship between social boundaries and the areas to which they apply. These boundaries are constituted and produced within a social and territorial space.[25] The essay emphasizes the problems related to the potential absence of overlapping between social and territorial boundaries. This reflects difficulties in the self-definition of a collective identity, in relation to a certain space, as expressed in internal conflicts between groups holding opposing definitions of "us."[26] Such conflicts are linked to the time dimension of collective identity.[27] The incongruity of social and territorial boundaries is expressed in the internal dispute over traditions and modes of remembering. Cultural institutions, such as television news, cannot easily use the past to interpret current developments. Ceremonial symbolic practices are possible when identity is constituted over a well-defined space. However, when this is not the case, an imagined community is produced also by other means, and not only by historical narrative practices. Cultural institutions have to develop other devices to activate inclusion and exclusion and to regulate internal conflicts.

Notes

1. J. Fiske, *Television Culture* (London: Methuen, 1987), 282.

2. E. Hobsbawm, "Introduction," in E. Hobsbawm and T. Ranger, eds., *The Invention of Tradition* (Cambridge, U.K.: Cambridge Univ. Press, 1983).

3. Later developments, like the Oslo Accords (1993), posed a challenge to the normative definition of collective identity, but they are beyond the scope of this chapter.

4. B. Kimmerling, "Boundaries and Frontiers of the Israeli Control System: Analytical Conclusions," in B. Kimmerling, ed., *The Israeli State and Society Boundaries and Frontiers* (New York: State University of New York Press, 1989), 271–72. These opposing views of "us" lead necessarily to different definitions of "them." The primordial approach sees no difference within the category of "them"; therefore, there is no distinction between the Israeli–Arab and Israeli–Palestinian conflicts.

5. S.I. Lustick, *Unsettled States, Disputed Lands* (Ithaca, N.Y.: Cornell Univ. Press, 1993), 12.

6. Central Bureau of Statistics, *Statistical Abstract of Israel* 47 (Jerusalem: Central Bureau of Statistics, 1996), 55.

7. Lustick, *Unsettled States*, 41–46.

8. S.I. Lustick, "Israeli State-Building in the West Bank and Gaza Strip: Theory and Practice," *International Organization* 41 (1987), 165.

9. Lustick, *Unsettled States*, 366.

10. Between May 1968 and November 1987, there were 1,957 news items shot in the occupied territories, and between December 1987 and January 1990 there were 862. This represents a four-fold increase in the coverage of the subject by Israel Television news.

11. It should be noted that six years later (June 2, 1995), during the peace process with the Palestinians, Israel Television news covered a fire that caused much larger damages without using historical references.

12. Y. Zerubavel, *Recovered Roots: Collective Memory and the Making of Israeli National Tradition* (Chicago: University of Chicago, 1995), 22–36.

13. D. Handelman and E. Katz, "State Ceremonial of Israel—Remembrance Day and Independence Day," in D. Handelman, ed., *Models and Mirrors: Towards an Anthropology of Public Events* (Cambridge, U.K.: Cambridge Univ. Press, 1990).

14. Zerubavel, *Recovered Roots*, 31–36.

15. It should be noted that news magazine reports are meant to offer a longer and in-depth coverage of current developments. The news magazine is broadcast on Friday evenings and is prepared by the news department of Israel Television.

16. R. Barthes, *Elements of Semiology* (London: Cape, 1973).

17. I. Irwin-Zarecka, *Frames of Remembrance: The Dynamics of Collective Memory* (New Brunswick, N.J.: Transaction Publishers, 1994).

18. H. Lefebvre, *The Production of Space* (Oxford: Blackwell, 1991), 51.

19. Y. Loshitzky, "Images of Intifada Television News: The Case of Nahalin," in A.A. Cohen and G. Wolfseld, eds., *Framing the Intifada: People and Media* (Norwood; N.J.: Ablex, 1993), 160–75.

20. The sequence was part of a report that was broadcast on December 13, 1987, and which described events in Nablus that day. The particular sequence was shot in close-up, stressing the potential familiarity of the soldier in the frame.

21. B. Anderson, *Imagined Community* (London: Verso, 1991).

22. A. Giddens, *The Consititution of Society* (Cambridge, U.K.: Polity Press, 1984), 185.

23. Hobsbawm, "Introduction," 13.

24. P. Elliott, "Press Performance as Political Ritual," in H. Christian, ed., *The Sociology of Journalism and the Press* (Keele, U.K.: University of Keele, Sociological Review Monograph no. 29, 1980), 141–77; D. Chaney, "The Symbolic Form of Ritual in Mass Communication," in P. Golding, G. Murdock, and P. Schlesinger, eds., *Communicating Politics: Mass Communication and the Political Process* (Leicester, U.K.: Leicester Univ. Press, 1986), 115–32.

25. Giddens, *The Constitution of Society*, 164–65; and P. Schlesinger, *Media, State and Nation: Political Violence and Collective Identity* (London: Sage, 1991), 173.

26. On the importance of territorial boundaries for collective identity, see Lustick, *Unsettled States*, and B. Kimmerling, "Between the Premordial and the Civil Definitions of the Collective Identity: Eretz Israel or the State of Israel," in E. Cohen, M. Lissak, and U. Almagor, eds., *Comparative Social Dynamics: Essays in Honor of S. N. Eisenstadt* (Boulder, Colo.: Westview, 1985), 262–82.

27. Schlesinger, *Media, State and Nation*, 174.

11

Memories of 1945 and 1963

American Television Coverage of the End of the Berlin Wall, November 9, 1989

David Culbert

The Berlin Wall, which came down on November 9, 1989, is a visual story whose meaning is found in the euphoria of masses of persons spontaneously removing, as they moved from East to West Berlin, the quintessential symbol of the Cold War. The events of November 9 were the stuff of banner headlines in newspapers all over the world; sometimes a dramatic event truly symbolizes a change in a system of alliances or the reshaping of a country's national identity. Such was the meaning of November 9, 1989: it marked the end of the Cold War and signaled the inevitable reunification of Germany, divided since 1945 by the ideological concerns of the United States and the Soviet Union.[1]

American network television, in an era before cable television had made major inroads, and before anyone considered the Internet as a competing news source, covered the story visually. NBC's Tom Brokaw happened to have flown to Berlin a day ahead of his CBS and ABC competitors; on November 9 he stood on a platform in front of the Brandenburg Gate to record East Berliners, who climbed the wall in celebration, undeterred by water cannons—a frosty, nonlethal form of crowd control—used by East German authorities on a cold November night. Unnoticed by German scholars who have subjected the events of November 9 to minute scrutiny, Brokaw also recorded a short interview in English with Guenter Schabowski, the East German Politburo spokesman, who announced the lifting of border restrictions. Schabowski spoke to Brokaw a few minutes after his historic press conference for German and foreign journalists on the evening of November 9.[2] The Schabowski interview in English is important confirmation of what had just been said in German, and helps contextualize explanations offered later by Schabowski and others who claimed to have lifted travel restrictions without having first cleared this with armed East German border guards.[3]

Network television defined its visual worth in the coverage of the euphoric crowds on the night of November 9. No gifted reporter, confined to words, and no still photographer, however successful in capturing a visual microcosm, could hope to compete. The end of the wall, after all, is not the tearing down of a concrete structure, but the image of masses of East Germans surging across to the capitalist West, their emotions marking the end of a Communist alternative to capitalism. The crowds tell the story, and it is a story in no way untrue even if, unlike the conventional ending of a fairy tale, those East Germans failed to live happily ever after in a capitalist Germany controlled by rich West Germans.[4]

There is more to the story of November 9 than depicting euphoria. Television news tries to offer perspective, to give events a meaning that allows the viewer to understand what he or she is seeing. Here network television offered important cathartic assistance. American viewers, including the President of the United States, George Bush—who watched television coverage of November 9 with great interest—sensed that American support for a united Germany required coming to terms with 1945 and 1963; in other words, the legacy of Nazi Germany and John F. Kennedy's remarkable speech given in Berlin on June 26, 1963, where one phrase, in German, captured all the media attention: "Ich bin ein Berliner" ("I am a Berliner"). Kennedy's remarks, incidentally, were not presented in front of the Brandenburg Gate, where he would have proved an easy target for border marksmen, but in front of the West Berlin City Hall. Kennedy offered fine words, but nothing more, reflecting his administration's decision to accept the Berlin Wall as permanent.

How did network television producers assemble the components to contextualize the events of November 9? The anchor for each network offered personal opinion; persons such as the president were shown on-camera. But the story of context is best seen in terms of selected file footage, archival footage, and sound bites provided by various "experts" incorporated into edited stories prepared to accompany what the anchor said. It is thus network film editors and producers, in New York and London, who helped viewers make sense of November 9, a process that focuses—but also restricts—memory. Another source of unintended contextualization is the larding of commercials interrupting the story. When the story is the collapse of one economic system and the triumph of another, collective meaning is found in the television commercials extolling consumer product decisions of minor moment. As Walter Goodman, the brilliant *New York Times* television critic, noted, after watching television coverage of Berlin: "Instead of campaigning for the pulling down of the Berlin Wall, Berliners will go shopping. . . . The choice between one model car and another may be a trivial and distracting sort of exercise, but in a century that has seen such horrors committed under the banners of one ideology or another, perhaps there is something to be said for the simple desires, stoked by television strictly for profit, for work-saving gadgets, well-supplied tables, attractive surroundings and a touch of luxury.[5]"

American commercial television news asks viewers to accept the visual authority of a single anchorman. In the 1960s and 1970s, before cable television, almost 80 percent of American television viewers watched the evening news, broadcast nationally for thirty minutes to coincide with an early dinner hour. By 1989, a vast percentage of this audience had vanished. As a *Wall Street Journal* story's headline proclaimed, "CBS Has Worst-Ever November." In November 1989, for example, the most-watched television program in America was a sitcom, *Roseanne,* in which an overweight comedienne offered wisecracks that went down well with millions of viewers. A.C. Nielsen, using a so-called scientific system of measurement, reported that of 92.1 million American homes with television sets, 23.6, or 21,735,600 homes, were tuned to *Roseanne,* for a 35 percent audience share. (In November 1989, each rating point represented 921,000 homes.) Thus even the most-watched sitcom attracted only a third of those who watched the evening network news in the early 1970s. In 1989, evening network news ratings were way down, to market shares of 15.1 percent for NBC; 13 percent for ABC; and 12 percent for CBS. Even if the market share was way down, it still meant that nearly fourteen million American homes were watching Tom Brokaw speak from Berlin at a time when the newspaper with the largest circulation in America, *The Wall Street Journal,* sold two million copies per day.[6] In sum, commercial network television news reached a far larger mass audience in America than any competing medium of information, albeit not every single citizen.

Thanks to the Vanderbilt Television News Archive's videotaping system and its printed finding aids, which index every daily news broadcast, including the reporter introducing the feed, commercials, and timings to the tenth of a second (including, in 1989, Cable Network News, or CNN), it is easy to study television coverage of the fall of the Berlin Wall.[7] Also most helpful is a breathless, wholly laudatory account, *Anchors: Brokaw, Jennings, Rather and the Evening News,* written with the complete cooperation of each network anchor. As a malicious *New York Times* reviewer noted, "It would be a good

idea, however, to read *Anchors* before the increasing numbers of viewers fleeing the evening news render anchormen obsolete." One entire chapter of
Anchors is devoted to Tom Brokaw and his trip to Berlin.[8]

ABC's handsome Canadian anchorman opened *World News Tonight with
Peter Jennings* with a tease: "The prisoners in the prison state are free to go ...
the most stunning news to emerge from the so-called Communist bloc in
thirty years." ABC's Don Kladstrup offered shots of the wall being torn down,
cutting to the puffy figure of Guenter Schabowski, a "member of East
Germany's ruling Politburo." Soon viewers are taken to Washington, D.C.,
where ABC's Brit Hume, speaking in front of the White House, tells us, in
voice-over, about George Bush's latest press conference, where, Hume con-
fides, the president "is scrambling to keep pace with developments." The
camera shows Bush in the Oval Office, a map of Germany on his desk;
Secretary of State James Baker is to his left; Bush fields questions from reporters:

> Q.: This is a sort of great victory for our side in the big East-West battle, but
> you don't seem elated.
>
> BUSH: I am not an emotional kind of guy.[9]

Peter Jennings then reports that the German Parliament in Bonn greeted
news of the collapse of the wall by standing spontaneously to sing the German national anthem, not reminding viewers what that might sound like.
Barrie Dunsmore, in Berlin, speaks about reunification, adding that, "the
possibility of another Adolf Hitler is not very realistic." In Washington, a
short reaction story is punctuated with some Nazi archival footage as part of
a story about the possibility of German reunification. The broadcast concludes with Peter Jennings reviewing the history of the wall, including Ronald
Reagan's speech before the Brandenburg Gate, on June 11, 1987: "Mr.
Gorbachev, tear down this wall."[10] Jennings recalls the killing by East German border guards on February 6 of the last East German to try to scale the
wall. Overall, the broadcast includes effective file footage, notes the historical significance of what has happened—the end of the Cold War—specu-
lates cautiously about German reunification, and reminds viewers, through
the Nazi file footage and the reference to Hitler, that there is a Germany of
1945 that must be reckoned with on November 10, like it or not.

CBS Evening News with Dan Rather opens with the singing, by the German Parliament in Bonn, of the German national anthem, a melody all too
familiar to listeners as "Deutschland, Deutschland ueber Alles," the official
national anthem of the Third Reich. No matter that this tune was originally
Austria's national anthem, or that officially, in 1952, West Germany decided

that only the third verse ("Einigkeit und Recht und Freiheit" ["Unity and Justice and Freedom"]) would be sung. American viewers could not understand the words, but could hardly fail to associate the tune with the Third Reich—a grim aural device for contextualizing the events of November 9 for American viewers. In Berlin, CBS's Allen Pizzey claims that the opening of the border "doesn't" open the way to unification. CBS includes good footage of crowd euphoria. Bill Plante sums up a studied confusion from Washington: "If the Cold War is really about to be over, no one here knows what happens next." After a filler report from Pentagon correspondent David Martin, the ideology of capitalism reveals itself in four straight commercials—Nabisco Shredded Wheat; Puritan Salad Oil; Sears and its low prices; and Maalox antacid for indigestion. What better way to contextualize the end of the Cold War than to replace decisions about competing ideological systems with the tale of two feckless men struggling to decide whether an oat bran cereal or Nabisco Shredded Wheat should be consumed for breakfast. Nabisco's pitch insists that no matter what one might have heard about a causal relationship between bounding good health and oat bran, nothing can possibly give better good health than eating shredded wheat for breakfast. The Maalox Moment suggests that all America is awash in indigestion; to save the day, carry bottles of Maalox in the car, at the ready.

Dan Rather returns from the string of commercials to introduce two experts from academe, brought to his New York studio to tell us what the events of the day mean. The performance by the academics should remind every other academic of the difference between criticizing television news and being part of television news. Michael Mandelbaum, introduced as a Fellow of the New York Council on Foreign Relations, offers apocalyptic analysis, the sort offered by Chicken Little: "The sky is falling."[11] Professor Mandelbaum, cliché at the ready, wonders how the West will "stem the tidal wave." He notes that "things are literally out of control" and that "Germany is a wild card." His comments suggest that a Maalox Moment is at hand.

Different—but no more enlightening—is the analysis of Stephen Cohen, from Princeton, a splendid scholar doing something for which he is poorly prepared.[12] Cohen is not to be rushed into hasty speculation; he is not to be rushed into any speculation. He asks: "Does anybody want German reunification? Not the Poles, not the Russians." Dan Rather interjects rather timidly: "The Germans." Cohen: "Which Germans?" Cut to a welcome commercial interruption. So much for academics brought on board to give special insight. CBS concludes with a report on Alzheimer's, noting that no cure is in sight. Viewers who watched the fall of the wall on CBS made a poor choice.

East Germans on top of the Berlin Wall at the Brandenburg Gate on November 9, 1989. They are using umbrellas to fend off East German water cannons. Courtesy of NBC News.

NBC's *Nightly News with Tom Brokaw* is unique. Brokaw was in Berlin on November 9, standing on a platform in front of the Brandenburg Gate, as he noted in his opening "on the most historic night in this wall's history." In *Anchors,* Brokaw—a strikingly handsome man, incidentally, the sort once referred to as a matinee idol—declares that his greatest worry is that he had to borrow a colleague's overcoat, at least one size too large, because his L.L. Bean jacket was not heavy enough for a November evening in Berlin. Only a professional haberdasher would see the problem.[13] More significant is Brokaw's ability to direct the NBC cameraman to show East German water cannons failing to reduce the ardor of East Germans standing on top of the wall near the Brandenburg Gate, drenched, cold, but exuberant in a way so easy to see, an opportunity given to every NBC viewer. Those East Germans, some with umbrellas, embody the end of the East German state; it is a visual story; NBC's Tom Brokaw was there to tell viewers what it felt like. This is a glorious moment for the medium of television, and a defining moment for a system of anchor celebrities not likely to last much longer.

Guenter Schabowski, Communist Party propaganda chief during his November 9, 1989, interview with Tom Brokaw in English. Courtesy of NBC News.

Brokaw then cuts to his interview, in English, with Guenter Schabowski. Not knowing his official title, he identifies him as "Communist Party propaganda chief." What Schabowski says in English to Brokaw comes just after Schabowski's press conference on the evening of November 9, where he amazed hundreds of German and foreign reporters (the latter listening to a simultaneous translation) by noting the sudden end to East German travel restrictions. Tom Brokaw's interview is a significant part of the story of how the wall came down.

What follows is an exact transcription of what was aired, including body language:

Scene: partying Germans passing bottles of champagne to each other in the street. Rampant jubilation.

Voice-over (BROKAW): Along the wall tonight, jubilation as the word spread. East Germans are being told if they apply for visas tomorrow morning they will be granted immediately and they can leave through the Berlin Wall checkpoint.

Cut to press conference, where East German officials on a dais, including

Schabowski, respond to questions in German. Simultaneous translation into English. A puffy, rather bloated Schabowski looks and sounds harried.

Voice-over (BROKAW): We first heard about this tonight almost by accident in the closing minutes of a news conference with Guenter Schabowski, the Communist Party propaganda chief.

Cut to small, ill-lit office, obviously not big enough to film reaction shots of Brokaw. Schabowski finishes reading some papers; he takes off his glasses. Partial establishing shot of Brokaw with Schabowski.

Voice-over (BROKAW): When I sat down with him for an interview, he was still learning about the new policy.

Close-up (BROKAW): Mr. Schabowski, do I understand correctly, citizens of the GDR can leave through any checkpoint that they choose for personal reasons? They no longer have to go through a third country?

Close-up (SCHABOWSKI): Uh. They are not further forced to leave GDR by, uh, uh, transit, uh, through another country.

BROKAW: It is possible for them to go through the wall at some point?

SCHABOWSKI *(cutting Brokaw off):* It is possible for them to go through the border. *(Smiles)*

BROKAW: Freedom to travel?

SCHABOWSKI: Yes, of course. It is no question of tourism. It is the permission of leaving GDR. *(Schabowski gestures, pointing his finger in the air.)*

BROKAW: One of the ways that you would prove your good intentions is to hold elections, which you have announced that you are willing to do. When?

SCHABOWSKI *(looking away):* This question is to be decided, is still to be decided. If you fix a date, I think it is a second step. The first step is to, uh, have the conditions for ef-election, of free elections. And the conditions must be discussed. *(Places hand over his mouth; points with index finger; then holds chin.)*

BROKAW: You have spent most of your adult life as a prominent official in the party, in the Communist Party in the GDR. Given what has happened in the *(reaction shot of Schabowski, hand over his mouth)* last three months, do you think the personal investment that you've made in the Party has been a mistake, or a waste?

SCHABOWSKI *(fiddling nervously with shirt pocket, inside suit jacket, near his left shoulder):* It was not mistake. I'm. I'm a convinced Communist, you see . . . Of course we—

BROKAW *(interrupting):* Even now?

SCHABOWSKI: I. Even now. On the other hand *(hand on chin),* of course we see the troubles and we see the mistakes and there is a lot of work which we have to do. And we see the mistrust of the people, uh, and, uh, we understand that it is a very, very, difficult task. But it is a task.[14]

Remember that Schabowski feels his English is good enough—and it is—to risk an interview with an unknown American television reporter just after he has given the public signal for the collapse of communism, knowing that Mikhail Gorbachev in Moscow has insisted that force may no longer be used to keep East Germans inside their own country. All in all, a remarkable interview, both for Brokaw and Schabowski and for the medium of television.[15]

History has been hard on Guenter Schabowski, a scapegoat for East Germans seeking retribution since 1989. In December 1999, seventy years old, suffering from diabetes, he entered prison for three and a half years, convicted by a unified Germany's court system of complicity in East Germany's policy to shoot citizens who tried to escape over the wall. At the time of his sentencing, Schabowski offered an apologia for the actions of what he termed a "failed regime." As he stated, "those who died at the wall are part of the burden we inherit from our misguided attempt to free humanity from its plagues. As a former supporter and protagonist of this world view, I feel guilt and shame when I think of those who died at the wall."[16]

Tom Brokaw, excited about his interview, and no doubt feeling a touch of jet lag, then referred to the current German Chancellor as Helmut Schmidt, soon correcting himself ("I meant Helmut Kohl"), apparently presuming that one chancellor named Helmut was as good as another.

The broadcast cut to NBC's London bureau for some contextualization. French political commentator Olivier Todd says, "I like Germany so much I want two of them forever. Deep down most French feel that way."[17] Cut to footage from Leni Riefenstahl's 1935 glorification of Nazi Germany, *Triumph of the Will*, a "subtle" editor's statement about how much to trust the Germans. As if that were not enough, the London story cuts to an interview with former Irish cabinet minister Conor Cruise O'Brian, who refers to the economic threat of a reunified Germany as a "Fourth Reich." NBC's broadcast concludes with color footage of Kennedy's 1963 speech in Berlin, used in voice-over, in part, as images elide with recent shots of mass demonstrations in East Berlin just before the collapse of the wall—JFK is made to anticipate the events of November 9, when his original speech did just the opposite. In sum, NBC's broadcast offered viewers mixed signals—Brokaw's euphoria in Berlin versus the visual reminders of a German past and future threat in reports from London and New York. Still there is no question that NBC covered November 9 far, far better than CBS or ABC.

How about cable? Anyone who viewed the fall of the wall on CNN got precious little. CNN, with Lou Waters and Susan Rook, opened its Atlanta evening news not with the story of the end of the Berlin Wall, but with the crash of a Navy jet in an Atlanta suburb, a crash in which nobody was hurt. Too poorly funded, or too thrifty, CNN covered the fall of the wall entirely with file footage purchased elsewhere, using Doug Janes on the telephone to describe the day's events. Talk about throwing away the potential of a visual medium. In November 1989, CNN clearly deserved the contempt with which it was held by competing television news organizations. Still, when CNN, in Washington, sought to contextualize the day's events by speaking to selected political leaders—sort of a man-in-the-Congress interview—what Stephen Solarz, Democrat from New York, said was the stuff of effective on-camera interviews: "The Berlin Wall has become a functional irrelevancy."

In terms of unintended irony, one of many CNN commercial interruptions provided a wonderful commentary on the events of November 9. Grape Nuts cereal, like East Germany, has a past it hopes to live down. The cereal was formerly pitched to the elderly. Commercials showed handsome elderly models in improbably good shape who claimed that a bowl of Grape Nuts explained why they never gained weight and excelled in every sort of senior athletic endeavor. In November 1989, Grape Nuts hoped to reposition itself to meet the needs of a health-conscious younger generation. The commercial features a fine figure of a man who tells us that he is thirty-five. (East Germany celebrated its fortieth anniversary in October 1989.) The Grape Nuts on-camera spokesman dares not be too enthusiastic about the same old breakfast cereal, now somehow just right for today's youth: "The taste ... it's not fancy ... but it's really good.... And feeling good about it." Triumphalist capitalism. An end to ideology ... with Grape Nuts.

What, in sum, does American television coverage of November 9, 1989, offer as to meaning? First, television offers a story with closure. We see a powerful visualization of freedom—those exuberant crowds pouring over and through the wall are not celebrating a sports upset. Nor are they promising to live happily ever after in a state of suspended bliss. What is freedom? We see it, and we see it every time television footage of those crowds on November 9 is aired. Second, the Cold War is over. Third, German reunification is inevitable, even if some network producers and some on-camera interviews suggest otherwise. The surging crowds at the wall will prevail against the doubters. Fourth, the events of November 9 indicate the triumph of capitalism over communism. It really is simple; it really is obvious; and television images tell the story, memorably.

Some other conclusions are less obvious, or could not have been predicted in November 1989. For example, the extraordinary difficulties of what Peter

Schneider, in *The Wall-Jumper*, termed the walls inside the minds of East and West Germans.[18] Reunification includes the terrible realization that in some ways cultural expectations in East and West Germany, after forty years, truly have created two very different societies. Of course, the difficulties and tensions of reunification since 1990, all highly publicized, are the key to world acceptance of German reunification. Hardliners are mollified by all those problems, as yet unresolved. When I raised this matter in a talk I gave on November 10, 1999, in Frankfurt-an-der-Oder, right on the Polish border, a German professor in the audience bluntly rephrased my delicate words: "You mean we got gypped."[19] Perhaps that directness also indicates the contempt so many West Germans feel for Ossies.

American television producers relied on file footage to provide contextualization, in a way that invited little thoughtful reflection. Images were asked to speak for themselves, though many file images spoke at best obliquely, if at all. Some events were deemed of no moment to American viewers. No network reminded anyone of the Berlin airlift; no network mentioned the Holocaust specifically; no network mentioned the uprising in East Berlin on June 17, 1953, though this would have been inevitable in any German television story about November 9. Instead, collective memories of a Germany to be feared, or hated, or never forgiven, were encapsulated in momentary bits of visual history—*Triumph of the Will;* Hitler's troops parading past Napoleon's Arch of Triumph in Paris, 1940; Kennedy's 1963 Berlin speech; and Ronald Reagan's June 1987 challenge to Gorbachev: "Tear down this wall."

Some comments about journalistic performance are in order. This was not a CNN story; the 1991 Gulf War was. CNN's coverage reveals the amateur status of cable in 1989. For network news, Berlin 1989 is but part of a downward trajectory of American viewing preferences for a thirty-minute evening news program, from 80 percent of all homes with televisions in America (virtually every single home) in the early 1970s, to 57 percent in 1989, to 45 percent in 1999, and still falling. It seems clear that network evening news will go the way of the newsreel, but for different reasons. November 9 network news was a time of intrusive commercial interruptions. A full 25 percent of the thirty-minute program was given over to pitches for breakfast cereals, cheap motel rooms, relief from stomach gas—all commercials in which the viewer is encouraged to make a choice, but between products for which demand must be artificially created. Nobody growing up in America needs to be reminded about commercials—the rich outpouring assures a process of desensitization. But to look at November 9, 1989, when a choice of economic systems was given definitive answer, is an opportunity to think about just how trivial are the "choices" offered by capitalist ideology: "And now a word from our sponsor." November 9, 1989, will be remembered in terms of moving images; it is television's story. No matter that Brokaw, Jennings, and Rather (the latter two arrived for November 10) could not ask a question without using an interpreter. No matter that *The New York Times* offered splendid, overwhelming, coverage in print. The visual center of the wall was the Brandenburg Gate; this was the visual backdrop for crowds who came and responded emotionally before cameras set up to record the actions of crowds. November 9 is a crowning achievement for television news; it will be remembered in terms of ecstatic, euphoric crowds, whose collective response captures the spirit of a song of another people no longer in bondage: "Free at last, free at last, Thank God Almighty, we are free at last."

Notes

1. Philip Zelikow and Condoleezza Rice, *Germany Unified and Europe Transformed: A Study in Statecraft* (Cambridge, Mass.: Harvard Univ. Press, 1995); see also Jonathan Osmond, "The End of the GDR: Revolution and Voluntary Annexation," in Mary Fulbrook, ed., *German History Since 1800* (London: Arnold, 1997), 454–73.

2. See Guenter Schabowski, *Der Absturz* (Berlin: Rowohlt, 1991), 301. He describes himself as "so-called media spokesman for the SED—Sogenannter Medien-Verautwortlicher der SED." Schabowski's notes and the piece of paper from which he read at the November 9 press conference are reproduced in Thomas Fleming and Hagen Koch, *Die Berliner Mauer: Geschichte eines politischen Bauwerks* (Berlin: Bebra, 1999), 115–17. Schabowski was born on January 4, 1929. He was the notorious editor-in-chief of the Party newspaper, *Neues Deutschland*, 1968–1985, and a member of the Politburo's Central Committee, 1984–1989.

3. See Roger Cohen, "Haphazardly, Berlin Wall Fell a Decade Ago," *The New York Times*, November 9, 1999, A1. This article concerns the testimony of Harald Jaeger, border guard from 1961 to 1989, who opened the Bornholmer Strasse gate about 11 P.M., the first formal opening of the wall. Jaeger recalls having watched Schabowski on television, then calling his superior, Colonel Rudi Ziegenhorn, for orders. There were none to be had. Schabowski, *Der Absturz*, 302–11, describes the press conference with no mention of the NBC interview. Egon Krenz later claimed the wall was to have been opened at 4 A.M.; Schabowski says his notes of the meeting said "at once."

4. The problems of reunification since 1989 can hardly be a secret. For a good overview, see Mary Fulbrook, "Ossis and Wessis: The Creation of Two German Societies," in Fulbrook, *German History*, 411–31.

5. Walter Goodman, "The Video Age and the Wall That Opened," *The New York Times*, November 20, 1989, III, 22.

6. Kevin Goldman, "CBS Has Worst-Ever November as NBC Tops TV 'Sweeps' Ratings," *The Wall Street Journal*, November 30, 1989, II, 6; Jeremy Gerard, "ABC Sur-

passes CBS in Evening News Ratings," *The New York Times,* November 29, 1989, C22; Felicity Barringer, "CBS News May Face More Cuts," *The New York Times,* September 9, 1999, C8; and Robert Goldberg and Gerald Jay Goldberg, *Anchors: Brokaw, Jennings, Rather and the Evening News* (New York: Carol Publishing Group, 1990), 30–36.

7. See John Lynch, "Vanderbilt Television News Archive," *Historical Journal of Film, Radio and Television* 16:1 (1996), 81–83.

8. See Goldberg and Goldberg, *Anchors,* 254–68, including interview with ABC producers as well as Brokaw. See the review by Mary Perot Nichols, *New York Times Book Review,* October 14, 1990, 12.

9. See "Remarks and a Question-and-Answer Session with Reporters on the Relaxation of East German Border Controls," November 9, 1989, *Public Papers of the Presidents of the United States: George Bush 1989—Book II—July 1 to December 31, 1989* (Washington, D.C.: GPO, 1990), 1488–90. See also "Memcoms," memorandums of telephone conversations between Bush and Kohl, recently declassified by the Bush Presidential Library and excerpted in *Newsweek.*

November 10, 1989

BUSH: "I want to see our people continue to avoid especially hot rhetoric that might by mistake, cause a problem . . .

KOHL: Thank you. Give my best to Barbara. Tell her that I intend to send sausages for Christmas."

(*Newsweek,* November 8, 1999, 44.)

10. See "Remarks on East-West Relations at the Brandenburg Gate in West Berlin," June 12, 1987, *Public Papers of the Presidents of the United States: Ronald Reagan 1987—Book I—January 1 to July 3, 1987* (Washington, D.C.: GPO, 1989), 634–38. The entire speech on video is available from Steve Branch, Audiovisual Archives, Ronald Reagan Presidential Library, FAX 1–805–579–9428.

11. Michael Mandelbaum is currently Professor of American Foreign Policy at the Johns Hopkins School of Advanced International Studies.

12. Stephen Cohen is Professor of Russian History at Princeton and author, among many books, of the best biography in English of Bukharin.

13. The breathless tale of the coat is found in Goldberg and Goldberg, *Anchors,* 265.

14. NBC broadcast, November 9, 1989, 5:31:40 to 5:34:20, Vanderbilt Television News Archive. For background, see Goldberg and Goldberg, *Anchors,* 259–63.

15. Brokaw could not figure out why Schabowski agreed to the interview; according to the Goldbergs, *Anchors,* 259–60, "today American anchors are surprisingly well-known abroad." I screened Brokaw's coverage of November 9 in Berlin in September 1999, and in Frankfurt (Oder) the next month, and not a single person in either audience had ever heard of, or seen, Tom Brokaw. How many Americans can identify even the best-known news presenter on any German television news program?

16. Quoted in Edmund L. Andrews, "Long After the Wall, Questions About Punishment," *The New York Times,* December 26, 1999, A3.

17. The same quip is described as one of French President Francois Mitterrand's favorites: "Germany was such a splendid place, it was a good thing there were two of

them." Roger Cohen, "For the Wall's Fall, East Germans Are Given Their Due," *The New York Times,* November 10, 1999, A3.

18. Peter Schneider, *The Wall Jumper* (New York: Pantheon, 1983), 119: "It will take us longer to tear down the Wall in our heads than any wrecking company will need for the Wall we can see." Schneider was no more prescient than anyone else about the end of communism. In his "If the Wall Came Tumbling Down," *The New York Times Magazine,* June 25, 1989, VI, 70, he concludes: "There is no 'human right' of German unification and there will continue to be two German states." In early August 1989, Martin Loiperdinger and I made a day trip to East Berlin. Neither of us had the faintest sense that there was any change whatsoever in the air.

19. Thanks to Rainer Rother, who invited me to explore the subject, visually, at "The Media and Political Change in Europe," Martin-Gropius-Bau, September 1999, a building literally part of the Berlin Wall, two blocks from the Brandenburg Gate; thanks too to Gerhard Jakob, with whom I stood in the crowd before the Brandenburg Gate on the evening of November 9, 1999, and who invited me to speak at Europa-Universitaet Viadrina, Frankfurt (Oder), the next night. Thanks too, to my research assistant, James Hughes.

12 Television

The First Flawed Rough Drafts of History

Philip M. Taylor

Television, the predominant mass medium of the second half of the twentieth century (at least in industrialized countries) remains largely neglected by historians as a primary archival source. Radio, sometimes referred to as "the forgotten medium," has suffered a similar fate, even though it remains a primary source of news, information, and entertainment for millions of people (especially in developing countries). Where the mass media are concerned, mainstream history has just begun to accept the press and the cinema as legitimate "windows into the past." So what is it about the newer media of broadcasting that generally makes historians nervous about utilizing them in their archival research? Why indeed is it still rare to find a history textbook of the twentieth century—which is distinct from all other centuries before it by virtue of the mass media—that embraces these important forms of communication as a central theme? Typically, there are occasional references or side-glances to the media, but the emphasis tends to remain on those people and events that "make" history rather than on how those people and events were observed, portrayed, and perceived by the rest of humankind. Of course, that relatively recent and growing breed of media historians are more sympathetic to the realization that the mass public are not simply passive observers of history but, via the mass media, are actual participants in the life and times of "the great and the good." But even they get terribly frustrated at the reluctance of so-called mainstream historians to embrace the media as a primary source for how the doings of the few are mediated to the many. Equally, it has to be conceded that they have repeatedly failed to have their research findings integrated into the mainstream of historical research.

Media historians and that other, even newer, subspecies—the cultural historian—gather together at conferences and are unanimous in their condemnation that the "big names" do not condescend to attend. When they occasionally do—Stephen Ambrose talking about *The Longest Day* or A.J.P. Taylor on the Ministry of Information in World War Two—the media historians congregate afterward to whisper about how what they have just heard reveals how much the "big names" do not really understand the media. But is this not due more to the failure of media and cultural historians to drive home their conviction that the media really are significant rather than to the failure of mainstream historians to see what is blatantly obvious to the already converted? Or is it due to the nature of the media themselves? We have long referred to newspapers as "the first rough drafts of history," but most historians would deride social scientists for regarding the press as either a reliable or indeed as a primary source of information. Perhaps, in their heart of hearts, because they do actually understand the media, historians understand that broadcasting suffers from similar deficiencies.

There are some well-known logistical obstacles. Broadcasting has developed, whether in its public service or commercial manifestations, as an *industry* and, as such, it feels no obligation to preserve its output for subsequent scrutiny. Its very immediacy gives it its potency, and within the industrial context, if there is an urge to preserve the output, it is for subsequent repeat broadcasting or for sale to other broadcasters. This is hardly conducive to introducing coherent archival policies. As a result, there is no broadcasting organization anywhere in the world that holds a complete collection of its output from the moment it began transmission. Long-standing organizations like the BBC have large and unique holdings, but they are nonetheless incomplete. And because of the commercial opportunities for selling such material on to other broadcasting organizations, the costs of accessing this material are usually beyond the limited budgets of academic research. As a result, scholarly output about the BBC, for example, is usually confined to research undertaken at the BBC Written Archives Centre at Caversham without the author having actually heard or seen the programming that was heard and seen by the audience at the time.

Most historians are still trained to analyze paper documentation, and it is not unnatural that they should feel most at home with the written word. After all, the written word remains their own primary medium for their own professional output. But when program makers with larger budgets access the surviving audiovisual material in order to make "television history," the historians are usually still unhappy. The rows between historians and program producers over the making of the BBC's 1960s series *The Great War* are now legendary, and although many of the lessons learned were rectified in the making of Thames Television's *The World at War* and subsequent good television history, the tension remains. It is, therefore, astonishing that it was not until 1999 at the IAMHIST (International Association of Media and History) scholarly conference hosted by the University of Leeds that, finally, program makers and historians sat down together to discuss the issues in terms of how to move forward together.

As Nicholas Pronay pointed out at the Leeds conference, history program production is currently undergoing enormous popularity, as is shown by the presence of The History Channel on most satellite and cable services. This new popularity may be linked to the usual *fin de siecle* retrospectiveness about the departing century, the only century about which we have an (albeit incomplete) audiovisual record. As an aside, however, it is a damning testimony to the power of the media as well as to the impotence of the historical profession to convince the mass public that the new millennium didn't begin until January 1, 2001. But still too few historians are utilizing television in particular as a primary source material for the second half of the twentieth century. And this can't simply be explained away by excessive research costs or the lack of National Television Archives. A great deal of broadcasting output *has* survived, often admittedly more by accident than design, and I would hazard a guess that indeed a higher proportion of broadcast material has survived than has cinema production output. This material may be in centers like the Vanderbilt Television Archive (since 1968) or in the National Film and Television Archive, or it may be in the personal collections of individual academics who have (since the early 1980s) embraced the video recorder as a means of building up their own source materials. It is also relatively cheap for an individual or an academic department to decide to record, for example, all the news output on any given event—such as the death of Princess Diana or the Kosovo conflict. But this relatively random process serves neither the significance of broadcasting in the twentieth century nor the twentieth century itself.

With the new millennium, moreover, things can only get worse for two reasons. Broadcasting, as we traditionally understand it, is undergoing massive technological change. With the digital, multichannel, and interactive era unfolding, it will be virtually impossible to preserve all television output, especially once interactive services allow the viewer to determine not just what they want to watch and when, but even what camera angle they wish to view the output from. The age when it was possible to gauge with relative accuracy what a proportion of the population was watching at any given time may therefore appear to be passing, but in fact the fragmentation of the audience across a multichannel, digital environment allows for even greater accuracy of the measurement of who is watching what and when. Just as when one calls a help line of a mobile phone company, the receiver in the call center knows who is calling without the caller having to identify him or herself, so also can digital broadcasters identify the viewer of a particular program in the same way and on the same principle as the "cookie" leaving an identifying mark when one visits a website while surfing the Internet. But the motives for identifying a particular audience are once again commercial—for advertising directed at specific target groups, for example—and are not designed to serve the archival needs of future historians. And as more and more broadcasters move to the Internet as a form of program delivery, how much more difficult it will be for those future historians to utilize records that are not currently being preserved if they are to talk sensibly about the information revolution.

The second reason that television is becoming more difficult relates to the massive expansion of broadcast services. Whereas it was once possible—even though it was not done—to preserve the broadcast output of Britain's or America's terrestrial broadcasting stations when they were fewer in number, it is now almost inconceivable to imagine *all* the output of the hundreds and thousands of broadcast stations ever being preserved for posterity. We can't even talk any more about *broad*casting in the old sense of the word. Whereas once we had national services like CBS or the BBC, which would see their remit as providing a variety of programming—news, documentaries, quiz shows, current affairs, films and dramas—in one evening's output, now we have specific channels for all of those types of programming. This *narrow*casting—CNN, the Cartoon Channel, MTV, and the like—enables the viewer to select a particular genre of programming and leads to even further fragmentation of the audience. How will future historians cope with this, especially as that audience is now a global one with a truly international reach for the most successful programs?

This issue could perhaps be resolved if we decided now to select particular channels for future posterity. I would guess that most historians, with their predisposition toward "facts," would instinctively prioritize news and current affairs programming for future scrutiny. Such selectivity would, in itself, be making the same mistake as that made by news and current affairs program producers who provide for us these first audiovisual rough drafts of history. This is because news programs do not necessarily reveal all the facts on a given day about events that are taking place. Television news may have become since the 1960s the most preferred and trusted medium of news provision for audiences in developed countries, but that does not mean it is the most reliable or accurate source. It is very much a *flawed* first rough draft of history, and any future historian utilizing it as a primary source of evidence must be aware of the factors that make it so.

These can be summarized essentially as industrialized pressures that militate against the creation of an accurate window on the world. Perhaps we expect too much of our news. We have been brought up in a liberal western tradition whereby certain standards in news dissemination have come to be expected—impartiality, accuracy, reliability, and truthfulness. Yet in reality, to borrow Walter Lippmann's phrase, the "pictures inside our heads" about the happenings of the world around us beyond our direct experience are mapped out for us by news-gathering *organizations,* which operate according to financial, technological, and corporate constraints. News gathering is a very expensive business. Foreign news in particular requires reporters to be dispatched with crews and equipment to faraway lands for indefinite periods and thus unlimited expense and hotel costs. Consequently, the decision to dispatch a reporter to cover a news story is a serious one, and the significance and relevance of the story for the home audience is a determining factor. This partly helps to explain why only two or three of the world's twenty or so conflicts receive media attention at any given time. The result is what might be termed "forgotten wars," about which little is known to the majority of people who rely on the media not so much to tell them what to think, but certainly what to think about.

Rightly or wrongly, most editors today, especially in the United States, do not believe their audiences to be interested in foreign affairs. The decline in the number of foreign correspondents since the end of World War II is especially marked. In 1945, American news organizations deployed around 2,500 reporters on overseas assignments, but by the mid-1970s that number had fallen to around 500. Having said that, wars in which national troops are employed show a reverse trend. There were around 450 reporters covering the Normandy Landings in 1944, but by the time of the Persian Gulf War in 1991, there were around 1,500 journalists in Riyahd and another 1,500 waiting to secure accreditation. As Gen. Michael Dugan said, "1,500 is not an unmanageable number, but it is a number that cries out for management."[1] This in turn reveals another constraint on the journalist attempting to gather an accurate picture of events. The "fog of war" is itself difficult enough for journalists to penetrate, but the growing breed of professional information officers that now accompany reporters into battle also influences what can or cannot be said or shown to a watching global audience.

The profession of the war correspondent is around 150 years old, and it is no coincidence that the practice of modern military censorship is about the same age. Ever since the Crimean and American Civil Wars, soldiers have feared journalists and have constructed all sorts of obstacles to prevent them from getting not so much at the truth but certainly at the whole truth.[2] The time-honored justification for military censorship is that no journalist should reveal information that might prove useful to the enemy, thereby jeopardizing the lives of the very troops whom the journalists are accompanying into battle. With the arrival first of cinema and subsequently television cameras, this fear increased considerably, especially as technology provided journalists with the ability to report live from the battlefield. An unwitting shot of a road sign in the background of a report might reveal invaluable information to a watching enemy, and so very careful scrutiny of copy and pictures now takes place in the name of operational security.

Most experienced journalists understand this, but since the 1980s, with the arrival of Electronic News Gathering (ENG) technology *and* a dramatic increase in the number of freelance reporters caused by increased commercialization and competition among the world's media organizations, the problem is compounded. Such freelancers are often young, inexperienced, and quite ruthless in the lengths they are prepared to go to get a story. During the Kosovo crisis in 1999, there were more than three thousand reporters of all kinds attempting to cover the story, and many of the freelancers were "loose cannons" who respected neither their military minders nor their more experienced and contracted colleagues.

Perhaps, in one sense, they are right to do so. It is too often forgotten that the record of military-media relations throughout the twentieth century is one far more of cooperation than conflict. Journalists who attached themselves to troops theoretically to observe conflict actually became participants by the distorted and one-sided reports they produced. Journalists are often every bit as patriotic as the soldiers, and they are given access for very good military reasons—namely, the soldiers need popular and, therefore, media support for their endeavors. Since the First World War, an increasingly professionalized group of public affairs or public information officers has grown in significance in order to feed a hungry press corps, and inevitably the military agenda influences considerably the media agenda. One need only recall during the first week of the 1991 Gulf War that global television audiences were mesmerized by shots taken by cameras mounted on the nose of precision-guided weaponry prior to the screen going blank. Those pictures were supplied to the media by the military. There were no pictures (until long after the war) of missiles missing their targets. Indeed, this media reliance on the military for the story created some frustration among journalists and helps to explain why they behaved the way they did when the time came to take pictures for themselves—namely, when the Iraqi Scud missiles began to fall over Saudi cities only to be intercepted by Patriot missiles fired by the American-led coalition forces.

We now know that those Patriot missiles were not as accurate as was portrayed at the time. We also know now that less than 10 percent of the weapons deployed against the Iraqis were "smart" weapons. At the time, however, the media—and television in particular—portrayed the progress of the Gulf War as a "smart," clean, video game–type war in which death was largely absent. Nothing could have been further from the truth, especially for the Iraqi forces in occupied Kuwait and southern Iraq. But by amplifying the peripheral to a central media theme, a completely distorted impression was conveyed, and the picture-hungry medium of television was the magnifying glass instead of the window.

This leads us to a distinction between what might be termed "real war" and "media war." Real war is about the brutal, nasty business of people killing people. Media war, on the other hand, is merely an audiovisual representation of that reality, which by its very nature is a mediated version of events. The one does not necessarily reflect accurately the other. Television news reports in evening bulletins may stretch to three minutes—barely enough time to report the complexity of world events. They need pictures, and since wars and conflicts are dangerous places, it may simply be impossible to get them. And diplomacy is even more difficult to report. Shots of limousines driving up to a building, men in suits getting out of the car and walking to the door, "photo-ops" of the delegates followed by men sitting around a table, are hardly the stuff of exciting television. It is really only when a crowd gathers to demonstrate—as in Seattle in 1999 for the World Trade Organization talks—that such events become newsworthy, and then only if the news organization has decided to send a reporter in the first place. Whereas analysts of news coverage once used to talk about "bad news" being the principal criterion of newsworthiness, now they talk about the "dumbing down" of the news. All these developments hardly fill the historian with confidence about the value of television news as an archival source.

Compressing the events of the world into a package of three-minute bulletins determined by the availability of pictures of bad news stories undeniably provides a distorted view of reality. But it also reveals that we do indeed expect too much of the news; for news is in fact a part of the entertainment industry, and is becoming more so. Television news is increasingly tabloidized as news programs compete for audiences by delivering "infotainment," focusing mainly on human-interest stories.[3] A few years ago, the most important piece of equipment in an American newsroom was a helicopter, so that exciting pictures of a crime scene could be relayed before the police arrived. One need only think of the coverage of the O.J. Simpson car chase to illustrate this point. The ability of networked news to "go live" drives the nature of the coverage. The arrival of twenty-four-hour live news services like CNN, Sky News, or BBC Live 24 means that they have an enormous amount of air time to fill and thus, in theory, have more time to concentrate on stories at greater length and depth. But apart from events like the Gulf War, audiences rarely watch live TV news for twenty-four hours at a time. However, by devoting considerable resources to global news gathering, such services are often able to relay stories of significance more quickly than traditional diplomatic or political communications systems. This is why computer screens in the White House have CNN running in a small box on the top right-hand side of the monitor. Over the past ten years, numerous officials have testified to the pressures created by the so-called CNN Effect.[4] They argue that live television coverage decreases the time they once had for decision making. Whereas once, intelligence reports would come in raising issues of actual or possible concern for policy and the policy makers, secure in the absence of public scrutiny or media pressure, could take time to consider their options and possible actions, now they no longer enjoy such temporal luxury. Pictures may be being transmitted of a highly emotive nature—television is at its best when it plays to the heart rather than the head—and images of refugee women and children create additional pressures on policy makers to do something to stop the screen suffering. Somalia in 1992 provides a classic example of this "push" impact of television, and few who saw them will forget the pictures of American forces landing on Somali beaches lit up by the lights of the waiting media crews. But Somalia also illustrates the "pull" impact of television, because several months later, pictures of a dead American airman being dragged through General Aideed's camp shocked sufficient American viewers to jam the White House telephone exchange. Within days, American troops were withdrawn from Somalia.

The notion of foreign policy being determined by television images is an alarming one. Television-weaned politicians like President Clinton and Prime Minister Tony Blair are renowned for their "spin doctoring" because they recognize the importance of ensuring that their own political agenda dominates the media agenda rather than the other way round. Mostly they are quite successful at this, but they cannot guarantee success, as the Monica Lewinsky affair or the humanitarian crisis in Kosovo illustrates. Part of the reason for this again relates to the growth of the freelancer. A professional journalist did not in fact take those pictures of the dead American airman in Somalia. Somalia had become too dangerous for reporters and most had actually left by that time. However, a Reuters news crew gave their camera to their driver (the infamous "technicals") with instructions to film anything interesting. Perhaps the most influential amateur footage in recent times was the video recording taken of the Rodney King beating, which led to the Los Angeles riots. There was once a time when respectable TV stations would never have transmitted such poor quality footage. But in the age of the mobile phone and the palmcorder, ordinary citizens are given greater opportunity to serve as eyewitness reporters. Hence, the rules that have traditionally governed the responsibilities of reporters as a profession have changed considerably—as was illustrated perfectly in the mid-1990s when a Greece-Turkey crisis was precipitated by a group of journalists who decided to stake a claim to a disputed island in the Aegean Sea.

Live reporting reveals further problems. Because the expensive satellite time has been booked, many stations feel compelled to "go live" to a reporter "on the spot" even if nothing is happening. The result is either a live report of what has already happened or encouragement by the anchor to get the reporter to speculate on what might happen later in the day. Increasingly, nonspecialized reporters either waffle about events they do not fully understand or reiterate uncritically what they have been told by official spin doctors. This tells us more about the nature of modern reporting than it does the doings of the world.

All this paints a rather depressing picture of the modern journalist and, by implication, the modern politician who succumbs to the emotive power of the news reports. However, it in part derives from the expectation of the historian as a seeker of the truth. In theory, historians and journalists are cousins, because they both seek the same thing. The difference is that the journalist is governed by deadlines measured in hours, minutes, and now seconds in "real-time," whereas the historian has the luxury of a greater length of time to sift, reflect, and cross-check. Indeed, if the historian of the future decided to rely upon one single media source, he or she would gain a pretty distorted impression of the past. But no self-respecting historian would do this. They would research a variety of media sources—in the event that they had survived. My own experience of researching the Gulf War, largely from media sources, is that provided one looks at a significant cross section of sources—newspapers, radio, television (packaged and live)—it is indeed possible to gain a fairly accurate impression of events. Almost ten years since the publication of *War and the Media: Propaganda and Persuasion in the Gulf War*,[5] I would estimate that only around 3–5 percent of the text has been proven wrong or inaccurate by the subsequent release of information. And for all our frustration about the "dumbing down" of certain sections of the media, it is in fact possible now to gain more access to more media outlets than ever before.

This is because the enormous growth of the Internet during the past ten years has revolutionized research into contemporary history. For somebody to be reasonably well-informed, one once had to rely upon the morning paper over breakfast, radio reports in the car on the way to work, and an evening television news bulletin; now one can access thousands of online newspapers, radio programs, and television stations around the world. Whereas once an expert on Tanzania might lament the absence of any western media coverage on events in that country, now they can access media from that country at the click of a mouse. Although less than 5 percent of the world's population has logged on to the World Wide Web, specialists in advanced industrialized countries have access to more information than ever before. Of course, they will still need to treat that information in exactly the same way as historians treat all evidence—with skepticism, caution, and with cross-verification constantly in mind. On the Internet, ordinary citizens with access to a computer, whether expert or not in a given subject, become reporters of the world's events, continuing the massive growth and fragmentation of the profession of journalism in our information age. The Kosovo conflict of 1999 revealed all of the possibilities, as well as the pitfalls. The traditional media, operating under restrictions in Belgrade and excluded altogether from Kosovo, were no longer the exclusive mediators of news about the conflict. Television as a weapon of war—in the information war—was still significant enough for NATO to target Serbian transmitters and even the state-run station, RTS. But it was on the Internet that citizens from NATO countries, and indeed Serbian citizens, could gain access to the other side's point of view. While we could watch NATO spokesmen delivering the official line live (so why do we need journalists to mediate?) from the State Department, the U.K. Ministry of Defence of SHAPE headquarters, we could also check how the Serbs or the KLA responded on the "Serbinfo" website. Equally, we could read what ordinary Serb citizens were thinking as they corresponded in chat rooms while NATO bombers flew over their homes.

As the postmortem of Kosovo unfolds and as the military embarks upon its usual lessons-learned exercise, communications and media scholars are beginning to examine the media record in greater detail.[6] What they are finding should surprise no contemporary historian, especially those who have studied the Gulf War of 1991. The western media demonized Slobodan Milosevich; they framed stories in terms of Serb aggression or genocide in Kosovo; they were (largely) uncritical of NATO aggression, especially in terms of the legality of the conflict; and—Greece apart—they were largely supportive of the justness of NATO's humanitarian cause. They echoed the official agenda and they failed to get the whole story, largely because a combination of Serb aggression and NATO air strikes had made Kosovo itself an extremely dangerous place from which to report. It was because of this information vacuum from the very heart of the conflict that propaganda by both sides could flourish. Those who regard the role of the media in such circumstances as the torch bearer for "the truth" either fail to appreciate the sheer operational constraints on the media in wartime or cling to some old-fashioned notion that the media are simple observers of events rather than actual and significant participants within them.

An increasingly sophisticated NATO information machine, let alone the Serb authorities, understood these phenomena only too well. The world's press corps may have been horrified by the bombing of colleagues in Radio-Television Serbia's main building in Belgrade, but anyone monitoring the output of this government-controlled media outlet could guess that it would indeed be a target. Its explicit footage of the consequences of NATO mistakes, such as the bombing of a civilian convoy, reinforced the official Serb propaganda line that the Kosovo Albanians were fleeing the bombing, not genocide. Because genocide was the line western leaders were plugging in their "just war" justifications, satellite transmissions from CNN and Sky News echoed their statements as they were beamed across Europe, including back into Serbia itself. One can only speculate as to what press corps colleagues in Iraq felt at this outcry, given that there was no similar reaction when Iraqi TV was bombed off the air in 1991. Serb TV, however, was soon up and running again—an indication in itself of how significant the Serb authorities regarded it as a weapon of war. Indeed, as NATO air strikes continued over more than eighty days, with no fatal NATO casualties, the information "weapon" was perhaps the only way Serbia could strike back. And if it could do this by keeping its own population "on message" through domestic television, while sowing seeds of doubt via the Internet among the logged-on populations of NATO and other countries, then it was determined to win the one battle it perhaps stood a chance of winning.[7]

Given the importance that modern governments attach to the television presentation of their policies, in peace and war, there should surely be no more argument about the significance of the media as a source of historical evidence. Yet it took thirty years for historians to be convinced of the significance of the surviving footage of Neville Chamberlain or Stanley Baldwin as they addressed the nation in the 1930s via the newsreels. The tragedy for historians thirty years from now is that they will have only a patchwork of surviving evidence for the television appearances of President Clinton or

Prime Minister Tony Blair in the absence of coherent national and international broadcasting and communications archival policies. As a result, the final interstate conflict of the twentieth century, from the media point of view, will remain every bit as much of an evidential vacuum as it was an informational vacuum during the war itself.

This is surely a contradiction in terms. If there were no consistent reporting from Kosovo during the war itself, how would future historians benefit from the absence of such material? We return to the nature of broadcasting as an industry. News organizations, with all their commercial pressures, make decisions about what stories, especially foreign stories, they need to cover. They spend a great deal of time and money on market research about their audiences. If those audiences are less and less interested in foreign news, this may tell us as much, if not more, about the nature of our societies than it does about the contemporary media. What is not being reported upon, or how two or three out of twenty or so current conflicts around the world are decided upon as being newsworthy, is an important element in understanding not so much this particular "window on the world," but upon the smaller number of panes of glass that the media chooses to let us see through.

Moreover, a major finding of the Leeds Gulf War research project was the desire of British audiences *not* to see on their television sets the realities of what modern war can do to real people.[8] Yet, to my knowledge, no scholar in any discipline has picked up on this tantalizing line of research. And as the war fades increasingly into history, it will become even more difficult for any empirical sociologist or other social scientist to do so—a genuine lost opportunity, and a tragedy due perhaps once again to old-fashioned academic conservatism and artificial disciplinary boundaries. For communications as a process of persuasion, rooted in technology but requiring creative applications with deep-seated cultural, political, and psychological consequences, is the ultimate multidisciplinary subject. Yet, despite this, the ball remains firmly rooted to the ground during and since the Kosovo conflict.

Another hindrance to further progress has been the growing antagonism between scholars and practitioners. Many media scholars are highly critical of media performance, rightly or wrongly. Practitioners such as journalists deeply resent such criticism; the knee-jerk reaction is to complain that academics have no idea of the "real world" of journalism and have no understanding of its operational constraints. It is a very similar problem to historians and historical film and television producers. In Britain, there is a fascinating phenomenon whereby the media periodically attack media studies as a discipline that ill-prepares students for the "real world" of media work. The charges are that this fastest growing university subject of the 1990s is too theoretical, too divorced from reality, and too over-subscribed in a world where there are not enough jobs to go around. Journalists employed as academics to teach such students are "poachers turned gamekeepers," rather in the same way as any journalist who criticizes his or her fellow journalists are rounded on like in a shark attack.[9] This all says a great deal about the pressures of modern journalism in an increasingly competitive, results- and deadline-driven commercial environment.

The point is that in a "knowledge economy," academia and industry simply have to work closer together. There is certainly no advantage in us staying in our ivory towers looking down on what we see as the demise of analytical journalism into infotainment. We have keen and committed students who are bright and able—and we have three or four years to get them to think about the ethical, moral, and legal issues that they'll be grappling with upon graduation, when they do enter the so-called real world. The reporting of Kosovo was a classic example of why this is necessary for the future—and survival—of serious journalism that will be of value to future historians. During the spring of 1999 at NATO headquarters, a press corps consisting of only a handful of specialized defense correspondents, was seen live on television by a global audience to be asking stupid questions about issues they little understood, if at all. This is a perfect formula for an increasingly professional corps of official information officers to hijack the media agenda with talk of "collateral damage," "BDA" (bomb damage assessment), and other such jargon to provide a smokescreen for what is really happening, as distinct from what they say is happening.

As in the Gulf War, such information officers were able to provide the media with footage of precision-guided weapons hitting their targets—footage that was taken not by the media but by military cameras mounted on these so-called "smart" weapons. It was only when Serb television provided alternative footage of what had happened when the smart weapon cameras had gone blank that this ability to dominate the media agenda was challenged, which in turn agitated the unspecialized press corps to ask slightly more probing questions. In other words, information competition is the sole motivation that prompts the news media to do the job we used to think it was paid to do. As Daniel Hallin demonstrated a long time ago with his work on Vietnam,[10] only when the media refused to accept uncritically what the military was telling them after 1968 did the official authorities begin to "shoot the messenger." Equally, during the Kosovo conflict, only when the British government began to criticize the BBC's John Simpson for his reporting from Belgrade were we provided with a clue that this particular journalist was attempting to do his job of reporting fairly and impartially within a public service tradition.

That tradition, of course, requires the journalist to report both sides of an argument or dispute. In wartime, this is almost impossible and invariably unacceptable to governments who want to keep public support for "our boys" doing the fighting.[11] As the public service tradition retreats in the face of commercialization—a problem more acute in Britain than in the United States—perhaps our focus needs to shift from the news media to the new media. Whatever the reasons for our mass media having become what they have become, and however they might turn out in the future, consumers of nonmediated news now have a rich new source of easily accessible information on the Internet, a resource that is bound to grow both qualitatively and quantitatively. As such, these are exciting times for scholars. But will they regard the Internet to be as disposable a resource as they have regarded television programming? If the answer to this is "yes," then historians of the next wave of the information revolution are in big trouble. A crisis is already brewing with conventional archives. In Britain now, with its Thirty Year Rule, only a tiny fraction of government records reach the Public Record Office. How can historians legitimately argue that they have a comprehensive record of U.K. government activity in the 1960s when in reality less than 5 percent of the paper produced is retained? With digital information technology, most of the material could in fact be preserved on formats that take up far less space than paper. But what is first required is a general acceptance on the part of the historical profession that information—including that conveyed by our mass media—is essential to understanding our contemporary world. We will still need to use historical skills in evaluating the significance of one piece of information over another. We will still need to understand the processes by which that information is gathered, evaluated, and disseminated. But we first need access to that information in archival forms. Television may be flawed, but it *is* a first rough draft and, as such, as precious a resource as any first draft of a manuscript by history's traditional creative communicators—like writers, novelists, and authors. Why do we still not value it as such?

Notes

1. General Dugan, "Generals versus Journalists" in H. Smith, ed., *The Media and the Gulf War* (Washington, D.C.: Seven Locks Press, 1992), 60.

2. P. Knightley, *The First Casualty: The War Correspondent as Hero, Propagandist and Mythmaker from the Crimea to Vietnam* (New York: Harcourt Brace Jovanovich, 1975). To this often cited work must now be added Stephen Badsey, ed., *The Media and International Security* (London: Frank Cass, 2000); Susan Carruthers, *The Media at War* (London: Macmillan, 1999); and Peter Young and Peter Jesser, *The Media and the Military: From the Crimea to Desert Strike* (New York: St. Martin's Press, 1997).

3. Despite the public protestations from journalists about the "dumbing down" of the news, a few of them are prepared to go on record as conceding this. See the special issue of *The Historical Journal of Film Radio and Television* 20.1 (2000).

4. For the growing literature on this subject, see in particular W. Strobel, *Late Breaking Foreign Policy: The News Media's Influence on Peace Operations* (Washington, D.C.: U.S. Institute of Peace Press, 1997); and Philip Seib, *Headline Diplomacy: How News Coverage Affects Foreign Policy* (Westport, Conn.: Praeger, 1997).

5. Philip M. Taylor, *War and the Media: Propaganda and Persuasion in the Gulf War,* (Manchester, U.K.: Manchester Univ. Press, 1992), 2nd edition, 1998.

6. See the forthcoming "anniversary" special issue of the *European Journal of Communications.*

7. See Philip M. Taylor, "Propaganda and the Web War: Kosovo—The information war," *The World Today* 55.6 (June 1999), 10–12; and Philip M. Taylor, "WWW1: The World Wide Web Goes to War," in D. Gauntlett, ed., *Web.studies* (Oxford and New York: Arnold, 2000).

8. David Morrison, *Television and the Gulf War* (London: John Libbey, 1992).

9. In recent years, this has happened to two prominent British television journalists. The first was Martyn Lewis, who was strongly criticized by his colleagues for arguing that the media should give more attention to "good news" stories. The second was Martin Bell, now an independent Member of Parliament, who criticized the "sanitization" by news editors of British TV news coverage of the Bosnian war, suggesting that this failure to report the war in all its horror minimized its significance in the eyes of the British television audience.

10. Daniel Hallin, *The Uncensored War: The Media and Vietnam* (Oxford, U.K.: Oxford Univ. Press, 1986).

11. For an elaboration of this argument, see Philip M. Taylor, "The Military and the Media: Past, Present and Future" in Stephen Badsey, ed., *The Media and International Security,* 177–202.

IV | Television Production, Reception, and History

13 | The History Channel and the Challenge of Historical Programming

Brian Taves

The History Channel was launched at the beginning of 1995 as an offspring of the eleven-year-old Arts & Entertainment network (A&E). In subsequent years, The History Channel has increasingly become a standard part of basic cable packages, both in the United States and in the United Kingdom. Emerging with the evolving proliferation of cable stations that began in the 1980s, The History Channel has joined the constellation of channels devoted to specialized non-news nonfiction entertainment for particular audiences, including nature (Animal Planet), gardening (Home & Garden Network), Travel Channel, and such generalized documentary channels as Discovery and The Learning Channel (TLC). This essay examines the inherently problematic nature of such an endeavor as The History Channel, together with how The History Channel has accomplished its own goal of finding a commercial niche.

At the outset, there is a temptation to put the name "History Channel" in quotes, given the simultaneous grand nature of such a designation and the expectations such an appellation raises from a scholarly standpoint. The very concept of a History Channel spawns obvious questions, extending from how history will be told to what modes of address will be used. However, initially an even more practical issue needs to be asked: How does one analyze a specific television channel? There is little existing academic literature to provide a model for how a commercial cable channel may be examined, and network or public broadcasting channels are too radically different in their origin, audience focus, and commercial needs to be treated analogously. From a practical standpoint, analyzing a particular channel is possible principally through examining the range of programs that are broadcast—specific series and episodes. Accordingly, this essay is based on the primary experience of closely watching a representative sample of The History Channel—over thirty full hours. Much of the fare that originated elsewhere and was being rerun on The History Channel had already been viewed in its first run by the author. Some of the shows were selected at random, including one full day's documentary programming. Others were chosen based on various personal interests, or on subjects where my own expertise was sufficient to evaluate the accuracy of the presentations.[1] Overall, this essay delineates not only the types of history presented in a variety of series and programs, and the differences in stylistic modes, but also how they manifest certain trends in programming, most apparent in the contrast between old and newly commissioned work. This essay also looks at The History Channel's integration of historical fiction into the broader nonfictional context.

Secondly, the apparent patterns formed by the selection of programs are discussed, in terms of the philosophy governing the choice of programs and scheduling practices, as well as the practical commercial considerations. To provide a sense of comparative possibilities, other channels governed by similar criteria and seeking to serve similar ends are noted. Recurring throughout all of these topics is the way in which certain styles of documentary production pose a perilous trend for historical accuracy in television historical documentaries on The History Channel and related channels.

The potential range of programming, and its evolution over time, may be adequately discussed in an essay of this length, since The History Channel is relatively new and its methods and presentations have remained constant. The History Channel has yet to experience a wholesale alteration of its choice of programming and the philosophy behind those selections that seem to be a benchmark of upheavals in management thinking at most networks. Throughout The History Channel's brief broadcast history, many of its offerings are repeated, not only within the broadcast day but with the passage of weeks and months as well, meaning that the total number of different series is comparatively small.

The History Channel clearly enunciates its mission with the mottoes "all of history, all in one place," "where the past comes alive," and most recently "the official network of every millennium," fulfilled primarily through various types of documentaries, as well as fictive work with a historical background. The approach is not the specialized one of the academy or a social science, but instead a form of popular history, similar to the standard presentation of nineteenth-century school books.[2] The History Channel's website makes clear its appeal to the traditional amateur history enthusiast, with an

ALL OF HISTORY. ALL IN ONE PLACE.

DAYTIME PROGRAMS

A new journey into the past begins every day. The History Channel proves that there's more to stimulating daytime TV than soaps and talk shows. Tune in and enhance the quality of your daytime viewing.

HISTORY THEATER:

If all the world's a stage, history is its theatre. This show features outstanding theatrical presentations, from both the U.S. and England, set in historic periods. Presented in the form of multi-episode series, it's a new way to watch compelling stories unfold day after day while you enjoy quality television.

HIGH POINTS IN HISTORY:

A virtual anthology of historical documentaries, *High Points* offers a wide range of perspectives on greatness. Shows that cover some of the most important events and people from the past, and that take viewers back to the places and the moments that still stand out for the way they've shaped who we are today.

THE REAL WEST:

Buffalo Bill, General Custer, Dodge City. Now there is an entire series devoted to exploring some of America's most enduring myths and legends. *The Real West* covers some of the subjects Americans love best in an enlightening and entertaining way, like cowboys, outlaw gangs and boom towns. It provides unusual close-ups, not just of the best known stories, but of fascinating sidelights, such as Wild West Shows, Wild, Wild Woman and the Texas Rangers.

YEAR BY YEAR:

YEAR BY YEAR travels back in time to chronicle the events that stand out and define some of history's most interesting years. Each episode is focused on a single year, and combines documentary newsreels and historic footage so that you'll experience it, not just as it looks to us today, but how it was seen and reported by the people at the time.

The History Channel promises "All of History. All in One Place." Courtesy of A&E Television Networks.

abundance of trivia, such as "Today in History," and factoids designed to appeal to school-age youth and older potential audiences.[3] The emphasis is on commemorating the lives of memorable individuals and elucidating events recognized as important from the perspective of western culture, a focus which has caused some criticism of The History Channel, particularly the large quantity of programming dealing with war.[4] (The war-related programming has helped The History Channel preclude major competition from another, more obscure cable offering, The Military Channel.) Overall, the interpretation of what constitutes history is unusually broad, including not only political, contemporary, military, and social, but also scientific and technological history, together with history targeted at children. The topics span not only time—from the beginning of civilization through Operation Desert Storm—but all parts of the globe.

A single day's programming may be organized around a specific theme, often a historical anniversary. For instance, on December 29, 1996, the anniversary of the admission of Texas to the Union was celebrated with four hours of programs about the state, on the state's founding fathers, the Alamo, the Mexican War, and the Texas Rangers. The release of Oliver Stone's *Nixon* (1996) was noted with an evening that included dialogues with Stone, historians of the Nixon era, and earlier television interviews shot during the former president's retirement. There are also seasonal presentations, such as *Christmas Unwrapped: The History of Christmas* in December 1997, and *Celebrating the Green: The History of Saint Patrick's Day* and *A Short History of Ireland* in March 1998. A 1999 Halloween tribute, "Devils and Demons Week," included documentaries from *Witchcraft* to *The Evil Eye* (on voodoo) to *Hitler and the Occult*.[5]

Daily programming is organized loosely under such broad categories as *High Points in History, In Search of History,* and *History Alive*. Most of these series function as anthology-style slots within which a variety of very different programming can be scheduled, largely composed of preexisting miniseries and single documentaries. Other series, like *Our Century,* have at least some focus, such as the miniseries *Korea: The Unknown War* (1990). By contrast, in a single week (March 23–27, 1998) the category *In Search of History* spanned hour-long documentaries on such varied topics as *The Cavemen, The Pirate's Lost City, The Monkey Trial, The Hidden Glory of Petra,* and *Madam President*. Another major portion of The History Channel's programming focuses on military history, with such series as *Secrets of World War II, Air Combat, Masters of War, Combat at Sea,* and *Weapons of War*.

The History Channel's start-up expenses were kept relatively low by initiating little production in comparison with the amount of older material

THE HISTORY CHANNEL

ALL OF HISTORY. ALL IN ONE PLACE.

PRIME TIME SCHEDULE

- Vertical niche. Easy brand for front-line employees to sell. A concept your subscribers will easily understand.
- High-demand programming appeals to your formers, nevers, light viewers and men and women in all regions.
- The History Channel offers powerful local tie-ins with museums, historical societies and civic groups.
- Every weekday The History Channel offers 1 hour of commercial-free classroom programming.

TIME	SUN	MON	TUE	WED	THU	FRI	SAT
8PM ET 7PM CT 5PM PT	MODERN MARVELS		HISTORY ALIVE The story of American history and beyond.				
9PM ET 8PM CT 6PM PT	HISTORY SUNDAY		MOVIES IN TIME Outstanding historical motion pictures and mini-series, with interviews with expert historians and journalists.				HISTORY ALIVE The story of American history and beyond.
10PM ET 9PM CT 7PM PT	Historical specials						
11PM ET 10PM CT 8PM PT	WEAPONS AT WAR		OUR CENTURY The history of man in conflict.				

DAYTIME SCHEDULE

TIME	MON	TUE	WED	THU	FRI
9AM ET 8AM CT 6AM PT	HISTORY CLASSROOM				
10AM ET 9AM CT 7AM PT	AMERICAN HISTORY SHOWCASE				
11AM ET 10AM CT 8AM PT	HISTORY THEATRE				
12N ET 11AM CT 9AM PT	HIGH POINTS IN HISTORY				
1PM ET 12N CT 10AM PT	THE REAL WEST				
2PM ET 1PM CT 11AM PT	YEAR BY YEAR				
3PM ET 2PM CT 12N PT	AMERICAN HISTORY SHOWCASE				
4PM ET 3PM CT 1PM PT	HISTORY THEATRE				
5PM ET 4PM CT 2PM PT	HIGH POINTS IN HISTORY				
6PM ET 5PM CT 3PM PT	THE REAL WEST				
7PM ET 6PM CT 4PM PT	YEAR BY YEAR				

ET= Eastern Time, CT= Central Time, PT= Pacific Time

WEEKEND SCHEDULE

TIME	SAT	SUN
8AM ET 7AM CT 5AM PT	AMERICAN HISTORY SHOWCASE	THE HISTORY CHANNEL ON CAMPUS
9AM ET 8AM CT 6AM PT	HISTORY FOR KIDS	HISTORY FOR KIDS
11AM ET 10AM CT 8AM PT	YEAR BY YEAR FOR KIDS	YEAR BY YEAR FOR KIDS
12N ET 11AM CT 9AM PT	MODERN MARVELS	AUTOMOBILES
1PM ET 12N CT 10AM PT	OUR CENTURY	
2PM ET 1PM CT 11AM PT	CRUSADES IN THE PACIFIC	MOVIES IN TIME
2:30PM ET 1:30PM CT 11:30AM PT	AMERICA AT WAR	
3PM ET 2PM CT 12N PT	THE REAL WEST	
4PM ET 3PM CT 1PM PT	WEAPONS AT WAR	MOVIES IN TIME
5PM ET 4PM CT 2PM PT	AUTOMOBILES	THE WORLD AT WAR
6PM ET 5PM CT 3PM PT	POWER & THE GLORY	
6:30PM ET 5:30PM CT 3:30PM PT	FIRST FLIGHTS	VICTORY AT SEA
7PM ET 6PM CT 4PM PT	MODERN MARVELS	AUTOMOBILES

A typical week of programming at The History Channel. Courtesy of A&E Television Networks.

shown.[6] This consisted primarily of documentaries and historical fiction originally produced in England, or for PBS or A&E (a fact that has made The History Channel perhaps the closest direct follower of PBS in terms of content, despite the necessity of succeeding as a commercial station). With programming choices initially driven by the types of shows readily available, The History Channel has evidenced a surprising openness to nontraditional forms of television historical documentary, such as regional and social history. One of the most unique ideas on The History Channel was *American History Showcase* (1995–1997), a daily series of documentaries and dramatizations from museums and historic sites across the country, with presentations ranging from the film at the U.S. Naval Memorial Visitor's Center to productions from various sponsoring agencies, such as agricultural groups. Many diverse productions were shown that were otherwise not in general television circulation, variable by topic as well as approach and (inherently) quality.

Other documentaries, from a range of sources, serve to elucidate familiar subjects from perspectives different from those to which audiences in the United States are accustomed.[7] For instance, one of the subseries of *Our Century,* entitled *The Century of Warfare,* included *Vietnam* (1994), a one-hour British documentary from Nugus/Martin Productions. *Vietnam* offers a different perspective on the conflict, lacking many details that would have been expected in a United States–produced history of the war, such as the assassination of Diem. Instead, other emphases are substituted, especially the role of Australian and South Korean troops. The result is less reflective of a diverging moral or political viewpoint than the fact that the primary (British) audience is one for whom the subject would have different concerns. Similarly, *Locomotion* (1994) is a four-part, four-hour British documentary miniseries on the history of trains, with only one episode covering the rail industry in the United States. Although scarcely constituting alternative views of history, and not necessarily superior from either a historical or production standpoint, such programming enriches the mix of The History Channel's offerings. Exposing audiences to history from another nation's viewpoint is a healthy alternative to the frequency with which such documentaries are domestic products centered on the United States, even if the dominant "other" perspective is only that of another English-speaking country.

Mining the abundant supply of existing historical productions, from which the best can be selected, is a wise strategy that may bring renewed attention to quality series, including such classic World War II documentaries as *Victory at Sea* (1952–1953) and *The World at War* (1973–1975). Segments of the 1962–1963 *Biography* series for CBS, narrated by Mike Wallace, have been repackaged by The History Channel as *Perspectives—High Points in History*. For instance, two segments of *Perspectives* shown back-to-back were about the space pioneers Wernher von Braun and John Glenn. Both programs reflect the intensely patriotic, celebratory approach that made the shows so typical of their time and a staple of 1960s and 1970s films shown in classrooms. The Von Braun segment, made in 1960, sidesteps any moral concerns about his past Nazi connections to transform his life story into that of a German boy's interest in rocketry, which did result in the V-2 but was also a step toward the dream of sending humankind into outer space. Von Braun's life is constructed according to the myth of the ability of the United States to attract foreign talent as a free nation of immigrants, Americanizing them in the great melting pot and thereby triumphing over old world adversaries—in this case the Soviet Union in the Cold War space race. The John Glenn segment, made in 1964 (prior to his business and political careers) is similar in its narrative strategy, this time adopting the myth of the common man whose diligence and courage allowed him to become the first American to orbit the Earth. The predictable narrative approach of such shows, transforming life stories into American legends, may make them seem fusty to some modern audiences. Yet in other respects they remain rewarding, since they were able to draw from the elaborate film libraries maintained by the networks as the basis for their own documentaries, allowing abundant and accurate background footage.

More recent miniseries demonstrate how The History Channel can bring deserving shows a wider audience. The four-hour, four-part British series *Churchill* (1992), written and narrated by Martin Gilbert, his official biographer, provides an absorbing introduction to the life of the prime minister that is equally effective for those already familiar with the man and his times. The series retains interest through combining well-known events with new interpretations and little-known but significant facts, such as the state of Churchill's health in wartime, or his initial miscalculations regarding Stalin. The interviews in *Churchill* are generally not with his best-known associates, but with those who knew him on a daily basis as relatively minor office or personal staff, giving a different perspective from the near-official versions of events by more famous individuals.

The History Channel's penchant for technological history, as well as its use of independent production, is illustrated by *First Flights* (1993), an exemplary history of aviation hosted by Neil Armstrong—one of his very few such appearances. The selection and use of the historical footage is ideal and edited with unusual skill. While each episode concentrates on a specific aspect of aviation, such as the principles and mechanics of aerodynamics that make the flight of helicopters possible, *First Flights* is also grounded in the historical development of flying in the context of world events. The scientific explanations are challenging, while still comprehensible to a layman who closely follows the narration, demonstrating that such a documentary series can be both entertaining and highly educational.

When The History Channel goes beyond showing documentaries made before its inception, its choice of works and the presentation and treatment it gives them becomes increasingly problematic. The History Channel makes extensive use of historical fiction, replaying features and miniseries set in the past. Many of these are hosted by Sander Vanocur, with commentaries by historians ranging from academics to journalists on issues ranging from costuming to the broader interpretation of events. The History Channel touts these programs with the slogan: "See the great epics that depict our past. Then get the inside story on what really happened through interviews with expert historians and journalists. History has never been so entertaining!"[8] The selections range from the highly fictive, such as *Shogun* (1980) and *The Blue and the Gray* (1982), to the stylized, like *I, Claudius* (1977) and *Reilly—Ace of Spies* (1983), to those intended to be more factual, such as *Edward and Mrs. Simpson* (1979), *Sadat* (1983), and *George Washington* (1983). The features are equally wide-ranging in their subject matter and treatment of history, from *PT-109* (1962) to *The Last Days of Patton* (1986), and from *The Private Life of Henry VIII* (1933) to *Mary, Queen of Scots* (1971). A precise historical reconstruction of a specific World War II event, like *The Dambusters* (1955), is followed the next evening by one with the most minimal historical content, John Wayne in *The Flying Tigers* (1942).

The movies themselves are frequently shown in the most diminished way possible, failing to allow for the film's textual integrity, and on occasion artistry. Historical films tend to be long because of their subject matter, but The History Channel routinely edits features into a standard time slot of two or at most three hours, and they are cut even further than ordinary commercial breaks would require, so as to allow time for the historian's comments. For instance, the epic polar adventure, *The Red Tent* (1971), was squeezed into a standard two-hour time slot. This means that a picture originally running 121 minutes was cut to less than 90 minutes, considering the time for commercials and commentary. By contrast, the Turner movie channels (TBS, TNT, and TCM) usually show this same film in a longer slot, so that it does not have to be cut. As well, only pan-and-scan versions of wide-screen films are shown on The History Channel. Considering that one of the most accurate aspects of historical movies is often their sets and costumes, such films ought to be shown in a letterboxed format, which would allow the decor to be better appreciated, as is done by the Turner movie channels and by American Movie Classics (AMC).

The use of historical fiction brings to prominence another flaw found both in this aspect as well as the documentary programming. Despite The History Channel's range of presentations and willingness to use films made over a forty-year period (and sometimes older), it fails to articulate, or even recognize, the way in which these programs themselves are part of history, artifacts that are endemic to the time of their production. For instance, *Churchill* is a more modern documentary, one that interrogates its heroically regarded subject and does not hesitate to point out flaws in his thinking and behavior. Nonetheless, it does not seek to undercut its subject or diminish his vital importance to an Allied victory. This basic indifference to its own medium, and the history of television and film, and exhibition, may be at the root of some of the problems with The History Channel's own productions.

Apart from presenting older documentaries and those that have been produced independently, The History Channel has also sponsored original creations, often in conjunction with its parent network, A&E, and cross-premiered on both stations to publicize The History Channel to the larger pool of existing A&E viewers.[9] Best of these was *The American Revolution* (1994), with which The History Channel sought at its inception to establish itself as a credible new source of historical programming. The narration by Bill Kurtis carefully explores the Revolution in a comprehensive, thorough manner, marked by interviews with historians, who develop clear characteristics and interpretations of the events during the six-hour running time. Stars ranging from William Daniels to Cliff Robertson read selections from the writings of various patriots, and the consistent use of their voices in specific roles helps to provide a familiarity and personality so often lacking in screen portrayals of the nation's founders. The conflict is told, both in its broad aspects as well as in details and incidents, such as the treason of Benedict Arnold, synthesizing the events in a manner that is both intellectually and emotionally affecting. Using a range of graphics of the period, together with maps and other illustrations, mixed with battle re-creations, the exceptional photography by I-Li Chen far surpasses the usual documentary palette to provide a colorful perspective on the sights of the eighteenth century, especially musketry and battle.[10]

Unfortunately, *The American Revolution* is an exception among The History Channel's original programming, an area in which their record is equivocal at best. At the other extreme is *Crusades* (1995), a four-hour, four-part miniseries that transforms documentary into a comedy star vehicle. *Crusades* was written and hosted by Terry Jones, a Monty Python veteran, whose qualification seems to have been the comedy troupe's treatment of the Middle Ages. Jones dresses in a suit of armor or reclines on a Roman beach, aiming to be hip and irreverent in concentrating on the more salacious aspects of medieval life, such as the activities of camp followers. Instead, he only achieves wan humor and pure subjectivity.

Crusades contains about as much history as the 1935 Cecil B. DeMille movie of the same title—except that viewers rightly expect a greater measure of accuracy when the label "documentary" is invoked. The natural skepticism that serves as a built-in defense mechanism for a historically inaccurate movie is substantially diminished when assuming on faith the "truth" of a documentary. A fictional treatment is bound to raise at least some questions, if nothing more than whether a given star portrayed a real person, in the proper costume and make-up. While distortions in historical movies are usually justified on grounds of dramatic necessity, when a documentary approaches its subject in a deliberately incomplete or less than accurate manner, it takes advantage of a unique form of reception while failing to accept the accompanying responsibility. The factors giving rise to such ahistorical tendencies in narration and style so permeate modern documentaries as to be deserving of fuller analysis, in relation to both The History Channel and similar television stations.

While The History Channel can fill programming time for a comparatively low cost by relying on preexisting material, trying to finance quality new productions at an equivalent rate is nearly impossible. One misguided attempt earned The History Channel its principal spate of negative publicity from historians and media watchdog groups: *The Spirit of Enterprise,* a series of documentaries about the development of specific companies, to be funded by the respective corporations, who would provide additional advertising support.[11] Despite a hasty withdrawal to a more ostensibly objective position, The History Channel's ready use of existing documentaries from a variety of sources produced in England and the United States, along with use of other sponsored films such as the *American History Showcase* series, indicates how little consideration is given to the role of the financial interest in the final product. Indeed, sponsored documentaries have a long pedigree in the market of educational, instructional, and documentary films, whether shown in schools or community organizations. Their promotional or propagandistic content is seldom questioned, and it must have seemed an easy potential step for The History Channel to forthrightly join in continuing this tradition as a way to finance a lavishly produced series. (The principal other criticism of The History Channel has been over its treatment of the various months devoted to women's history or that of minority groups, and the programming shown during these times.)[12]

The growth of the modern television documentary industry has been largely determined by the need for fresh programming by a number of non-fiction cable channels with limited audiences and resources, including not only The History Channel but also Discovery, TLC, and Animal Planet.[13] A sense of the finances involved can be realized by noting that the budget of a typical episode of *Biography* (1993–present), the *leading* series on The History Channel's parent company A&E, is $60,000 apiece. Segments can be produced in as little as a week (the one on Yitzhak Rabin after his assassination) to a single day (the *Biography* on Sonny Bono produced immediately after his death). By contrast, the *American Masters* biographical shows presented on PBS since 1986 take six to eight months to produce and edit and have a budget of $500,000–$600,000 apiece.[14] An hour's flagship fare costs an equivalent amount on Discovery, but the channel may also spend less than $8,000 for a half-hour afternoon program.[15] Using the funding that the cable channels are willing to offer, contracts are usually awarded primarily on the basis of the lowest bid. The commissioned companies churn out documentaries inexpensively and quickly, often on topics that can be filmed cheaply or where public domain footage is easily available. Hastily constructed documentaries are pieced together according to assembly-line standards, cutting corners to maintain a profit—deficiencies that are not only evident to the historian but to any thoughtful viewer. Such productions are marked by such flaws as slipshod chronology, minimal research and analysis, and a fragmented narration highlighting the lack of any unifying thesis. The producers would justifiably complain that no more can be expected; shortcomings are inevitable given the budgets and schedules with which they must work.

Examples may be found in several of The History Channel's original programs. One of the oft-shown prestige series is *The Real West* (1993), a Greystone Communications production, with Craig Haffner as executive producer, but with responsibility for individual episodes farmed out to various different producers. A few of the episodes live up to their potential, such as "Stagecoach and The Pony Express," despite such embarrassments as re-created footage with vintage bandits in obviously modern clothes. While using chronological organization, narration is often vague, with facts and details following one after another but only loosely linked. In the episode entitled "Chief Joseph and the Nez Perce War," keeping track of the battles between Indians and U.S. military forces is almost impossible because of confusing narration and graphics, including misleading maps.

Seldom do the filmmakers bring expertise to the subject of the documentary or an overall viewpoint to the assemblage of footage. Instead, they rely on a few commentators to provide some coherence, usually historians, who are allowed to contribute in front of but not behind the camera. They are most often seen in interview excerpts, "talking heads" interspersed to lend a veneer of depth and analysis that is otherwise absent. There is little effort to make interview and narration complimentary, and they may even be antithetical, cut together without trying to reconcile them. In the episode of *The Real West* entitled "The Mexican War," the narration clearly intends to portray the United States as the aggressor, but the evidence cited supports the justice of President Polk's actions. All save one of the historians suggest that the conflict must be seen within the context of mid-nineteenth-century foreign policy morals and the inevitable impetus of the westward movement; yet the lone dissenter is given the final word.

Preexisting documentary material may be modified in such a way that it loses all sense. In The History Channel series *History for Kids* (1995–1997), two silly and unenlightening hosts jokingly present portions of old newsreels for children ages seven to thirteen, with stories ranging from the important to the insignificant, giving equal emphasis to wars, natural disasters, and marble-shooting championships. In *History for Kids,* newsreel stories are recycled to represent an entire year, but they are extracted from their original weekly release format with the narration unchanged. Hence, listening to *History for Kids*: "1937" would lead a youngster to assume that aviatrix Amelia Earhart was found after her disappearance over the Pacific, as the original newsreel narration, showing ships and planes quickly gathering to search for her aircraft, had confidently predicted. The *History for Kids* hosts did not bother to point out the enduring mystery of her fate before jumping on to the next topic; the series was not prepared with the care given the reassembling of the old *March of Time* newsreels by topic for an earlier generation in 1951–1952. Despite the shoddiness of this offering for younger viewers, with the bulk of its programming at an intellectual level appropriate for high school students, educational use of The History Channel is encouraged and is a major part of the joint outreach with A&E.

As a commercial channel, The History Channel lacks the possibility of the uninterrupted attention of a PBS audience, so much of The History Channel's original programming is created in recognition of the fact that it must appeal to the fragmented attention of the channel surfer. Most commercial television series are constructed so that the narration proceeds in a simple, slow manner that will allow a viewer to comfortably join at any point. For a documentary, this structure requires a multi-act structure (typically including the introduction and sometimes adding a brief conclusion), with each major segment roughly eight minutes in duration, the narration beginning anew and recapitulating what has been previously stated after each commercial interruption.

Too often the result of this approach is that the program is also best experienced in a disjointed manner, where the faults will not be as obvious. The shallowness and plodding style of *The Real West* will inevitably dissatisfy viewers who remain throughout its duration. Indeed, *The Real West* is assembled so that episodes may become a source of television specials on topics as diverse as Native Americans or the birth of Texas; one of the better episodes, "The Alamo," was expanded in 1996 from a one-hour segment to a two-hour special.[16] Some episodes appear to have been cobbled together from shorter segments, such as "Fathers of Texas," a joint biography of Stephen Austin and Sam Houston. By contrast, a series that was not originally produced for The History Channel, like *First Flights*, was created for more than the casual audience, achieving greater quality by rewarding serious attention with an organized presentation that successfully transmits knowledge.

No less problematic than the content in such documentaries are the frequently inappropriate visuals. Modern independent documentary filmmakers must rely on a variety of institutional and private archives, without access to the free in-house corporate and studio film libraries that embellished such a series as *Biography* (1962–1963, shown on The History Channel as *Perspectives*). At the same time, modern documentarists are unable to afford adequate research among archives. The result is predictable: images and narration that frequently do not reinforce one another. The stylistic pattern of most *Real West* episodes is standard. Many images are ill-chosen and only vaguely relevant to the narration, such as picture-perfect shots of western vistas unrelated to the subject. Illustrations may represent a different time than is described: in the portion of the episode "The Mexican War," on the invasion of Mexico, General Winfield Scott is represented as he appeared fifteen years later in a Civil War–era engraving. Further confusion arises from the repetitious use of the same visual on a particular subject in completely different periods—or out of chronological sequence altogether—rather than locating images appropriate to the time in question.

In many cases, valid still images from the historical periods in question, such as contemporary engravings, paintings, or folk art—all of which require research to locate—are largely abandoned. Rather than images directly related to the subject at hand, vaguely sixteenth- through nineteenth-century artwork is used as a type of stock footage. Sometimes such images are superimposed in an awkward attempt to create the appearance of movement. Increasingly, period material is entirely replaced by freshly staged reenactments, often filmed in tiresome slow motion in an attempt to prolong the running time of the new footage as long as possible. Such footage extends from original scenes of actors in costume to long shots of weekend Civil War buffs reliving a battle. A similar tactic is the use of old historical epics, whether virtually anonymous European-produced films or public domain movies such as *Captain Kidd* (1945)—continually exploited for scenes of pirate and naval action—or such easily recognizable Hollywood epics as *Cleopatra* (1963). To rely on an excessively re-creative treatment as the dominant visual strategy too often becomes a way to elide the research appropriate to the documentary purpose. As well, since vintage still images create editorial dissonance when placed in conjunction with re-creations, the latter style tends to become the dominant mode of representation.

This style ill serves the subject matter and presents the viewer with less accurate visuals than the traditional approach of searching archives for appropriate images from the time. For example, in the A&E/The History Channel original series *Nautilus* (1995), on the history of submarines, the episode on World War I entitled "To War in Iron Coffins" is composed almost entirely of re-creations. "To War in Iron Coffins" imitates such movies as *Das Boot* (1981) by concentrating on shots of dimly lit, cramped submarine interiors, with grimy actors in repetitive close-ups as the crew. Yet when a more expensive scene is called for, such as the sinking of a ship, instead of showing still images of the event, it is approximated by an underwater pan of a helmet and boot descending to the bottom of a tank doubling for the ocean floor.

This same deliberate substitution of fictional filmmaking techniques is found in The History Channel original documentary *The Man in the Iron Mask* (1998), which was inspired by the theatrical release of a new movie of the classic Alexandre Dumas novel. With a topic involving such a famous king as Louis XIV, and spanning decades of his reign, paintings and engravings are surely not difficult to find and would seldom be governed by copyright restrictions. Hence, the choice to use re-creative images is a conscious decision rather than one driven by cost. The documentary relies largely on live-action footage to supposedly show the arrest and imprisonment of the man in the iron mask, with actors dressed in shoddy costumes, while limited hand-held camera movement tries to conceal the lack of settings. Heavy borrowing is made from the public domain 1929 Douglas Fairbanks feature *The Iron Mask*, although the movie is never identified. Even what might seem to be elemental requirements of period illustrations are avoided; government archives of the eighteenth century are repeatedly referred to, but only photographs of a modern warehouse are shown.

The visuals of modern commercial documentaries tend to be designed around three needs: movement, color, and minimal expenditures. It can be cheaper to film new footage, whether actors or the weekend battlefield re-creations of amateur historians, or to use stock footage from public domain historical films, than the more conventional route of searching for appropriate images of the time in archival resources. (Perhaps the most clichéd single shot in documentaries today is of a costumed arm writing the words that a narrator is quoting rather than actual period images appropriate to the document in question.) However, this re-creative tendency, especially when coupled with feature-style sound tracks and editing, also indicates documentary film-makers are trying to imitate fictional film techniques, allowing filmmakers who might prefer to be working in this form to approximate it. This is surely the reason Terry Jones chose to turn *Crusades* into yet another variation on the familiar comedic formulas associated with his career. Such an approach is hardly confined to The History Channel; a crescendo of this technique appeared in TLC's *Atlantis Uncovered,* which not only uses flashy editing rhythms but musical themes lifted, without credit, from Bernard Herrmann's score of *Vertigo* (1958).

The use of live footage is also invariably color, not the black and white that implies historicity. Giving audiences the stylistic equivalent of modern, fictional work seems to offer a way to persuade peripatetic channel surfers to pause rather than react negatively to the traditional documentary style. In the words of one Discovery president, "We're in this frame-by-frame battle to get people to stay. . . . People feel if they watch 10 to 15 minutes of our programming they get nuggets," as Discovery tries to be one of the three or four networks that viewers alternate between.[17] Twenty years ago, this re-creative technique was reserved for such speculative series exploring the mysteries and legends of history as the syndicated *In Search of . . .* (1976–1982), when it was used as a technique signifying a pseudo-documentary style; today it has become a mainstream approach in commercial television documentaries. Indeed, the same style has also become a staple of "reality-based" shows supposedly offering a glimpse, based on re-creations of police activities, such as *America's Most Wanted* or *Cops* (TLC has its equivalent, *Trauma! Life in the ER*). Surely serious documentary filming deserves to be treated in a manner that signifies a greater recognition of the distinction between history, re-creation, and speculation.

These tendencies are not unique to The History Channel's original programming and even more noticeably afflict many of the documentaries, particularly on historical subjects, on such similar cable commercial cable channels as A&E, Discovery, and TLC.[18] The latter two provide a point of comparison with The History Channel, especially since they parallel the relationship of A&E and The History Channel. Discovery Channel, founded in 1985, spawned TLC as an offshoot in 1991, with Animal Planet and Travel Channel subsequently joining the Discovery lineup. Discovery began when the rise of cable made it possible to appeal to more specialized viewers and advertising rather than the mass audience required by networks. Like The History Channel, Discovery began by mining the lode of existing documentaries before gradually expanding into steadily more original shows, both coproduced in-house but primarily contracted to freelance filmmakers.[19] Discovery programming can be redubbed into any language for a range of countries, as culturally and geographically distant as India and Southeast Asia. However, this need for easy overseas resale and export to any country compels documentaries on the nonfiction commercial cable channels to follow noncontroversial, educational lines. They avoid the topicality of journalistic documentaries once produced by the American networks (and now only found on PBS); as a Discovery programming chief noted, documentaries on Watergate, Tianamen Square, or the occupation of Tibet are unlikely subject matter.[20] However, documentaries on infamous parts of history have been popular on The History Channel; some of its best ratings were for a 1998 documentary on the Ku Klux Klan.[21]

All of these stations draw at least some of their inspiration from PBS, although each is situated differently from it. The History Channel, like its parent, A&E—with its motto, "time well spent"—consciously strives to achieve the cultural mantle of PBS, coming the closest to resembling it of all the nonfiction commercial cable channels. Without labeling themselves ostensibly as family programming, in the way of such networks as Disney Channel, PAX, or Family Channel, The History Channel, Discovery, TLC, and Animal Planet also broadly seek the same family entertainment market.[22] Discovery typically adds to the mix male viewers, who watch less television, while TLC claims to offer advertisers access to upscale adults ages twenty-five to fifty-five, split evenly between both sexes.[23] By contrast, The History Channel's bedrock support is considered to be men, middle-aged and older; hence the emphasis on programming dealing with war, weapons, and technology, especially during its weekend lineup, as a counteroffering to sports broadcasting.[24]

Unlike the Anglocentric focus of PBS, A&E, and The History Channel, many of the historical documentaries for TLC and Discovery are produced on the European continent, with American rights sold for relatively small fees. These not only display the familiar problems in narration and style, but are even more haphazardly constructed and lacking in coherence before dubbing into English. On occasion, these various documentary channels have sponsored competing original programs on similar topics; for instance, in the space of a single year, 1994–1995, original six-hour documentary miniseries on the American Revolution were sponsored by The History Channel (*The American Revolution*) and TLC (*The Revolutionary War*), and in 1997, PBS sponsored a series of equal length on the same topic (*Liberty! The American Revolution*).[25] However, the focus of The History Channel and TLC series are different; the TLC version concentrates on a military perspective, while The History Channel's version is more wide-ranging in analyzing the causes and events of the conflict, spanning not only battlefields but the political dimensions.

While The History Channel has its specific and comparatively narrow focus to itself, TLC bears some similarities but takes its mission more broadly, as its name indicates, and is not committed to a specific discipline. Discovery began by emphasizing natural science, but has since widened its focus; its own publicity has labeled Discovery the channel of the outer world, while TLC is the realm of thought and ideas.[26] TLC provides the primary competition with The History Channel in seeking the educational market of school-age children.[27] TLC approaches a variety of different types of subject matter, especially in the areas of archaeology and anthropology; a specialty is documentaries on Egyptology, many of which are muddled and barely coherent. Even among the best of such programs, the subjects may be sensationalized by placing them in an inappropriate modern context, as when Bob Briers wondered whether Pharaoh Tutankhamen was the victim of a "serial killer" in his series, *The Great Egyptians* (1997). Typical of The History Channel's competition in Egyptology is *The Face of Tutankhamun* (1992), a four-hour series produced by the BBC in association with A&E, written and presented by Christopher Frayling. The four parts range from the discovery of Tut's tomb and its excavation, to the decay of Egypt's artifacts, whether in museums or at the archaeological sites themselves, concentrating on a revisionist approach to Howard Carter and his generation's lack of thorough, modern methods.

This contrast is a key difference between The History Channel and its competition from Discovery and TLC.[28] Discovery and TLC have dived unashamedly into programming on aliens and UFOs—a field where The History Channel has, for the most part, not followed. TLC and Discovery give historical shows such fantastic-sounding titles as *Terra X* (a series),

An example of one of The History Channel's rare attempts to compete with Discovery and TLC in one of their specialties.

Mystery of the Ghost Galleon, or *Curse of the Cocaine Mummies.* Together with Discovery, TLC also includes a far greater quantity of speculative programs, from alien-landing documentaries to the "what ifs" and "maybes" of history, such as *Mysteries of the Unexplained.* A TLC program such as *Atlantis: In Search of the Lost Continent* (coproduced with RAI) is fundamentally not a documentary, but an hour of speculation, in which the son of Edgar Cayce is as authoritative a voice as an acknowledged historian. TLC's *Atlantis Uncovered* eschews any pretense of historical analysis of the myth to reach the astonishing conclusion that because leaders of Fascist Germany were intrigued by the legend of Atlantis, it must therefore also be essentially evil. By contrast, the History Channel documentary "Las Vegas Hotels" (1998) on the series *Modern Marvels* avoids the obvious temptations of sensationalism and glitz to instead offer an intelligent chronicle of the development of a cultural combination of architecture and entertainment.[29]

This is the key difference: The History Channel has been content to remain largely within the bounds of history, catering to more specialized viewers. The History Channel has accepted the inherent audience limitations in its specialized subject matter, generally refusing to shift toward sensationalized or trivial subject matter. This is in contrast to much of the programming of rivals Discovery and TLC and their attempt at a more mainstream appeal; for instance, TLC alone has made three Princess Diana biographies, pre- and post-divorce, and another after her death.[30] Similarly, Discovery has expanded into publishing and retail stores, competing with such other museums and organizations as Smithsonian and National Geographic, which are both also becoming increasingly involved in television production and video sales, all ultimately appealing to the same market. The History Channel has only expanded beyond its base to sponsor an annual antique automobile race, and in 1997 affiliated with such organizations as the National Trust for Historic Preservation and the Civil War Trust in sponsoring historical tours to be pitched during certain programming.[31] Only in making home video sales an important second outlet for the distribution of product that airs on their networks have all the nonfiction commercial cable channels, like PBS, followed a similar marketing strategy.[32]

Although much of the programming on The History Channel is far from reaching the potential of the subject matter, it seems to have achieved a rare degree of scholarly focus in its mix of programming. It is utilizing the range of several decades of valuable existing quality documentaries, providing an outlet for programming too seldom seen after its initial premiere. Only in its original programming, plagued by low budget requirements that result in second-rate work, is The History Channel doing a disservice to its field. Yet such work for The History Channel is only part of a growing tendency, one that is even more pronounced at other commercial cable channels. The History Channel's strength's are unique to it; its weaknesses are, for the most part, those of its counterparts among commercial documentary channels and the perils of such filmmaking. The plateau of seriousness and guiding philosophy behind The History Channel's choice of programming has been sound (despite some poor selections), and will hopefully remain in place, establishing for The History Channel a preeminent niche that distinguishes it from other historically oriented offerings of nonfiction networks.

Notes

1. Supplementary information on this programming was taken from The History Channel sections of the *A&E Monthly* magazine.

2. David Bauder, "Making Television and History, at the Same Time" (AP), *The Florida Times-Union*, May 7, 1998, at <http://www.jacksonville.com/tu-online/stories/050798/ent_Shistory.html>.

3. Eileen Flick, "Review of The History Channel," March 10, 1996, at <http://www.usc.edu/users/help/flick/Infofilter/history_channel.html>.

4. Jaime Yassin, "The 'History Channel' Gives Us War, Bubblegum and Not Much Else," *Extra!* (May–June 1998) at <http://www.charm.net/~marc/chronicle/media_june98.html>.

5. Melanie McFarland, "History Channel Spends Some Time on the Dark Side," *Seattle Times*, October 22, 1999, at <http://www.seattletimes.com/news/entertainment/html98/mel_19991022.html>.

6. For instance, see Barry Layne, "Col Pact makes History," *Hollywood Reporter*, April 6, 1994, at <http://www.hollywoodreporter.com/archive/hollywood/archive/1991–1994/00024539.asp>.

7. The History Channel even showed a documentary series on Adolf Hitler produced by German television. Bauder, "Making Television and History, at the Same Time."

8. History Channel publicity.

9. Harriet Winslow, "What's Next? Network Target: Arts, History, Entertainment, Growth," *The Washington Post TV Week*, January 14, 1996, 6, 46.

10. Tony Scott, "*The American Revolution*," *Variety*, November 21, 1994.

11. Yassin, "The 'History Channel' Gives Us War, Bubblegum and Not Much Else"; the issue was discussed on the H-film (History and Film) listserv on July 10, 1996.

12. For instance, see "History Channel Fails Hispanics," *La Prensa San Diego*, September 24, 1999, at <http://www.ncmonline.com/commentary/1999–10–01/history.html>.

13. "When Discovery Sinks Roots," *The Washington Post*, February 14, 2000, A8. Overall, the marketplace demand for historical documentaries has grown beyond the bounds of basic film production programs, with at least one academic program now specifically in "historical documentary filmmaking" sponsored in 2000 by George Washington University.

14. Noel Riley Fitch, "This is Everybody's Life," *Los Angeles Times Calendar,* April 26, 1998, 5; Noel Riley Fitch, "Bibliography of Biography Programs," *Los Angeles Times Calendar,* April 26, 1998, 95; Harriet Winslow, "What's Next?"

15. Bill Edelstein, "Producers hitch stars to docus," *Variety,* April 3–9, 1995, 10.

16. Ken Ringle, "The History Channel Remembers the Alamo," *The Washington Post,* February 25, 1996, G9.

17. Ruth Otte, quoted in MS, "The Discovery Channel Looks for Next Frontier," *Broadcasting,* June 11, 1990, reprinted in Discovery Channel publicity portfolio.

18. I first outlined some of these tendencies in a posting to the H-film (History and Film) listserv on March 4, 1998.

19. Kathryn Harris, "Mind Over Rock Videos," *Forbes,* January 21, 1991, reprinted in Discovery Channel publicity portfolio.

20. Dennis Wharton, "Channeling the market: Q & A with Greg Moyer," *Variety,* April 3–9, 1995, 22.

21. Bauder, "Making Television and History, at the Same Time."

22. "When Discovery Sinks Roots," *The Washington Post.*

23. Harris, "Mind Over Rock Videos"; David Tobenkin, "Discovery Tops Basic Cable Poll," *Hollywood Reporter,* December 13, 1993, at <http://www.hollywoodreporter.com/archive/hollywood/archive/1991–1994/00021591.asp>; "Question and Answer: The New Learning Channel," publicity flyer, The Learning Channel organizational file, Motion Picture/Broadcasting/Recorded Sound Division, Library of Congress.

24. Bauder, "Making Television and History, at the Same Time"; Yassin, "The 'History Channel' Gives Us War, Bubblegum and Not Much Else."

25. Tony Scott, "*The American Revolution*"; Patricia Brennan, "'The Revolutionary War': A Passion for Freedom," *The Washington Post TV Week,* November 26, 1995, 7, 46; Harriet Winslow, "'Liberty!' The American Revolution Without the Song and Dance," *The Washington Post TV Week,* November 23, 1997, 7, 48.

26. "Question and Answer: The New Learning Channel."

27. Joe Flint, "TLC's Mixed Bag of Blessings," *Variety,* April 3–9, 1995, 28.

28. A discussion of these tendencies occurred on the H-film (History and Film) listserv on February 26–27, 1998.

29. "History Channel Studies Hotels in Las Vegas," *Las Vegas Review Journal,* August 3, 1998, at <http://www.lvrj.com/lvryj_home/1998/Aug-03-Mon-1998/lifestyles/7958116.html>.

30. Fitch, "This is Everybody's Life."

31. "Denton to Host The History Channel Great Race XVII," at <http://www.denton-chamber.org/greatrace/>; "History Channel Looks Forward to Travel Business," *Media Daily* 5 (November 12, 1997) at <http://www.mediacentral.com/Magazines/MediaDaily/OldArchives/199711202.html>; Bauder, "Making Television and History, at the Same Time."

32. Video availability is frequently announced at the show's conclusion, and it is not only the leading programs that are so available, but hundreds of other titles as well, many of which would seem so specialized in their subject matter as to lack sufficient commercial draw.

14 | Rethinking Television History

Douglas Gomery

Writings about the early history of U.S. television have long concentrated on the rise of dominating national networks. Whether coming from a textual, personal, or national approach, historians have shaped television history for the United States from solely the network perspective. Yet based on principles of social, demographic, policy and urban history, we should rethink this seemingly "obvious" historical analysis, attend to TV's early history at the local level, and then integrate and synthesize a complete historical analysis of the coming of television to the United States.

Let us begin with Monday the twenty-first of January 1957, a day when nearly all Americans watched TV. This day of high viewing totals symbolizes the potential of the new medium to unite and inform a nation, while revealing a snapshot of basic trends of historical change. The choice of January 21, 1957, is not arbitrary. To those who heralded TV as "a window on the world," this day was an historical one because of the extensive live coverage of the second inauguration of Dwight David Eisenhower. "Ike" and the Republicans appreciated that a nation would be watching and prepared a proper and unprecedented TV spectacle they hoped would mesmerize a nation of whom three-quarters had TV sets. On the prior Friday, for example, they held a mock parade, as technicians from the three networks timed the exercise and sought to deal with subzero freezing weather. Republican officials took no chances, even bringing in Cecil B. DeMille to direct the inaugural balls. DeMille, reported *The Washington Evening Star,* demanded "take" after "take," shouting to Republican volunteers: "Please, ladies and gentlemen, let's try it again."[1]

The networks heralded their coverage as "historic," to be covered in more detail and seen by more people than any event ever telecast. For the forty-third presidential inauguration, both CBS and NBC heralded the first use of videotape, with newly developed Ampex apparatus to "re-broadcast" the actual swearing-in ceremonies. NBC replayed the noon swearing-in by Chief Justice Earl Warren at 12:45 P.M.; CBS followed at 12:55 P.M. The trade press reported "no discernable difference between the live and the recorded versions of the ceremony." A whole nation saw their first view of videotape in action, and NBC and CBS told proudly of their technical achievement. NBC boasted that it was airing the swearing-in twice, "mainly for the benefit of schoolchildren who miss the event while having lunch."[2]

Ampex had introduced its two-inch machines six months earlier at the annual convention of the National Association of Broadcasters. By the end of November of 1956, CBS was secretly using it for West Coast feeds of *Douglas Edwards and the News,* but not telling viewers. It was the much-praised use of videotape for the 1957 inauguration that formally kicked off a new TV era. The videotape equipment was a $45,009, reel-to-reel apparatus the size of an office desk. But its use at the inaugural led to innovation, and so shortly afterward, CBS began to reinvent prime time by prerecording *Arthur Godfrey's Talent Scouts,* one of its most popular programs, to enable Godfrey to go off to Africa "on safari" in late February 1957 and still keep *Talent Scouts* on its highly rated Monday night schedule.[3]

Inaugural coverage was indeed extensive. CBS and ABC commenced at 11:30 P.M. and ended five hours later. NBC started a half hour earlier and continued to 4:45 P.M.—fifteen minutes past when the parade ended. The DeMille-directed inaugural balls started at 11:15 P.M., after the local news. The networks reported a total of $380,000 in lost advertising as late-morning game shows, like *Strike It Rich,* and afternoon soap operas, such as *Search for Tomorrow* and *The Guiding Light,* were canceled. In an era well before satellite distribution, the networks paid dearly to tie up much of AT&T landline capacity and microwave facilities. The big names of the news— David Brinkley and Chet Huntley (NBC), Walter Cronkite and Edward R. Murrow (CBS), and John Charles Daly (ABC)—hosted for their respective networks. NBC technicians led the way by laying one hundred miles of coaxial cable and five hundred miles of wiring, and utilizing twenty cameras and fifty microphones. NBC boasted that "No special event coverage takes more elaborate technical arrangements than Inaugural Day. More than a mile of the presidential parade route had to be covered with special camera placements, power sources, and audio loops, making Washington the TV capital of the world for the day."[4]

In the end, the three networks spent—directly or in monies lost by pre-empting advertising-based entertainment programming—some $682,000. The relatively high ratings for a pure news event set a record as an estimated 90 percent of the country tuned in at some point that afternoon. In a poll conducted just after January 21, 1957, Sindlinger and Company reported that there were some 122,230,000 persons in the United States over the age of twelve who revealed they sought out TV coverage, abandoning the radio. But the networks did not simply give away all profit making. For example, while CBS officially started at 11:30 A.M., at 11:00 A.M. Arthur Godfrey hosted an "Inaugural Preview" as part of his regular morning show. Two TV favorites of the day—Lawrence Welk and Guy Lombardo—made the inaugural balls popular telecasts. *TV Guide* called the inauguration the "biggest spectacular of them all" and praised TV's elaborate coverage of the event by writing: "The nation's television audience will get a far better view of President Eisenhower's inaugural ceremonies next Monday than all but a handful of on-the-spot spectators." Yet *TV Guide* also highlighted that week an appearance by Bing Crosby on *The Phil Silvers Show* and Jerry Lewis's return to television. Indeed it was Lewis—not the president—who graced the *TV Guide* cover that inaugural week.[5]

It was no wonder. Prime-time fare, even the evening of inaugural day, drew far more TV watchers per program than any portion of the celebration for the president. While heralding their inaugural coverage, the three major networks never contemplated abandoning sponsored prime-time programming. CBS knew it had millions to lose, from *Arthur Godfrey's Talent Scouts* at 8:30 P.M., followed by *I Love Lucy* at 9:00 P.M., followed by *December Bride* and *Studio One*. During the 1956–1957 TV season, *I Love Lucy* ranked first in the ratings, with *December Bride* capturing most of the 49.0 rating and *Talent Scouts* doing almost as well, holding the audience from *Lucy's* lead-in. These three shows constituted the core of the biggest night of TV through the middle 1950s. And, while it was not fully appreciated at the time, Lucy was leading a revolution—toward Hollywood's domination of prime time on its way to becoming a classic through filming original and repeatable episodes forever rebroadcast.[6]

NBC countered Godfrey and Lucy with *Twenty-One*. (ABC was no serious factor in 1957.) *Twenty-One* was a quiz show with a developing nation star—Charles Van Doren—who was later disgraced as having been coached as he "won" $104,500 on the evening of January 21, 1957. Millions watched Van Doren break the magical $100,000 winnings marker in dramatic fashion. It would be more than a year before the nation learned that Van Doren's mental powers had not really been tested that night; they had seen only an amateur actor well coached by producer Dan Enright. From the moment Columbia University instructor Van Doren walked onto the stage of *Twenty-One* on November 28, 1956, for his first "contest" with fellow New Yorker Herbert Stempel, he gradually rose to stardom that was acknowledged late that winter with his face adorning the cover of *Time* magazine. Van Doren played his role well, muttering to himself constantly, letting the viewers "see" him think by frequently scratching his chin and then suddenly blurting out: "Oh, I know!"[7]

By January 21, Van Doren was doing so well in his role as New York intellectual, NBC and Enright placed *Twenty-One* directly opposite *I Love Lucy*. It was almost as if this intellectual show aimed at New Yorkers was finally going national. When defeated on March 11, 1957, by yet another New Yorker (Enright demanded contestants live close to the studio so he could keep them on a tight leash), the NBC brass breathlessly announced the network had signed Van Doren to add to the ratings of *Today*. Yet this New York centric "test" of intellectual ability never toppled the Queen of comedy or even matched the drawing power of Godfrey's lead-in. It proved only an aberration in TV history.[8]

That very night of January 21, a long-lived star was discovered a half-hour before Van Doren's performance. Twenty-five-year-old Patsy Cline won *Talent Scouts*, and this Washington, D.C., local TV veteran, now a legend of country music, burst onto the national stage. Godfrey, while home on his farm south and west of the nation's capital, had caught Cline performing on a local Washington, D.C., television show. She had a great voice and style but no national reputation—she was ready for discovery. Godfrey long captured a nation's fancy by finding budding stars, regularly ranking in TV's top ten. (Indeed, during the 1951–1952 TV season, *Talent Scouts* ranked number one. Godfrey loved to tug at the heartstrings of his audience and was still at the peak of his powers when 1957 began with him gracing the cover of *TV Guide*. Lever Brothers Company, owner of Lipton's Tea, Gillette, and Toni products for women's hair, sponsored *Talent Scouts*—through advertising agency Young and Rubicam—for telecast to eager CBS affiliates. In terms of audience composition, *Talent Scouts* drew a largely female audience to whom Godfrey sold tea and women's hair products.[9]

Cline represented the link between local and national. She had been appearing on local TV in Washington for more than a year before the "debut" and "discovery" by Godfrey. Backed by Godfrey's in-house big band, not the classic country combo she normally worked with, Cline sang what would later constitute one of her signature tunes—"Walkin' After Midnight." Her "talent scout" mother and the twenty-five-year-old Cline broke down as

Godfrey declared her the winner: "Don't go away, Patsy honey, you done won this. . . . Bless your little heart; sit down before you have a heart attack."[10]

Patsy Cline's appearance was no "stroke of lightning," but the careful work by a local TV producer, Connie B. Gay, who was the king of country music in and around the nation's capital. He facilitated local TV interaction with the national programming. Gay had persuaded Godfrey to give Cline a look on a Saturday night local Washington, D.C., broadcast on December 8, 1956. Godfrey must have liked what he saw, because on the following Monday morning his chief assistant, Janette Davis, contacted Patsy Cline to set the January 21 booking.[11]

Three days before her Monday night appearance, Cline traveled to New York City and passed on her usual date—scheduled by *TV Guide*—to perform not as a "hillbilly girl singer," but as a New York–style torch singer. Patsy picked a country favorite, "A Poor Man's Roses (or a Rich Man's Gold)," to sing on *Talent Scouts;* Godfrey preferred the bluesier "Walkin' After Midnight." While the rest of nation was watching Eisenhower and Nixon being celebrated, Patsy Cline was at Godfrey's Fifty-third and Broadway studio, rehearsing her number. Godfrey was not present; indeed, Patsy Cline and Arthur Godfrey would not meet until minutes before her live performance that evening.[12]

Television fans in Washington saw and heard nothing new. They had become fans of Patsy through her regular appearances on Connie B. Gay's *Town and Country Jamboree* and *Town and Country Time* shows on Channel 7. Indeed, that very evening of January 21, 1957, on the local Washington ABC television affiliate, *Town and Country Time* went on without Patsy Cline. Her discovery on *Talent Scouts* was not even mentioned in *The Washington Post*. Even *The Star*'s TV writer Bernie Harrison wrote: "Patsy Cline walked off with top honors on Godfrey's *Talent Scouts* Monday night, singing her new Decca recording. . . . Patsy is another of the Connie B. Gay country team to hit it on country fan Godfrey's show." Harrison worked for the company that not only published the most widely circulated newspaper in the nation's capital, but also owned WMAL-TV, the station that broadcast the *Town and Country* shows of Connie B. Gay.[13]

Godfrey simply let the nation learn what they were missing. With one of Gay's local stars winning *Talent Scouts*, there is an absorbing link made on a typical day of 1957 that pushes us to examine TV as both national and local, where forms of an emerging TV industry were still being defined. While most persons are only vaguely familiar with Charles Van Doren and Arthur Godfrey, as the twentieth century ends, Patsy Cline—local TV star—has

Country music legend Patsy Cline, in a publicity photo about the time she was becoming a star on Washington, D.C., television. Courtesy of Douglas Gomery collection.

been the subject of a movie biography, an essay on heroine worship in the *New York Times*, the star of three plays by impersonators depicting her tragic life, the seller of a half a million CDs and cassettes per annum thirty years after her death, and an inspiration to music makers of many genres.[14]

Rethinking TV Historiography

The day of January 21, 1957, was a peak for the early days of television, consisting of special programming fare in the late morning and throughout the afternoon, but also of a typical synergy of national network and local fare. How should we thus rethink the analytical techniques for researching and writing the history of television in the United States? While television as a mass medium seems always to have been with us, the struggle for its control was defined in the 1950s. And the writing of the history of television—of this complex programming mixture—buttressed by all the vexing problems of "contemporary historical analysis," would benefit by recognizing this mixture of national and local appeal, and the developing economic history of the TV business.

Presently the history of the advent of television begins (and ends) with the studies of ascendancy of the U.S. national networks. This can be easily appreciated by contrasting the vast array of books on CBS news and newsman Edward R. Murrow with the sole book-length entry on the history of local news, about the journalistic efforts at KDKA in Pittsburgh. Following historian Thomas Bender's admonition to link "parts and wholes," we need to connect national TV through network programming and policy making (the whole) to the specifics of local viewing, production, and audience use (the parts). This best begins with the contradictions surrounding the stated FCC policy goal of "localism." While network economics pressured a national system, policy makers were positioning stations in local communities and asking owners, managers, and programmers to direct their efforts to their community. In short, we need to follow what Bender and a generation of social historians have taught us; recognize the limits of "national" history, and seek to look at TV's historical development from the bottom up.[15]

The best first step is to turn the problem on its head and move directly from the national to the local. This is in line with the 1952 national allocation plan for analog television, the "Sixth Report and Order," which elevated local programming to a top policy goal. The commission sought to push the new medium to develop live local programming as expressed in the FCC's "Public Service Responsibility of Broadcast Licenses," issued six years earlier, which called for "programs of local interests, activities and talent." As an example, the commission praised a Missouri station's airing of a local hill-billy quartet: "Public acceptance has been phenomenal, partly *because of the interest of rural people in the type of entertainment afforded but also because the entertainers are all local people and well known in the community*" (original ital-ics). The commission recognized that mounting live local shows did not represent a profit-maximizing strategy, but simply plugging into a network "abdicated [a station's] local responsibilities."[16]

The "Sixth Report and Order" further underscored "localism" as a top priority, as it prescribed licenses for TV stations community by community, not in some national network scheme. The commission did not want local stations to simply become "network spigots." Licensees understood, and be-tween 1952 and 1965 applicants promised that an average of a third of their broadcasting day would be devoted to local programming. Here we confront the reality of national network forces and the ideal of a local medium re-sponding to local needs and concerns.[17]

But how best to analyze local TV as an expression of FCC and policy-making desires? Let us follow what the FCC wrought by first analyzing the place of television in urban history. The FCC allocated TV stations to cities, and this is where we best begin. But cities have histories, and TV historians need to look at their changing social make-up through time and how that composition changed the nature of the TV audience. Thus, by moving from urban history through social and demographic analysis—all the while recog-nizing that this is a regulated industry consisting of businesses seeking to maximize profits—we can properly synthesize the parts into a new and more complete understanding of the history of television in the United States.

Washington, D.C., as a Key to Broadcasting History

Since TV markets blanket urban communities by FCC design, there is no better way to test this historiographic approach than by beginning with Sam Bass Warner, who simply asked in his now-classic *American Historical Review* article, "If the World Were Philadelphia. . . ." For media historians, one community needs to take precedence—Washington, D.C. Media historians tell us only of a Washington as a site of national news events such as inaugu-rations, but Washington, D.C., was also an important, growing, vital urban place, where those who were making the policy of TV regulation lived, worked, and tuned in. FCC Commissioners, members of Congress, and the presi-dent all watched TV at home in Washington, D.C., and through the 1950s saw and heard what they had wrought. On a daily basis, from 1946 on, when the first experimental TV station in the nation's capital began operation from a hotel across the street from the FCC's headquarters, government officials walked over and saw how TV worked and then returned to their offices to further ponder the politics of license allocation. In short, Washington TV stations influenced national communications policy far more than any other set of stations in the United States as they fed back into the loop of policy making.[18]

Indeed the three most powerful politicians in 1957 Washington—President Dwight Eisenhower, Speaker of the House Sam Rayburn, and the majority leader of the U.S. Senate (later president) Lyndon Johnson—all followed the development of TV closely from their homes and offices in the nation's capital. Speaker Rayburn in 1934 even helped create the FCC; two decades later his nephew Robert Bartley was a member of the FCC. Appointed in 1952 by President Harry Truman as a favor for Rayburn, Bartley provided a direct pipeline to his uncle. Newton Minow has written that one day shortly after being nominated by President John F. Kennedy to head the FCC, he called on Rayburn, who put his arm around Minow and said, "Just remember one thing, son. Your agency is an arm of Congress; you belong to us. Remember that and you'll be all right."[19]

When Eisenhower reappointed nephew Bartley, Rayburn wrote the president that he and his sister were grateful, and "you could not have done anything in the world for me that I would appreciate more than the reappointment. . . . I shall always remember this gracious and fine act on your part." Personally, Rayburn loved to watch Washington TV stations as a way to relax. A close aide noticed that the divorced Rayburn used TV as an antidote for loneliness and claimed the syndicated *Lone Ranger* his favorite show. He also loved local broadcasts of Washington Redskins football and Senators baseball.[20]

Eisenhower knew the value of an FCC appointment when he filled the Speaker's request. Ike appreciated the fact that he was the first TV president. Elected as the freeze on the granting of new TV licenses was being lifted, when only about a third of Americans owned a TV set, by the close of his presidency in January 1961 nearly every American who so desired had a set. Eisenhower was an avid television fan, arguing that as an "average American" he loved everything Arthur Godfrey did. Ike loved NBC newscaster John Cameron Swayze and complained bitterly in October of 1956 when NBC replaced Swayze with Huntley and Brinkley. He knew the movers and shakers of the new TV industry, from both David Sarnoff and William Paley to the heads of the major advertising agencies to talented performers such as Robert Montgomery, who advised the president on TV matters. First Lady Mamie Eisenhower was an even bigger TV fan. Longtime White House correspondent Ray Scherer recalled that when he was assigned to escort Charles Van Doren around the White House after Van Doren joined *Today*, Mamie lit up like an average fan as he introduced her to TV's newest star.[21]

Indeed, Ike was there when Sarnoff called on him to formally open NBC's newly owned and operated $4 million all-color facility in the nation's capital. Ike dedicated the new WRC on May 22, 1958, making his first appearance in color as president from Washington. FCC chair John C. Doerfer and three other FCC commissioners also attended, hearing Sarnoff state, "We are highly honored, Mr. President, by your presence here today, and on behalf of my associates, as well as myself, I should like to express to you our most sincere thanks and appreciation for taking out of your busy day the time to honor us with your presence. Having had the privilege of serving under you in both war and peace, I know first hand how deep is your interest in all forms of communication."[22]

Lyndon Baines Johnson ruled the U.S. Senate in 1957. Here was yet another Godfrey fan. Like Ike and Sam Rayburn, Johnson watched TV news constantly; less well known is that he and Lady Bird were also big *Gunsmoke* fans. They should have been, given where they owned a CBS affiliate. If Rayburn and Eisenhower appreciated the power of TV and were among its biggest fans, Johnson became a millionaire because of his family ownership of a TV station. Johnson needed money to feed his political obsession, and that money came from his clout with the FCC. Johnson acquired and long maintained the lone television station in Austin, enabling him to raise the wave of prosperity of TV innovation into American culture, society, and economy. There can be no doubt that Johnson, more than any modern politician, even Ronald Reagan, made his fortune through TV.[23]

These three powerful men followed social historian Howard Gillette's dictum: "[Washington has long served] as a workshop in which to try out new policy initiatives." They influenced the FCC, Rayburn in particular, to allocate to the nation's capital four of the first VHF television stations in the United States, the most on a per population basis of any city in the United States. Through April 1952, with the lifting of the freeze, there were more than one hundred stations on the air, and only two much larger urban areas, New York and Los Angeles, had more TV stations. Far bigger metropolitan regions, such as Boston and Pittsburgh, had fewer; similar-sized communities, such as Denver and Portland, Oregon, had none. Moreover, the commission used its ruling about Washington, D.C., to explain its precepts for station allocation, noting that "maximum opportunity for local expression and development of community activity [should be] afforded."[24]

The Washington metro area, where these first TV signals reached, represented most of the typical traits of twentieth-century urban development. Urban historian Carl Abbott reminds us in his *American Historical Review* study of the nation's capital as city: "Washington as everyday community has remained embedded in its regional environment. Despite frequent comments about its isolation from the American mainstream, [Washington's] residents have maintained many old regional relationships while accommodating and constructing new claims and connections." In particular Washington, D.C., functioned—through the period where television was innovated into American society and culture—as a southern capital city, dominated by representatives and senators from the South, defining the border of northern Virginia. Yet as TV was becoming a force in U.S. society, Washington was being transformed by an influx of northerners. Here important demographic forces were remaking Washington from the northernmost southern city to the southernmost northern city, shoving the nation's capital onto the tail of megalopolis.[25]

During the late 1940s and through the 1950s, Washington, D.C., was becoming richer, more suburbanized, and more racially divided. Because its boundaries were fixed by federal law, the District of Columbia never expanded beyond its original borders, following the suburbs. These four social traits differentiated Washington as an urban place. As a consequence, after World War II the percentage of metro area citizens living inside the District of Columbia fell on a regular basis. At the end of World War II, two of three metro residents lived inside D.C. By 1960, after the region's population doubled and television was a presence in nearly every household, only one of three metro residents resided inside the District. The well-off and white fled, leaving D.C. a poor African American enclave, which by 1960 had become the first major jurisdiction in the United States with a majority African American population.[26]

Indeed, historian Carl Abbott finds the constantly changing demographic status of the nation's capital as its defining post–World War II characteristic. Still, as television was becoming fully diffused, the nation's capital remained best characterized as a southern urban place. In the 1950s, the majority of Washingtonians had been born elsewhere, principally the South. Since many stayed and located in Washington, because it seemed safe and familiar on the border of the South, they continued to identify themselves as southerners. With the proximity of Washington to rail lines south, they would often travel back home for family reunions, weddings, and funerals, thus permitting family, social, church, and musical networks to remain intact, despite geographical dislocation. Television would also help fill this function of constructing and maintaining a mythic vision of the familiar, while newcomers confronted the frenzy surrounding a growing federal government. The history of the coming of TV to the nation's capital as a community was defined by this from the South with continual community transformation.[27]

Important Big City TV Stations

The four VHF television stations in the nation's capital were all on the air before the 1950s commenced. Two were in the hands of electronics manufacturers with designs on cornering TV set sales. DuMont's WTTG came on line in 1946; the Radio Corporation of America and its subsidiary, NBC, followed a year later with WNBW. Local newspapers owned the other two stations. WMAL went on the air in 1947, licensed to the then-dominant afternoon daily, *The Washington Evening Star*. In 1949 when WOIC went on the air, it was licensed to Bamberger Broadcasting; a year later the *Washington Post* took control.[28]

Notably for media historians, since the *Star* and the *Post* both owned TV stations, these dailies covered the local TV scene with a great deal of space and care. In response, their rivals for mass newspaper circulation, *The Times-Herald* and *The Daily News*, often investigated the emerging TV scene, knowing that two of the four stations were in the hands of their press rivals. Thus, the newspaper coverage of early TV in Washington, D.C., is rich and, supplemented by ratings data and oral histories, demonstrates that Washington metro residents quickly and lovingly embraced television. In one study done of viewing on a prime-time Monday night in November 1950, the Washington area led both New York and Los Angeles, each with more stations, in percentage of sets in use. In 1950 *The Times-Herald* correctly noted, "The nation's eyes are focused on Washington."[29]

When Washington's first station began transmissions in 1946, there were only 150 sets in the entire metropolitan area. By 1954, nearly 200,000 homes owned TV sets, representing more than three-quarters of the area's households. Four years later, in 1958, there were television sets in 90 percent of living rooms in the Washington metro region. Through the early 1950s, D.C.'s four stations dealt differently with a changing metro region and the unknown nature of the TV business. RCA used its NBC-owned-and-operated station to build its prestige in front of policy makers. In 1946 John Royal, an NBC vice president, testified that his company wanted to "carry the sight and sound of Washington events into every American home that can be reached by a television network. . . . As a source of television program material, Washington is a city which has no parallel in the United States." NBC alone carried the opening of Congress each January, and it devoted the most airtime to presidential inaugural ceremonies every fourth year. However, the station felt this fulfilled its public interest obligations, and so aired little local programming other than football and basketball contests by area universities.[30]

In contrast, DuMont was a far weaker company, with a far more vulnerable network. In short, DuMont's owned-and-operated WTTG, channel 5, in Washington, D.C., was neither the owned-and-operated station (or O&O) of a rich manufacturer nor the exploited progeny of an expanding media empire. Without much network programming to fill its day and with no newspaper promotion support, WTTG presented a great deal of live local programming, beginning most notably in 1947 with regular telecasts of Washington Senators baseball games. WTTG exploited contacts in the nation's capital. In 1951, for example, as the Korean War heated up and as parent company DuMont bid for radar contracts, WTTG programmed *Guide Right,* a weekly variety show supplied by the U.S. Army and Air Force, and *Keep Posted,* a series of televised lectures by government officials on the escalating dangers of communism. All were cheap to produce, and all garnered sympathy for DuMont officials seeking valuable government contracts.[31]

The newspaper-owned stations had stronger ties to the local community. Profits from the *Post*'s television station, WTOP on channel 9, affiliated with CBS, were used in the early 1950s to help the newspaper play catch-up to its long dominant rival, *The Evening Star.* Thus *Post* management chose to draw profits from everything CBS piped down the line rather than spend money televising either special events or live local programming. WTOP did even less than WNBW in terms of local programming. Prior to the purchase of the *Times-Herald* in 1954, "more than one reporter remembered asking [publisher Phil] Graham for a raise and, as Sam Zagoria [a fellow reporter] recalled it, hearing [Graham] reply, 'Sam, did you get a check the last week from *The Post?* The funds for that [check] came from WTOP. We lost money here [at the newspaper]." During those years, the *Post* shamelessly used newspaper space to promote network fare, splashing advertisements for CBS shows across its entertainment page while listing what the competition had to offer in small type.[32]

The station in the nation's capital that operated closest to what the FCC had in mind when it allocated its license was the *Star*'s WMAL-TV, an ABC affiliate. Local programming thrived at WMAL because of access to a limited network schedule. The *Star,* a rich afternoon daily, one of the most profitable in the country, was owned by a family willing and wealthy enough to wait for the ABC-TV network to grow. The *Star*'s local owners saw TV fulfilling the same supplementary role radio long had for them, a means of promoting the newspaper and protecting its circulation leadership. The *Star* boasted about WMAL-TV's accomplishments in news, heralding in 1949, at the end of its second year on the air, the prestige of being the first TV station in the land to broadcast a documentary on the Nuremberg trials, the first to televise a hearing from Capitol Hill, and the first to televise from inside the White House.[33]

Washington, D.C., Local TV Experiments

Through its first decade on the air, WMAL alone experimented with many forms of local programming, from the talking heads of *Meet Your Congress* to the highly targeted *Modern Woman*. None of this was surprising or exceptional. But during the 1955–1956 and 1956–1957 TV seasons, WMAL's live, locally produced country music shows, *Town and Country Time* and *Town and Country Jamboree,* ranked as particular favorites of Washingtonians. Beyond the marble museums and halls of government deliberations, southerner's nostalgia gave rise in the 1950s to a country music nexus equal at the time to Nashville. It was here where the intersection of urban forces, social history, and demographic change intersected to forge a local schedule on WMAL dominated by country music.[34]

New white immigrants to the nation's capital embraced country music as a reminder of "back home." As a community on the edge of the South, white Washingtonians—in the city and suburbs—watched and listened to WMAL's average of an hour of live country music local programming per day to sweep away their anxieties. While the significant migration of African Americans out of the South has received significant historical analysis, movement occurred for poor and aspiring whites as well. The poor were pushed from the farm because of sick economic conditions and natural disasters. They moved to the nation's capital, starting in the Great Depression, and in accelerating rates during World War II, to find higher paying, steady work. No city represented more of a lure than the headquarters of the war effort, yet all new immigrants felt a sense of loss as they were invariably overwhelmed by the city. For the white southerners moving to Washington, D.C., this manifested itself through Connie B. Gay's country music offerings.[35]

Televising eight hours a week of locally produced, live country music was certainly not what the *Star* had envisioned for WMAL-TV. But by the close of the 1953–1954 TV season they had grown frustrated watching rival stations make more money, and so hired Booz, Allen, Hamilton, a consulting firm, to suggest ways of increasing profits. Consultant Fred Houwink delivered his report during the summer of 1954. The *Star* management liked what he had to say and hired Houwink as the new general manager of WMAL. Houwink followed his own advice and promptly boosted WMAL's

signal reach into the predominantly white suburbs. This meant higher ratings, greater revenues, and an instant increase in profits. Policymakers noticed the change; FCC commissioners—including Robert Bartley—praised
the new "Super Power Channel 7."[36]

Houwink next looked for new programming. He had already noticed
Connie B. Gay, a local radio personality who pioneered the country format
in the D.C. area, successfully tapping into transplanted white southerner's
desires for music from back home. Gay had moved his collection of country
stars into DAR Constitution Hall and constantly filled its nearly four thousand seats. His "Club Hillbilly," in suburban Prince Georges County, Maryland, regularly turned away customers. "Hillbilly Cruises" down the Potomac
River helped make Jimmy Dean a star. Area fans also flocked to see and hear
other local Gay discoveries: guitarist Roy Clark and "girl singer" Patsy Cline.[37]

Houwink knew that throughout cities on the "border South," where rural
southerners had moved, advertisers long supported barn dances on radio.
Moving them over to TV made sense: costs were low, and advertisers eagerly
bought advertising, especially local beer distributors and auto dealers. After
only weeks on the job as WMAL general manager, Houwink contacted Gay,
and on an otherwise quiet Monday night in January 1955 *Town and Country
Time*, starring Jimmy Dean, premiered at 5:00 P.M. Five nights a week, Dean
and company faced off against *Pinky Lee* on WRC and a B-western movie
on WTOP. Not surprisingly, the *Post* did not even mention the debut of
Town and Country Time; the *Star* gave over nearly a full page to herald the
top "western and Country Music program on television. Local! Live!"[38]

By midway through 1955, *Town and Country Time* moved into second
place in its time slot. Local advertisers loved the surveys, which indicated
three or four persons crowding around their TV sets (more women than
men) to see and hear Dean, Clark, and Cline, and national guest stars. No
one was surprised that ten months later, in October 1955, as the new TV
season commenced, WMAL launched a three-hour live Saturday night *Town
and Country Jamboree*. The *Star* regularly proffered huge advertisements on
its television page, heralding the appearance of big-name guests, from country music legends Roy Acuff and Kitty Wells to newcomers like Johnny Cash
and Elvis Presley. Overnight *The Jamboree* moved WMAL into second place
in the late Saturday night hours.[39]

Town and Country programming helped Houwink reap the rewards of an
economic boom taking place in the D.C. suburbs. At this point, the migration to suburban Maryland and Virginia made Washington, D.C., the second fastest-growing metro area in the nation. During one stretch of the
early 1950s, enough buildings had been built in the D.C. suburbs to house

Connie B. Gay (applauding) promotes one of his WARL country music concerts along with local figure Horace Lohnes (with hat in hand). Courtesy of the Library of American Broadcasting, University of Maryland.

all the families in a Jacksonville, Florida, or Sacramento, California. The well-off whites in a booming Bethesda, Maryland, and a flourishing Fairfax County, Virginia, had thrust the Washington metro area to second place in family income in the nation, and to number one in retail sales per family. And these new suburbanites loved watching Jimmy Dean, Patsy Cline, and company on TV—achieving ratings that equalled national programming of the day.[40]

As the 1956–1957 TV season commenced, ratings were so high that Connie B. Gay, with Houwink's consent, mounted a third show, *Town and Country Matinee*, starring George Hamilton IV, which aired each weekday afternoon. College sophomore Hamilton was Gay's next discovery, a good looking "boy" from back home in North Carolina who was to be the *Town and Country* empire's answer to that unprecedented musical phenomenon, another white southern teen heartthrob, Elvis Presley. *TV Guide*'s annual preview edition, issued in September 1956, celebrated *Town and Country* as a true local success story, describing how crowds of supposedly sophisticated Washingtonians lined up each Saturday night to get a chance to be a part of the *Town and Country Jamboree* and listen to Patsy Cline and Jimmy Dean sing their latest hits.[41]

Gay aspired to expand. Patsy Cline's success on January 21 led CBS to commission Gay to produce a live morning show to go up against NBC's long-running hit, *Today*. Jimmy Dean, George Hamilton IV, and the gang premiered *Country Style* at 7:00 A.M. on Monday, April 8, 1957, live from a Washington, D.C., studio. They repeated the telecast at 8:00 A.M. for the west coast. *Variety* noted that there was "Nothing Hayseed About Connie Gay" and heralded the possibility that, like Lawrence Welk emerging from Los Angeles eighteen months earlier, a "local [TV] show breaking into network TV" might become a hit. Meanwhile at WMAL, Houwink replaced *Town and Country Jamboree* with a late movie, *Town and Country Time* with the syndicated *Three Musketeers*, and most importantly, fully plugged the station into the expanding schedule of ABC-TV network programs. But Gay had overreached, and by the end of 1957 *Country Style* had been canceled. Gay cashed in. The "Golden Age" of live, local country music on television in the nation's capital ended. ABC had caught up, and the end of this local era came just as the networks were "Hollywoodizing" television for a mass medium.[42]

Implications for the History of Television

In 1990, media historian David Nord wrote, "Before communication historians rush to jump onto the latest trend an adequate foundation needs to be laid in the economic and institutional history of the mass media."[43] This essay suggests that institutional history needs to be defined by social, demographic, urban, and policy historical factors. Further, this essay has put these historiographic methods to a test—analyzing the practice of local TV in general, and focusing on where the picture met the public, where the particulars of the Washington, D.C., community met the generalities of the whole—becoming a TV nation. Here we not only see the nation's capital as the locus of TV policy-making, but also as a community where recently transplanted urban whites embraced live, local country music as policy makers crafted the rules the would make modern television practice. The January 21, 1957, programming day made this point of linking national and local history-making—TV style—through programming and persons from Washington, D.C.—from the president to Patsy Cline.

This is more than a simply a case study, because of the centrality of the Washington community as home to the policy makers who watched TV develop on the local level as they made policy for the nation. While they spoke of the ideal of localism, and Connie B. Gay delivered, in the end the policy makers—led by Eisenhower, Rayburn, and Johnson—acceded to the economics of networking. But this case study does lead to four important implications for the remaking of TV historiography:

First, it is not always best to confront an issue head-on. From the case study of WMAL in Washington, D.C., the media historian can learn of the development of both the ABC and CBS networks and their local affiliates. Thus, while this might on the surface seem to be simply a local case study, this analysis has profound implications for national network study. The possibility for live and local *Town and Country* programming came to be because of the slow growth of the ABC-TV network. ABC leaped over its rivals and caught up by "going Hollywood." While an individual Hollywood show cost a great deal to produce, when spread over hundreds of stations—either through syndication or on a network—its profits overwhelmed live local programming, where full costs fell to a single station. Hollywood made all other fare into a second-best solution. Localism nearly vanished, reducing all representations of the community to a single TV genre—local news.[44]

We need more in-depth case studies of what the development of network television meant for local audiences, "from the bottom up" as in the case of Washington, D.C.'s white country music fans, and we need to cease lamenting the sad disappearance of live elite drama beamed in from New York City. We need a blend of the wholes and parts for all TV history, not the networks that offered live performance and major news coverage to appeal to elites for favorable treatment by policy makers. Historians of television ought to cease only examining CBS and NBC simply because they boasted themselves as high-culture 1950s programmers. Surely CBS' *Country Style* betrays that false image; so did the mega-hit *Beverly Hillbillies* seven years later.

Second, media historians need to rethink and integrate key concepts of urban (and suburban) history as the key bases for television history. The suburbanizing of America, a fundamental tenet of late twentieth-century U.S. social history second to none, can clearly be seen in Washington, D.C., as whites fled to escape new African American neighbors and how television enabled advertisers and programmers alike to reach across urban borders to make profits through mass entertainment and culture. In Washington, in particular, anxious suburban whites who had come north to get government jobs during the Great Depression and World War II embraced Connie B. Gay's programs that filled their homes with the sights and sounds of a mythic home they had reluctantly abandoned or never really knew. Suburbanites, usually thought of as faithful watchers of only sanitized 1950s network TV, embraced local shows aimed at their multiple video needs.[45]

Migration was key, indeed demographic change as destiny. A next step in research on Washington should focus on its growing African American population, moving up from the South, whom local D.C. television stations virtually ignored until the pressure exerted during the civil rights movement of the 1960s. During the early days, WTTG alone recognized the D.C. African American population when, for a time, it featured the weekly series of Reverend Elder Lightfoot Solomon Michaux. Preaching from his Church of God, Michaux had skillfully used radio to help feed thousands during the Great Depression; his religious services worked even better on TV, with an elegant mix of choirs, preaching, and pleading.[46]

Third, we media historians need to use policy, urban, social, and demographic methods to refocus on crucial links between the usually separately studied mass media. Two of the owners of TV stations in Washington, D.C., were far more famous for their newspapers, the *Post* and the *Star*, than their TV operations. Indeed their official histories make invisible their TV profits and participation. Yet during the early 1950s the *Star*, with a circulation of a quarter of a million (America's fifth-largest daily), was being affected by suburbanization in a positive way, as it helped create the audience needed for WMAL's profitable *Town and Country* programs, and in a negative way, as suburbanization exacerbated delivery problems for the afternoon daily. Inexorably the *Star* moved back its long-held noon deadline, thus making the paper increasingly irrelevant to the very suburban commuters its advertisers so wanted to court. Suburbanites chose to relax with *Town and Country Time*, not by reading the *Star's* version of the news written ten hours earlier. The *Post* ascended to local newspaper dominance by milking WTOP-TV. In the end, TV profits (based on advertisers wanting to reach suburbanites) enabled the *Post* to buy out its rival, the *Times-Herald*, gain a morning monopoly, and two decades later take over the complete business in the U.S. capital.

Popular music history needs to be repositioned with television at its focus after the arrival of this new medium. In this case study, the seemingly abrupt end of the Connie B. Gay country music empire was directly linked to TV history, but also came about because of the emergence of rock 'n' roll. TV responded by bringing Dick Clark's locally created *American Bandstand* to the ABC-TV national network, where rock 'n' roll triumphed as the dominant musical form for white teens, as opposed to country music. (In Washington, *The Milt Grant Show* went on the air on August 19, 1957, and for four years as a teen dance party rivaled *American Bandstand* on the local level.) The end of the Connie B. Gay country music shows (locally and on CBS) simply proved the point that "hillbilly" music of the late 1950s needed to reinvent itself and crossover to white teenagers, as Joli Jensen has shown in her 1998 book, *The Nashville Sound.*[47]

Fourth, this study of Washington illuminates the key importance of Washington, D.C., as a TV community, because it alone offered the feedback between programming and national policy-making. NBC fed live plays and news events to protect its valuable license, as did CBS and to a lesser extent ABC and DuMont. Yet ironically for the FCC's avowed tension of local programming achieved by homegrown producers for their own communities, a quintessential example in *Town and Country* programming was fulfilling the commission's very call, yet never enough to turn 1950s communications policy. Country music programming may have worked for the masses of white working-class folks, but they hardly represented what the policy makers valued and preferred.

Indeed while Washingtonians were embracing Jimmy Dean and Patsy Cline's brand of local programming, across town Republican and Democratic policy makers were killing the very policy that made its appearance possible. Policy makers did not see country music for the masses as an achievement of good FCC policy. Both preferred more serious, politically based or high art local programming as a proper policy fulfillment. Neither got what they wanted, and Hollywood as an economic force recrafted TV as a national social force, with local entry coming only in news and sports. We historians need to be careful not to see the past as an inevitable march toward the present.[48]

In sum, the history of TV needs to be written not simply about the wholes—the networks that dominated—but also of the parts from the local level, analyzed from the rich approaches of policy, urban, social, demographic, and economic historiography. This essay has tried to initiate this process of rethinking TV historiography, offering a beginning. Many fascinating and important questions remain unanswered: How did the desires of transplanted white Southerners as the first generation of TV viewers actually use TV in the 1950s? How did African Americans living in D.C. respond to this "white" television? Once these and other questions are answered for communities around the country, we can then fully appreciate and complete our understanding of the emergence of TV during the 1950s.

Notes

1. "Rehearsal Parade Cuts 5 Minutes Off Schedule," *The Evening Star*, 18 January 1957, A1; "Mercury Hits 8, Relief Due for Inauguration," *The Evening Star*, 18 January 1957, A1; John Rossin, "G.O.P. Promenaders Take Their Orders from Film Director in Good Grace," *The Evening Star*, 18 January 1957, B1.

2. "Networks Firm Details of Inaugural Coverage," *Broadcasting*Telecasting*, 21 January 1957, 88; "Inauguration Top Radio-TV Show," *Radio Television Daily*, 22 January 1957, 1, 23. Craig Allen, *Eisenhower and the Mass Media: Peace, Prosperity, and Prime-Time TV* (Chapel Hill: Univ. of North Carolina Press, 1993), offers a fine case study of the use of television by this president, yet contains no mention of the significant image-making power of the presidential inauguration spectacle.

3. Crosby S. Noyes, "Thousands Witness Inauguration," *The Evening Star*, 21 January 1957, A1, A4; "CBS-TV, NBC-TV Record Inaugural Swearing-In Ceremony," *Broadcasting*Telecasting*, 28 January 1957, 68; "Use of Ampex VTR," *Broadcasting*Telecasting*, 28 January 1957, 72; "VTR: Out of the Lab, Onto the Firing Line," *Broadcasting*Telecasting*, 1 April 1957, 120–21; "Monday TV Preview," *The Washington Post and Times Herald*, 21 January 1957, B17. "The Device That May Revolutionize Television," *TV Guide*, 26 January–1 February 1957, 22–23.

4. "Full Inaugural Coverage," *Broadcasting*Telecasting*, 14 January 1957, 78, 80; Lawrence Laurent, "Television Has Got Us Covered for Inauguration," *The Washington Post and Times Herald*, "TV Week," 20 January 1957, G3; "Inauguration Top Radio-TV Show"; NBC Press Release: "NBC Devoted More TV Time to Inaugural Coverage Than Any Other Network," found in NBC Press Release Collection, Library of American Broadcasting, College Park, Maryland.

5. "Your Box Seat for the Inauguration," *TV Guide*, 19–25 January 1957, Washington-Baltimore edition, 6–7, A3, A29; "CBS-TV, NBC-TV Record Inaugural Swearing-In Ceremony"; "Use of Ampex VTR"; "How People Spend their Time," *Broadcasting*Telecasting*, 25 February 1957, 36.

6. "Advertiser Expenditures—Network," *Television*, Data Book 1957, 55–80; *TV Guide*, 19–25 January 1957, A33–A34.

7. There is a great deal written about quiz shows in the middle 1950s, still best summarized in Kent Anderson, *Television Fraud: The History and Implications of the Quiz Show Scandals* (Westport, Conn.: Greenwood, 1978). As to the state of hysteria during late January 1957, press coverage was extensive; for a typically gushing reaction see "Know-It-All," *Newsweek*, 29 January 1957, 60.

8. Thomas A. DeLong, *Quiz Craze: America's Infatuation with Game Shows* (New York: Praeger, 1991) notes the 21 January date on page 213; see also 214–28. See also

"Quiz Winner Tops $100,000," *The Washington Post and Times-Herald,* 22 January 1957, C8, and Bernie Harrison, "On the Air," *The Washington Evening Star,* 22 January 1957, A31, both which noted the growing obsession.

9. "The Stuff That Stars Are Made Of," *TV Guide,* 5–11 January 1957, 8–11; "Advertiser Expenditures—Network";"TV Costs," *Sponsor,* 19 January 1957, 35–40; Evelyn Konrad, "The Y&R Story," *Sponsor,* 19 January 1957, 27–32.

10. "Patsy Cline: The Birth of a Star," compact disc from Razor & Tie, RE 2108–2, issued 1996, includes the introduction of her "talent scout," her performance, and the announcement by Godfrey that she won.

11. Ellis Nassour, *Honky Tonk Angel: The Intimate Story of Patsy Cline* (New York: St. Martin's Press, 1993), 57, 66–69.

12. Nassour, *Honky Tonk Angel,* 66–75; Jones, *Patsy: The Life and Times of Patsy Cline,* 126–34.

13. *TV Guide,* Washington-Baltimore edition, 19–25 January 1957, A18, and Bernie Harrison, "On the Air." According to *TV Guide,* on the 19 January 1957 edition of *Town and Country Jamboree,* there were three featured numbers: "She's My Baby" from Jimmy Dean, the host, "Your Cheatin' Heart" from featured "girl singer" Dale Turner, and "Slave of a Hopeless Love" by Patsy Kline [*sic*]. Such was Patsy Cline's lack of fame to the writers and editors of Philadelphia-based *TV Guide.*

14. For an analysis of the "Posthumous Patsy Cline," see Joli Jensen, *The Nashville Sound: Authenticity, Commercialism, and Country Music* (Nashville: Vanderbilt Univ. Press, 1998). Donald Clarke finds her "highly regarded and influential in his *The Rise and Fall of Popular Music* (New York: Penguin, 1995), 481.

15. Thomas Bender, "Wholes and Parts: The Need for Synthesis in American History," *The Journal of American History* 73 (June 1986): 120–36. The two most influential recent books of TV history are William Boddy, *Fifties Television: The Industry and Its Critics* (Urbana: Univ. of Illinois Press, 1990), and Lynn Spigel, *Make Room for TV: Television and the Family Ideal in Postwar America* (Chicago: Univ. of Chicago Press, 1992). Both are network focused. An exception is Lynn Boyd Hinds, *Broadcasting the Local News: The Early Years of Pittsburgh's KDKA-TV* (University Park: Pennsylvania State Univ. Press, 1995). Michael D. Murray and Donald G. Godfrey, eds., *Television in America* (Ames: Iowa State Univ. Press, 1997) delivers twenty-two case studies of pioneering local stations, but sadly with no consistent historiographic approach.

16. Federal Communications Commission, *Public Service Responsibility of Broadcast Licensees* (Washington, D.C.: FCC, March 7, 1946), 37–39.

17. Federal Communications Commission, "In the Matter of Television Assignments," 41 FCC 148 (1952), more popularly known as the "Sixth Report and Order." In *FCC Annual Reports: 15th Annual, ending Fiscal Year ended 30 June 1949* (Washington, D.C., USGPO, 1949), 41–54, we learn that before the freeze on granting new TV licenses, the TV allocation plan called for limited localism, with no stations planned for Colorado, Idaho, Kansas, Maine, Mississippi, Montana, Nevada, New Hampshire, North Dakota, South Carolina, South Dakota, Vermont, or Wyoming. As to promises made, see Kenneth A. Cox and Nicholas A. Johnson, "Broadcasting in America and the FCC's License Renewal Process" 14 FCC (2nd) 1 (1968). Localism as a policy goal has been well analyzed in Dennis McQuail, *Media Performance: Mass Communication and the*

Public Interest (London: Sage, 1992); Tom A. Collins, "The Local Service Concept in Broadcasting," *Iowa Law Review* 65 (1980): 553–635; and E.W. Kelley, *Policy and Politics in the United States: The Limits of Localism* (Philadelphia: Temple Univ. Press, 1987).

18. Sam Bass Warner's influential plea for historiographic change: "If the World Were Philadelphia: A Scaffolding for Urban History, 1774–1930," *American Historical Review* 74(spring 1968), 26–43; Thomas T. Goldsmith, letter to Allen B. DuMont, 10 May 1945 and letter from Thomas T. Goldsmith to Alan Hartnick, 20 April 1960, both found in the Goldsmith Papers, Records of the Allen B. DuMont Laboratories, Manuscript Division, Library of Congress. See also Library of American Broadcasting, Oral History 1466, Les Arries Jr., 20 December 1995, and Oral History 1467, Larry Richardson, 31 October 1995.

19. Newton Minow, book review of William Cary, *Politics and Regulatory Agencies, Columbia Law Review*, volume 68 (1968), 383–84; Gerald V. Flannery ed., *Commissioners of the FCC, 1927–1994* (Lanham, Md.: Univ. Press of America, 1995), 99–101; Robert W. McChesney, *Telecommunications, Mass Media, and Democracy: The Battle for the Control of U.S. Broadcasting, 1928–1935* (New York: Oxford Univ. Press, 1994), 191–208.

20. Barry Cole and Mal Oettinger, *Reluctant Regulators: The FCC and the Broadcast Audience* (Reading, Mass.: Addison-Wesley, 1978), 16–17; Sam Rayburn letter to Dwight D. Eisenhower, 6 June 1953, Sam Rayburn file, Box 952, president's personal file, Dwight D. Eisenhower Papers, Dwight D. Eisenhower Library, Abilene, Kansas; D.B. Hardeman and Donald C. Bacon, *Rayburn: A Biography* (Austin: Texas Monthly Press, 1987), 418.

21. *Eisenhower and the Mass Media*, 7–8, 15–16, 31; Oral History of Ray Scherer by Douglas Gomery, 22 May 1998, copy in possession of the author.

22. Laurence Laurent, "WRC-TV to Dedicate Its New Home Today," *The Washington Post and Times Herald*, 22 May 1958, B3; Oral History of Ray Scherer; William Hedges Collection, Library of American Broadcasting, College Park, Maryland, Box 132, file 1958A.

23. Robert A. Caro, *The Years of Lyndon Johnson: Means of Ascent* (New York: Knopf, 1990), 80–118, covers in some detail the manipulations of the radio station in the 1940s, as the book ends in 1949. Robert Dallek, *Lone Star Rising: Lyndon Johnson and His Times, 1908–1960* (New York: Oxford Univ. Press, 1991), covers more of Johnson's life and treats the radio manipulation on pages 247–65 and the television gestation of even more wealth on pages 409–16. See also Oral History of Ray Scherer by Douglas Gomery, 22 May 1998, copy in possession of the author, and *Variety*, 9 December 1964, 1.

24. Howard Gillette, "A National Workshop for Urban Policy: The Metropolitization of Washington, 1946–1968," *The Public Historian* 7 (winter 1975): 7. On the crucial allocation of broadcast television stations, see "In the Matter of Television Assignments," 41 FCC 148 (1952). Note that on 30 September 1948 the FCC announced a freeze on the granting of new TV licenses, which it thawed on 14 April 1952 with the issuance of the "Sixth Report and Order." For Washington, D.C., station allocation, see Bamberger Broadcasting Service, Inc. et al, 211 FCC Reports 211 (1946), quotation at 222. On a personal level, longtime FCC Commissioner Robert Emmet Lee has

written an autobiography, *In the Public Interest* (Lanham, Md.: Univ. Press of America, 1996), which offers example after example of Washington, D.C., media to illustrate Lee's points.

25. Carl Abbott, "Dimensions of Regional Change in Washington, D.C.," *American Historical Review* 95 (December 1990), 1368. See also Jean Gottmann's valuable study, *Megalopolis: The Urbanized Northeastern Seaboard of the United States* (Cambridge, Mass.: MIT Press, 1961), as to Washington's changing urban and social status in the years after the Second World War.

26. "Television's Magic Carpet Beckons Eager Washingtonians," *The Washington Evening Star*, 18 March 1946, C3; "The Washington Radio Market," *Broadcasting*Telecasting*, 29 March 29, 1948, 33–34. See also Russell Baker, *An American in Washington* (New York: Knopf, 1961); Howard Gillette, *Between Justice and Beauty* (Baltimore: Johns Hopkins Univ. Press, 1995); Eunice Grier, *People and Government: Changing Need in the District of Columbia, 1950–1970* (Washington, D.C.: Washington Center for Metropolitan Studies, 1970); and Francine Curro Cary, ed., *Urban Odyssey: A Multicultural History of Washington, D.C.* (Washington: Smithsonian Institution Press, 1996).

27. The key articles are Carl Abbott, "Dimensions of Regional Change in Washington, D.C.," *American Historical Review*, 1367–94, and Ray Allen, "Back Home: Southern Identity and African-American Gospel Quartet Performance," in Wayne Franklin and Michael Steiner, eds., *Mapping American Culture* (Iowa City: Univ. of Iowa Press, 1992), 112–35. Allen's book, *Singing in the Spirit: African-American Sacred Quartets in New York City* (Philadelphia: Univ. of Pennsylvania Press, 1991), provides a model of local historical cultural analysis that we TV historians ought to seriously study. On Washington, D.C., as a southern community of popular culture, see Mark Opsasnick, *Capitol Rock* (Riverdale, Md.: Fort Center Books, 1996), 10–12, 18–22.

28. Bamberger Broadcasting Service, Inc., et al., 211 FCC Reports 211 (1946); Thomas T. Goldsmith, letter to William Sayer, 20 November 1945, Records of the Allen B. DuMont Laboratories, Manuscript Division, Library of Congress; Howard Fields, "'Temporary' W3XWT Blossomed into Indie Poorhouse, WTTG," *Television/Radio Age*, May 1985, A3–A4; "CBS Sells Interest in WTOP," *Broadcasting*Telecasting*, 11 October 1954, 64; "The Rich Rewards of Pioneering," *Television*, March 1968, 27–51; Jeff Kisseloff, *The Box: An Oral History of Television* (New York: Viking, 1995), 61–68; *12th Annual FCC Report, Fiscal Year Ended 1946* (Washington, D.C.: USGPO, 1946), 9–17.

29. "Washington Is Source of Nationwide TV Interest," *Washington Times-Herald*, 16 July 1950, 12.

30. Testimony of John Royal, Box 105, Folder WRC 1946, National Broadcasting Company Records, State Historical Society of Wisconsin, Madison, Wisconsin; "WNBW," *Television*, July 1947, 10, 39; WRC-Television and Radio, Folder 313, NBC Collection, Library of Congress, Recorded Sound Division; David Sarnoff, *Looking Ahead* (New York: McGraw-Hill, 1968), 125–45.

31. Library of American Broadcasting, Oral History 1143, Neal Edwards, 17 April 1978; William McAndrew, memo to Carlton Smith, 26 January 1948, Box 596, Folder 23, NBC Collection, State Historical Society of Wisconsin; Kisseloff, *The Box: An Oral*

History of Television, 206–09, 222–24; memo from Carl McCardle, Assistant Secretary of State, 9 February 1953, Department of State, Record Group 59, Series 911.44, National Archives, Washington, D.C.; "DuMont Turns Its Corporate Back on TV Network," *Broadcasting*Telecasting*, 29 August 1955, 80.

32. Chalmers M. Roberts, *The Washington Post: The First 100 Years* (Boston: Houghton Mifflin, 1977), 262.

33. License renewal forms from this period are found in the records of the Federal Communications Commission, Record Group 173, National Archives. David Weinstein, "Capitalizing on the Capital: WMAL-TV," in Michael D. Murray and Donald G. Godfrey, eds., *Television in America* (Ames: Iowa State Univ. Press, 1996), 61–79, nicely capsulizes WMAL's history until 1953. See also Library of American Broadcasting, Oral History 1133, Fred S. Houwink, 11 April 1979, and Oral History 1138, John William Thompson Jr., 27 March 1978, and "WMAL Launches TV Service," *The Washington Evening Star*, 4 October 1947, A12; "WMAL-TV, 2 Years Old," *The Washington Evening Star*, October, 2, 1949, A6; "WMAL-TV," *Broadcasting*Telecasting*, special issue of July 1951, 56, 84–85; Joseph C. Goulden, "The Evening Star," *Washingtonian*, January 1970, 28–33, 64–69; John Morton, "Saving the Star," *Washingtonian*, November 1975, 108–11, 165–74; "ABC Fights for Survival," *Business Week*, 10 July 1954, 52–56; Leonard Goldenson, *Beating the Odds* (New York: Scribner's, 1991).

34. By the middle 1950s, live local country music shows were airing on television stations throughout the South and West. The key point is that a border city like Washington, D.C., would not be expected to be a center of such activity. For an astute and helpful analysis of what the border of North and South means, see Edward L. Ayers, "What We Talk about When We Talk about the South," in Edward L. Ayers, Patricia Nelson Limerick, Stephen Nissenbaum, and Peter S. Onuf, eds., *All Over the Map: Rethinking American Regions* (Baltimore: Johns Hopkins Univ. Press, 1996), 62–82.

35. E. Barbara Phillips, *City Lights: Urban-Suburban Life in the Global Society*, 2nd edition (New York: Oxford Univ. Press, 1996), 201–3; Wladislava S. Frost, "Cities and Towns Mobilize for War," *American Sociological Review* 9 (February 1944), 85–89; Samuel Lubell, "So You're Going to Washington," *Saturday Evening Post*, 7 February 1942, 18–19, 62, 64; Lewis M. Killian, *White Southerners*, revised edition (Amherst: Univ. of Massachusetts Press, 1985), passim. On southerners migrating to D.C., see Laurie M. Sharp, *Social Organization and Life Patterns in the District of Columbia* (Washington, D.C.: Bureau of Social Science Research, Inc., 1965); Joseph T. Holl, *Hard Living on Clay Street* (New York: Anchor, 1973); Frederick Gutheim, *Worthy of a Nation* (Washington, D.C.: Smithsonian Institution Press, 1977); and James N. Gregory, "The Southern Diaspora and the Urban Dispossessed: Demonstrating the Census Public Use Microdata Samples," *The Journal of American History* 82 (June 1995), 111–34.

36. Oral History 1133, Fred S. Houwink, and Oral History 1138, John William Thompson Jr. See also "WMAL Makes Switch," *The Evening Star*, 21 September 1955, A14.

37. Oral History 1133, Fred S. Houwink; also, from copies in possession of the author, Oral History of Connie B. Gay, 1 April 1976; Oral History of George T. Merriken, 13 November 1996; Oral History of Thomas R. Winkler, 6 June 1993; Oral History of Jan Gay, 25 May 1993. On Connie B. Gay's early activities see "Washington's Hillbilly Impresario Goes Far in 5 Years," *The Washington Evening Star*, 13 September

1951, B1, and "Our Respects to Connie Barriot Gay," *Broadcasting*Telecasting*, 2 February 1959, 81.

38. Oral History 1133, Fred S. Houwink; Oral History of Connie B. Gay. The advertisement is found in the *Star*, 16 January 1955, E6. A key article is "Why Sponsors Hate to Leave the Barn Dance," *Sponsor*, 3 May 1954, 42–43. See also *Sponsor*, 11 July 1955, 30; *Sponsor*, 17 October 1955, 33; *Business Week*, 10 March 1956, 30–31; *Sponsor*, 14 May 1956, 29; *Radio-Television Daily*, 16 July 1956, 7.

39. Oral History of Connie B. Gay; Oral History of George T. Merriken; Oral History of Thomas R. Winkler; Oral History of Jan Gay. Roy Clark's autobiography, *My Life* (New York: Simon and Schuster, 1994), 29–70, colorfully describes his experiences working for Connie B. Gay and with Jimmy Dean. The ratings information is from Hargrett Library, Rare Book and Manuscript Library, University of Georgia, Arbitron TV Collection, ARB Television Audience Reports, Washington, D.C. Television Audience for April 1–7, 1954, March 10–April 5, 1955, October 8–14, 1955, December 1–7, 1955, February 1–7, 1956, April 7–13, 1956, October 8–14, 1956, December 1–7, 1956, February 1–7, 1957, May 6–12, 1957, June 1–7, 1957 and October 8–14, 1957.

40. Oral History of Connie B. Gay; Oral History of George T. Merriken; Oral History of Thomas R. Winkler; Oral History of Jan Gay. The ratings information is from Hargrett Library, same dates as listed above. See also *Radio Daily-Television Daily*, 23 May 1956, 3; *Broadcasting*, 23 April 1956, 30; *Broadcasting*, 11 March 1957, 71; *Television, Data Book for 1955*, 178; *Broadcasting*Telecasting 1955–56 Yearbook*, 83. *Broadcasting Yearbook of 1958* reported on A15, A26, A51, and A93 that in the D.C. area by March of 1958 that nine in ten area households had TV sets, with the greatest concentration in the suburbs.

41. "The Town and Country Story," *TV Guide*, Washington, D.C.-Baltimore edition, 15 September 1955, A7–A8; Oral History of Connie B. Gay; Oral History of Thomas R. Winkler; Oral History of Jan Gay; and Oral History of George Hamilton IV, 31 August 1996, copy in possession of the author. Dale Vinicur, *George Hamilton IV* (Hamergen, Germany: Bear Family Records, 1995), 25–32, describes Hamilton's Washington, D.C., experiences. From a far different perspective, Richard Revere noticed the rural side of the nation's capital in his "'Hick Town' or World Capital?" *New York Times Magazine*, 17 April 1955, 13, 56, 58, 60.

42. Oral History 1133, Fred S. Houwink, and Oral History 1138, John William Thompson Jr.; Oral History of Connie B. Gay; *TV Guide*, 8 April 1957 (Washington, D.C.-Baltimore edition), A28; "Nothing Hayseed About Connie Gay," *Variety*, 20 March 1957, 35, 43; "Country Stylist," *New York Times*, 8 September 1957, X17. Gay's efforts as a network producer failed and he turned to other ventures, as did Jimmy Dean and Patsy Cline. See "Our Respects to Connie Barriot Gay," *Broadcasting*, 2 February 1959, 81, and "Pappy's Advice and Country Music Launched Gay's Radio-TV Empire," *The Star*, 18 August 1960, 37.

43. David Nord, "Intellectual History, Social History, Cultural History . . . and Our History," *Journalism Quarterly* 67 (winter 1990): 645–48.

44. For more on this important transition, see Matthew Murray, "NBC Program Clearance Policies during the 1950s: Nationalizing Trends and Regional Resistance,"

The Velvet Light Trap 33 (spring 1994): 37–48, and Phyllis Kaniss, *Making Local News* (Chicago: Univ. of Chicago Press, 1991), 13–70.

45. For more on this important historical theme, see Jack Temple Kirby, *Rural Worlds Lost: The American South 1920–1960* (Baton Rouge: Louisiana State Univ. Press, 1987).

46. Constance M. Green, *Secret City: A History of Race Relations in the Nation's Capital* (Princeton, N.J.: Princeton Univ. Press, 1967), 238–40; Oral History 1466, Les Arries Jr.

47. See Joli Jensen, *The Nashville Sound: Authenticity, Commercialism, and Country Music* (Nashville: Vanderbilt Univ. Press, 1998).

48. David Hackett Fischer, *Historian's Fallacies: Toward a Logic of Historical Thought* (New York: Harper, 1970), 12–13, clearly and carefully warns of the pitfalls here.

15

Nice Guys Last Fifteen Seasons

Jack Benny on Television, 1950–1965

James L. Baughman

On Sunday evening, October 28, 1950, Jack Benny, America's most popular radio comedian, made his network television debut. People finally saw what most had only heard. For more than fifteen years, Benny had crafted a vain, insecure persona. And his very first line continued the tradition of the preoccupation with self: "I'd give a million dollars to know how I look!" And the anxiety: "If I'm a success tonight, all right. If not, I'll kill myself."[1]

Benny had no cause for concern. For the next fifteen seasons on network television, *The Jack Benny Show* generally enjoyed good to excellent ratings. "The Rock of Radio," William Saroyan wrote in 1955, had become "the Tower of Television."[2] In the early 1960s, with the comedian approaching 39 plus 31 years of age, he still had his fans. *The Jack Benny Show* was one of the few weekly programs President Kennedy tried not to miss.[3]

That Benny's show survived for so long is extraordinary. Of the hundreds of network TV series aired in evening prime time between 1947 and 1995, only eleven had longer runs.[4] And he succeeded in a medium where most series failed after short runs. *Variety* estimated that over a three-year period, beginning with the 1952–1953 season, just over two-thirds of all TV programs left the air.[5] "People get tired of you a lot quicker on TV than they do on the radio," wrote comedian Steve Allen. "They pick you up faster, but they drop you faster, too."[6]

Benny's video durability has its scholarly uses. Generalizations about television's beginnings can be tested against one major player's history. From the vantage point of an individual performer, one observes a calculated transition from radio to television. Benny's status as a network radio star af-

Unlike many of his radio contemporaries, Jack Benny not only survived his transition to television but flourished for fifteen seasons. Here Benny is pictured in a skit with singer Connie Francis during an episode from the 1960s. Courtesy of the Wisconsin Center for Film and Television.

forded him remarkable control over his initial television career. In that regard, the comedian proved both prescient and backward-looking. In some instances, he correctly anticipated what TV was to become; at other times, he held out, ultimately in vain, for other outcomes. All in all, by lasting so long, Benny's program provides a window on the great transformations of television, from the first years of often-awkward live telecasts to a period of relative product standardization. Finally, Benny's extended television career suggests, if only by comparison to the video fates of his peers, something about the advantages of his style of comedy as well as his long-nurtured public "personality."

Benny's program endured upheavals in how and where network TV programs were assembled. In June 1953, or two-and-a-half years after the comedian first appeared on CBS, some 81.5 percent of all network programming was telecast live. In mid-1965, that percentage had fallen to 25.2 percent.[7] Virtually all network telecasts in 1950 originated from New York. By 1965, only ten of ninety-six network entertainment shows were produced there.[8]

The medium's changing look can be seen in the popularity ratings of TV programs. The most-watched series of the 1950–1951 season was *The Texaco Star Theater*. Hosted by Milton Berle, *Star Theater* commanded an extraordinary 61.6 rating, which meant that more than six of every ten television households in America were tuned in. Two hour-long programs offering original dramas, *The Fireside Theater* and *Philco TV Playhouse*, followed; a pair of comedy revues, *Your Show of Shows*, starring Sid Caesar and Imogene Coca, and *The Colgate Comedy Hour*, with a variety of hosts,[9] placed fourth and fifth. All came from New York.

Few in 1950 would have recognized the television and performers that were dominant the year *The Jack Benny Show* left the air. The five most-watched programs in 1965 were a Western *(Bonanza)*, several situation comedies, and the action program *The Fugitive*. All were filmed in Southern California. The ratings leaders of 1950–1951 had departed, not all voluntarily. The one-time "King of Television," Milton Berle, was plotting a restoration—an expensive weekly variety show—which proved a disaster for ABC.[10] Sid Caesar was relegated to performing in summer stock and battling alcoholism[11]; Imogene Coca's 1963–1964 situation comedy, *Grindl*, had been canceled after one season. The *Colgate* hosts were dead or made only occasional TV appearances. And the old dramatic anthology series had disappeared.

Nor did Benny's immense radio following guarantee longevity in the newer medium. Although radio programs and players began filling network TV schedules in the late 1940s and early 1950s, very few remained on the air at the end of the decade. Fred Allen never found the right vehicle for his talents; Bob Hope simply never mounted a weekly TV program. Popular radio series, notably *Amos 'n' Andy*, had relatively brief TV lives.[12] The newest medium's great successes, including Berle and Lucille Ball, had modest radio ratings and middling film careers. Berle, *Newsweek* reported with only some exaggeration, "was a flop in radio and a poor bet in the movies."[13]

For his part, Benny had few doubts about entering TV, yet he was determined to control, as much as any individual star could, his video destiny. And the comedian's plans and preferences for the "home screen" contrasted sharply with those of some network executives and major television critics.

Newspaper and magazine columnists who regularly wrote about broadcasting, led by Jack Gould of the *New York Times* and John Crosby of the *Herald Tribune*, as well as Gilbert Seldes of the *Saturday Review*, forcefully shared a vision for the newest medium.[14] All insisted that television not mimic radio, but be distinctive. At worst, TV should rely on a number of entertainment forms, notably the best of legitimate theater. Seldes and others believed television should be live rather than on film. A live telecast, they averred, gave viewers the sensation of seeing a theatrical performance.[15]

Relatedly, they wanted television to be a New York–based medium. This had a self-serving aspect. If TV production shifted to California, the New York journalists would be far removed from sources and stories. On a disinterested level, these New Yorkers preferred the stage over the motion picture and shared a disdain for Hollywood and things Southern Californian.[16] Not surprisingly, the critics' favorite radio comedian in the 1940s had not been Benny, who had originated his radio show from Hollywood, but Fred Allen, who produced his program in New York. Allen hated Hollywood; many of his jokes and comic routines mocked Los Angeles and the movie industry. California, he once remarked, was "a great place to live, if you're an orange."[17]

The networks shared some but not all of the critics' hopes for the newest medium. In the early 1950s, two networks, CBS and NBC, operated a virtual duopoly over TV, with ABC and Du Mont being marginal players.[18] Both CBS and NBC accepted the then-conventional wisdom that people preferred live broadcasts. "Transcriptions" would leave consumers feeling cheated. For the same reason, the networks avoided rebroadcasting programs in the summer, choosing instead to offer special replacement shows.[19] Advertisers agreed; Benny's 1947 contract with his sponsor, the American Tobacco Company, had specified that his radio show be aired live.[20] "The fact that you are on live will always be a handicap," Groucho Marx wrote Fred Allen in 1953. "But apparently there is nothing you can do about it."[21]

Unlike the leading critics, the networks did not abhor Hollywood. Although wary of the major studios' gaining control over program production, CBS and NBC recognized that some, if not most, TV production would eventually be transferred to Southern California. The New York City area lacked the talent and facilities of the movie colony. By 1952, both networks had constructed production facilities in and around Hollywood and permitted some of their stars to originate their shows on the West Coast.[22]

In other ways, however, the heads of CBS and NBC differed intensely over the newest medium. NBC's chief programmer between 1949 and 1956, Sylvester L. Weaver Jr., agreed with those critics who wanted television to be different and not imitate radio—or motion pictures. Both film and radio had seen their audiences decline in the late 1940s, Weaver maintained, by attending too much to formulas. Television would not be able to sustain and augment demand by offering, à la network radio, the same programs week-in, week-out. Irregularly scheduled special programs, which he eventually dubbed "spectaculars," would maintain TV.[23] Although NBC did air weekly series and Berle's Texaco show appeared every week, one of the network's most popular early variety programs, *The Colgate Comedy Hour*, had rotating hosts, as did *Four Star Revue*.[24]

CBS's programming philosophy clashed sharply with Weaver's. Audiences preferred the weekly series, contended Frank Stanton, president of CBS, Inc. With the same program telecast every week, he told *Business Week* in 1956, "the public knows what's on, looks forward to it, makes plans around it, develops the habit of the time-period. If it isn't a regular show, it's not television."[25]

Stanton had no better proof of the value of "habit" than Jack Benny's radio program on NBC. Within a few years of his first regularly scheduled show, in 1932, Benny had become the single most popular radio performer in America. Moreover, Benny was able to maintain his ranking, while most rivals saw their audiences invariably decline. In the late 1940s, his program led all others in the ratings.[26] For a generation of Americans, listening to his Sunday evening show had become a welcome ritual. Recalled one columnist, "Jack Benny on the radio at 7 o'clock Sunday night was almost as obligatory as church on Sunday morning, and in many families, more so."[27]

Benny and his writers developed what for radio comedy proved an original and compelling idea.[28] Discarding the then-dominant vaudeville revue model of radio comedy, they organized the show around situations and verbal exchanges involving the lead's comic imperfections. He was, in other words, both star *and* comic foil. Everyone else on the program—his valet, his coworkers, his girlfriend, Mary Livingstone—usually had the best lines. Benny made himself an unavoidable target. He portrayed himself as cheap, vain about his looks, age, musical and acting talents, and faintly effeminate.[29] Yet his writers carefully made his "flaws" comical—and forgivable. They were the characteristics of relatives and friends, individuals whose frailties were amusing rather than off-putting. "He was," Joseph Boskin observed, "everybody's Miser: a family relation, a close friend or neighbor, a distant businessman or banker." Benny, Boskin added, "could be petty, cowardly, scheming—even egotistical and mildly tyrannical—but never was he overwhelming disdainful."[30]

Then, too, most listeners understood it was an act. Benny appeared at the end of the show to dispel—or try to dispel—the notion that he really was cheap or mean. It did not always work. A Cleveland attorney demanded that Benny pay Rochester more[31]; Southerners objected to a program during which his black valet accidentally struck Benny.[32] And there was the often-noted incident of a hat-checker who returned a generous tip: "Mr. Benny, please leave me some illusions."[33] Such stories notwithstanding, studies of radio audiences, and a keener sensibility about the "mass mind," permit historians to acknowledge that most Americans knew that Martians had not actually landed in New Jersey on Halloween 1938, and that Jack Benny probably was something other than a penny-pinching, egotistical twit.[34]

Most listeners realized that there were two Bennys: a character in a radio comedy, and a kind and unassuming off-stage figure. In frequent press interviews, often conducted on his birthday, February 14, Jack spoke of his willingness to spend money. He owned eighty cashmere sweaters and about forty jackets. His daughter had her own phone line; he even volunteered his real age.[35] He also denied any ambiguity to his sexual orientation. In a February 1954 television program, for example, following a sketch in which Jack dreams of marrying Mary and starting a family, he brings both Mary and his daughter Joan on stage. "As most of you know," Benny notes, Mary is his wife and Joan his daughter.[36]

The "two Bennys" strategy had not only made him, he later boasted, "the all-American miser,"[37] but helped to topple the balance of power in network radio. In the late 1940s, most prominent NBC performers, led by Benny, switched to CBS after owner William Paley signed them to lavish new contracts that promised significant tax savings. The exodus of Benny and other NBC stars gave CBS the radio ratings leadership in 1949–1950.[38]

"Paley's raid" proved to be the last act in the great network radio ratings wars of the 1940s. A TV-set purchase boom, which commenced in 1948, began to eat away at radio's audience. The number of homes with TV sets rose from 940,000 in 1948 to 3.9 million two years later.[39] Initially, radio stars as different as George Burns and Edward R. Murrow hesitated. "Most people who were still successful on radio didn't go into television right away," recalled George Burns, Benny's best friend. "None of us knew it then, but having a successful radio show was about to become as important as being nominated to run for vice-president on a ticket with Tom Dewey."[40]

Benny started acknowledging that he would do some television shows. "It is now generally accepted," Benny wrote early in 1951, "that eventually television will completely dominate nighttime entertainment."[41] Other prominent comedians were entering television.[42] The question for Benny, then, was when to take the plunge. It would be his decision. Such was his popularity that both his sponsor and CBS in effect left the matter to him.[43]

One caution was TV's minority status. Despite robust sales, TV sets could be found in only 2.3 percent of all households in 1949.[44] Benny toyed with doing two TV programs that fall, then waited a year; he would enter television when more homes had TVs.[45] But he could not hesitate indefinitely. In New York City, where television had spread rapidly, the Hooper ratings for his radio program fell from 26.5 in 1948 to 4.8 in 1951.[46]

A related concern was technological. With nearly all network telecasts being live, Benny wanted network-affiliated stations to be connected by the coaxial cable. Until then, affiliates without a direct hook-up to New York carried on a delayed basis poor quality kinescopes of live telecasts. Even so, when Benny finally did his first network program, in late October 1950, the coaxial cable only reached as far west as Missouri.

Continuing to wait left the newest medium—and celebrity status—to a comic whom few peers genuinely liked. The week of May 16, 1949, Milton Berle adorned the covers of both *Time* and *Newsweek*.[47] The prominence awarded the brash Berle, "the thief of bad gags," dismayed most of his fellow comedians. When someone, as a publicity stunt, proposed erecting a statue of Berle at New York's Herald Square, Fred Allen remarked, "That will be the first time that people shit on a statue."[48] Benny's radio program had treated "Mr. Television" with a mix of contempt and unease. A June 1948 show referred to Berle's penchant for stealing jokes.[49] A year later, singer Hoagy Carmichael discussed a song he had been writing, "I bought a television for my girl. And now she's in love with Milton Berle."[50]

Painfully related to Berle's ascendancy was the likelihood of network radio's obsolescence. Benny's radio program occasionally offered a harrowing prospect—that fame in radio might not matter in a few years. In a May 1, 1949, satire of *The Treasure of the Sierra Madre*, Mary meets Jack in a Mexican bar.

MARY: You look like a derelict. What's the matter?

JACK: It's a long story. I used to be a famous comedian. I had a big house, a swimming pool, and everything. Then all of a sudden, I'm a bum.

MARY: What happened?

JACK: Television.

316 | James L. Baughman

MARY: Television? What's that?

JACK: I don't know, but the wrestlers have all good writers now.[51]

In a September 1950 sketch, Benny arrives to do his radio program only to find to his horror that a TV show is being telecast in the studio normally reserved for him. He confronts two TV crewmen, played by Mel Blanc and Frank Nelson.

JACK: What's going on here?

NELSON: Can't you see; we're in the middle of a television program?

JACK: Television! But I'm supposed to do a radio show in this studio.

MEL (puzzled): What kind of show?

JACK: Radio?

MEL (puzzled): Radio?

NELSON: Think back, Joe, *you can remember.*

Later, Benny realizes the crew members do not recognize him.

JACK: I'm Jack Benny.

MEL: Jack who?

BENNY: Benny.

NELSON: Think back, Joe, *you can remember.*

Benny subsequently discovers that *all* of the studios are being used for television. Confronting a CBS executive, Benny cries, "For nineteen years I've been in radio, nineteen years, and a little thing like television comes in and disrupts everything."[52]

Facing the challenge of a new mass medium, Benny looked backward. He shared Ed Wynn's conviction that TV was little more than a live performance of a stage show. And Benny was a vaudeville veteran who had continued to perform onstage in the 1940s. "People tell me that television is a completely new medium," he remarked in September 1950. "I don't think so. I'm going to give them the same kind of entertainment I do on stage appearances. It's the same type of show I used to do at the Orpheum in vaudeville days."[53] When Benny finally did his TV program, he conveyed none of the anxiety that had been so apparent to viewers of Fred Allen and others making their video premieres. Benny, *The New Yorker's* Philip Hamburger noted, "was not going to be frightened by anything as ridiculous as a television camera."[54]

Perhaps Benny should have been uneasier. A move to television had to take into consideration the comedian's motion picture career, which had been far from impressive. Indeed, his fifteen films were so unsuccessful that they became the basis for jokes on his radio program. In an otherwise admiring 1948 profile, Cleveland Amory wondered if Benny would last on television. His failure in movies suggested that his humor would not translate visually.[55]

Benny went ahead, though without much of his radio "family." Although Don Wilson, his announcer, would of necessity be a regular, not all members of the Benny ensemble would appear in every episode. The first program featured Eddie Anderson, playing Rochester, his valet, and Arnie Auerbach as Mr. Kitzle, a friend who drops by Jack's home. (During the visit, Mr. Kitzle asks Benny for a cigarette, and Jack points to his vending machine.) The show included no other radio cast members.

As with many of his radio programs, the sketches on Benny's first program had a show-within-a-show quality, in this instance, Benny's preparations for his TV premiere. In the opening scene, Jack informs Rochester of his television plans. Benny's parrot promptly lays an egg. Benny then decides to call Dinah Shore, one of the medium's first stars, to ask her to appear on his program. Using a pay phone—in his living room—Benny negotiates with Shore. He had seen her on a Bob Hope show, though he confessed to having had a poor view. "I couldn't get near the screen; it was so crowded in the store."[56]

Many critics felt he leaned too much on his radio image and routines, especially his cheapness. Calling the program "something of a letdown," Jack Gould complained that, "It had too much familiar radio and not enough original video."[57] Terrence O'Flaherty of the *San Francisco Chronicle* wondered if Benny could "continue to milk the same old pinch-penny gag week after week in the manner that makes him happy and rich."[58]

If some critics had tired of Benny's act by the time he entered TV, the comedian's image was so recognizable—and popular—that it gave him an automatic advantage in the new medium. As two show business reporters observed, "Benny's professional character is by now so well established that TV audiences had only to see his first set—with coin phone and cigarette machine installed in his living room—to know what was coming. What comes is natural and likable . . . it's the payoff of a lifetime in show business."[59] Acknowledging that "there was nothing new about Benny, except that you see him now," Larry Wolters of the *Chicago Tribune* found him "completely at home in television. Those who liked him in radio—and that includes 50 million or more people—are going to like him even better on TV."[60]

Benny's second program commanded less enthusiasm among critics. Three months after his debut, on January 28, 1951, Benny returned to TV, live from New York. This time, he had two guest stars—Frank Sinatra and Faye Emerson, one of TV's first celebrities. Ever hopeful of a career breakthrough, Jack tried to present himself as a potential screen lover to Emerson. As in the first show, Wilson and Anderson appeared; another member of the radio ensemble, Frank Fontaine, did several bits mocking the mentally disabled. There were scenes in Jack's very modest New York City hotel room.[61] The humor overall seemed strained. Gould wrote of "a rather uninspired presentation" and "the lack-luster quality of the material."[62] Bill Irwin of the *Chicago Sun-Times,* who had hailed the first show, admitted that the second program "was something less than sensational."[63] Benny, *Variety* complained, continued to rely too much on radio references to his age, cheap accommodations, and the like, gags "that had an all-too-familiar twang."[64]

Benny's final two programs proved more successful. Both had opening monologues by Benny, followed by one extended sketch with guest stars. None of the radio ensemble—not even Wilson—appeared in the April 1 show. Instead, the program revolved around Jack's attempts to break into serious drama by crashing a rehearsal of a television play, starring Claudette Colbert and Basil Rathbone, and being directed by actor-director Robert Montgomery. Benny's abandonment of his radio formula won Jack Gould's praise. He hailed the comedian's "sense of showmanship and his personal courage." "In one swoop he ditched the whole time-worn works and started out afresh."[65] In the last 1950–1951 show, Benny chances upon golf pro Ben Hogan at a country club; unaware of Hogan's identity, Benny proceeds hilariously to "correct" Hogan's swing. Both sketches were more sustained and less contrived than the shorter bits in the first two programs. And both played on different aspects of Benny's vanity: his claims to be what everyone (but Jack) knew he was not—a great dramatic actor and a great golfer.[66]

Benny did six shows in the 1951–1952 season. His strategy was to mix it up. Some programs relied more on members of the radio cast; others were built around guest stars.[67] All tried to make maximum use of TV through visual gags. On the March 9, 1952, show, Benny dresses up as Gracie Allen. (Gazing at himself in a mirror, he confesses, "I don't look so bad.")[68] Six weeks later, the show featured violinist Isaac Stern; it closed with radio cast regular Dennis Day wildly imitating momentary singing sensation Johnnie Ray, in front of a formally attired Benny and symphonic orchestra.[69]

The final 1952 episode, with no guest stars, similarly seized upon television's visual possibilities. Jack is about to leave for England to play at the London Palladium. With Benny departing, his next-door neighbors, the Ronald Colmans, regulars on his radio show, dispatch their butler to retrieve various items Benny has borrowed from them. Over the course of the sketch, the manservant, and eventually a two-man moving crew, take end and coffee tables, silverware, lamps, mirrors, and even shirt studs Jack had been about to put in his trunk. By the end of the show, the living room is nearly bare.

In the last routine, reworked from some past radio programs, an agent brings three female singers, the "Landrew Sisters," to be in Jack's London act. Jack had been hoping for young and attractive performers. What he (and the audience) see are two decidedly plain-looking women, the third is short and fat. As they stand before him, Jack says nothing initially. He takes a long look, pauses, then puts on his glasses, pauses, removes his glasses, cleans them, and then looks again. The threesome sings "Did You Ever Seen a Dream Walking?" and offer a choreographic disaster (the plump one has to be lifted up after doing a plié). A burly mover walks in and, looking at one of the women, cries, "Hello, mother."[70]

Where Benny did his show reflected an industry trend. He launched his television career in New York, which meant some cracks about the expense of living in the city. "I've been in town a week, and twenty bucks went like that!"[71] With the coaxial cable connecting Los Angeles to the East Coast, all of Benny's 1951–1952 programs were live from Hollywood, though Benny later occasionally made the trek back east.[72] Benny followed the pattern of George Burns and Gracie Allen, who originally did their show live from New York, and then on film from a California studio. Two new TV stars, Lucille Ball and Desi Arnaz, resisted network and advertiser pressure to originate their new series, *I Love Lucy*, from New York. After extended negotiations, CBS permitted Ball and Arnaz to film the program in an old Hollywood studio.[73]

Whatever merits the critics saw in producing series in New York, Benny would only do so on a temporary basis. And, under the terms of contracts with CBS and his sponsor, Benny would control the program's point of origination. Indeed, a 1950 amendment to Benny's CBS contract, signed on the eve of his television premiere, specified that the performer would produce his TV program in Los Angeles once the laying of the coaxial cable permitted West Coast originations.[74] Even before the move, the end theme on Benny's TV show was not "Love in Bloom," his musical signature, but "Hooray for Hollywood."

Benny had long preferred the West Coast. He and his wife had moved to California in 1935, part of a mass migration of radio talent from New York. Advertising agencies, which had produced most radio shows, had encouraged the shift. They saw Hollywood as a excellent source of celebrity guests; it also offered better facilities.[75] In September 1947, *Variety* reported that twenty-two of twenty-eight network comedy programs originated from

Jack Benny (right) followed the lead of his best friend, George Burns (left), who with his wife, Gracie Allen, originally did their TV show live from New York before soon moving it to California to produce it on film. Courtesy of the Wisconsin Center for Film and Television.

Hollywood, with the remaining six from New York.[76] Then, too, for much of this group, living in and around the movie colony was a reward for many long and hard years on the road and in New York. Fred Allen might stay in Manhattan, joking that he met a better class of people on the subway. But Benny delighted in the advantages Allen ridiculed, the ease (then) of driving around and the warm climate.[77] Most of Benny's friends resided in Beverly Hills, where he lived. He could play golf year-round; in 1949 and 1955 interviews he indicated he tried to play a round every day.[78] His wife Mary, to whom he was devoted, much preferred living and shopping there. They had a large, $250,000 (in 1948) home, with a swimming pool and eight servants, as well as another home in Palm Springs.[79]

Location figured in the show itself. There were occasional, though not many, references to the smog and Griffith Park.[80] In another program, aired during the first World Series featuring the Los Angeles Dodgers, Benny briefly sports a Dodgers cap.[81] The Beverly Hills Police Department became a target: its number was unlisted, the police dogs were poodles, and one needed a reservation to see the desk sergeant.[82]

More importantly, being based in Hollywood permitted Benny, as he had on radio, to recruit guest stars from the movie colony. The off-camera Benny, with his gentle, self-effacing manner, had made many friends in a community of large egos.[83] Performers who rarely if ever appeared on television agreed to do shows with Benny. Those making their TV debut on his program included Claudette Colbert, Barbara Stanwyck, Marilyn Monroe, Jimmy Stewart, and Humphrey Bogart.[84] A single episode featured Dick Powell, Fred MacMurray, Kirk Douglas, and Dan Dailey. In the late 1960s, relegated to doing specials, Benny continued to bring Hollywood talent to the home screen. He persuaded Gregory Peck not only to appear on his show, but also, in a stiffly Lincolnesque manner, to do a song and dance with him.[85]

Few TV personalities matched Benny's record in casting film stars, especially in the early days when many studios discouraged performers from appearing on TV and telecasts were live. "Every one of us was scared to death of television—including me," Claudette Colbert recalled.[86] Guests on Berle and Cantor shows, for example, were often unimpressive. Cantor relied heavily on such lesser lights as Cesar Romero.[87] Berle was notorious for bullying performers during rehearsals. Berle, George Burns wrote, "only interrupted those guests whose acts he thought he could improve. It was just a coincidence that that turned out to be everybody."[88] Benny, in contrast, treated his guests with the greatest respect. They were, after all, friends as well as performers. They "could be sure that Benny would not make them look silly," William A. Henry III noted.[89] "I trusted Jack implicitly," Colbert remembered. "When he asked me to appear, I couldn't turn him down . . . to know Jack was to both love and trust him."[90]

While securing impressive guests, Benny in other ways remained cautious about television. During the 1952–1953 season, he did eight programs; the next year he appeared every three weeks. Only beginning in the fall of 1954 did he agree to do a show every other week; his program alternated with other CBS comedies for the next six seasons.

Benny therefore only partially fit the Stanton model of TV scheduling. The comedian did not share the CBS president's conviction that a weekly television comedy show could be successful. Although Benny's radio program had appeared every seven days, TV production made many more demands. Others concurred. After long careers in vaudeville, film, and radio, Burns and Allen found doing a TV series to be enormously labor-intensive. "Television," Burns wrote, "was really the toughest thing we'd ever done."[91] On TV, performers had to memorize lines; on radio, they could read from a script. Benny himself more than once on radio had alluded to his having to turn a page. There was blocking and costuming. All in all, TV was too much work.[92]

Benny had other reservations about a weekly series. He worried about what show business executives called the "fatigue factor." Simply put, if seen too often, performers might wear out their welcome. This was less of a problem with radio, when people only *heard* a comic. But TV came much closer to being a virtual presence in someone's home. In an article about doing television, Benny noted the similarity of some TV programming to feature films. He suspected that viewers might tire of even a great movie star like Cary Grant if he or his films appeared on television every week.[93] CBS ultimately allayed the comedian's fears. The network had been pressing the comedian to go weekly since the mid-fifties and Benny finally relented in 1960.[94] By then, the biweekly scheduling of series had all but disappeared.

Benny similarly moved to film slowly. He had never adhered to the notion, shared by many critics and broadcasters, that a successful TV program had to be aired live. "If the show is good," he commented in 1949, "the audience will like it."[95] Still, he waited until the 1953–1954 season to do a filmed program.[96] Sponsor pressure ended under the terms of his 1955 contract with American Tobacco, which left the decision to him, though only four of his sixteen programs were to be rebroadcast.[97] As late as the 1958–1959 season, however, a majority of Benny's programs originated live.[98] The next season, all but two of fourteen were on film or tape.[99]

In relatively short order, networks and advertisers had discovered that audiences would accept filmed programming. Indeed, Benny's earlier contract had specified that any transcriptions of his radio program had to be destroyed within three weeks of the original air date.[100] In the mid-1950s, however, filmed reruns of *I Love Lucy* and *Amos 'n' Andy* had accrued impressive ratings.[101] By the decade's end, prerecorded programming, repeated in the summer, had become the norm. Television, the *New York Times* reported, "clearly seems to be moving to a philosophy of film."[102]

By then, the great debate over television programming—which had divided critics and the networks—had essentially been resolved. Stanton's one-time rival, Weaver of NBC, had been fired, replaced by figures far more inclined to the CBS model; a revived ABC relentlessly and successfully scheduled Hollywood-made series.[103] More and more programs were produced in the movie colony. New York was rapidly becoming little more than an administrative center, the site of network news divisions, a few game shows, and soap operas. *The Hallmark Hall of Fame*, a dramatic anthology program with New York's theatrical pretensions, had moved west in 1953.[104] Even Berle, so associated with New York, had transferred his program west in 1955. He and his wife had "decided that we would move to California. It was where so many of our friends had gone; it was where television was going."[105]

As for Benny, the ratings hardly bore out his misgivings about a weekly show. Benny ranked tenth in the 1960–1961 Nielsens. Scheduled against NBC's immensely popular *Bonanza* in 1961–1962, *The Jack Benny Show* fell out of the top twenty-five.[106] Shifted to Tuesday nights at 9:30, Benny rose again to twelfth place in 1962–1963, and fourteenth in 1963–1964. Yet such numbers could be deceiving. The schedule-makers had proven generous. In 1963–1964, CBS had given him a good "lead-in," the rural comedy *Petticoat Junction*. It had finished fourth the same year Benny ranked fourteenth. Moreover, Benny's own program faced weak competition on ABC and NBC.[107]

The real test came during the 1964–1965 season. To the horror of numerous TV critics and Benny himself, CBS had begun to depend heavily on comedies like *Petticoat Junction* with a rural flavor and characters. Benny suddenly no longer fit the network's plans. Returning to NBC for the 1964–1965 season, Benny was scheduled against a new CBS rural character sitcom, *Gomer Pyle, U.S.M.C. Gomer Pyle* destroyed him in the ratings, leaving Benny furious. "I'm getting murdered by something called 'Gomer Pyle,' and ninety percent of the people I talk to don't know what or who 'Gomer Pyle' is," he complained. "I don't understand anything about this business anymore."[108]

The medium had eventually discarded him, as it had so many others. Yet one has to control for age. Benny could not remain, his protestations not-withstanding, permanently thirty-nine. When NBC canceled his weekly series in 1965, the comedian was seventy-one and losing a step.[109]

Then, too, broadcast programming itself had changed by the time the Benny program left the air. By the 1960s, most popular sitcoms were organized around situations and characters rather than individual stars. There were exceptions to be sure, notably Lucille Ball's *The Lucy Show* and *Here's Lucy*. In the case of Benny, although the comedian had usually awarded other cast members prominent roles and the best lines, it remained his program. Sitcoms in the 1960s, in comparison, tended to consist of interchangeable parts. When Andy Griffith quit his popular program in 1968, it continued and prospered for several years as *Mayberry R.F.D.* Griffith himself struggled to restore his small-screen standing. Only after eighteen years and three failed series did he regain a large video audience, with *Matlock*.[110]

All told, Benny should not have cried too loudly. Unlike Cantor, Burns, Wynn, and many more radio veterans, Benny had not only survived the transition to television, he had flourished. Only a few other early fifties entertainment programs, including Ed Sullivan's variety hour and comedies starring Red Skelton and the Nelson family, could match the Benny show's durability.[111]

The program's format helped. *The Jack Benny Show* was far less taxing than the hour-long variety shows that Berle, Cantor, and others had hosted in the early 1950s. The revues were physically exhausting and hard to sustain in terms of quality.[112] A sitcom made relatively fewer demands on the writers and the lead. It also proved the more durable program type. *Variety* called the sitcom "the basic staple of the tv spectrum."[113] The *Tribune*'s Larry Wolters well appreciated Benny's choice of vehicles. Praising the comedian for not hosting a variety program, Wolters suggested that Benny better understood the nature of the new medium. "The [first] Benny show was intimate and friendly, aimed at the home audience," Wolters wrote. Benny thus "avoided the showy, the elaborate and pretentious in television."[114]

Then, too, unlike many of the frantic emcees of TV's golden age, Benny wore better. His demeanor worked to his advantage. Unlike Berle, in so many ways his opposite, Benny rarely screamed and never mugged before the camera. He was the party guest who would, in fact, be invited back. In a 1951 tribute to Benny, Goodman Ace wrote, "Television has the problem of keeping its stars from wearing out their welcome. The best way to keep them fresh and welcome is to keep them from becoming overbearing."[115] No one ever accused Benny of having an overpowering personality. He himself argued that "the essential quality of a great comedian is humility and sincerity, and I don't feel that this type of performer will ever tire his audience."[116]

In that regard, the essential vulnerability of Benny's character explained much of his appeal. Several generations of Americans laughed at the situations resulting from, or barbs directed at, the conceited and niggardly figure Benny portrayed. The character's familiarity—and harmlessness—invariably made him comical. "Jack Benny did almost everything wrong," *The Los Angeles Times* observed in an editorial tribute:

> When he played the violin, it sounded like a cat fight. His old Maxwell [automobile] kept breaking down. He was always short of money—or said he was. And he couldn't keep track of his age. . . . The only thing Benny did right in his 65 bumbling years as a comedian was to make people laugh. And he never made fun of others, only of himself. Everybody on his show was always cleverer than he was. And he took all of his defeats with a vague wave of the hand and the look of a martyr.[117]

Even Benny, before saying good night at the end of each program, was laughing at the foolishness of "the other Benny."

Benny's lack of a strong regional or religious identity also helped to extend his career in television. Perhaps only Bob Hope was the more assimilated American comic.[118] Raised in Waukegan, Illinois, just north of Chicago, Benny did not have a New York comic's machine-gun delivery. His "accent" was indistinguishably Midwestern. He was a Jew, though he rarely brought it up—and always celebrated Christmas on his program. Audiences "never identified Benny as a 'Jewish' comedian," wrote a Fred Allen biographer.[119] He was cheap, but no Shylock. When, as a spoof of self-serving radio contests in the mid-1940s, Benny launched a "Why I can't stand Jack Benny" competition, only three of the 270,000 letters were deemed anti-Semitic.[120]

Unlike much of his original competition, Benny had little difficulty surviving the spread of television into smaller communities in the western and southern states. The same could not be said for Berle. A 1957 *Television Magazine* article reported, "Berle's humor, it is held, with its inherent Eastern big-city appeal, attracted a smaller percentage of the total audience as it grew to national proportions." Sid Caesar, too, was considered a victim of the extension of TV into small-town America; being scheduled against Lawrence Welk did not help.[121] Ironically, Berle had temporarily reversed his ratings slide by transforming his TV persona into the put-upon figure à la Benny.[122] In contrast, Benny never had to reinvent himself.

For some fifteen years, Benny was able to prosper on TV—and substantially on his own terms. He exercised unusual power over his television career. Stanton might want his series on every week, but Benny resisted for ten years. New York critics might prefer that TV be a local production, but Benny would not leave Los Angeles except on a temporary basis. Any consideration of television's beginnings must take into account the preferences of performers like Benny. They, too, had some say in the shape of the newest medium.

Notes

The author thanks Steven H. Chaffee, Roland Marchand, Philip Ranlet, and Steven Ross for commenting on earlier drafts of this essay, as well as Jack Kapfer, Alinda Nelson, and Inger Stole for their assistance.

1. Videotape, *The Jack Benny Show,* 28 October 1950, UCLA Film and Television Archive; Bill Irwin, "Benny a Wow in TV Debut," *Chicago Sun-Times,* 30 October 1950, 2:7. All videotapes cited here are in the UCLA archive.

2. William Saroyan, "Jack Benny's Thirty-Nine Years," *Look,* 1 November 1955, 52. Benny finished ninth in the A.C. Nielsens in 1951–1952, twelfth in 1952–1953, sixteenth in 1953–1954, and seventh in 1954–1955. Tim Brooks and Earle Marsh, *The Complete Directory of Prime Time Network TV Shows 1946–Present,* 6th ed. (New York: Ballantine Books, 1995), 1258ff.

3. Jim Bishop, *A Day in the Life of President Kennedy* (New York: Random House, 1964), 100.

4. Brooks and Marsh, *Complete Directory,* appendix 4.

5. Cited in minutes of Friday Meeting with Management Committee, n.d. [1956], Radio-Television Department files, Box 2, J. Walter Thompson Papers, Duke University.

6. Steve Allen, *The Funny Men* (New York: Simon and Schuster, 1956), 16.

7. *Broadcasting Yearbook 1963* (Washington, D.C.: Broadcasting Magazine, 1963), 20; *Broadcasting Yearbook 1966* (Washington, D.C.: Broadcasting Magazine, 1966), D37.

8. *New York Times,* 20 March 1965, 95. See also James L. Baughman, "Take Me Away from Manhattan: New York City and American Mass Culture, 1930–1990," in *Capital of the American Century: The National and International Influence of New York City,* ed. Martin Shefter (New York: Russell Sage Foundation, 1993), 126.

9. During the 1950–1951 season, they included Eddie Cantor, Martin and Lewis, and Fred Allen.

10. Milton Berle, *Milton Berle* (New York: Dell, 1975), 351.

11. Sid Caesar, *Where Have I Been? An Autobiography* (New York: Crown, 1982), 183–85.

12. Alan Havig, *Fred Allen's Radio Comedy* (Philadelphia: Temple Univ. Press, 1990), 211–13; Robert Taylor, *Fred Allen: His Life and Wit* (Boston: Little, Brown, 1989), 290–94; memo, Fred Wile Jr. to Joseph H. McConnell, 8 May 1951, Niles Trammell Files, NBC Records, Box 115, State Historical Society of Wisconsin (hereafter, SHSW); Arthur Frank Wertheim, *Radio Comedy* (New York: Oxford Univ. Press, 1979), 385–87, 390–91, 393–94. African American protests of *Amos 'n' Andy* shortened the program's TV life. See Melvin Patrick Ely, *The Adventures of Amos 'n' Andy: A Social History of an American Phenomenon* (New York: Free Press, 1991), 205–42; Thomas Cripps, "*Amos 'n' Andy* and the Debate over American Racial Integration," in *American History/Ameri-*

can Television: Interpreting the American Past, ed. John E. O'Connor (New York: Frederick Ungar, 1983), 33–54.

13. "Television's Top," *Newsweek,* 16 May 1949, 56; Wertheim, *Radio Comedy,* 387–89.

14. Unpublished analysis by Patrick McGrady of television criticism, in Fund for Republic Proceedings, 10 October 1958, Fund Papers, Box 63, Princeton University; Michael Kammen, *The Lively Arts: Gilbert Seldes and the Transformation of Cultural Criticism in the United States* (New York: Oxford Univ. Press, 1996).

15. William Boddy, *Fifties Television: The Industry and Its Critics* (Urbana: Univ. of Illinois Press, 1990), 73ff, 80ff.

16. Boddy, 74–75; Ben Gross, *I Looked and I Listened: Informal Recollections of Radio and TV* (New York: Random House, 1954), 289–92.

17. Quoted in Allen, *Funny Men,* 38. See also Alan Havig, "Fred Allen and Hollywood," *Journal of Popular Film and Television* 7, no. 3 (1979): 273–91; Taylor, *Fred Allen,* 246–51; Joe McCarthy, "Introduction," *Fred Allen's Letters,* ed. McCarthy (Garden City, N.Y.: Doubleday, 1965), ix.

18. CBS claimed 46 percent of home viewing hours in 1956, compared to 36 percent for NBC and 18 percent for ABC. Memorandum, George Bristol to all TV network salesmen, 14 February 1957, copy in NBC Records, Box 140.

19. Milt Josefberg, *The Jack Benny Show* (New Rochelle, N.Y.: Arlington House, 1977), 269. As late as March 1958, Frank Stanton of CBS was assuring the FCC that "useful as film may be, it is the live quality, the sense of seeing the actual event or performance taking place before your eyes, that is the real magic of television. To confine television largely to film is to confine its excitement, scope and impact." James L. Baughman, "Television in the 'Golden Age': An Entrepreneurial Experiment," *Historian* 47 (February 1985), 182–83. See also David Morton, *Off the Record: The Technology and Culture of Sound Recording in America* (New Brunswick, N.J.: Rutgers Univ. Press, 2000), 50–54.

20. Contract, 6 March 1947. Broadcasting a recorded program required special permission. See American Tobacco Co. (ATC) to Benny, 1 February 1951. The only exceptions were for same-day broadcasts necessitated by differences in the time zones. See ATC to Benny, 30 April 1948, Benny Papers, Box 82, Special Collections, UCLA.

21. Marx to Allen, 4 September 1953, Marx Papers, Box 1, Library of Congress.

22. "N.Y. Studio Shortage Critical," *Variety,* 17 January 1951, 29; "TV's Time of Trouble," *Fortune* 44 (August 1951), 131, 132; "Networks Go Hollywood: TV City," *Life,* 1 December 1952, 97; Martin B. Campbell to D.A. Frank Jr., 25 January 1949, Niles Trammell Files, NBC Records, Box 115; "Western Approach," *Time,* 24 November 1952, 85; script, *The All Star Revue,* 3 November 1951, 53, copy in Charles Isaacs Papers, Box 1, Arts-Special Collections, UCLA.

23. Weaver speech to Chicago Economics Club, 15 June 1953, and remarks, NBC TV Affiliates Meeting, Chicago, 18 November 1953, copies in Broadcast Pioneers Library, Washington, D.C.; Richard Austin Smith, "TV: The Coming Showdown," *Fortune* 50 (September 1954): 138–39, 164; "Television: The New Cyclops," *Business Week,* 10 March 1956, 80; Jack Gould, "Creative Spark," *New York Times,* 21 November 1954, 2:9; Baughman, "Television in the 'Golden Age,'" 186–87, 189–90; Vance Kepley Jr., "From 'Frontal Lobes' to the 'Bob-and-Bob' Show: NBC Management and Pro-

gramming Strategies, 1949–65," in *Hollywood in the Age of Television*, ed. Tino Balio (Boston: Unwin Hyman, 1990), 45–48, 49.

24. George Rosen, "'What Next?' Dilemma," *Variety*, 14 February 1951, 1, 55.

25. "Television: The New Cyclops," 80; "Sarnoff Drives to Put NBC Out Front in TV," *Business Week*, 16 February 1957, 92.

26. Harrison B. Summers, ed., *A Thirty-Year History of Programs Carried on National Radio Networks in the United States, 1926–1956* (New York: Arno Press, 1971), 165ff; Cleveland Amory, "Jack Benny's $400 Yaks," *Saturday Evening Post*, 6 November 1948, 25. An on-air promotion by one of Benny's sponsors reportedly caused some 62 million Jell-O box tops to be sent to the comedian. See "Radio I: A $140,000,000 Art," *Fortune* 17 (May 1938), 51.

27. David B. Wilson, "Forty Years of Healing Laughter," *Boston Globe*, 6 January 1975, copy in Benny Papers, Box 56, University of Wyoming.

28. As Benny himself frequently admitted, he relied heavily on his writers. "He couldn't ad-lib a sneeze at a pepper factory," his valet, Rochester, declared in a 1959 telecast. Videotape, *The Jack Benny Program*, 18 October 1959. At the same time, Benny closely supervised his productions. See "The Quiet Riot," *Newsweek*, 3 November 1952, 62–63; Amory, "Jack Benny's $400 Yaks," 81–82; Wertheim, *Radio Comedy*, 316; Mary Livingstone Benny and Hilliard Marks, *Jack Benny* (Garden City, N.Y.: Doubleday, 1978), 217; Gross, *I Looked and I Listened*, 128; Bill Davidson, "Buck Benny Rides Again," *Saturday Evening Post*, 2 March 1963, 30; "Life Begins at 39," *Newsweek*, 13 April 1959, 98; Fred De Cordova, *Johnny Came Lately* (New York: Simon and Schuster, 1988), 109.

29. For excellent analyses of the evolution of the Benny radio program and its characters, see Wertheim, *Radio Comedy*, chapter 7; Michele Hilmes, *Radio Voices: American Broadcasting, 1922–1952* (Minneapolis: University of Minnesota, 1997), 192–99, and Gary Giddins, *Faces in the Crowd: Players and Writers* (New York: Oxford Univ. Press, 1992), 3–13. Much more speculative is Margaret McFadden, "'America's Boy Friend Who Can't Get a Date': Gender, Race, and the Cultural Work of the Jack Benny Program, 1932–1946," *Journal of American History* 80 (June 1993): 113–34.

30. Joseph Boskin, *Sambo: The Rise and Demise of an American Jester* (New York: Oxford Univ. Press, 1986), 179. See also William A. Henry III, "Mr. Benny and America—The Long Romance," in *Jack Benny: The Radio and Television Work* (New York: HarperCollins, 1991), 7.

31. Amory, "Jack Benny's $400 Yaks," 84.

32. The episode, Jack Benny wrote, "brought the heaviest mail we ever received on the program." Jack Benny and Joan Benny, *Sunday Nights at Seven: The Jack Benny Story* (New York: Warner Books, 1990), 107.

33. J.P. Shanley, "Mr. Benny Accompanied by Bells," *New York Times*, 21 November 1954, 2:9.

34. See Hadley Cantril, *The Invasion from Mars: A Study in the Psychology of Panic* (Princeton, N.J.: Princeton Univ. Press, 1940); Lawrence W. Levine, "The Folklore of Industrial Society: Popular Culture and Its Audiences," *American Historical Review* 97 (December 1992), 1369–99, esp. 1371–72, 1374.

35. See, e.g., Fredda Dudley Balling, "A Myth Is as Good as a Smile," 1955 manuscript, copy in Benny Papers, Box 89, UCLA. A recent history of Benny's talent agency contended that the comedian was, in fact, a spendthrift "in and out of debt most of his

life." Dennis McDougal, *The Last Mogul: Lew Wasserman, MCA, and the Hidden History of Hollywood* (New York: Crown, 1998), 161.

36. Videotape, *The Jack Benny Show,* 7 February 1954. Earlier, during Benny's second TV show, he admitted during a long opening monologue that he and Mary were married. Script, *The Jack Benny Television Program,* 28 January 1951, Benny Papers, Box 42, UCLA.

37. Benny and Benny, *Sunday Nights at Seven,* 85.

38. McDougal, *The Last Mogul,* 162–63; Sally Bedell Smith, *In All His Glory: The Life of William S. Paley* (New York: Simon and Schuster, 1990), 261–64; "CBS Steals the Show," *Fortune* 48 (July 1953), 79; B.C. Duffy to Barton, et al., n.d., Barton Papers, Box 75, SHSW; "Points covered at meeting with Salesmen," 29 November 1948, Niles Trammell Files, NBC Records, Box 115. Sally Bedell Smith argues persuasively that Paley, in signing Benny, was not considering the comedian as a future television star. See *In All His Glory,* 268–69.

39. U.S. Department of Commerce, *Historical Statistics of the United States; Colonial Times to 1970,* 2 vols. (Washington: U.S. Government Printing Office, 1975), 2:796.

40. George Burns and David Fisher, *All My Best Friends* (New York: Putnam, 1989), 262; Joseph E. Persico, *Edward R. Murrow: An American Original* (New York: McGraw-Hill, 1988), 300.

41. Jack Benny, "From Vaudeo to Video via Radio," *Collier's,* 24 March 1951, 81; Arthur Altschul, "Jack Benny Considers His Future," *New York Times,* 10 April 1949, copy in Benny papers, Box 89, UCLA.

42. "Big Time Comics Invade TV," 81–84; George Rosen and Mary Scott Welch, "TV's Old-New Stars Prove that Laughs Begin at 40," *Look,* 10 April 1951, 78, 80–81, 83–86; George Rosen, "Vets Solidify Tele's Standing," *Variety,* 8 November 1950, 29.

43. Benny's last radio sponsor, the American Tobacco Company, specified that Benny had to offer the company the option to sponsor his entry into television. See contract, 6 March 1947, Benny papers, Box 82, UCLA. A year or two earlier, Pat Weaver, then working for ATC, had filmed some Benny sketches to measure his impact on television. The films "convinced me Jack Benny would be effective on television." Weaver, *The Best Seat in the House: The Golden Years of Radio and Television* (New York: Knopf, 1994), 154.

44. Christopher H. Sterling and Timothy R. Haight, *The Mass Media: Aspen Institute Guide to Communication Industry Trends* (New York: Praeger, 1978), 372.

45. Benny actually made his TV debut on 8 March 1949 to celebrate the start of Los Angeles station KTTV. The appearance was not telecast nationally. Wertheim, *Radio Comedy,* 391; memorandum, Wick Crider to Jack Denove, 26 July 1949, copy in Barton Papers, Box 75; Jack Quigg, "Jack Benny Gives TV Cold Shoulder," *New York Daily Compass,* 14 September 1949, copy in Benny Papers, Box 89, UCLA. See also Harry MacArthur, "Jack Benny's TV Is Certain, But He's Moving to It Carefully," *Washington Star,* 26 February 1950, copy in Benny Papers, Box 89, UCLA; and Jack Benny, "From Vaudeo to Video," 81.

46. Milton MacKaye, "The Big Brawl: Hollywood vs. Television," *Saturday Evening Post,* 2 February 1952, 100.

47. "The Child Wonder," *Time,* 16 May 1949, 70–72, 75–77; "Television's Top," *Newsweek,* 16 May 1949, 56–58.

48. Quoted in Jeff Kisselhoff, *The Box: An Oral History of Television, 1920–1961* (New York: Viking, 1995), 304. See also Allen, *Funny Men*, 76.

49. Characteristically laughing at his own joke, cast member Phil Harris cries, "I'll bet Milton Berle's got that written down already." Jack replies, "Written down? He's doing it on television right now." Script, *The Jack Benny Program*, 27 June 1948, 10, Benny Papers, Box 33, UCLA.

50. Script, *The Jack Benny Program*, 15 May 1949, 12, Benny Papers, Box 34, UCLA.

51. Script, *The Jack Benny Program*, 1 May 1949, 12, Benny Papers, Box 34, UCLA.

52. Script, *The Jack Benny Program*, 10 September 1950, 11, 20, Benny Papers, Box 35, UCLA.

53. Bob Thomas, "Benny to Appear on Regular TV Program," *St. Louis Post-Dispatch*, 7 September 1950, clipping in Benny Papers, Box 89, UCLA. See also Ed Wynn's comments in *Variety*, 20 July 1949, 1, and Arthur Altschul, "Jack Benny Considers His Future."

54. *The New Yorker*, 11 November 1950, 98.

55. Amory, "Jack Benny's $400 Yaks," 89.

56. Script, *The Jack Benny Television Show*, 28 October 1950, Benny papers, Box 42, UCLA; videotape, *The Jack Benny Show*, 28 October 1950. Note that during this period the actual title of Benny's program varied from script to script and production to production.

57. Jack Gould, "Jack Benny Show Has Video Debut," *New York Times*, 30 October 1950, 33. See also idem., "Viewpoint on Comedy," *New York Times*, 5 November 1950, 2:11. Gould was one of several New York critics harsh toward Benny's debut. See Goodman Ace, "Big Bargain from Waukegan," *Saturday Review*, 11 November 1950, 31.

58. O'Flaherty, "Jack Benny Hits the Video Trail," *San Francisco Chronicle*, 2 November 1950, 25.

59. Rosen and Welch, 84. See also John Horn, "Jack Benny Sits in a Golden Rut," *New York Star*, 7 November 1948, clipping in Benny Papers, Box 89, UCLA.

60. "Jack Benny's Plunge into TV Refreshing One," *Chicago Tribune*, 1 November 1950, 2:4. See also review in *Variety*, 1 November 1950, 31.

61. Script, *The Jack Benny Television Program*, 28 January 1951, copy in Benny Papers, Box 42, UCLA; video in UCLA Film and Television Archive.

62. *New York Times*, 29 January 1951, 28.

63. *Chicago Sun-Times*, 31 January 1951, 2:5.

64. *Variety*, 31 January 1951, 23.

65. Script, *The Jack Benny Television Program*, 1 April 1951, Benny Papers, Box 42, UCLA; videotape, UCLA FTV; *New York Times*, 2 April 1951, 35. Dorothy Collins substituted for Wilson in both the April and May 1951 programs; Rochester, Mary Livingstone, and Bob Crosby appeared in the second program. See also "Talent Will Out," *Variety*, 4 April 1951, 28.

66. Script, *The Jack Benny Television Program*, 20 May 1951, Benny Papers, Box 42, UCLA; Josefberg, *The Jack Benny Show*, 385–86. *Variety*, 23 May 1951, 37, was less enthusiastic about the Hogan show.

67. "'The Quiet Riot,'" *Newsweek*, 3 November 1952, 62–63. In a December 1952 interview, Benny insisted that this approach was consistent with what he was doing in

radio. His radio program had no set format, he argued, and his TV show would be similarly free of a definite structure. His radio program had, in fact, occasionally involved a long sketch, often a spoof of a popular film. Some featured guest stars; some did not. The common convention was the opening monologue and a farewell. Typescript of story in *Los Angeles Times* or *New York Times*, 18 December 1952, Benny Papers, Box 89, UCLA. See also Irving Fein, *Jack Benny: An Intimate Biography* (New York: Putnam, 1976), 62; Larry Wolters, *Chicago Tribune*, 13 May [1956], clipping in Benny Papers, Box 33, University of Wyoming.

68. Videotape, *The Jack Benny Program*, 9 March 1952.

69. Videotape, *The Jack Benny Show*, 20 April 1952.

70. Videotape, *The Jack Benny Program*, 1 June 1952. See also Fein, *Jack Benny*, 67–68. A November 30, 1952, sketch similarly relies heavily on visual humor. As Jack is about to go to sleep, his bed is transformed into a giant baby cradle. Two burglars enter, only to discover that everything in the room has been booby-trapped. One opens a dresser drawer and gets squirted by a seltzer bottle; another opens the secretary door and is struck by a punching bag. Inside the safe is a live tiger. Videotape, *The Jack Benny Program*, 30 November 1952.

71. Script, *The Jack Benny Television Show*, 28 October 1950, 4, Benny Papers, Box 42, UCLA.

72. All of Benny's early TV scripts included an announcer's notation indicating if the program was live and the origination point. The 1951–1952 scripts are in the Benny Papers, Box 43, UCLA. Although the sixth script is missing, the video survives and the episode clearly appears to have been produced in Hollywood and live, if only because Don Wilson trips over a line. As late as November 1960, Benny did a program from New York. See script, *The Jack Benny Program*, 20 November 1960, Benny Papers, Box 48, UCLA.

73. James L. Baughman, "'Show Business in the Living Room': Management Expectations for American Television, 1947–56," *Business and Economic History* 26 (winter 1997), 722.

74. See paragraph four, amendments to employment agreement, CBS to Benny, 25 October 1950, and contract, ATC and Benny, 22 June 1955, 3, Benny Papers, Box 94, UCLA; Arthur Altschul, "Jack Benny Considers His Future"; Bob Thomas, "Benny to Appear on Regular TV Program." Like Benny, Jimmy Durante, one of the hosts of NBC's *All Star Revue*, similarly moved his show to Hollywood soon after the coaxial cable reached the Pacific. See script, "All Star Revue," 1 December 1951, Isaacs Papers, Box 1. On the cable reaching Los Angeles, see *Los Angeles Times*, 2 September 1951, 4:9, and 5 September 1951, 2:1. Please note that page numbers are not available for a few of these articles because they were accessible only as clippings in Benny's personal papers.

75. Benny also made the move hoping for a film career. "Radio II: A $45,000,000 Talent Bill," *Fortune* 17 (May 1938), 122; Ely, *Adventures of Amos 'n' Andy*, 196–97; Michele Hilmes, *Hollywood and Broadcasting: From Radio to Cable* (Urbana: Univ. of Illinois Press, 1990), 62–63, 71; Benny and Marks, *Jack Benny*, 70; Benny and Benny, *Sunday Nights at Seven*, 99.

76. Cited in Havig, *Fred Allen*, 269. Benny's 1947 ATC contract specified that his program would originate from Hollywood.

77. Baughman, "Take Me Away," 122; Havig, "Fred Allen and Hollywood." Frank Sinatra, a New Jersey native, came to prefer California very early in his show business career. Yet doing *The Bulova Show* in 1951 had forced him to live in New York. During the second Benny TV show, Jack remarked to Sinatra, "I remember how crazy you used to be about living in California. You used to say you wouldn't want to live anywhere else." Sinatra replied, "That's right, Jack." Script, *The Jack Benny Television Program*, 28 January 1951, Benny Papers, Box 42, UCLA.

78. Arthur Altschul, "Jack Benny Considers His Future"; Phyllis Battelle, "Jack Benny, As Seen Off-Mike," *Los Angeles Herald-Express*, 2 May 1955, clipping in Benny Papers, Box 89, UCLA.

79. Amory, "Jack Benny's $400 Yaks," 81; Benny and Benny, *Sunday Nights at Seven*, 180, 203, 205, 208.

80. The Sportsmen's singing commercial in the June 1, 1952, episode refers to Los Angeles's smog. In the November 30 show, Benny says the bench in a sketch had been taken from Griffith Park. Videotape, *The Jack Benny Program*, 30 November 1952.

81. Videotape, *The Jack Benny Program*, 18 October 1959.

82. Fein, *Jack Benny*, 185; Benny and Benny, *Sunday Nights at Seven*, 243–44.

83. Amory, "Jack Benny's $400 Yaks," 81; Benny and Marks, *Jack Benny*, 87–88; Benny and Benny, *Sunday Nights at Seven*, 59–60, 113–15, 214. Much of Hollywood turned out for Benny's 1974 funeral, which reportedly drew the largest crowd since Humphrey Bogart's in 1957. "Thousands Watch Hollywood Farewell to Benny," *New York Times*, 30 December 1974, 26.

84. Walter Ames, "Benny Demands Parts Fitted to Guest Stars," *Los Angeles Times*, 20 December 1953, 4:1, 8, clipping in Benny Papers, Box 89, UCLA; Fein, *Jack Benny*, 181.

85. Peck sang "The Shadow of Your Smile." Of doing the show, Peck, according to Benny's agent, said "he never had more fun in his entire life" Fein, *Jack Benny*, 260.

86. Benny and Marks, *Jack Benny*, 186.

87. Romero was twice Cantor's guest star during the 1951–1952 season. Scripts for *Colgate Comedy Hour*, 1951–1952, Cantor Papers, Box 22, Special Collections, UCLA. In 1952–1953, Berle's guests included Dennis King, Robert Merrill, Eva Gabor, Boris Karloff, Don Ameche, Basil Rathbone, and Paulette Goddard. Scripts for *The Texaco Star Theater*, Berle Papers, Box 3, Arts-Special Collections, UCLA.

88. Burns and Fisher, *All My Best Friends*, 271–72. See also "Television's Top," 58.

89. Henry, "Mr. Benny and America," 18; Fein, *Jack Benny*, 181.

90. Benny and Marks, *Jack Benny*, 186.

91. Burns and Fisher, *All My Best Friends*, 276.

92. Hal Humphrey, "Benny Has It Figured," *Los Angeles Daily Mirror*, 23 October 1953, 33, copy in Benny Papers, Box 89. TV's greater demands on the performer, one of Benny's writers argued, was ultimately his undoing. His television show suffered because Benny could not supervise the program as closely as he had the radio version. See Josefberg, *The Jack Benny Show*, 390.

93. Benny, "From Vaudeo," 81; Benny and Benny, *Sunday Nights at Seven*, 279–80. See also Bill Irwin, "Jack's His Own Best 'Gimmick,'" *Chicago Sun-Times*, 23 August 1952, copy in Benny Papers, Box 89; Bob Thomas, "Benny to Appear on Regular TV Program." Jerry Lewis and Dean Martin had similar concerns and carefully limited

their TV appearances in the early 1950s. See Robert Strauss, "The Devil Made Him Do It," *Los Angeles Times, Calendar,* 26 February 1995, 88.

94. Roland E. Lindbloom, "Benny Past and Present Master of Situation Comedy," *Newark News,* 21 March 1954, copy in Benny Papers, Box 89, UCLA; clippings, Marie Torre, *New York Herald Tribune,* 25 April 1960, and *New York Times,* 8 May 1960, in Benny file, *Herald Tribune* morgue, Center for American History, University of Texas.

95. Arthur Altschul, "Jack Benny Considers His Future." Benny had apparently encountered little difficulty persuading his sponsor to permit him to prerecord some of his radio programs. See, e.g., American Tobacco Co. to Benny, 9 May 1952, allowing Benny to record four programs. Benny Papers, Box 94, UCLA. Other radio performers, however, had been pressuring the networks to accept more recorded programming. See William S. Paley, *As It Happened: A Memoir* (Garden City, N.Y.: Doubleday, 1979), 231–32; Ben Gross, "Looking and Listening," *New York Daily News,* 10 March 1950, clipping in Niles Trammell Files, NBC Records, Box 115.

96. The notation for the script for *The Jack Benny Program,* 6 December 1953, indicates the show was filmed in July. Benny Papers, Box 43, UCLA. This was the first script to carry this note.

97. Contract, American Tobacco Co. and Benny, 22 June 1955, 2. Benny Papers, Box 94, UCLA.

98. Of fourteen 1958–1959 scripts in the Benny Papers, nine carry the "live" notation, three were taped, and two filmed. Some scripts are missing. Benny Papers, Box 47, UCLA. Videotape was just becoming available to performers like Benny in the late 1950s. By the 1970s, most prime-time series were taped.

99. Fourteen of fifteen scripts for the 1959–1960 season are in Benny Papers, Box 48, UCLA. Notations indicate that ten were videotaped.

100. See clause 15 of March 6, 1947 contract.

101. *Sponsor,* 26 December 1955, 2; *Broadcasting,* 17 July 1961, 29.

102. *New York Times,* 14 July 1957, 2:9. See also Cecil Smith, "Booming Hollywood May Become TV Capital Too," *Los Angeles Times,* 2 October 1955, 4:1, 5.

103. Kepley, "From 'Frontal Lobes,'" 53, 55; James L. Baughman, "The Weakest Chain and the Strongest Link: The American Broadcasting Company and the Motion Picture Industry," in Balio, ed., 91–114.

104. Albert McCleery to John Glendinning, 11 August 1953, McCleery Papers, Box 6, Arts-Special Collections, UCLA; George Rosen, "Television's West Side Story," *Variety,* 13 November 1957, 29.

105. Berle, *Milton Berle,* 347. See also memorandum, vice president in charge of programs [NBC] to all members of the Hollywood staff, 15 December 1954, copy in McCleery Papers, Box 8.

106. *Bonanza* was scheduled a half-hour before his show. Benny decided to sample the Western and became so absorbed that he forgot to switch to his own program. See Josefberg, *The Jack Benny Show,* 386.

107. Benny had originally opposed following *Petticoat Junction.* Fein, *Jack Benny,* 239–40. In 1963–1964, he faced a short-lived dramatic anthology program, *The Richard Boone Show,* on NBC, and a circus drama, *The Greatest Show on Earth,* on ABC.

108. Bill Davidson, "Who Killed Your Favorite TV Show?" *Saturday Evening Post,* 27 February 1965, 87.

109. Benny, for example, appeared stiff and not terribly funny in his last regular program. He made poor use of his guest stars, the Smothers Brothers, who, in their own variety show several years later, severely challenged the rules of network comedy and political commentary. Videotape, *The Jack Benny Show*, 16 April 1965.

110. The three flops were *The New Andy Griffith Show*, *The Headmaster*, and *Salvage I*. See Brooks and Marsh, *Complete Directory*, 447–48, 660–61, 735, 897; Joan Barthel, "How to Merchandise an Actor on TV," *New York Times Magazine*, 25 October 1970, 26, 28.

111. Benny's success on TV undermines McFadden's argument that his character deflected tensions in the 1930s and 1940s, thus explaining his popularity. His miserliness hardly fit the economy of the 1950s; economic anxieties had been greatly relaxed by the time Benny came to television.

112. Rosen, "'What's Next' Dilemma," 1, 55; Virginia MacPherson, "Funny Folk Finding TV Work Perilous," [United Press] clipping, n.d., in Isaacs Papers, Box 1. See also Goodman Ace, "The Cobalt Blues," *Saturday Review*, 20 January 1951, 30–31.

113. "Key to TV: Keep 'Em Laughing," *Variety*, 3 January 1962, 1.

114. Wolters, "Jack Benny's Plunge," 2:4. See also Ace, "Big Bargain," 31.

115. Ace, "Bright New Star: Jack Benny," *Saturday Review*, 1 December 1951, 39. See also Jack Mabley, "Benny Avoids Over-Exposure," *Chicago Daily News*, 2 June 1956, clipping Benny Papers, Box 33, University of Wyoming.

116. Benny, "From Vaudeo," 81.

117. "Jack Benny," *Los Angeles Times*, 29 December 1974, 6:2.

118. Wertheim, *Radio Comedy*, 132; Henry, "Mr. Benny and America," 5, 12.

119. Taylor, *Fred Allen*, 238. See also Wertheim, *Radio Comedy*, 132; Giddins, *Faces in the Crowd*, 9; Benny and Benny, *Sunday Nights at Seven*, 163; Frank Rich, "TV's New Jew," *New York Times*, 23 November 1996, 17; Joseph Boskin and Joseph Dorinson, "Ethnic Humor: Subversion and Survival," *American Quarterly* 37 (spring 1985), 90.

120. Amory, "Jack Benny's $400 Yaks," 86.

121. "Is There a Programming Crisis?" *Television Magazine* 14 (February 1957), 93; Caesar, *Where Have I Been?* 162–67; Stanley Frank, "Television's Desperate Numbers Game," *Saturday Evening Post*, 7 December 1957, 150; Robert W. Sarnoff, "What Do You Want from TV?" *Saturday Evening Post*, 1 July 1961, 44; Arthur Frank Wertheim, "The Rise and Fall of Milton Berle," in O'Connor, *American History; American Television*, 74, 75–76. In 1954, NBC's estimates of households with TVs indicated that most states with percentages of below 50 percent were in the South or the Plains. Hugh M. Beville to Fred Horton, 19 March 1954, NBC Records, Box 142.

122. Berle, *Milton Berle*, 335, 339, 346–48; Lynn Spigel, *Make Room for TV: Television and the Family Ideal in Postwar America* (Chicago: Univ. of Chicago Press, 1992), 145–51; Gross, *I Looked and I Listened*, 126–27; notes of interview with Goodman Ace, c. 1958, "Berle notebook," Martin Mayer Papers, Box 63, Columbia University. Scripts for the revamped Berle program are in his papers, Box 3.

16 Organizing Difference on Global TV

Television History and Cultural Geography

Michael Curtin

A few years ago, I received an unsolicited copy of a public relations videotape from AT&T offering an optimistic narrative of how the most recent communications revolution will alter our everyday lives. The opening shot of *Connections: AT&T's Vision of the Future* features the title scripted across a brilliant daylight image of a snow-covered Himalayan mountain peak. This shot then dissolves to the misty ambiance of a dimly lit weaving hut, occupied by a mustachioed, elderly man. The man rises slowly from a handloom and ambles across the shop to a low table, where a laptop computer is emitting a friendly electronic gurgle, signaling an incoming call. At the touch of a button, the screen lights up with the image of a twenty-something western woman, Lilly, who is telephoning from an airliner somewhere over the Pacific Ocean as she wings her way home to the United States. The conversation (which features simultaneous translation) soon adds a third link, as Lilly's Belgian fiancée joins the transcontinental deliberations regarding a special carpet that is being woven as a wedding present for the young American doctor who, in the words of Shri Nan, "has done so much for our village." By the end of the video, the narrative introduces characters who represent a variety of social, economic, and cultural identities as well as a host of new media technologies, ranging from satellite teleconferencing to computer-aided design to children's virtual reality games (which doting parents can remotely monitor, even while they are away at work). In every instance, the video suggests that communication technologies are working to overcome geographic barriers and resolve social tensions.

As has been the case for over thirty years, such corporate fantasies of the future prominently feature television as the master technology that connects people across vast spatial expanses, facilitating the circuits of production and exchange, as well as social interaction. Although there is a popular dimension to these fantasies, they are nevertheless inextricably connected to the historical project of capitalism, which is to alter and expand the operating spheres of profit-making enterprise. Many scholars have described this globalization process from a variety of perspectives and have marveled at the power of corporate enterprises that organize people and places around the world into an integrated economic system dominated by the abstract logics of commodification and exchange. We see this critique in the work of political economists, such as Immanuel Wallerstein and Alain Lipietz, as well as geographers like David Harvey and Edward Soja.[1] Yet the integrative project of capitalism that they describe so well is sometimes mistaken for a process of homogenization in the realm of popular culture. We encounter this confusion in the cultural critiques offered by scholars like Herbert Schiller, Ben Bagdikian, and Edward Herman and Robert McChesney, who contend that the rise of huge, transnational media conglomerates has led to the steady erasure of differences and the demise of local and national public spheres.[2] In their eyes, corporate leviathans have narrowed the spectrum of free expression, serving up a menu of cultural offerings that range from the inane to the banal. The diverse and animated discourse of a prior era has been displaced by a bland and indifferent, if hyperkinetic, stream of commercial images. We see a related concern about the fate of public culture in the work of postmodern and postcolonial scholars, such as Arif Dirlik, Masao Miyoshi, and Edward Said, each of whom suggests that the homogenizing power of corporate media is one of the key attributes of the current era of globalization.[3]

Many historians of mass media have adopted a similar logic in their work. Histories of printing, broadcasting, and cinema have tended to emphasize the ways in which media smooth out cultural differences and foster a national consciousness. Prominent television historians like Erik Barnouw, J. Fred McDonald, and Christopher H. Sterling and John M. Kittross have written the preeminent accounts of how television came to dominate national culture by single-mindedly pursuing a commercial logic that tended to favor uniformity over diversity, replication over innovation, and the national over the local.[4] Although these tendencies are mitigated somewhat by the rise of cable, the narrative trajectory in these histories is nevertheless toward homogenization, nationalization, and ultimately transnationalization.

Obviously, there is a kernel of truth in these critiques. Billions of people around the world have participated in nearly synchronous mediated experiences: the collapse of the Berlin Wall, the Tiananmen uprising, the Persian

Gulf War. Furthermore, music television and satellite sports events seem to have facilitated the rise of a global youth culture that shares a fascination with everything from Michael Jordan to "Macarena," lending further credence to the putative power of television institutions to shape transnational popular culture.

Nevertheless, it is important to draw a fine—but crucial—distinction between integration and homogenization, between globalization and the emergence of a global village. Here television histories are particularly important, because they can offer richly detailed accounts of the actual strategies of cultural institutions, which have aimed not at producing global similarity, but instead at organizing local differences toward profitable ends under a global regime of consumer capitalism. Although it is true that huge media conglomerates attempt to shape and delimit the range of ideas in circulation at any given time, one must be careful not to fall into the trap of believing that the purpose of corporate television is to erase difference and create a dull homogeneity of thought, experience, and lifestyle.[5]

As AT&T's *Connections* suggests, televisual images of the modern world are not those of homogenization, but of uneven development. The video depicts a hierarchy in which the labor of some people is valued differently than others and in which the representation, placement, and movement of actors helps to define relations of power. Moreover, *Connections* naturalizes a process of differentiation that is justified by the "invisible hand" of modernization. Some people have more status, more power, and more mobility simply because they are further along the path of modernization. Interestingly, telecommunications—and more specifically, television—is situated at the center of this set of relationships. It mediates between near and far, between past and present, between up and down the social scale. Lilly can render assistance to Himalayan villagers on the far side of the world because television has grown ever more flexible, transparent, and inexpensive. The technology allows Lilly to transcend social, spatial, and linguistic barriers so that she can sustain a meaningful long-distance relationship with inhabitants of a pastoral mountain village. Conversely, television enables Shri Nan to enjoy the benefits of contact with the modern world, while at the same time allowing him to continue living in an "idyllic" locale high in the Himalayas. Television both links peoples at the global level and helps to secure their identities at the local level.

Connections does not present a world in which lifestyles and imagery tend toward uniformity. Rather it elaborately delineates a set of cultural and class differences that are seemingly voluntary, "colorful," and authentic, thereby obscuring an unequal global division of labor. In the Himalayan sweatshop, at the local level, the tensions created by what Anthony Giddens refers to as *distanciation* and what David Harvey has described as *time-space compression* have been artfully managed.[6] One can wear a yak hat, work at a hand loom, and operate a sophisticated communication and computing device without a trace of antipathy or disorientation. There is diversity within a global unity, but, as Doreen Massey argues, it is a diversity formed "not so much out of a home-grown uniqueness, as out of the specificity of position within the globalized space of flows."[7] Thus, one's place is not so much a matter of authentic location or rootedness, but more a matter of one's relationship to economic, political, technological, and cultural flows. Place is produced and reproduced in relation to constantly changing patterns of flow. Furthermore, each person knows his or her place, not because of an organic connection to a particular locale, but in large part because of his or her relation to a dynamic set of media representations about place and about modernization.

On one level, television works to mediate social tensions by helping to shape one's sense of place, but on another level, it continually disrupts one's sense of place by contributing to the process of capitalist development. Historically, television is one of many electronic technologies that businesses have used to overcome spatial barriers in the pursuit of new sites for production, marketing, and resource extraction. Rather than creating a homogeneous space of operation, these communication technologies have made capital more mobile and hence even more sensitive to the differences between places. Since businesses now have more choices as to where they will locate, they have become increasingly sensitive to perceptions of place. It is not coincidental, for example, that *Fortune, Forbes,* and *Money Magazine* now run feature stories on the "best" places to live, work, and invest. As a result, localities must work ever more diligently to promote themselves as a favorable climate for business investment. Paradoxically, "the less important the spatial barriers," says David Harvey, "the greater the sensitivity of capital to the variations of place within space, and the greater the incentive for places to be differentiated in ways attractive to capital. The result has been the production of fragmentation, insecurity, and ephemeral uneven development within a highly unified global space economy of capital flows."[8] In other words, it is precisely because capitalist firms have carved out global spheres of operations that the differentiation between places becomes increasingly important. Accordingly, *the central mission of television is not to homogenize, but constantly to organize and reorganize popular perceptions of difference within a global economic order.* The medium is a tool for localizing and naturalizing a hierarchy of values and attitudes about places. It repeatedly works to anchor and orient one's perception of how power and wealth should be distributed.

Global television links peoples around the world, while also helping them to secure their identities on a local level. Courtesy of Photofest.

In this way, it helps to manage the process of uneven development—one of capitalism's defining features—primarily under the banners of modernization and global citizenship.

Having begun with the contemporary example of AT&T's *Connections*, this chapter looks back to the dawn of satellite television to demonstrate a remarkable consistency in the themes and strategies of corporate television. Despite profound changes in capitalism, consumer culture, and electronic media, one still can discern a number of patterns in television's global imagery. Even in its early years, television was envisioned as a medium that would help to organize political identities across national boundaries and within local communities. It worked both to create a unified space of operations and to regulate differences within this global context. The essay begins by looking at the relationship between television and the global aspirations of the New Frontier during the early 1960s. It then turns to the dilemma of local television in Chicago at precisely the same moment. Both cases show how television's attempts to transform spatial relations and organize cultural differences were intimately connected to particular notions of modernization and citizenship.

TV, Modernity, and Global Citizenship

President Kennedy's inaugural address, in which he made a vigorous call to arms in defense of the Free World, was followed only a few months later by a now-famous critique of television in which Newton Minow, chairman of the Federal Communications Commission (FCC), referred to the medium as a "vast wasteland" of vacuous entertainment and specifically connected the urgency of television reform to the foreign policy of the New Frontier. Minow's speech positioned the medium at the very center of public debate about the future—not simply of the nation or the economy—but of the world.

That same year at the University of Detroit, David Sarnoff, chairman of RCA—a corporation that had a major stake in virtually every aspect of what many then saw as a communications revolution—predicted that by the end of the decade, global television audiences of one billion people would be watching the same program at the same time via satellite transmission and simultaneous translation. "In a world where nearly half of the population is illiterate," argued Sarnoff, "no other means of mass communication could equal television's reach and impact on the human mind."[9] Many government policy makers at the time agreed with Sarnoff; as Newton Minow remarked, he expected a day in the not-too-distant future when "a broadcast from a studio in New York will be viewed in India as well as in Indiana, will be seen in the Congo as well as Chicago."[10]

As with most major policy objectives of the New Frontier era, this utopian portrayal of an emerging global village was juxtaposed with portentous images a monolithic communist threat. Poised against the homogenizing onslaught of the communist powers, the community of the Free World supposedly offered a haven of liberal pluralism and material plenitude. Consequently, television policy makers like Newton Minow launched a reform campaign against an undifferentiated "wasteland" of prime-time programming.[11] According to government leaders and social critics, television's purpose should be both to bring together ever larger audiences around the world and to celebrate differences. Indeed, liberal critiques of monolithic communism and Madison Avenue converged on the issue of homogenization of popular culture. Whether driven by totalitarian or commercial imperatives, television reformers widely feared and reviled what they saw as the ascendancy of middlebrow culture, resulting in an interminable flow of monotonous imagery. From their perspective, prime-time television offered viewers a severely limited range of choices that failed to take into account the diverse tastes, preferences, and needs of the audience. Paradoxically, however, television's other key mission was to bring together citizens of the Free World so that they might partake in electronically mediated communal experiences. Television, in the eyes of these critics, must help to make the world both an integrated and diverse social system.

Such seemingly contradictory policy objectives can best be analyzed by placing them in a wider historical context that draws attention to the relationship between mass communication and empire,[12] for the Kennedy administration faced a challenge that was very much like those that confronted leaders of imperial regimes during the nineteenth century. Like Britain and Russia one hundred years earlier, the U.S. government sought to use new communication technologies to organize its sphere of strategic influence and to assert its leadership role. Yet, unlike its predecessors, the sprawling Free World alliance was comprised in large part of states that had emerged from broad-based independence movements that had toppled colonial regimes during the post–World War II era. These newly independent states were premised on notions of popular sovereignty. Therefore, unlike the imperial era, the United States could not solidify its alliance by simply brokering with local power elites or subjugating local populations by force of arms. Instead, the coordinating power of strategic communications had to be complemented by the mobilizing power of mass communication. Accordingly, U.S. leaders believed that television's most important potential was its ability to reach past local elites and vie for the uncertain loyalties of citizens in Africa, Asia, and Latin America. Cold War television offered a way to help geographically dispersed peoples to imagine themselves as part of an extra-local social order.[13] It would assist them in finding their place as citizens of the Free World.

It therefore makes sense that the 1964 Olympic Games were among the first major events broadcast globally via U.S. satellite.[14] For viewers in the emerging nation-states of the postcolonial world, the games provided an arena in which to explore one's new national identity and one's relationship to others in countries around the globe. Moreover, the games provided a

The 1964 Olympics were among the first major events telecast globally via U.S. satellite television. Courtesy of Photofest.

ritualistic site for Cold War struggle, a location where national and suprana-tional differences could be tallied and organized mathematically. Viewers could develop affinity for their national team and, in turn, see their team as part of a superpower alliance. In 1964, due to the fact that television was still a new technology in many parts of the world, the audiences for the 1964 games were comparatively modest in size. Yet within a decade the games rapidly extended their appeal to viewers around the world. What is most significant, however, is the fact that from this very early moment of global television, the medium was imagined not as a homogenizer, but as an *organizer of difference*. Another form of programming that was similarly pro-moted and widely popular in the early years of transnational television was the global beauty contest. Again, the significance of these programs was that they both incorporated local concepts of beauty into a global system, and they suggested a hierarchy for organizing these differences.[15] At the apex of the global pyramid of sports and beauty was, of course, the United States.

Such competitive entertainments were complemented by explicit U.S. government efforts to dramatically expand informational programming about international issues. Of particular importance during this era was the docu-mentary genre, which was characterized as an important tool for interpret-ing the increasingly complex flood of information about global events. During the early 1960s, the three major U.S. television networks produced scores of

Global beauty contests, such as this 1965 Miss Universe pagent, were widely popular in the early years of transnational television. Courtesy of Photofest.

documentaries about international issues that were broadcast during prime time in America and then distributed via a rapidly growing global syndication market. One of the key narrative challenges confronting these programs was to manage questions of political and cultural difference. Given the incredible diversity within the "Western" alliance, documentaries of this era seemed to ask: How would one recognize the boundaries of the Free World? What similarities and differences exist within the alliance? And what characteristics set the Western world apart from the Communist bloc?[16]

For example, ABC's *Cambodia: The Peaceful Paradox* (1962) examined that country's avowed aspiration to opt out of the superpower struggle then developing in Southeast Asia.[17] The documentary not only pondered Cambodia's move toward political neutrality, but also puzzled over a host of differences between this Southeast Asian society and Western societies. In one scene, for example, traditional dancers adorned in elaborate silk costumes show up at a highway construction site to entertain laborers who are toiling away with hand tools instead of bulldozers. The documentary acknowledges such "unique" behavior, categorizes it as a colorfully exotic premodern ritual, and then employs it as justification for U.S. economic and political intervention in Southeast Asia. What the documentary cannot fathom, however, is the notion that Cambodia might wish to pursue an independent course, and that it may wish to define development and security in entirely different terms.

The documentary's perspective on international issues was largely shared by the foreign policy establishment during the 1960s and perhaps found its most systematic expression in Walt Rostow's influential book, *Stages of Economic Growth: A Non-Communist Manifesto*.[18] Rostow, who became a key presidential advisor during the Kennedy and Johnson administrations, argues that all societies naturally pass through comparable stages in their progress toward modernity, a path that, not surprisingly, culminates in a social order remarkably like that of the United States. The teleology of this process may explain in part why many confuse the concepts of globalization and homogenization. Rostow contends that when societies reach the final stage, they will have similar standards of living and similar social outlooks. Although this suggests a uniform outcome, in reality Rostow's stages functioned as a hierarchy of differences that legitimized U.S. leadership and justified the suffering of millions of people in the "less developed" regions of the globe. In other words, it is presumed that all peoples and all societies share the same ambition—modernization—which can only be achieved by enduring an inevitable and seemingly neutral process of development. In the long term such an approach promises future equality, while in the short term justifying an unequal distribution of power and wealth. Global leadership and authority in this scheme belong to the most developed societies, and signs of difference inevitably relegate one to the periphery.

Although Rostow's approach is imbued with the distinctive social science discourse of the Cold War era, the process of modernization proved to be anything but scientific or inevitable. Instead, newly independent states struggled with tremendous social and economic burdens that were compounded by ethnic and cultural tensions inherited from the colonial era. Rather than a united Angola or a unified India, policy makers like Rostow were well aware that many regimes had a very tenuous hold on power. At the most fundamental level they confronted a crisis of legitimacy. On whose authority did these new governments rule? The premodern and colonial regimes that preceded them had literally embodied sovereign power in the physical representation of the ruler. They legitimized their authority through the trappings and rituals of the court, through elaborate ceremonies connecting the ruler to a supernatural deity, and through the awesome exercise of the monarch's military might. Yet, in the modern era, governments must foster a different constellation of legitimating imagery. Elections, inaugurations, and the quotidian operations of a legal system—all dutifully monitored by the mass media—help to cultivate the notion that power flows from the will of the people.[19] It is the continuous and excessive circulation of images of a united and sovereign citizenry that is the foundation of state power in the modern era.

Similarly, U.S. pretensions to leadership of the Free World demanded the creation of a new set of legitimating images as well—ones that were far different from the colonial era. By what authority would the U.S. exercise power over a widely dispersed and culturally diverse group of people? Rostow's stages of development articulated a seemingly universal set of aspirations and provided both the promise of future equality and a justification for current hierarchies of difference that were spatially and culturally defined. It promised democracy and equality, while paradoxically practicing the politics of difference. This articulation of citizenship to modernization is thoroughly woven into the history of the television era at both the national and international levels.

Television therefore played an important role in the a process of spatial restructuring during the postwar era, helping to elevate the United States to a preeminent status among nations and to position citizens around the world in relation to a discourse of modernization. One can most explicitly see this process at work when examining the globalization of the medium. Yet, interestingly, a similar process was at work in the U.S. itself, where relations between regions, cities, and suburbs were undergoing profound changes. Television mediated these spatial transformations in strikingly similar ways, suggesting that modernization justified new conceptions of place in postwar America.

In Search of Chicagoland

The very same year that the U.S. government launched its first global communications satellite was also the year that the Federal Communications Commission took the unusual step of convening a special set of public hearings to investigate the demise of local television. Staged in Chicago during the spring of 1962, it was one of the few times in its history that the FCC explicitly took up the issue of local television, despite the fact that localism has been a foundational concept of U.S. media regulation since the 1920s.[20] As Christopher Anderson and I have explained elsewhere, the hearings began as a rather practical attempt to shore up and protect local broadcasters, but they became increasingly convoluted as participants began to reflect on more philosophical issues regarding relationships between city and nation, between Chicago and the Midwest, and between the many groups and factions within the city itself.[21] Commissioners wondered: What is television's role in producing and sustaining local identity? Should national networks be allowed to dominate local television channels, or should the government actively protect localities against powerful external influences? If government is to take action, then what exactly should it protect?

These questions were raised because Chicago once was a vibrant broadcasting center that produced hundreds of radio programs for local, regional, and even national audiences. Two of the most enduring media genres—the situation comedy and the soap opera—were developed, if not actually invented, in Chicago during the 1920s and 1930s.[22] This tradition carried over to the early years of television, as local producers experimented with a distinctive variety of live, low-budget programs that became widely known as the "Chicago School" of television. For example, Studs Terkel produced and acted in a popular weekly drama set in a neighborhood tavern, entitled *Studs' Place*. Dave Garroway pioneered a variety-talk show known as *Garroway at Large*, a format that would become the template for NBC's subsequent development of the *Today* show—which in fact lured Garroway from Chicago to network headquarters in New York City. Chicago was also fertile terrain for innovations in children's programming, ranging from *Bozo's Circus* to *Kukla, Fran, and Ollie*. Moreover, the late-night talk show format possibly reached its cerebral apogee in the hands of Chicago newspaper columnist Irving Kupcinet, whose weekly gabfest became renowned for thoughtful interviews with politicians, performers, and celebrities.[23]

In his testimony before the FCC in 1962, Ted Mills, a programmer at WNBQ, recalled "a burning kind of regional pride" that stimulated the creative community in Chicago during the early years of television. He and others were initially optimistic that the new medium would help the city sustain its status as a regional hub for the cultural production of a Midwestern identity. Yet Mills conceded that the logic of national consumer marketing and new technologies of network interconnection ultimately undermined their best efforts. After transcontinental television landlines were established in 1952, all three major networks used the new technology to centralize their control over programming and advertising. As television became an increasingly national phenomenon, regional advertisers fled to the national networks and local station management acceded to network pressures to reduce staff and cut costs. Mills concluded, however, "There is nobody to blame; unfortunately, regionalism is increasingly disappearing in the standardization of our mass economy."[24] The demise of Chicago broadcasting was characterized by Mills and many other critics of the period as a silencing of the

Garroway at Large was a pioneering variety-talk show in Chicago that became the forerunner of NBC's *Today*. Courtesy of Photofest.

region's voice, a draining away of its talent, and an imposition of a homogenizing cultural form from afar. This assessment of the plight of local broadcasting closely conformed to the liberal critique advanced by New Frontier policy makers like FCC chairman Newton Minow and presidential advisor Arthur Schlesinger Jr.[25]

What is remarkable, however, is that many middle-class Chicagoans did not share Mills' critique. For example, Mrs. P.J. Schultz enthusiastically embraced the logic of national network television by arguing that Chicago should not be seen as a regional production center so much as a suburb of New York and Los Angeles. "We do not have the mental climate here to make local live TV worth watching," she contended. "Neither are we an area where the news is made . . . I think we should be grateful for the networks' efforts to make us part of the informed nation and aware of what is going on in the world."[26]

Clearly, Mrs. Schultz had internalized the hierarchy of differences that was preferred by network officials. She had either overlooked or was unaware of the fact that during the pre–World War II era, Chicago was itself widely renowned as a cultural center because of its contributions to architecture, literature, academic scholarship, radio broadcasting, journalism, jazz, vaudeville, and sports. Although Mrs. Schultz could perhaps be excused for overlooking Chicago's high culture tradition, it is remarkable for her to forget the vibrant popular culture of the prewar era. It was not that Chicago objectively lacked its own cultural tradition; it was rather that the regime of national network television, along with other forces in postwar society, was working to reorganize perceptions of Chicago's place in the world.

One is reminded by Mrs. Schultz that network television had not so much homogenized as it had reorganized representations of particular places in concert with a reorganization of spatial and economic relations. Accordingly, the 1950s marked a significant turning point in the history of Chicago. From the mid-nineteenth century to the middle of the twentieth century, the city developed at the center of the vast railroad network that connected the agricultural heartland of the United States with East Coast markets and Great Lakes shipping routes. Its spectacular industrial growth during this period furthermore made Chicago a magnet for hundreds of thousands of immigrants.[27] Thus, the city's centrality as a cultural producer grew out of its role as a site of mediation between rural and urban, between immigrant and Anglo, between premodern and modern. These social and economic tensions were manifested in the popular culture of this period and, as scholars such as Michele Hilmes, Robert C. Allen, and Melvin Patrick Ely have shown, they were especially manifested in the programming of the radio era.[28] Although these tensions were not fully resolved by the early 1960s, Ted Mills was quite right to argue that times had changed both economically and culturally. A more fully integrated national consumer economy diminished Chicago's status as an important locus of cultural mediation. Moreover, World War II and the Cold War had fostered both institutional and ideological presumptions of national consensus. Indeed, local particularism was especially difficult to assert in the face of recurring solicitations to pull the country together in response to the growing "communist threat." Consequently, those who expressed opposition to the consolidation of a national network television system at the Chicago hearings had trouble formulating their arguments so that they might be taken seriously by the mainstream media.[29] In the eyes of many, network television was good for the economy and good for the nation. Chicago should subordinate its pretensions to cultural leadership and, in the words of Mrs. Schultz, "be grateful for the networks' efforts to make us part of the informed nation."

In the face of such presumptions, the commission nevertheless tried to fashion a set of standards for supporting local broadcasting. In part, the commission seemed motivated by political considerations. Newton Minow was a lawyer and political operative in Chicago prior to joining the FCC and therefore was well connected to members of the local Democratic Party, many of whom expressed concern about Chicago's fortunes in the postwar economic and political order. The commission's concerns also may have stemmed from a nostalgic response to the demise of the "Chicago School" and from anxieties about the ascendancy of middlebrow culture and Madison Avenue. Finally, the FCC seems to have been motivated by input from local community groups who felt that their voices were diminished by the new regime of network television.

Yet on what basis might the commission seek to intervene in the defense of local television? In this regard, the most vexing problem was defining the contours of locality. For even though the FCC had consistently endorsed the principle of localism since the very early days of broadcasting, the commission never elaborated much beyond referring to local stations as the "mouthpiece of the community." Not only does this confusion permeate the record of the 1962 FCC hearings in Chicago, but it is also reflected in internal memos among the commissioners and their staff during this period.[30] What marked the boundaries of locality? Could one really speak of Chicago without reference to the suburbs, the agricultural heartland, or the constellation of cities throughout the Midwest? Wasn't the city itself an amalgam of different factions vying for influence over the levers of social and economic power? What role then did television play in organizing these internal and external differences?

Ultimately, the FCC's regulatory initiative crumbled in the face of dominant notions of modernization and citizenship. For the prevailing assumption throughout the hearings was that the Chicago community was primarily constituted by white, middle-class consumers who lived in uneasy relation to a chaotic collection of "special interest" groups, those who had not yet evolved or assimilated. Chicago's many and diverse ethnic neighborhoods were characterized as either colorfully exotic (as was the case with references to the Gruza Serbian Folk Dancers and the Jolly Lumberjack German Dancers) or as potentially threatening (as with references to the rapidly expanding African American and Latino communities). Such urban diversity was managed and made understandable by the concept of modernization, which intimated a future in which all of Chicago's citizens might assimilate and rise to the status of middle-class suburbanites. Consequently, Chicagoans like Mrs. Schultz celebrated the rise of a national, postwar consumer culture and showed little concern about the politics of locality. For citizens like her, Chicagoland was a highly privatized, mediated, and abstract experience, perhaps not so different from their experience of national politics and consumer culture. They lived in single, detached, suburban homes, commuted to work on automobile expressways, and spent much of their leisure time listening to records or radio, or watching television. These Chicagoans embraced the novel opportunities offered by postwar prosperity. They seized the chance to transcend prior constraints of space and time, characterizing themselves as the modern standard against which one could measure the progress of other groups within and around the Chicago area. Thus, middle-class Chicagoans' perceptions of their locality had shifted in the postwar era, and television played an important role in redefining their sense of place and their relationships with others. By comparison, those in the urban ethnic neighborhoods also came to understand their experience in relation to a new set of images concerning space and motion. Over the course of the 1950s, television programs increasingly suggested that urban dwellers were either stuck in the city or that they aspired to rise up the social ladder and move out to the suburbs.[31] Television not only played an important role in refashioning relations between cities, but also relations within cities.

It is precisely this ongoing transformation of spatial relations that Doreen Massey describes when she writes, "The identity of a place does not derive from some internalized history. It derives, in large part, from the specificity of its interaction with the 'outside.' 'Places' have for centuries been complex locations where numerous different, and frequently conflicting, communities intersected."[32] Television histories can help us understand the specificity of these relationships as they change over time, for these interactions between the local and the "outside" are always mediated by shifting representations of the relative value and significance of places and communities.

Looking Backward

What then can we learn from this sixties retrospective? First of all, that globalization of media should not be confused with homogenization. Television has never worked to erase differences, but to organize differences so as to help manage processes of uneven development. It does this at the global, national, regional, and local levels through institutional practices, government regulations, modes of representation, and the organization and surveillance of audiences. As David Harvey suggests, "Any struggle to reconstitute power relations is a struggle to reorganize their spatial bases. It is in this light that we can better understand 'why capitalism is continually reterritorializing with one hand what it was deterritorializing with the other.'"[33] That is, capitalism does not simply attack or undermine existing spatial boundaries; it also seeks to produce new boundaries and new relationships. The role that media play in this constant process of change is increasingly drawing the attention of television historians who seek not to portray a seemingly inevitable process of corporate expansion, transnationalization, and homogenization, but to chart patterns and continuities while also maintaining a sensitive eye for the complexities, divergences, and reversals that characterize social struggles inscribed in space.

Another lesson to be drawn from a sixties retrospective has to do with the complexity of locales. As the Chicago experience suggests, even the most modern, prosperous, and seemingly powerful metropolitan areas in the 1960s were difficult to define and manage as coherent entities. Life then was not necessarily more centered or grounded than it is today. Instead, a tremendous amount of effort was invested in the struggle to identify Chicago's place in an increasingly globalized space of flows. Chicago was not a fully formed community that was suddenly subjected to a moment of disruptive transformation. It was instead a location that was evolving in relation to perpetual movements of people, ideas, goods, and capital. Scholarship that portrays television as a homogenizing force suffers from the presumption that localities were once stable, authentic entities, bereft of tensions and ambiguities.[34] Such nostalgia is not only misguided but fundamentally misleading. In contrast, television history offers a particularly promising point of entry for examining the complex historical interactions among different places, groups, and forces during the second half of the twentieth century. It reminds us that the relations between inside and outside are constantly subject to contest and reformation and that television's representations of locality play an important role in this process.

Finally, a 1960s retrospective shows that the experience of Chicago's television reformers anticipated problems that now confront many popular movements in the post-colonial world, for they too now must wrestle with complex identity issues and seemingly diffuse relations of power. Nationalist struggles against a colonial oppressor fifty years ago clearly marked out the boundaries between opposing camps, between inside and outside. Yet today many countries suffer problems that are very similar to those that confronted Chicagoans forty years ago: the emergence of internal rivalries, middle-class endorsement of values promulgated by cosmopolitan media institutions, and the seeming impotence of local public policy in the face of globalizing economic forces. Given such conditions, it is improbable that one can simply pull up the drawbridge and defend one's locality against influences from afar. Instead, scholars like Arif Dirlik have advanced the notion of "critical localism" as a strategic orientation that emphasizes the articulation of progressive forces at the local, national, and transnational levels.[35] Dirlik argues that defensive localized responses that unreflectively valorize traditional customs and identities run the risk of being not only politically regressive but self-defeating. Critical localism encourages one to explore new relationships between people, places, and power. In the context of television history, this requires that we develop an awareness of the many ways the medium plays upon and manages differences.

We can therefore find continuities between the early 1960s and the present as we note the ways in which television works to manage differences within a global capitalist order. Corporate fantasies of new communications technologies are but one way of constituting hierarchies of difference, and they suggest not a process of homogenization but of uneven development. In this sense, not much has changed since the dawn of the satellite era. Westerners still continue to imagine Shri Nan waiting patiently in his hut for the gift of televisual communication and for the opportunity to modernize himself, his business, and his village. And perhaps millions of Shri Nans around the world also see the medium as a ticket to prosperity and global citizenship. After all, the television receiver is more than a source of entertainment or information; it's also a key component of many people's dreams about the future. Yet the process of fashioning such "visions of the future" is the product of complex social struggles over the reterritorialization of space. Television history provides a unique vantage point for understanding such struggles, by showing how the medium has been used to promise equality, while it practices the politics of difference.

Notes

An earlier version of this essay was delivered at the Malcolm S. Forbes Center for Modern Culture and Media, Brown University, 1995. I would like to thank Sasha Torres for her generous hospitality and critical feedback.

1. Immanuel Wallerstein, *Historical Capitalism* (London: Verso Press, 1983); Alain Lipietz, *Mirages and Miracles: The Crises of Global Fordism* (London: Verso Press, 1987); David Harvey, *The Condition of Postmodernity: An Enquiry into the Origins of Cultural Change* (Cambridge, Mass.: Basil Blackwell, 1989); and Edward Soja, *Postmodern Geographies: The Reassertion of Space in Critical Social Theory* (New York: Verso Press, 1989).

2. Herbert I. Schiller, *Culture, Inc.: The Corporate Takeover of Public Expression* (New York: Oxford Univ. Press, 1989). Schiller's analysis of global media was first put forth in the late 1960s and has recently been reissued. See *Mass Communication and American Empire*, 2nd ed. (1969; reprint, Boulder: Westview, 1992). Ben Bagdikian, *The Media Monopoly*, 4th ed. (Boston: Beacon Press, 1992); Edward Herman and Robert McChesney, *The Global Media: The New Missionaries of Corporate Capitalism* (London: Cassell, 1997).

3. Arif Dirlik, "The Global in the Local," and Masao Miyoshi, "A Borderless World? From Colonialism to Transnationalism and the Decline of the Nation-State," in Rob Wilson and Wimal Dissanayake, eds., *Global/Local: Cultural Production and the Transnational Imaginary* (Durham, N.C.: Duke Univ. Press, 1996); Edward W. Said, *Culture and Imperialism* (New York: Knopf, 1994).

4. Erik Barnouw, *The Tube of Plenty: The Evolution of American Television*, a popular and abridged version of his three-volume work, *The Image Empire* (New York: Oxford Univ. Press, 1990); J. Fred McDonald, *One Nation Under Television: The Rise and Decline of Network TV* (New York: Pantheon, 1990); and Christopher H. Sterling and John M. Kittross, *Stay Tuned: A Concise History of American Broadcasting*, 2nd ed. (Belmont, Calif.: Wadsworth Publishing, 1990).

5. There is a substantial amount of scholarship arguing that this encounter between the global and the local results in the hybridization or indigenization of cultural forms. It suggests that culture is endlessly variable and complex and that the reception and appropriation of transnational cultural forms often result in variations that are a mix of the traditional and the modern. Furthermore, some scholars, such as Arjun Appadurai, contend that the transnational flow of cultural products is but one of several flows that shape modern culture. He argues that complexity, disjuncture, and difference are the outcome of these flows rather than homogenization. Arjun Appadurai, "Disjuncture and Difference in the Global Cultural Economy," in Mike Featherstone, ed., *Global Culture: Nationalism, Globalization and Modernity*, (Newbury Park, Calif.: Sage, 1990). Working from a South American perspective, Jesus Martin-Barbero makes a somewhat similar argument in *Communication, Culture and Hegemony* (Newbury Park, Calif.: Sage, 1993). The emphasis of this essay is not on reception, appropriation, or indigenization, but instead on the ways that television has historically worked to organize differences rather than to homogenize popular culture, even in the 1960s. Related

perspectives on more recent developments can be found in Richard Maxwell, *The Spectacle of Democracy: Spanish Television, Nationalism, and Political Transition* (Minneapolis: Univ. of Minnesota Press, 1995), and David Morley and Kevin Robins, *Spaces of Identity: Global Media, Electronic Landscapes, and Cultural Boundaries* (London: Routledge, 1995).

6. Anthony Giddens, *The Consequences of Modernity* (Stanford, Calif.: Stanford Univ. Press), and Harvey, *Condition,* 260–308.

7. Doreen Massey, "A Place Called Home?" *New Formations* 17 (summer 1992): 6.

8. Harvey, *Condition,* 295–96.

9. News release, Radio Corporation of America, 5 April 1961, Newton Minow Papers, Box 35, State Historical Society of Wisconsin (SHSW).

10. Newton Minow, "Vast Wasteland," address by Newton N. Minow to the National Association of Broadcasters in Washington, D.C., 9 May 1961, in F.J. Kahn, ed., *Documents of American Broadcasting,* 4th ed. (Englewood Cliffs, N.J.: Prentice Hall, 1984), 215. For a discussion of the Minow FCC and global television, see Michael Curtin, "Beyond the Vast Wasteland: The Policy Discourse of Global Television and the Politics of American Empire," *Journal of Broadcasting and Electronic Media* 37.2 (spring 1993): 127–45.

11. Andrew Ross discusses liberal pluralism and diversity in the 1950s and 1960s in *No Respect: Intellectuals and Popular Culture* (New York: Routledge, 1989), and William Boddy traces the liberal critique of television that first emerged in the 1950s in *Fifties Television: The Industry and Its Critics,* (Urbana: Univ. of Illinois Press, 1990), while Mary Ann Watson, *The Expanding Vista: American Television in the Kennedy Years* (New York: Oxford Univ. Press, 1990), and James L. Baughman, *Television's Guardians: The FCC and the Politics of Programming* (Knoxville: Univ. of Tennessee Press, 1985), discuss New Frontier television policy, as does Michael Curtin, *Redeeming the Wasteland: Television Documentary and Cold War Politics* (New Brunswick, N.J.: Rutgers Univ. Press, 1995).

12. Numerous scholars have discussed this relationship, including Schiller, *Mass Communication;* Harold Innis, *The Bias of Communication* (Toronto: Univ. of Toronto Press, 1951), and *Empire and Communications* (Toronto: Univ. of Toronto Press, 1950); Benedict Anderson, *Imagined Communities: Reflections on the Origins and Spread of Nationalism* (New York: Verso, 1983); Anthony Smith, *The Geopolitics of Information: How Western Culture Dominates the World* (New York: Oxford, 1980), 41–67; Brian Winston, *Misunderstanding Media* (Cambridge, Mass.: Harvard Univ. Press, 1986), 256–61; Carolyn Marvin, *When Old Technologies Were New: Thinking about Electrical Communication in the Late Nineteenth Century* (New York: Oxford, 1988); and James Carey, *Communication as Culture: Essays on Media and Society* (Boston: Unwin Hyman, 1989).

13. This perspective is explicitly elaborated in the development communications literature of this era. See, for example, Daniel Lerner, *The Passing of Traditional Society: Modernizing the Middle East* (Glencoe, Ill.: Free Press, 1958), and Wilbur Shramm, *Mass Media and National Development: The Role of Information in Developing Countries* (Stanford, Calif.: Stanford Univ. Press, 1964).

14. Policy makers who planned the development and launch of Telstar in 1962, the

first global communications satellite, explicitly discussed the importance of having the system in operation to carry the forthcoming Olympic Games around the world.

15. On global beauty contests, see Colleen Ballerino Cohen, Richard Wilk, and Beverly Stoeltje, *Beauty Queens on the Global Stage* (New York: Routledge, 1996).

16. Curtin, *Redeeming the Wasteland.*

17. Broadcast on ABC, March 27, 1962.

18. W.W. Rostow, *The Stages of Economic Growth: A Non-Communist Manifesto* (Cambridge, U.K.: Cambridge Univ. Press, 1960).

19. Note that even in authoritarian states, rulers feel compelled to stage events that symbolize popular support for the state and to circulate images of these events throughout society. Whether May Day parades in Moscow carried via television or Nazi rallies at Nuremburg captured on film by Leni Riefenstahl, the purpose of such coverage is to suggest that the sovereignty of the modern state ultimately is derived from the will of the people. Regarding premodern monarchs as the embodiment of state power, see Michael Rogin, *Ronald Reagan, the Movie: And Other Episodes in Political Demonology* (Berkeley: Univ. of California Press, 1987) and Michel Foucault, *Discipline and Punish: The Birth of the Prison* (New York: Pantheon, 1977). Regarding the shift to popular sovereignty, see Anderson, *Imagined Communities.*

20. On localism and FCC policy, see Thomas Streeter, *Selling the Air: A Critique of the Policy of Commercial Broadcasting in the United States* (Chicago: Univ. of Chicago Press, 1996). On the fate of localism from the very earliest years of radio, see Susan Smulyan, *Selling Radio: The Commercialization of American Radio* (Washington, D.C.: Smithsonian Press, 1994), and Robert McChesney, *Telecommunications, Mass Media and Democracy: The Battle for the Control of U.S. Broadcasting, 1928–1935* (New York: Oxford Univ. Press, 1993).

21. Christopher Anderson and Michael Curtin, "Mapping the Ethereal City: Chicago Television, the FCC, and the Politics of Place," *Quarterly Review of Film and Video* 16.3–4, (1999): 289–305.

22. See Melvin Patrick Ely, *The Adventures of Amos 'n' Andy: A Social History of an American Phenomenon* (New York: Basic Books, 1991) and Robert C. Allen, *Speaking of Soap Operas* (Chapel Hill: Univ. of North Carolina Press, 1985).

23. The most complete account of the "Chicago School" of television appears in Joel Sternberg, "Television Town," *Chicago History* 4.2 (summer 1975), 108–17. Also see Sternberg, "A Descriptive History and Critical Analysis of the Chicago School of Television, 1948–1954," (Ph.D. diss., Northwestern University, 1973).

24. Letter from Ted Mills to the FCC, 1 March 1962, "Inquiry into Local Television Programming in Chicago, Illinois," Federal Communications Commission, Docket No. 14546, vol. 1, 179–80, Box 7593, National Archives, Washington, D.C. Raymond A. Jones made similar comments in his testimony before the commission and pointed to a long list of performers who made their start in Chicago broadcasting, among them: Red Skelton, Don Ameche, Hugh Downs, Bob Newhart, Mike Wallace, George Gobel, Fibber McGee and Molly, Dave Garroway, Gary Moore, and Fran Allison. See Jones, American Federation of Television and Radio Artists, 19 March 1962, 157–77, Box 7593. Also see the testimony of James Weigal, broadcast announcer, 19 March 1962, 747–55, Box 7593; Lester A. Weinrott, former writer, director, and producer, 19

March 1962, 755–64, Box 7593. All testimony and correspondence related to the Chicago hearings are to be found in "Inquiry into Local Television Programming in Chicago, Illinois," Federal Communications Commission, docket 14546, National Archives, Washington, D.C. (hereafter identified as FCCNA).

25. This critique is rather fully elaborated in a special symposium issue, "Mass Culture and Mass Media," *Daedalus* 89 (spring 1960).

26. Letter to the FCC from Mrs. P.J. Schultz of Elmhurst, Illinois, Box 7594, FCCNA.

27. William Cronon, *Nature's Metropolis: Chicago and the Great West* (New York: Norton, 1991).

28. Michele Hilmes, *Radio Voices: American Broadcasting, 1922–1952* (Minneapolis: Univ. of Minnesota Press, 1997); Allen, *Speaking of Soap Operas;* and Ely, *The Adventures of Amos 'n' Andy.*

29. Interestingly, Baughman in *Television's Guardians* is as dismissive of the "special interest" groups as were the dominant Chicago newspapers in 1962.

30. Memo from Commissioner Robert E. Lee to Chairman Newton Minow, 27 March 1962, Newton Minow Papers, Box 8, SHSW.

31. Lynn Spigel, *Make Room for TV: Television and the Family Ideal in Postwar America* (Chicago: Univ. of Chicago Press, 1992); Nina C. Leibman, *Living Room Lectures: The Fifties Family in Film and Television* (Austin: Univ. of Texas Press, 1995); and Mary Beth Haralovich, "Sitcoms and Suburbs: Positioning the 1950s Homemaker," in Lynn Spigel and Denise Mann, eds., *Private Screenings: Television and the Female Consumer* (Minneapolis: Univ. of Minnesota Press, 1992).

32. Massey, "A Place Called Home?," 8.

33. Harvey, *The Condition of Postmodernity,* 238.

34. In addition to recent work done by critical geographers, anthropologists have thoroughly critiqued nostalgic notions of place and authenticity. See, for example, Arjun Appadurai, *Modernity at Large: Cultural Dimensions of Globalization* (Minneapolis: Univ. of Minnesota Press, 1996), and James Clifford, *The Predicament of Culture: Twentieth Century Ethnography, Literature, and Art* (Cambridge, Mass.: Harvard Univ. Press, 1988).

35. Dirlik, "The Global in the Local."

Selected Bibliography

Additional Sources for Researching Television as Historian

Kathryn Helgesen Fuller-Seeley

Books

Altschuler, Glenn C. and Grossvogel, David I. *Changing Channels: America in TV Guide.* Urbana: Univ. of Illinois Press, 1992.

Anderegg, Michael, ed. *Inventing Vietnam: The War in Film and Television.* Philadelphia: Temple Univ. Press, 1991.

Ball, Rick. *Meet the Press: Fifty Years of History in the Making.* Foreword by Tim Russert. New York: McGraw-Hill, 1998.

Barnouw, Erik. *A History of Broadcasting in the United States.* 3 vols. New York: Cambridge Univ. Press, 1966–1970.

———. *Tube of Plenty: The Evolution of American Television.* 2nd rev. ed. New York: Oxford Univ. Press, 1990.

Baughman, James L. *The Republic of Mass Culture: Journalism, Filmmaking and Broadcasting in America Since 1941.* 2nd ed. Baltimore: Johns Hopkins Univ. Press, 1997.

Benjamin, Burton. *Fair Play: CBS, General Westmoreland and How a Television Documentary Went Wrong.* New York: Harper and Row, 1988.

Bernardi, Daniel. *Star Trek and History: Race-ing Toward a White Future.* New Brunswick, N.J.: Rutgers Univ. Press, 1998.

Bernhard, Nancy E. *U.S. Television News and Cold War Propaganda, 1947–1960.* New York: Cambridge Univ. Press, 1999.

Boddy, William. *Fifties Television: The Industry and Its Critics.* Urbana: Univ. of Illinois Press, 1990.

Browne, Nick, ed. *American Television: New Directions in History and Theory.* Langhorne, Pa.: Harwood Academic Pub., 1994.

Bullert, B.J. *Public Television: Politics and the Battle over Documentary Film.* New Brunswick, N.J: Rutgers Univ. Press, 1997.

Caldwell, John Thornton. *Televisuality: Style, Crisis, and Authority in American Television.* New Brunswick, N.J.: Rutgers Univ. Press, 1995.

Comstock, George A. *The Evolution of American Television.* Newbury Park, Calif.: Sage Publications, 1989.

Curtin, Michael. *Packaging Reality: The Influence of Fictional Forms on the Early Development of Television Documentary.* Columbia, S.C.: Association for Education in Journalism and Mass Communication, 1993.

————. *Redeeming the Wasteland: Television Documentary and Cold War Politics.* New Brunswick, N.J.: Rutgers Univ. Press, 1995.

Day, James. *The Vanishing Vision: The Inside Story of Public Television.* Berkeley, Calif.: Univ. of California Press, 1995.

Donovan, Robert J. and Scherer, Ray. *Unsilent Revolution: Television News and American Public Life, 1948–1991.* Washington, D.C.: Woodrow Wilson International Center for Scholars, and New York: Cambridge Univ. Press, 1992.

Engelman, Ralph. *Public Radio and Television in America: A Political History.* Thousand Oaks, Calif.: Sage Publications, 1996.

Godfrey, Donald G., compiler. *A Directory of Broadcast Archives.* Washington, D.C.: Broadcast Education Association, 1983.

Hammond, Charles Montgomery Jr. *The Image Decade: Television Documentary.* New York: Hastings House, 1981.

Haralovich, Mary Beth, and Lauren Rabinowitz. *Television, History, and American Culture: Feminist Critical Essays.* Durham, N.C.: Duke Univ. Press, 1999.

Himmelstein, Hal. *Television Myth and the American Mind.* 2nd ed. Westport, Conn.: Praeger, 1994.

Hinds, Lynn Boyd. *Broadcasting the Local News: The Early Years of Pittsburgh's KDKA-TV.* University Park, Pa.: Pennsylvania State Univ. Press, 1995.

Kisseloff, Jeff. *The Box: An Oral History of Television, 1920–1961.* New York: Viking, 1995.

Koppel, Ted, and Kyle Gibson. *Nightline: History in the Making and the Making of Television.* New York: Times Books, 1996.

Lynch, Christopher Owen. *Selling Catholicism: Bishop Sheen and the Power of Television.* Lexington, Ky.: Univ. Press of Kentucky, 1998.

MacDonald, J. Fred. *One Nation under Television: The Rise and Decline of Network TV.* New York: Pantheon Books, 1990.

Marc, David. *Demographic Vistas: Television in American Culture.* Foreword by Horace Newcomb. Rev. ed. Philadelphia: Univ. of Pennsylvania Press, 1996.

Marling, Karal Ann. *As Seen on TV: The Visual Culture of Everyday Life in the 1950s.* Cambridge, Mass.: Harvard Univ. Press, 1994.

Mickelson, Sig. *The Decade that Shaped Television News: CBS in the 1950s.* Westport, Conn.: Praeger, 1998.

Murray, Michael D., and Donald G. Godfrey, eds. *Television in America: Local Station History from Across the Nation.* Ames, Iowa: Iowa State Univ. Press, 1997.

O'Connor, John E. *Teaching History with Film and Television.* Washington, D.C.: American Historical Association, 1987.

O'Connor, John E., ed. *American History/American Television: Interpreting the Video Past.* Foreword by Erik Barnouw. New York: Ungar, 1983.

————. *Image as Artifact: The Historical Analysis of Film and Television.* Malabar, Fla.: R.E. Krieger, 1990.

Paget, Derek. *No Other Way to Tell It: Dramadoc/Docudrama on Television.* Manchester, U.K.: Manchester Univ. Press; New York: St. Martin's Press, 1998.

Ritchie, Michael. *Please Stand By: A Prehistory of Television.* Woodstock, N.Y.: Overlook Press, 1994.

Roman, James. *Love, Light, and a Dream: Television's Past, Present, and Future.* Westport, Conn.: Praeger, 1996.

Rosenthal, Alan. *Writing Docudrama: Dramatizing Reality for Film and Television.* Boston: Focal Press, 1995.

Rosenthal, Alan, ed. *Why Docudrama? Fact-Fiction on Film and Television.* Carbondale, Ill.: Southern Illinois Univ. Press, 1999.

Rosteck, Thomas. *"See It Now" Confronts McCarthyism: Television Documentary and the Politics of Representation.* Tuscaloosa: Univ. of Alabama Press, 1994.

Rowan, Bonnie G., and Cynthia J. Wood. *Scholar's Guide to Washington, D.C., Media Collections.* Washington, D.C.: Woodrow Wilson Center Press, 1994.

Shiers, George, compiler. *Early Television: A Bibliographic Guide to 1940.* New York: Garland, 1997.

Slotten, Hugh R. *Radio and Television Regulation: Broadcast Technology in the United States, 1920–1960.* Baltimore: Johns Hopkins Univ. Press, 2000.

Smith, Anthony, with Richard Paterson, eds. *Television: An International History.* 2nd ed. New York: Oxford Univ. Press, 1998.

Sobchack, Vivian, ed. *The Persistence of History: Cinema, Television, and the Modern Event.* New York: Routledge, 1996.

Spigel, Lynn. *Make Room for TV: Television and the Family Ideal in Postwar America.* Chicago: Univ. of Chicago Press, 1992.

Stark, Steven D. *Glued to the Set: The Sixty Television Shows and Events that Made Us Who We Are Today.* New York: Free Press, 1997.

Stempel, Tom. *Storytellers to the Nation: A History of American Television Writing.* New York: Continuum, 1992.

Sturken, Marita. *Tangled Memories: The Vietnam War, the AIDS Epidemic, and the Politics of Remembering.* Berkeley, Calif.: Univ. of California Press, 1997.

Toplin, Robert Brent, ed. *Ken Burns's The Civil War: Historians Respond.* New York: Oxford Univ. Press, 1996.

————. *Perspectives on Audiovisuals in the Teaching of History.* Washington, D.C.: American Historical Association, 1999.

Udelson, Joseph H. *The Great Television Race: A History of the American Television Industry, 1925–1941.* Tuscaloosa: Univ. of Alabama Press, 1982.

Watson, Mary Ann. *The Expanding Vista: American Television in the Kennedy Years.* New York: Oxford Univ. Press, 1990.

Wilk, Max. *The Golden Age of Television: Notes from the Survivors.* New York: Delacorte Press, 1976.

Zielinski, Siegfried. *Audiovisions: Cinema and Television as Entr'actes in History.* Translated by Gloria Custance. Amsterdam: Amsterdam Univ. Press, 1999.

Articles

Abrash, Barbara, and Daniel J. Walkowitz. "Sub/Versions of History: A Meditation of Film and Historical Narrative." *History Workshop Journal* [Great Britain] 38 (1994): 203–14.

"American Film and Television Archives." *Historical Journal of Film, Radio and Television* [Great Britain] 1996 16(1): 13–98.

Aron, Stephen. "The West as America: A Review of the Latest Ken Burns Documentary." *Perspectives: American Historical Association Newsletter* 34:6 (1996): 1, 7–10.

Attie, Jeanie. "Illusion of History: A Review of *The Civil War.*" *Radical History Review* 52 (1992): 95–104.

Auster, Albert. "All in the Family: The Kennedy Saga and Television." *Journal of Popular Film and Television* 19 (1991): 128–37.

———. "*The Missiles of October:* A Case Study of Television Docudrama and Modern Memory." *Journal of Popular Film and Television* 17 (1990): 164–72.

Ballard-Reisch, Deborah. "*China Beach* and *Tour of Duty:* American Television and Revisionist History of the Vietnam War." *Journal of Popular Culture* 25 (1991): 135–49.

Bartone, Richard C. "*Victory at Sea:* A Case Study in "Official" Telehistory." *Film & History* 21 (1991): 115–29.

Beidler, Philip D. "Making a Production Out of It: *Victory at Sea* and American Remembering." *Prospects* 22 (1997): 521–34.

Bindas, Kenneth J., and Kenneth J. Heineman. "Image Is Everything? Television and the Counterculture Message in the 1960s." *Journal of Popular Film and Television* 22 (1994): 22–37.

Blight, David W. "Homer with a Camera, Our 'Iliad' without the Aftermath: Ken Burns's Dialogue with Historians." *Reviews in American History* 25:2 (1997): 351–59.

Boritt, Gabor S. "Ken Burns's 'Civil War.'" *Pennsylvania History* 58:3 (1991): 212–21.

Bösel, Anke. "Ken Burns's Film Series 'The Civil War:' An Attempt at American Self-Definition." *American Studies* [Germany] 40:2 (1995): 283–89.

Breitbart, Eric. "From the Panorama to the Docudrama: Notes on the Visualization of History." *Radical History Review* 25 (1981): 115–25.

Brown, M. Elaine Dolan. "The Television War: Treatment of Gender and the Vietnam Experience in Network Television Drama in the 1988–89 Season." *Vietnam Generation* 1 (1989): 68–73.

Burns, Ken. "Baseball, the American Epic." *Proceedings of the American Antiquarian Society* 104:2 (1994): 243–60.

Burns, Ken; Cripps, Thomas, interviewer. "Historical Truth: An Interview with Ken Burns." *American Historical Review* 100:3 (1995): 741–64.

Burns, Ken; Thelen, David, interviewer. "The Movie Maker as Historian: Conversations with Ken Burns." *Journal of American History* 81:3 (1994): 1031–50.

Burns, Ken; Weisberger, Bernard A., interviewer. "'The Great Arrogance of the Present Is to Forget the Intelligence of the Past.'" *American Heritage* 41:6 (1990): 96–102.

Buttlar, Lois. "Media Coverage of the Black Americans' Struggle for Civil Rights." *Ethnic Forum* 8 (1988): 81–87.

Calavita, M. "Public Television: Politics and the Battle over Documentary Film." *Cineaste* 23 (1998): 59.

Censer, Jane Turner. "Videobites: Ken Burns's 'The Civil War' in the Classroom." *American Quarterly* 44:2 (1992): 244–54.

Cohn, William H. "History for the Masses: Television Portrays the Past." *Journal of Popular Culture* 10 (1976): 280–89.

Cornfield, Michael. "What Is Historic about Television?" *Journal of Communication* 44 (1994): 106–16.

Culbert, David. "Television's Vietnam and Historical Revisionism in the United States." *The Historical Journal of Film, Radio and Television* [Great Britain] 8 (1988): 253–67.

———. "Television's Visual Impact on Decision-Making in the USA, 1968: The Tet Offensive and Chicago's Democratic National Convention." *Journal of Contemporary History* [Great Britain] 33 (1998): 419–49.

Curtin, Michael. "Packaging Reality: The Influence of Fictional Forms on the Early Development of Television Documentary." *Journalism Monographs* 137 (1993): 1–37.

Davis, Susan G. "'Set Your Mood to Patriotic:' History as Televised Special Event." *Radical History Review* 42 (1988): 122–43.

DeCredico, Mary A. "Image and Reality: Ken Burns and the Urban Confederacy." *Journal of Urban History* 23 (1997): 387–405.

Dick, Ernest J. "History on Television: A Critical Archival Examination of *The Valour and the Horror*." *Archivaria* [Canada] 34 (1992): 199–216.

Doneson, Judith E. "History and Television, 1978–1988: A Survey of Dramatizations of the Holocaust." *Dimensions* 4 (1989): 23–27.

Duncan, Dayton. "'Never Take No Cutoffs': The Filmmaker's Saga." *Montana* 47:1 (1997): 73–77.

Dupont, Nancy McKenzie. "Television and Louisiana History: A Demonstration of a Partnership." *Louisiana History* 36 (1995): 467–73.

Edgerton, Gary. "Ken Burns's America: Style, Authorship and Cultural Memory." *Journal of Popular Film and Television* 21 (1993): 50–62.

———. "Ken Burns's American Dream." *Television Quarterly* 27 (1994): 56–64.

———. "Ken Burns's Rebirth of a Nation: Television, Narrative and Popular History." *Film & History* 22 (1992): 118–33.

Fabian, Ann. "A West for the Masochists among Us." *Western Historical Quarterly* 28:3 (1997): 311–14.

Freedman, Carl. "History, Fiction, Film, Television, Myth: The Ideology of *M*A*S*H*." *Southern Review* 26 (1990): 89–106.

Freehling, William W. "History and Television." *Southern Studies* 22 (1983): 76–81.

Frisch, Michael. "Oral History, Documentary, and the Mystification of Power: A Case Study Critique of Public Methodology." *International Journal of Oral History* 6:2 (1985): 118–25.

Gardner, Lloyd. "The Cold War According to CNN." *Perspectives: American Historical Association Newsletter* 37:4 (1999): 15–19.

Gerber, David A. "Haley's *Roots* and Our Own: An Inquiry into the Nature of a Popular Phenomenon." *Journal of Ethnic Studies* 5 (1977): 87–111.

Gomery, Douglas. "Rethinking TV History." *Journalism and Mass Communication Quarterly* 74 (1997): 501–14.

Gray, Herman. "Television, Black Americans, and the American Dream." *Critical Studies in Mass Communication* 6:4 (1989): 376–86.

Green, James. "Making 'The Great Depression' for Public Television: Notes on a Collaboration with Documentary Filmmakers." *Perspectives: American Historical Association Newsletter* 32:7 (1994): 3–6.

Greenberg, Douglas. "'History Is a Luxury': Mrs. Thatcher, Mr. Disney, and (Public) History." *Reviews in American History* 26:1 (1998): 294–311.

Hung, Nguyen Manh. "*Vietnam: A Television History*, A Case Study in Perceptual Conflict between the American Media and the Vietnamese Expatriates." *World Affairs* 147 (1984): 71–84.

Jenkins, William D. "Why TV Needs Historical Consultants." *Organization of American Historians Newsletter* 18 (1990): 6, 23.

Jordan, Daniel P., Richard R. Johnson; George A. Colburn; and Douglas D. Adler. "Reaching Out to New Constituencies beyond the Classroom." *History Teacher* 12 (1979): 319–27.

Koeniger, A. Cash. "Ken Burns's *The Civil War:* Triumph or Travesty?" *Journal of Military History* 55 (1991): 225–33.

Lancioni, Judith. "The Rhetoric of the Frame: Revisioning Archival Photographs in *The Civil War.*" *Western Journal of Communication* 60 (1996): 397–414.

Lang, William L. "Lewis and Clark and the American Century: A Review of Ken Burns's PBS Series on the Corps of Discovery." *Montana* 48:1 (1998): 56–61.

Lewis, Jan, and Peter S. Onuf. "American Synecdoche: Thomas Jefferson as Image, Icon, Character, and Self." *American Historical Review* 103:1 (1998): 125–36.

McFeely, William S. "Notes on Seeing History: The Civil War Made Visible." *Georgia Historical Quarterly* 74 (1990): 666–71.

McKerns, Joseph P. "Television Docudramas: The Image as History." *Journalism History* 7 (1980): 24–25, 40.

McPherson, Tara. "'Both Kinds of Arms': Remembering *The Civil War.*" *Velvet Light Trap* 35 (1995): 3–18.

Marber, Allen S. "Presidential Promotion and the Use of TV: An Historical Process." *Essays in Economic and Business History* 14 (1995): 305–18.

Marcus, Daniel. "NBC's 'Project XX': Television and American History at the End of Ideology." *The Historical Journal of Film, Radio and Television* [Great Britain] 17:3 (1997): 347–66.

Merron, Jeff. "Murrow on TV: *See It Now, Person to Person*, and the Making of a 'Masscult Personality.'" *Journalism Monographs* 106 (1988): 1–36.

Mittell, Jason S. "Invisible Footage: *Industry on Parade* and Television Historiography." *Film History* [Australia] 9 (1997): 200–18.

Moore, Shirley Ann Wilson. "Television, the West and the Real West." *Western Historical Quarterly* 28 (1997): 296–98.

Morrison, Michael A., and Robert E. May. "The Limitations of Classroom Media:

Ken Burns's *Civil War* Series as a Test Case." *Journal of American Culture* 19 (1996): 39–49.

Morrow, Lance. "The History-Devouring Machine." *Horizon* 21 (1978): 18–23.

Nelson, Richard Alan. "Sources for Archival Research on Film and Television Propaganda in the United States." *Film History* 3 (1989): 333–40.

O'Connor, John E. "Edward R. Murrow's Report on Senator McCarthy: Image as Artifact." *Film & History* 16 (1986): 55–72.

———. "The Moving Image Media in the History Classroom." *Film & History* 16 (1986): 49–54.

Protinsky, Ruth A., and Terry M. Wildman. "*Roots:* Reflections from the Classroom." *Journal of Negro Education* 48 (1979): 171–81.

Rakove, Jack N. "Jefferson Perceived." *Journal of the Early Republic* 17:4 (1997): 677–85.

Rankin, Charles E. "Not Such a Pretty Picture: Complexity and Understanding in the West." *Western Historical Quarterly* 28 (1997): 298–304.

Rollins, Richard M. "*The Adams Chronicles* and the American History Survey." *Teaching History: A Journal of Methods* 2 (1977): 54–57.

Rollins, Peter C. "HBO's Version of Neil Sheehan's Epic: Old Wine in New Bottles?" *Perspectives: American Historical Association Newsletter* 37 (1999): 33–35.

———. "Historical Interpretation or Ambush Journalism? CBS vs. Westmoreland in *The Uncounted Enemy: A Vietnam Deception* (1982)." *Purview Southwest: Proceedings of the Southwest and Texas Popular Culture Association Meeting* (Stillwater, Okla.: Southwest and Texas Popular Culture Association, 1989), 195–233.

Rosteck, Thomas. "Irony, Argument, and Reportage in Television Documentary: *See It Now* versus Senator McCarthy." *Quarterly Journal of Speech* 75 (1989): 277–98.

Slotkin, Richard. "'What Shall Men Remember?': Recent Work on the Civil War." *American Literary History* 3 (1991): 120–35.

Sollors, Werner. "*Wurzeln: Roots* in West Germany." *American Studies International* 17 (1979): 40–45.

Thomson, David. "History Composed with Film." *Film Comment* 26 (1990), 12.

Thornton, Bob. "Communicating History through Television, Videotape, and Films." *Baptist History and Heritage* 12 (1977): 156–65.

Tibbetts, John C. "The Incredible Stillness of Being: Motionless Pictures in the Films of Ken Burns." *American Studies* (Lawrence, Kans.) 37:1 (1996): 117–33.

Toplin, Robert Brent. "Television's Civil War." *Perspectives: American Historical Association Newsletter* 28 (1990): 1, 22, 24.

Tucker, Lauren R., and Hemant Shah. "Race and the Transformation of Culture: The Making of the Television Miniseries *Roots*." *Critical Studies in Mass Communication* 9 (1992): 325–36.

Vlastos, Stephen. "Television Wars: Representations of the Vietnam War in Television Documentaries." *Radical History Review* 36 (1986): 114–32.

Walkowitz, Daniel J. "Telling the Story: The Media, the Public, and American History." *Perspectives: American Historical Association Newsletter* 31:7 (1993): 1, 6–9.

Watson, Mary Ann. "Adventures in Reporting: John Kennedy and the Cinema Verite Television Documentaries of Drew Associates." *Film & History* 19 (1989): 26–43.

White, Duffield. "Television Non-Fiction as Historical Narrative." *Journal of Popular Culture* 7 (1974): 928–33.

White, Mary Alice, et al. "Where do Seventeen Year Olds Get Their History Information—From School or From Television?" *History Teacher* 22 (1989): 329–32.

Willett, Ralph. "Twisting the *Roots:* Fiction, 'Faction' and Recent TV Drama." *Umoja: A Scholarly Journal of Black Studies* 4 (1980): 11–20.

Worland, Rick. "From the New Frontier to the Final Frontier: Star Trek from Kennedy to Gorbachev." *Film & History* 24 (1994): 19–35.

Archives and Internet Resources

International Alliance of Theatrical Stage Employees, Motion Picture Technicians, and Artists, sponsor. "History and Research–Film and Television Industry Links" website, featuring extensive listing of links to television archives, historical sites, journals, museums, boards and organizations. <http://www.iatse.lm.com/flmhist.html>

Library of American Broadcasting, Hornbake Library, University of Maryland, College Park, Md. 20742. (301) 405–9160. Founded in 1972 as the Broadcast Pioneers Library, the Library of American Broadcasting holds a wide-ranging collection of audio and video recordings, books, pamphlets, periodicals, personal collections, oral histories, photographs, scripts, and vertical files devoted exclusively to the history of broadcasting. <http://www.lib.umd.edu/UMCP/LAB>

Library of Congress, Motion Picture, Broadcasting and Recorded Sound Division. Includes programs deposited for copyright, primarily network prime-time programs; NBC Television Collection; NET Television Collection; PBS Collection. <http://lcweb.loc.gov/rr/mopic>

National Archives, Motion Picture, Sound and Video Branch, 8601 Adelphi Road, College Park, Md. 20740–6001. (301) 713–7060. CBS Evening News collection; C-SPAN Collection; MacNeil-Lehrer News Report Collection; Television Interviews 1951–1955 Collection. <http://www.nara.gov.research/bymed/moint.html>

Northwestern University Media Resources Center, sponsor. "I Saw It on TV: A Guide to Broadcast and Cable Programming Sources." Multimedia, film, and broadcasting resources on the Internet. <http://www.library.nwu.edu/media/resources/tvguide.html>

Temple University Computer Center and Rice University Data Applications Center, sponsor. "Media Web." A loose coalition of film/tv/video webmasters that seeks to foster collaboration and coordination among media studies websites. The membership list offers excellent links to television and film history, theory, and production sites. <http://nt.riceinfo.rice.edu/outreach/mediaweb>

Timelapse, sponsor. "TV Link—Film and Television Website Archive." This rich site contains links to archives, museums, historical sites, and professional, academic, and fan sources on all aspects of television, film and media history and production. <http://www.timelapse.com/tvlink.html>

University of California at Berkeley library, sponsor. "Media Reference Sources and Information." Television, film, and media links. <http://www.lib.berkeley.edu/MRC/FilmRefMenu.html>

Vanderbilt Television News Archive, 110 Twenty-first Avenue South, Suite 704, Nashville, Tenn. 37203. ABC, CBS, NBC, CNN evening news broadcast collections, 1968–present. The collection holds more than 30,000 individual network evening news broadcasts and more than 9,000 hours of special news-related programming. The website offers an extraordinarily useful, searchable database of information. The collection has been abstracted with story level descriptions. The abstracts can be browsed by date or searched. The search returns specific items and the complete show. <http://tvnews.vanderbilt.edu>

Contributors

Carolyn Anderson is associate professor and undergraduate program director in the Department of Communication at the University of Massachusetts at Amherst. She has published dozens of essays on film and television and, with Thomas W. Benson, coauthored two books on the films of Frederick Wiseman. This chapter grows from her participation in a 1997 NEH Summer Seminar at the East-West Center, University of Hawai'i, on "The Politics of Representation in the Pacific Islands: Ethnography, Literature and Film," directed by Geoffrey White and Vilsoni Hereniko.

Steve Anderson is completing a Ph.D. in film, literature, and culture at the University of Southern California. His dissertation is entitled "History Written with Lightning: Film, Television and the Construction of the Past."

James Baughman is professor of journalism and mass communication at the University of Wisconsin at Madison. He is the author of *The Republic of Mass Culture: Journalism, Filmmaking, and Broadcasting in America since 1941*, 2nd ed., (Johns Hopkins, 1997).

David Culbert is professor of history at Louisiana State University, Baton Rouge. He is also editor of *The Historical Journal of Film, Radio and Television*.

Michael Curtin is associate professor in the Department of Communication and Culture at Indiana University and is currently writing a book about the globalization of media industries in East Asia. He is the author of *Redeeming the Wasteland: Television Documentary and Cold War Politics* (Rutgers, 1995), and coeditor of *Making and Selling Culture* (Wesleyan, 1996) and *The Revolution Wasn't Televised: Sixties Television and Social Conflict* (Routledge, 1997).

Thomas Doherty is associate professor of American Studies and chair of the Film Studies Program at Brandeis University. He is the author of *Projections of War: Hollywood, American Culture, and World War II* (Columbia, 1994) and *Pre-Code Hollywood: Sex, Immorality, and Insurrection in American Cinema, 1930–1934* (Columbia, 1999).

Gary R. Edgerton is professor and chair of the Communication and Theatre Arts Department at Old Dominion University. He coedits the *Journal of Popular Film and Television* and has authored a wide variety of books and articles on numerous topics addressing the relationship between media, history, and culture.

Kathryn H. Fuller-Seeley teaches American social history and media studies as an associate professor of history at Virginia Commonwealth University. She is the author of *At the Picture Show: Small Town Audiences and the Creation of Movie Fan Culture* (Smithsonian, 1996).

Douglas Gomery teaches media history and economics in the College of Journalism and Communication at the University of Maryland. He is the author of eleven books; the latest (with Ben Compaine) is *Who Owns the Media?* (Lawrence Erlbaum, 2000). His current work is focusing on television history and popular music.

Netta Ha-Ilan is a distance learning course developer and academic coordinator in the Department of Sociology and Communication at the Open University of Israel. She has completed her Ph.D. thesis entitled "Making Sense of the Occupied Territories in Israel Television News, 1968–1990," and her research continues to focus on the ways in which television news participates in the construction of collective identity in conditions of severe social controversy.

Robert Hanke is a senior research and teaching associate with the McLuhan Program in Culture and Technology, University of Toronto. He is currently teaching in the Communication Studies Programme at York University and the Arts & Sciences Programme at McMaster University. His work has appeared in journals such as *Film & History, Film Criticism, Communication Theory, The Western Journal of Communication, Critical Studies in Mass Communication, Public,* and *Communication,* as well as in edited books such as *Mapping the Beat: Popular Music and Contemporary Theory* (Blackwell, 1998), *Critical Approaches to Television* (Houghton Mifflin, 1998), and *Men, Masculinity and the Media* (Sage, 1992).

David Marcus is assistant professor in the Department of Communication at Wayne State University, where he teaches media and cultural studies. He has published on alternative media production and television treatments of American history. He is currently working on a book about the meanings of the 1950s and 1960s in contemporary American politics and popular culture.

Peter C. Rollins is a television producer/director and a film scholar. His *Will Rogers' 1920s: A Cowboy's Guide to the Times* (1976) has been shown over PBS and The Discovery Channel. His *Television's Vietnam: The Impact of Media* (1986) has been broadcast by WTBS and nearly two hundred PBS stations. *Hollywood as Historian,* rev. ed. (Kentucky, 1998) is an anthology for film that parallels the collection in hand. In his scholarly role, he edits *Film & History,* for which there is much information at <http://h-net.msu.edu/~filmhis>.

Brian Taves (Ph.D., University of Southern California) is a film archivist at the Library of Congress and is the author of *Robert Florey, The French Expressionist* (Scarecrow, 1987), *The Romance of Adventure: The Genre of Historical Adventure Movies* (Mississippi, 1993), and *The Jules Verne Encyclopedia* (Scarecrow, 1996).

Philip M. Taylor is professor of International Communication and director of the Institute of Communications at the University of Leeds, United Kingdom. The author of numerous books and articles, his most recent work is *British Propaganda in the Twentieth Century: Selling Democracy* (Edinburgh, 1999).

Chris Vos is on the History and Arts Studies faculty at the Erasmus University of Rotterdam, the Netherlands. His publications cover a wide range of subjects and in the last decade have focused on the relationship between television, film, and history. He has also produced a number of historical television documentaries for national broadcasting stations. His latest was awarded first prize at the 1999 Netherlands Film Festival for "Best Long Documentary."

Mimi White is professor in Radio/TV/Film at Northwestern University. She has published widely on film and television and is the author of *Tele-Advising: Therapeutic Discourse in American Television* (North Carolina, 1992) and coauthor of *Media Knowledge* (SUNY, 1992).

Television and Film Index

General Index

DATE DUE

APR 1 4 2002			

HIGHSMITH #45115